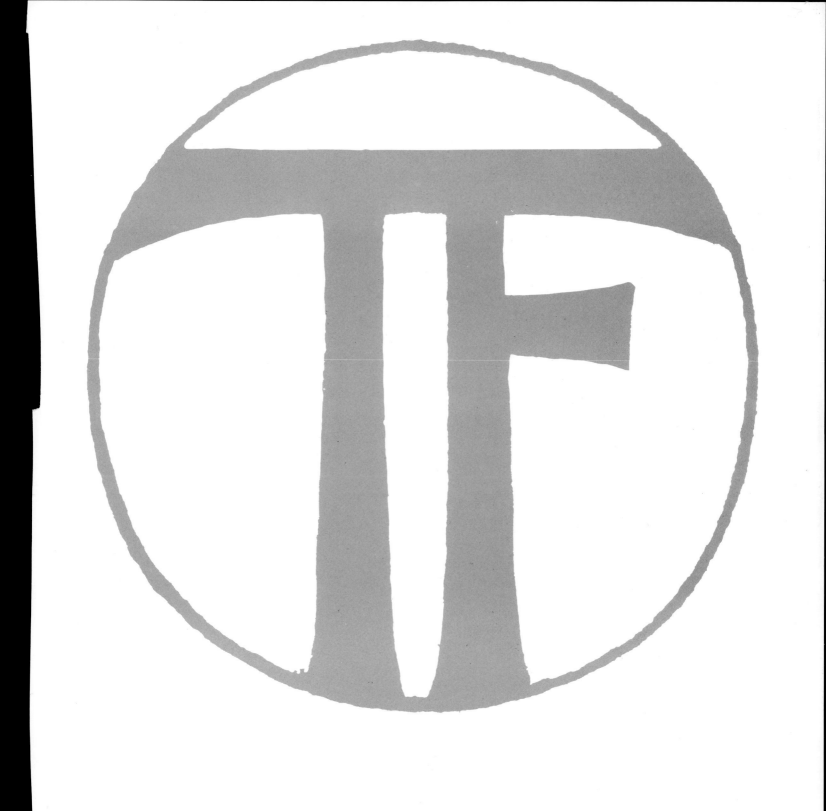

THEODOR FAHRNER **JEWELRY**

. . . between Avant-Garde and Tradition

ART NOUVEAU

ART DECO

THE 1950s

Ulrike von Hase-Schmundt

Christianne Weber

Ingeborg Becker

Schiffer Publishing Ltd

1469 Morstein Road, West Chester, Pennsylvania 19380

Produced by Brigitte Leonhardt and Dieter
Zühlsdorff,
FORUM for European Art and Culture,
Stuttgart and Heidelberg
Idea and conception: Brigitte Leonhardt and Dieter
Zühlsdorff
Catalog authors: Ulrike von Hase-Schmundt,
Christianne Weber, Ingeborg Becker.
Catalog editing: Brigitte Leonhardt
Photo editing: Gabriela Arnold
Title graphics: Carola Schmitz, Weingarten
Content graphics: Reinhold Burkart, Pforzheim
In collaboration with Manfred Geiger, Zürich
Graphic control: Manor Advertising Agency,
Pforzheim
Title photo: Peter Frankenstein, Marbach
Production coordination: Manor Advertising
Agency, Pforzheim, and Robert Wachs
Setup: Reinhold Burkart, Pforzheim, and Manfred
Geiger, Zürich

Translated from the German by,
Dr. Edward Force,
Central Connecticut State University.

Copyright © 1991 by Schiffer Publishing Ltd.
Library of Congress Catalog Number: 91-65661.

Printed in the United States of America.
ISBN: 0-88740-326-3

This title was originally published under the title,
*Theodor Fahrner SCHMUCK - . . . zwischen
Avantgarde und Tradition*
by FORUM für Europaische Kunst und Kultur,
Stuttgart.

We are interested in hearing from authors with
book ideas on related topics.

Published by Schiffer Publishing, Ltd.
1469 Morstein Road
West Chester, Pennsylvania 19380
Please write for a free catalog.
This book may be purchased from the publisher.
Please include $2.00 postage.
Try your bookstore first.

We thank:

Franziska Adriani

Gabriela Arnold

Anita Beckers

Torsten Bröhan GmbH

Hans-Peter Callsen

Dr. Marie-Louise Deissmann

R. & S. Diehl

Wolfgang Ehrlich

Hedwig Eichler

Flesser Collection

Marianne Geitel

Ursel Gronert

Dr. Ulrike von Hase-Schmundt

Meta-Maria Haseroth

Traudl Hauck

Max Hering

Robert Hiller

Dr. Karl Kreuzer

Ludwig Kuttner

Dr. Brigitte Marquardt

Beate Möllering

Lore Niemann

Beatrice Ost

Virginia J. Reinshagen

Astrid & Rainer Schill

Schneidewind-Wilksen Collection

Georgio Silzer

Telkamp Gallery

Udo Thomale

Martine & Rüdiger Urlass

Dr. G. Westermeier

Wiener Interieur

And all those who did not wish to be mentioned.

Baden State Museum, Karlsruhe

Museum of Applied Art, Cologne

Jewelry Museum, Pforzheim

City Museum, Düsseldorf

City Museum in the Prediger, Schwäbisch Gmünd

Württemberg State Museum, Stuttgart

Contents

Foreword and Acknowledgements
Ulrike von Hase-Schmundt:

THEODOR FAHRNER (1855-1919)

Contents of Factory Catalogs 1 and 2

79 FACTORY CATALOG 1 (to 1919)

Christianne Weber:

GUSTAV BRAENDLE THEODOR FAHRNER NACHF. (1919-1979)

Ingeborg Becker:

236 FASHION JEWELRY
or the problem of industrial production of luxury goods

Fashion and Jewelry in Art Nouveau • Haute Couture - Ready-made Articles - or Opposites Attract • Jazz Age and False Glamour - Fashions and Jewelry of the Twenties • The German Jewelry of the German Woman • The Graphics of FAHRNER JEWELRY Advertising

APPENDIX

We have long been accustomed to it. For renowned manufacturers of quality products for everyday use it has become self-evident: *the designers of the products are named; they are known to us!* The discriminating consumers have taken the position that they expect it and are disappointed or downright annoyed when designers' names are not given. Many automobile firms publicize the internationally known names of their coachbuilders; in the realms of furniture and fashion as well as kitchen utensils, in lighting and electronic entertainment (Porsche designs for Grundig!), they work together today, the producers and the designers, in a legitimate effort to link the good and also practical form with the necessity of economic success. This may well occur only when form and function, marketing, advertising and, last of all, the price affect each other sensibly, complete each other and form an inclusive union of all these factors. *We have become accustomed to it!* Artists, designers have an important function to fulfill, and we as consumers have the right to find out who is behind the objects with which we surround ourselves. It interests us to know who is responsible for a product that pleases us.

It was not very long ago that the designers' names became known to the "final purchaser"; not for very long have there been design exhibitions, design centers, and appropriate prizes and awards, by means of which a good product and those responsible for it are presented to a large public.

And yet, there are well-known cases from years ago: Peter Behrens and his collaboration with the AEG, the cooperation of Wilhelm Wagenfeld with the Württemberg Metal Goods Factory.

In more recent times, the Italian designers and "their" manufacturing firms have stepped into the limelight; whether Olivetti typewriters or Alessi boilers, one knows who produces these items, but one also knows that Ettore Sottsass, Michael Graves and Richard Sapper are responsible for the styling.

In the realm of industrially produced jewelry there were and are only a few firms that have named their artists, designers, pattern makers. And yet we know of exceptions: the designers of certain Scandinavian jewelry programs are known to at least the interested jewelry customer all over the world; American manufacturers and jewelers name their designers who set the style for the firm. A German manufacturer located near the border of The

Netherlands publicizes the names of those who design the outstanding jewelry of the house. After the collaboration of a Pforzheim firm with individually successful jewelry designers had led to extremely beautiful pieces of jewelry but, alas, to no commercial success, another jewelry manufacturer has gambled once again on the familiar name of an internationally known all-around designer.

Many years before, another jewelry manufacturer who called himself an "artist-manufacturer" had had success with this concept: Theodor Fahrner, who enjoyed international acclaim and great respect as a second-generation Pforzheim jewelry manufacturer until his death in 1919.

This man's extraordinary personality resulted in unusual methods. More extensively and successfully than his competitors (and only comparably with similar efforts in Britain), Fahrner, as a progressive, open-minded and particularly courageous entrepreneur, collaborated with artists from Darmstadt and Berlin, Munich, Stuttgart, Pforzheim and many other cities, and inspired them to design jewelry that he then produced in his "shop" and sold, citing the artist's name.

Theodor Fahrner himself — as has been stressed in a memoir — was artistically talented. But his ability to recognize corresponding talents in others, evaluate them and use them for his self-imposed task of achieving commercial success as a jewelry manufacturer through the high artistic and "technical" level of the jewelry created by his firm, seems to have been even greater.

Born in 1859 and imbued with the spirit of historicism in the years just after 1870, Theodor Fahrner recognized the signs of the times around the turn of the century, when "the artists went to work to free themselves from the chains of historical examples and achieve a timely, self-created expression of style" (R. Rücklin, in his evaluation of Fahrner in the Deutsche Goldschmiede Zeitung, 1919). The cooperation between the artists and manufacturers initiated by Theodor Fahrner paid off: the "artistic jewelry" made in not very large numbers by the "artist-manufacturer" Theodor Fahrner was a success. Fahrner's death caused a pause in, but not the end of, "Fahrner Jewelry", which meanwhile had won prizes at international fairs and exhibitions. What Gustav Braendle, as "Theodor Fahrner's Successor", produced in the following decades ranks — with new ideas in timely forms — only rarely lower than the jewelry that came into being under Theodor Fahrner's own direction.

Today Fahrner jewelry, whether produced in the "Theodor Fahrner Art Workshops" before 1919 or created by "Gustav Braendle — Theodor Fahrner Nachf.", has become valuable as collectors' items — and the object of a book that lives up to the highest expectations. "Theodor Fahrner JEWELRY between Avant-garde and Tradition" recognizes and honors a pioneer who practiced ninety years ago what is quite familiar to us in the field of jewelry today. As an open-minded and self-assured entrepreneur, he cooperated with selected artists, whom we would call designers today, for their mutual benefit, as well as for the benefit and pleasure of all those who — then as now — enhance their own quality of life because they know how to utilize the availability of capably and beautifully made things.

Have we all become accustomed to it?

Fritz Falk,
Schmuckmuseum Pforzheim

Wolfgang Beeh,
Hessisches Landesmuseum, Darmstadt

Wolfgang Till,
Münchner Stadtmuseum

Karl H. Bröhan,
Bröhan Museum, Berlin

Hilmar Ziegenrücker,
Galerie am Fischmarkt, Erfurt

Wieland Koenig,

Karl Bernd Heppe,
Stadtmuseum Düsseldorf

*T*he FORUM for European Art and Culture has set itself the task of making innovative artistic personalities and firms of the 20th Century in the realm of artistry and design known to a broad public through thoroughgoing scientific research. This can — as now in the case of Theodor Fahrner — also result in an inclusive display of his work, which is shown in numerous museums.

In 1979, after 125 years of changing history, the doors of the firm of Gustav Braendle Theodor Fahrner Nachf. in Pforzheim closed. Thus ended the exciting development of a formerly unimportant ring factory into one of the great creative jewelry firms of Europe.

At the end of the 19th Century, Theodor Fahrner, Jr. was one of the first to recognize the need to bring the goldsmithing profession up to date stylistically. He joined the new stylistic movement and hired free-lance artists, including painters, sculptors and architects, to design modern jewelry. At the first international exhibition in which he participated — the 1900 Paris World's Fair — this "artist jewelry" was an astounding success. While René Lalique enjoyed triumphal success with his capricious jewelry creations, Fahrner presented industrially produced steel jewelry in simple shapes; a greater contrast can scarcely be imagined. And yet both document the same artistic credo that the value of a piece of jewelry depends not on the value of the materials but on the artistic design, which must win the customer with a blend of material and form.

With his "design jewelry", which won much acclaim not only in Germany but particularly in England, he was able to establish his reputation as an "artist-manufacturer."

Despite his influential decision in favor of modern, partly machine-made jewelry, he maintained the tradition of the goldsmith's handicraft. In the newly founded "Studio for Goldsmithing Work", classic jewelry and avant-garde designs were created for small-series production.

The forms of his jewelry and the manifold techniques employed speak for the great artistic freedom that Fahrner allowed his designers. In his efforts to unite timely designs of high formal quality with quality workmanship and technology, he attained the principle of the Deutsche Werkbund long before it was founded.

Fahrner's commercial vision and artistic sensitivity can be seen in the fact that, instead of negating the ambivalence of his times between "individualism and mass society", he blended them congenially.

After Theodor Fahrner's death in 1919, his successor Gustav Braendle took over the business and the "FAHRNER-SCHMUCK" trade name. He continued the tradition with imaginative and avant-garde jewelry in the style of the twenties. The name of Theodor Fahrner remained a part of the new firm. The continuation of the firm's philosophy proved to be successful for Gustav Braendle too. But unlike Theodor Fahrner, he guarded his designers' names as a secret; in addition to his sons, only the painter Anton Kling was named as a free-lance designer. The new designs, in the international style of Art Deco, were acclaimed not only in Europe but also in the USA and Latin America.

The political development as of the mid-thirties led to an interruption of free artistic creativity in Germany. Extravagance contradicted the political view of the world; only simple, down-to-earth jewelry was wanted for the German woman. The lavish jewelry of Gustav Braendle could be sold only in the outside world. Two sons, who had contributed to the firm's creativity, died in the war. After World War II, Fahrner jewelry could not win back its former significance again.

In the foreground of this documentation is the attempt to illustrate the extent and creativity of this significant jewelry factory of Theodor Fahrner, known far beyond Europe, in a context of cultural history.

When the idea for this project was born four years ago, we were not aware of what great efforts would be needed for it. During the two world wars, most of the archives were destroyed, important records of the firm were lost, and much had to remain unknown despite intensive research. We hope that this exhibition will lead to the rediscovery of hitherto unknown documents and pieces of jewelry. A lot of traveling and tracking were needed to have the exhibition and the catalog show a representative cross-section of jewelry production in the period from 1900 to 1940; some 2500 examples were inspected. The choice was made not only on the basis of esthetic form, but also from the viewpoint of art history. That we could publish a goodly number of previously unknown documents despite the shortage of source material — among others, it was possible to name more than thirty of the firm's designers for the first time — we owe to the great effort and tireless research of our authors, Dr. Ulrike von Hase-Schmundt, Dr. Christianne Weber and Dr. Ingeborg Becker. We particularly want to thank them most heartily at this point. We also thank Dr. Joachim Becker, Lord Mayor of the City of Pforzheim, for his support and encouragement of the project. We thank Dr. Fritz Falk, Director of the Jewelry Museum, for his kind cooperation and his willingness to collaborate in making the exhibition become reality. In the same way, our thanks are due to the photographer, Peter Frankenstein, who photographed the pieces of jewelry with great sensitivity and tireless energy. Our advisors, Mr. Prof. Siegfried Cremer, Mr. Dr. Bernhard Odenkirchen and Mr. Dr. Claus Pese, are thanked for their factual counsel. For their financial support we thank Messrs. Manfred Müller, Günter Ruf of Stark-Druck and Eugen Müller of Meyle & Müller, as well as Mr. Wolfgang Daum of the Pforzheim City Treasury, all of them residents of Pforzheim.

Our thanks are also extended to the many residents of Pforzheim who were able to give us valuable information on the firm of Theodor Fahrner. The Fahrner pattern books of Mr. Hering and Mr. Arnold, which made it possible to date many pieces of jewelry, were priceless.

Last but not least, our special thanks go to all those who lent what were often their favorite pieces of jewelry and thus made this exhibition possible. In particular, we thank Mrs. Virginia J. Reinshagen, the granddaughter of Theodor Fahrner, Jr., and Mrs. Lore Niemann, daughter of Gustav Braendle, for their kind assistance and the loan of many important documents and pieces.

For their support of this project and much important advice, we also thank: Gabriela Arnold, Thekla Baader, Daniela Baaske, Erich Bahnmüller, Susanne Braendle, Bernd Brüwer, Reinhold Burkart, Prof. Dr. Gerda Buxbaum, Udo Dingler, Wolfgang Ehrlich, Mr. Essig (Pforzheim City Archives), Adam Fenz, Otto Fuchs, Traudl Hauck, Hildegard Huber, Hermann Huhn, Sr., Wolf D. Huwald, Dr. Nelly Jancar, Artur Klingel, Konrad Kreutel, Mrs. Kunze (Württemberg State Library, Stuttgart), Mrs. Leitz (FHG Library, Pforzheim), Lilo Müller, Hans Niemann, Heide Nies, Anne Reiss, Anneliese Römer-Hahn, Dr. Reinhard Sänger, Hans Schöner, Ursula Söllner, Robert Wachs, Achim Zöller M. A. (Boeres Archives, Seligenstadt).

Brigitte Leonhardt / Dieter Zühlsdorff
FORUM for European Art and Culture
August 1990

Ex libris 1912

P.M. Theodor Fahrner

Dates in the History of the Firm of Theodor Fahrner, Pforzheim (1855-1919)

Ulrike von Hase-Schmundt

More dates than products have survived from the first decades of the firm's life.

In April of 1855 the firm of "Seeger & Fahrner" was founded as a jewelry factory.[1] After Georg Seeger's early death, the firm of Theodor Fahrner, Sr. continued. The following dates can be found in the Pforzheim city directories:

1859 The jewelry factory was located on Rosenstrasse.[2]

1867 The jewelry factory was located at Luisenstrasse A116.

1867 at Luisenstrasse 23.[3]

1877 Founding of the Pforzheimer Kunstgewerbeverein (Pforzheim Commercial Art Society). Theodor Fahrner, Sr. is not listed among the founding members.

1881 Here for the first time the entry "ring factory" appears, which indicates a specialization, including for export.

1883 Death of Theodor Fahrner, Sr., age 60; Theodor Fahrner, Jr. was 24 years old. It is possible that he had already finished his training and took over the leadership of the firm at once.[4]

1884 Th. Fahrner appears in the directory as a "ring manufacturer."

1887 as a "jewelry manufacturer."

1891 The directory lists Theodor Fahrner, a jeweler, at Calwerstrasse 88. This may be an early branch office, or possibly a cousin with the same name.

1893 The firm's program is specified. Fahrner appears in the jewelry trade directory as: "Theodor Fahrner: Ring Factory, rings and pins", at Luisenstrasse 23.

1895 On August 1, a jewelry factory at Luisenstrasse 52 is listed as: "Ring Factory, pins, rings, brooches, patent on a safety pin and a brooch." The seven Fahrner siblings are named as the owners of the property at Luisenstrasse 23.[5a]

Shortly before 1900, to Fahrner's death in **1919,** designs were made by numerous artists. Involved were (alphabetically): *Max Benirschke, Friedrich Eugen Berner, Alfred (Max) Bernheim, Franz Boeres, Rudolf Bosselt, Paul Bürck, Karl Eugen Erhardt, Theodor Fahrner, Max Joseph Gradl, Ludwig Habich, Hermann Häussler, Adolf Hildenbrand, Patriz Huber, Bert Joho, Vera Joho (née Fahrner), Friedrich Katz, Georg Kleemann, Erich Kleinhempel, Ludwig Knupfer, Louise Matz, Ferdinand Morawe, Albin Müller,[5b] Julius Müller-Salem, Joseph Maria Olbrich, Egon Riester, Emil Riester, Fritz Wolber.*

1900 First international presentation of Fahrner jewelry at the Paris World's Fair. Fahrner received a silver medal for his creations.

1901 Introduction of the "TF" trade mark (see p. 68). Using this trade mark enabled exporting to Britain and collaboration with the firm of Murrle, Bennett & Co. of London (see p. 272). Expansion of production: "Gold articles, rings, pins, brooches, belt buckles."

What is probably Fahrner's first advertisement appeared in the catalog of the "Ein Dokument Deutscher Kunst" exhibition at the Mathildenhöhe in Darmstadt (see p. 263, #2).

---

1) Lit.: JGK 26, 1905, p. 161; Pforzheimer Generalanzeiger 99, 4/28/1905. Unexplained is the reference to "1856" as the year the firm was founded, on a letterhead of Theodor Fahrner, dated to between 1914 and 1919. A firm of Karst & Seeger in Pforzheim is listed for 1903.

2) Directories of the City of Pforzheim, from 1859 to 1933.

3) It could not be learned whether the firm moved at this time or the house numbers were changed.

4) Theodor Fahrner, Jr. had six sisters.

5a) In 1898 the property at Luisenstrasse 23 was bought by the firm of Andreas Daub. This could only have been a partial change, as the property at Luisenstrasse 23 is listed as being owned by the sisters Berta and Emma Fahrner until 1933. Lit.: Geschichte der Firma Andreas Daub e.V., Pforzheim 1938, p. 6.

5b) Catalog of the First Great Art Exhibition, Wiesbaden 1909. Third improved edition, Wiesbaden 1909, p. 102, no. 770. Original pieces could not be authenticated before that.

Listing of a branch office at Luisenstrasse 26; it was sold in **1907**. It is known that Fahrner worked extensively for "export to all countries." Rudolf Rücklin writes that this branch produced mainly plated jewelry for export to Britain (Cat. no. 1.106). In these years sales were handled by wholesalers, later sales were made directly to jewelers and jewelry stores.[6]

1902 The "Theodor Fahrner Studio for Goldsmithing Work" was cited.[7] In the same year, some 660 jewelry factories in Pforzheim were listed.

1903 Theodor Fahrner "Gold- und Silberwarenfabrik", Luisenstrasse 52.[8] A business card of 1913 has been preserved, bearing the following inscription:[9]

THEODOR FAHRNER
☙ PFORZHEIM ☙
GOLD- UND SILBERWAREN-
FABRIK · GEGRÜNDET 1855 ☙

In the Address and Handbook for the Deutsche Goldschmiedegewerbe, Leipzig 1903, page 7, the entry appears:

> *Fahrner, Theodor, Pforzheim, Luisenstr. 52. (1855.) Inh.: Theodor Fahrner Sohn. — Fabrikation von modernem, künstlerischen Schmuck in Gold (0,750 und 0,585 ff.), Silber und Doublé. Mittelfeiner und feiner Genre. — Estamperie mit eigenen Mustern. — Deutsch und Export nach allen Ländern.

1904 The ring factory was sold or abandoned.[10]

1905 Along with Theodor Fahrner, Heinrich Schütz is listed as an auditor of the funds of the Pforzheimer Kunst-

> Fahrner Th., Inh. Theodor Fahrner Gold- u. Silberwarenfabr., Broches, Braeclets, Anhänger, Kolliers, Gürtelschließen, Hutnadeln Fächerketten, Manschettenknöpfe, Blusen- und Westenknöpfe, Crav.-Nadeln, Messer, Bonbonnières, Cigaretten-Etuis, Bürsten etc., Luisenstr. 52

gewerbeverein.[11] The firm's entry appears in the directory as shown in box.

1910 Introduction of the term and trade mark "FAHRNER-SCHMUCK" (see p. 263). The number of employees at this time is estimated as 80 to 100.[12]

1911 "Theodor Fahrner Gold- und Silberschmuck, Luisenstr. 52/54."

1914 Membership in the Deutsche Werkbund (founded 1907); "D.W.B." included

> **Fahrner-Schmuck**
> **D.W.B.**
> Theodor Fahrner · Kunstwerkstätten

on the letterhead.

At this time too, individual orders, such as for the Berlin actress Maria Carmi (brooch with gold topaz).[13]

1916 Heinzelmann is named cabinetmaster. The number of employees is estimated at 30 to 40.[14]

1919 On July 22, Theodor Fahrner died after a long illness. At the end of the year, the firm was sold to Gustav Braendle of Esslingen by Martha Fahrner (Condition: all former employees had to be kept on). Braendle's cabinetmaster until **1938** was Friedrich Katz, who worked for the firm since **1900** as a fitter and patternmaker (see p. 108).

1921 Martha Fahrner gave the collection of the Pforzheim Kunstgewerbe School 67 pieces of Fahrner jewelry (the so-called Fahrner endowment (Fahrner-Stiftung, F.St. below), Inv.No. 3192/1-66).[15]

1925 In the directory, the firm is listed as "Braendle, Gustav, Theodor Fahrner Nachf., Inh. Gustav und Hermann Braendle, Luisenstrasse 52."

6)
Address and Handbook for the Deutsche Goldschmiedegewerbe, Leipzig 1903, p. 7. Rudolf Rücklin, in: DGZ XXII, 1919, p. 268.

7)
KuH 53, 1902-03, p. 255, illustration, p. 258.

8)
Directory 1903.

9)
Privately owned.

10)
R. Rücklin, DGZ XXII, 1919, p. 268.

11)
KGB Pfh. 12, 1905. The example at the Pforzheim Kunstgewerbeverein is included before p. 141.

12)
Estimated by Frau Dr. Jancar, daughter of the manufacturer Karl Scheufele, who lived near the Fahrners.

13)
Recalled by the goldsmith Konrad Kreutel, who became an apprentice at Fahrners in 1916.

14)
See note 13.

15)
Now owned by the Pforzheim Jewelry Museum.

The "Artist/Manufacturer" Theodor Fahrner, Jr.

Training and management of the firm. The history of the firm, hitherto recounted only in crude form, deserves to be amplified with comments on the personality and work of Theodor Fahrner, Jr. Here too, only a little had been preserved since an attack on Pforzheim on February 23, 1945 destroyed the firm's and family's archives as well as possessions of co-workers and a great portion of the city archives. Thus we must carefully assemble a mosaic. Theodor Fahrner was born in Pforzheim on **August 4, 1859,** the oldest of seven children and the only son of Theodor Fahrner, Sr. and his wife Pauline, née Schweikert.[1] Scarcely anything is known of his youth and schooling; only two letters to his parents, each dated January 1, of 1874 and 1875, remain, in which he expresses in loving loyalty — and enviably fine handwriting — his wishes for the new year (#1).[2] These letters were written in Pforzheim and, alas, tell nothing of his schooling, which may also have taken place elsewhere, perhaps in Strassburg, as was the custom in many Pforzheim families. Only from Rudolf Rücklin's memoirs do we learn of the course of his studies, which were to end with his taking control of his father's firm. "Theodor Fahrner, whose father ran a ring factory in Pforzheim, had practical training as a steel engraver and received his artistic instruction at the Pforzheim Kunstgewerbe School. At both the workbench and the school he showed his unusual artistic and technical capability, and he could take

[1]
See the family tree (p. 268). The Faber family tree is privately owned in Pforzheim.

[2]
Privately owned.

[3]
DGZ XXII, 1919, p. 268.

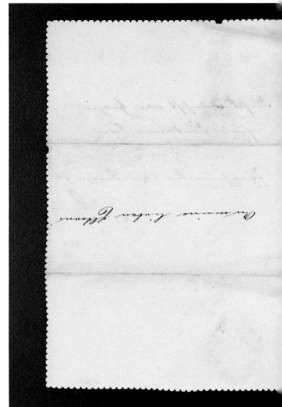

#1 (front and back)

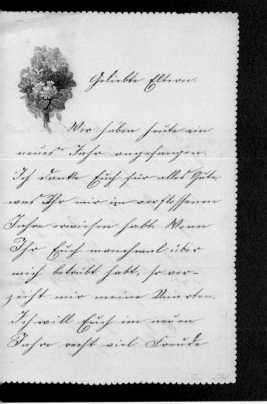

over the paternal factory as a capable technician and talented designer."[3] This training presumably ended with his father's death, for in 1884 Theodor Fahrner, Jr. is already listed in the directory as a "Ringfabrikant." Nothing is known of the firm's size or production methods at that time.

The time of great stylistic breakthroughs was making itself known — for Theodor Fahrner it was likewise a busy time of professional experience and personal development. At first he utilized the potential of his father's firm, which was obviously going well. Its products, of which little more than a set of rings has survived,

---

Letter by Theodor Fahrner to his parents, January 1, 1874 *(#1)*

To my beloved parents!

Today we have begun a new year. I thank you for all the good things that you have done for me in the past year. If you have worried about me at times, please forgive my misbehavior. I want to give you a great deal of joy in the new year. I want to study hard in school and obey my teacher. May God send you happiness and everything good in the new year. I particularly want to ask the Almighty to let you live long lives. This wish is from the heart of your thankful son Theodor. Pforzheim, January 1, '74.

---

probably represented the stylistic forms of dying historicism. Yet the stylistic breakthrough just before the turn of the century forced him to change his outlook. At this time, from 1895 on, come Fahrner's first technical inventions and innovations, patent and protection documents, that indicate an energetic effort to renew the business (see pp. 73ff). To a high degree, the young proprietor possessed both technical and artistic ability. Both of these,

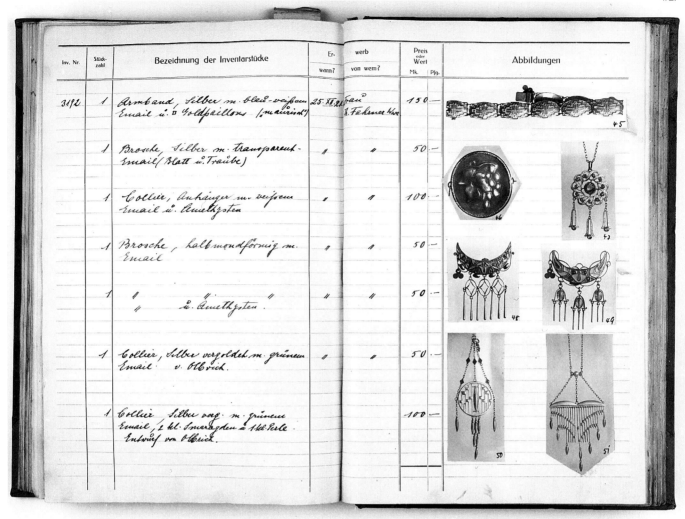

#2.
Double page from the "Inventory II.2 Illustrations" of the Pforzheim Kunstgewerbe School. The inventory includes purchases and gifts from 10/28/1912 to 12/3/1922 (see above).

#3.
Jewelry made at the Grand Ducal Kunstgewerbe School, Pforzheim, displayed at the Third German Commercial Art Exhibition in Dresden, 1906. From: Das deutsche Kunstgewerbe 1906, Munich 1906, p. 291.

4)
DGZ XXII, 1919, p. 269. In DGZ XII, 1909, p. 317, Rücklin wrote: ". . . is no artist. He is a modern businessman and manufacturer."

as seen in the repeated reports of his good jewelry designs,[4] were of good use to him in the years that followed, and gave his judgments a degree of artistic integrity that made a deep impression on the artisans and artists who worked with him.

Membership in the Pforzheim Kunstgewerbeverein — Gifts to the Kunstgewerbe School. It is possible that Fahrner was already a member of the Pforzheim Kunstgewerbeverein in these years, although no list of members is available. But in 1905 the "Kunstgewerbeblatt", journal of the Kunstgewerbeverein, includes the note that Fahrner was made an auditor of the group's funds. He was

#3.

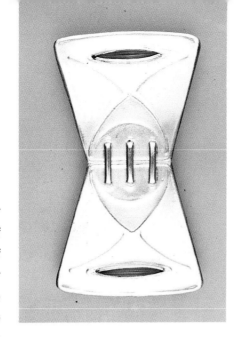

#4.
Belt buckle, 1905-06, designed by a student at the Grand Ducal Kunstgewerbe School, Pforzheim, and made by Theodor Fahrner. Pforzheim Jewelry Museum, Inv. No. Sch 2108.

also active in other areas: at intervals of about a year, pieces of jewelry as well as silver articles were given to the collections of the Kunstgewerbeverein and the Kunstgewerbe School. Some of them were listed as "gifts", others with prices noted, but presumably most of them were gifts. This probably applies most of all to the pieces that were added to the collection of the Kunstgewerbe School, where Fahrner had been a student. The most extensive gift of the Fahrner family was donated at Christmas in 1921, when Martha Fahrner, Theodor's widow, donated 67 pieces made between 1901 and 1919 to the school's collection (#2). The two collections now form the basis of the collection in the Pforzheim Jewelry Museum. Fahrner also promoted the designing ability of the school's students. A belt buckle made by Fahrner to such a design was displayed in Dresden in 1906 (#3, 4).

"The Artist-Manufacturer", "Artistic Jewelry"

In 1900 Rudolf Rücklin wrote something that sounds quite prophetic: "If we sum up . . . the jobs of the artist-manufacturer in brief, we find there is a great variety to them. He must be an artist in a certain sense, not a practicing one but a guiding one, not a virtuoso but a conductor. He must, selflessly and understandingly, grant the designing artist that freedom without which an original and individual work cannot come into being. He has the job of directing the work of the practicing technician, and directing it so that is it is true to the intentions of the design; whatever technical effect can be put into the design, he must know how to read out; it is his job to give the artist new inspiration, namely of a technical kind. And over and above all that, he must possess the qualities of a sober, far-seeing businessman who knows how to keep artistic inspiration and commercial calculation separate, never becoming tired of the former or incautious in the latter. He must be aware that he serves not only his own interests but also a high, ideal purpose, one that is of very special national significance and that the coming century will demand that we solve."[5] After Theodor Fahrner's death in 1919, Rücklin acknowledged that the person of Theodor Fahrner was his ideal.[6] In a 1900 article, Rücklin went into detail on the problems of producing jewelry in the factory, interestingly enough, not in reference to difficulties of a technical nature that might turn up, but in reference to the types of customers. He divided them into three levels:

The first class is composed of undifferentiated, typical buyers of low-priced, usually fashion-oriented mass-produced goods. As an unnamed contemporary art writer said in a harsh judgment: "Mush gives no echo, and in artistic terms, our people are mush!" The industry produced mass goods for this group.

The second class has "property and education", but does not risk buying the latest styles, especially daring artistic creations. "Here is a field for art, if only a modest one . . . Artistic power, though . . , strong and bold effects, are not wanted here" (p. 189). For this group the manufacturer makes "fine medium-priced goods."

The third class includes the real art lovers. They have the means and the knowledge of art, plus the interest in the

artists, new techniques, etc.. In Germany this group is still small, but it is growing. For this group the "artist-manufacturer" produces art works of personal individuality and independent artistic value." To do this, the following prerequisites are necessary for the manufacturer: He must know the art and artists of his time, must have an esthetic education, must possess high technical abilities, in order to realize designs that go beyond the normal technical level. Then too, the sales procedures for "works of art in precious metal" (p. 200) are different from those used for medium- and low-priced goods that can be sold via wholesalers or shops. Artistic jewelry must be introduced to the art trade and shown at art shows, art dealerships and salons. In this way the "United Workshops" of Munich and Dresden, "L'Art Nouveau" of Paris, etc., were already working. The best

#5.
Fahrner jewelry at the 1900 Paris World's Fair, as shown in: R. Rücklin, Das Schmuckbuch, Leipzig 1901, p. 249.

Abb. 223. **Schmuckstücke aus der Fabrik von Th. Fahrner, Pforzheim.**
Entwürfe von J. M. Gradl, München. Pariser Ausstellung 1900.

#6.
Theodor Fahrner's silver medal won at the 1900 Paris World's Fair.

way to finance this exclusive type of operation in the jewelry business was through "cheap, well-publicized and funded mass production" (p. 200) as a basis, just as had proved itself, for example, in the ceramic industry. Rücklin sees the inspiration for realizing his ideas in the jewelry business in Berlin, Hanau, Pforzheim and Schwäbisch Gmünd (end of the summary). The purposefulness with which Theodor Fahrner's work developed is a fascinating aspect of his life and work.

The 1900 Paris World's Fair - Max J. Gradl

At the beginning came the decision to take on a designer who was already famous at this point — Max J. Gradl of Munich (see pp. 92 ff). He was the first free-lance artist who collaborated with Fahrner and considerably influenced the program that had used the firm's own designs until then. The success of his first pieces encouraged Fahrner, who had hitherto taken part, presumably, only in the exhibitions of the Kunstgewerbeverein in Pforzheim, to show these pieces at the 1900 World's Fair in Paris (#5). When Max

J. Gradl moved from Munich to Stuttgart in 1901, his designs for Theodor Fahrner had already been awarded a silver medal in Paris.[7] Gradl's name did not, of course, appear in the fair catalog, but was made public later. In March of 1901 he was named "artistic advisor" to Fahrner.[8] The collaboration between Theodor Fahrner and Max J. Gradl lasted until at least 1910 and was not limited to jewelry designs. Around 1902, for example, Max J. Gradl also designed Fahrner's bedroom, which was built by the firm of Alfred Bühler in

7)
This medal is still owned by the family. Of 22 silver medals won by German jewelers and firms, 13 went to Pforzheim firms.

8)
See biography and catalog texts, plus Ostwald, Moderne deutsche Goldschmidedkunst, in: Westermanns Monatshefte, 45, 1901, pp. 797 ff.

#7.
Fahrner's bedroom, designed by Max J. Gradl, 1901-02.

Stuttgart (#7).[9] In addition to Fahrner, other noted Pforzheim firms, including L. Kuppenheim, Benckiser, Rodi & Wienenberger, D. F. Weber, Louis Fiessler, and F. Zerenner, were honored in Paris. But it is striking that it was he who subsequently succeeded in signing other great designers, whose names were seen more and more rarely in publications on the other firms. But Fahrner stubbornly pursued his goal, even after the exciting years of stylistic breakthroughs, of raising the artistic quality of wholly or partly machine-made jewelry to the level of artistic jewelry. He knew that this goal required constant innovation, and sought cooperative artists, though he obviously also discovered great talents among the designers who worked within the firm, especially Katz and Knupfer. This determined striving for quality must have impressed many artists who actually had nothing to do with the production of Pforzheim jewelry.

Cooperation with the Artists of the Darmstadt Art Colony

The path in the direction of artistic jewelry had been taken in the collaboration with Max J. Gradl, and the great success in Paris was proof that it had not been an exception. The forthcoming exhibition, "A Document of German Art", at Darmstadt in 1901 was surely the impetus to contract with members of the artists' colony for further jewelry designs. When and how the first

contacts were made is not known. It is also possible that the initiative was taken by the members of the art colony, for it was an economic necessity for the artists to arrange for the production of their designs. "For the production of the interior decor (of the artists' houses: author's note), a very unusual method was chosen. The artist placed his design on a tabletop, podium or the like, for the manufacturer. If the latter liked the design and wanted to produce it, then he received the exclusive right to the design, while the artist received a commission and the first piece produced. Thus everything was done that could afford the artist a free expression of his decorative ideals."[10] Excited by the entrepreneur's courage that Fahrner showed by presenting his unusual steel jewelry (Cat. no. 1.25) at the World's Fair, and by his subtle sensitivity for new artistic ideas, they may well have seen Fahrner as the ideal producer of their jewelry designs.

In retrospect, the contact between Fahrner and the artists appears to be a perfectly natural step. The so-called Darmstadt Experiment, generously promoted by Grand Duke Ludwig of Hesse and the Rhine and by the city of Darmstadt, coincided with Fahrner's conceptions. Paul Bürck, Rudolf Bosselt, Ludwig Habich, Patriz Huber and Joseph M. Olbrich could not resist the influence and enthusiasm of the Pforzheim jewelry manufacturer and put their designs in the service of the common goal: great artists designing for

9)
In November of 1902, photos of works by Max J. Gradl were displayed, showing furniture by Alfred Bühler of Stuttgart. One of these photos depicts the bedroom — described there as a bookcase — that could be identified by a photograph owned by a Fahrner descendant. Lit.: Richard Graul, Der Kampf um die Kunst im Mobiliar, and: Franck-Oberaspach, Künstler, Fabrikant und Publikum, in: Mitteilungen des Württembergischen Kunstgewerbevereins, 1903-04, No. 1, pp. 2-40.

10)
KGB Pforzheim, 1901, Vol. 8, No. 6, no page cited.

11)
DKD XIII, 1903-04, p. 40.

series production. Unlike the many reports that refer to the disaster of the Darmstadt exhibition, for Fahrner his collaboration with the artists was a long-lasting success. The number of their designs in the ensuing years went well beyond those involved in the exhibition. Patriz Huber in particular provided a great number of designs that could be sold in high price ranges. In "German Art and Decoration" of 1903 it was written: "Some of his brooches were sold by the thousands, not only in Germany but also in Paris and elsewhere outside the country."[11] The photographs of his jewelry in such respected journals as, for example, "The Studio" (in a special 1901-02 issue on jewelry and fans in London) meant very extra-ordinary recognition for Fahrner's accomplishments (#8).

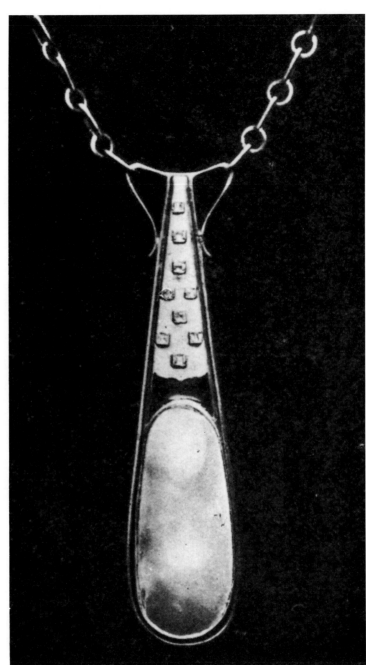

#8.
Necklace after a design by Joseph M. Olbrich, circa 1901, manufactured by Theodor Fahrner. Photo from Special Winter Number of THE STUDIO, A.D. 1901-1902 (Plate 3).

This success was all the more significant in that it had been the idea of the Darmstadt artist colony to give impetus to Hessian industry and make it grow. But the jewelry industry located in Hesse, especially in Hanau, had not been interested in this project. On the other hand, Theodor Fahrner, from Pforzheim in Baden, had stepped in and built the foundation for modern series production of art, very little of which was to been seen in Hanau during the following years.

#9a

The New Style.

It is clear that in terms of creating jewelry, the Darmstadt Experiment had succeeded and simultaneously showed that the modern style in Germany had inclined in a practical direction, that of factory production of jewelry. Fahrner had proved that modern jewelry was not bound to a need for expensive "reform" clothing, as was maintained by Behrens and Van de Velde. The fact that Fahrner's jewelry went very well with reform clothing, though, is shown by illustrations of a dress designed by Alfred Mohrbutter (#9a, 9b). On the illustrated black chiffon theater dress with brown taffeta sleeves, a bolero clasp (after a design by Patriz Huber) is worn on the matte gray velvet inset, which is decorated with malachite and lapiz lazuli. This variation of a belt buckle (Cat. no. 1.50) was the latest style in 1902-03: "Now, for example, belt buckles step far into the foreground, as in the prevailing blouse styles there was scarcely a dress without a blouse and not a blouse without a belt.

Boleros, worn loose, required something to hold them together across the breast; thus similar clasps were produced in smaller numbers . . ."[12] A further example of Theodor Fahrner's jewelry in combination with a reform dress was depicted in the "Deutsche Goldschmiedezeitung" of 1903, page 63: "a simple reform costume." with chain and brooch, possibly from a design by Max J. Gradl. These examples

#9b

show that Fahrner was trying to make his jewelry compatible with the latest styles, yet his pieces of jewelry were free of symbiosis with specific fashion concepts. He made chiefly necklaces and pendants, brooches, belt buckles, plus tie, hat and coat pins, all forms of jewelry that could be worn in many ways. Problems occurred for those Pforzheim firms that concentrated exclusively on the French-influenced Art Nouveau, such as the firm of Louis Kuppenheim with Hans Christiansen's beautiful pieces, which had won a gold medal at the Paris World's Fair. "The well-conceived simplicity, the simple, strict lines, the avoidance of any naturalistic effect of opulence: that affords a complete artistic picture that has nothing to do with art of the Lalique type" — thus comments R. Rücklin in a report on the Pforzheim jewelry industry in 1902, on the occasion of an anniversary exhibition in Karlsruhe, in the DGZ of 1903, page 3. This was the result of the firm's development away from the vegetative Art Nouveau and its adoption of the stylistic principles of the Darmstadt artists, following its own course free from that of French art. This was also the significance of Theodor Fahrner's work: he had quickly recognized the limitations of Art Nouveau for series production, and perhaps had also seen that in creating jewelry it could only be realized when its realization was in the hands of the famous Parisian jewelers. The purchase of the "swallow brooch" by René Lalique by the Pforzheim Kunstgewerbeverein had made the difference between the two types of production obvious. Through this very purchase it had become clear that another course had to be taken in the factory production of jewelry. Fahrner was aware of this fact, for on the one hand, he knew the technical requirements of manufacturing, and on the other, he was much too self-conscious to even think of the embarrassment of imitating the French luxury jewelry. He had recognized early that the Darmstadt course led to the solution of his major stylistic problem, and that may well have been the secret of his success as an "artist-manufacturer": he was almost the only one among all the Pforzheim manufacturers who produced high-quality artistic jewelry and avoided the narcotic effect of the French Art Nouveau.

Naturally it was not just artistic awareness that led his experiment in the right direction. It was important for the quality of his products that Theodor Fahrner gave his staff designers and the artists who provided designs for them both artistic and technical freedom. Friedrich Eugen Berner of Stuttgart, for example, whose flat stamped jewelry was certainly not above criticism, could offer similar designs to Fahrner, as several existing test pieces attest (see illustration, page 50). On the

12)
A. Mohrbutter, Das Kleid der Frau, 1904, pp. 44-45, DGZ 1903, pp. 43, 63.

Exhibitions

13)
DGZ XXII, 1919, p. 269.

14)
Appeared in Pforzheim.

15)
DGZ XXII, 1919, p. 269.

16)
Selected lit.: 1900 Paris
World's Fair, Amtl. Kat. der
Ausstellung des Deutschen
Reiches, Berlin (1900), p. 358;
Class 94, Display of the
Pforzheim Jewelry Industry,
No. 4402.

17)
J. M. Olbrich, Die Ausstellung
der Künstlerkolonie
Darmstadt 1901, p.
40,42,44,47,103,108,132

18)
Jubiläums-Kunst-
Ausstellung, Karlsruhe 1902,
p. 58.

19)
Franck-Oberaspach,
Feinmetall-Ausstellung April
1903, in: Mitt. des Württ.
Kunstgewerbevereins 1903,
No. 6, noted on pp. 357 ff.

other hand, the "small plastics" by Max J. Gradl or Ludwig Habich required, at least in part, different production methods, especially that of casting, which was done in sand at that time. Again and again it was stressed that Fahrner possessed a great regenerative power in these technical questions, for he insisted on the production of even those pieces that were difficult to realize.[13] Only by exhausting all of his technical abilities was it possible for him to make a success of the daring experiment of including free-lance artists in the jewelry business. In conclusion, it must be said that the precise price ranges of Fahrner jewelry could not be determined.

The Geometrical Ornament - The Years after 1902

It can be assumed that, about contemporaneously with his contact with the Darmstadt artists, Fahrner's collaboration with Professors Georg Kleemann, J. Müller-Salem and Fritz Wolber of the Pforzheim Kunstgewerbe School began.

Georg Kleemann, whose design drawings "Moderner Schmuck" of 1900 (#10)[14] already offered a remarkable variety, ranging from vegetative to strictly linear ornamentation, became a Fahrner designer around 1901. With the fresh, timely, symbolic designs of Wolber and Müller-Salem, Theodor Fahrner ended the era of vegetative Art Nouveau in his firm. With a good sense of artistic talent, he sought contact with the painter Ferdinand Morawe, the sculptor Franz Boeres and the architect Max Benirschke, whose jewelry designs were dominated by fascinating economy or simple geometry. The filigree jewelry so dear to Fahrner, for which he, as Rücklin states, made designs himself, was added to the program for 1908.[15] Other artists were obviously active for Fahrner for only short times, for example, Louise Matz of Lübeck and Erich Kleinhempel of Dresden. Their names also guaranteed the enduring success of the business and simultaneously give evidence of Fahrner's ability to attract. Fahrner's unbroken success since the 1900 World's Fair lasted until 1903, despite a financial recession, and was rightfully praised in the press and at exhibitions.

Exhibition Participation

Fahrner jewelry won prizes and praise in the press at the following exhibitions:

#10.
Georg Kleemann, Moderner Schmuck, 1900, no page cited.

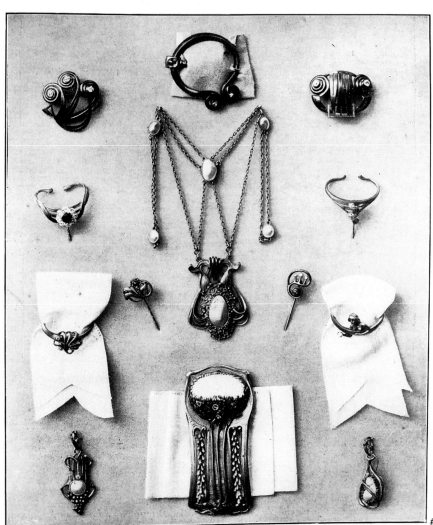

#11.
Jewelry by Theodor Fahrner exhibited at the 1900 Paris World's Fair (selection). Designed in part by Max J. Gradl.

#12.
Rings with jewels, after designs by Max J. Gradl, 1900 Paris World's Fair. Picture from DKD 1900, Vol. 6, p. 524.

#11

#12

1900: Paris World's Fair; as an individual exhibitor and as one of the Pforzheim industrial group, Theodor Fahrner received a silver medal (#11, 12).[16]

1901: Darmstadt, Exhibition of the Darmstadt Artists' Colony for 1901.[17]

1902: Karlsruhe, Anniversary Art Exhibition.[18]

1903: Stuttgart, Fine Metal Exhibition.[19]

1904: St. Louis World's Fair; Along with the Pforzheim Kunstgewerbe School, Fahrner exhibited in the hall of the Kunstgewerbeverein of Baden.[20]

1905: Munich: First Exhibition of the Munich Society of Applied Art.[21]

1906: Dresden, Third German Commercial Art Exhibition.[22]

1906: Karlsruhe, Jubille Expedition for Art and Commercial Art.[23]

1909: Stuttgart, Commercial Art Objects from Schwäbisch-Gmünd and Pforzheim.

1910: Brussels, World's Fair.[24]

1914: Cologne, Werkbund Exposition.[25]

1914: Malmö, Baltic Collection.[26]

1918: Kopenhagen, Werkbund Exposition.

20)
Weltausstellung in St. Louis 1904, Amtlicher Katalog, Berlin 1904: Group 31, No. 2309, p. 450; Group 37, No. 2448, p. 456. In Group 31 the citation appears: "Theodor Fahrner, Gold" and Silver Googs Factory. Specialty: Artistic Jewelry to original designs by leading artists." Group 37: "Theodor Fahrner, Jeweler."

21)
First Exhibition of the Munich Society of Applied Art, Munich 1905; jewelry: F. E. Berner Cat. No. 44-46, noted on p. 35.

22)
Das Deutsche Kunstgewerbe 1906, Catalog, Dresden 1906, jewelry by E. Kleinhempel, p. 252. Fahrner was honored with a gold medal. On p. 291 a belt buckle is shown at the right, made by Fahrner to a design from the Pforzheim Kunstgewerbe School (Inventory No. Sch 2108). The school displayed its own collection.

23)
KGB Pfh. XIII, 1906, pp. 27 ff.

24)
Theodor Fahrner also referred to this exhibition on a letterhead. It was noted in the Aukt. Kat. Fahrner-Schmuck, Munich, No. 153, 1990, p. x: Amtlicher Katalog für die Deutsche Abteilung der Baltischen Ausstellung, Malmö 1914, Berlin 1914.

25)
GK 31, 1910, p. 251; Brussels World's Fair 1910, Deutsches Reich Amtlicher Katalog 1910, p. 41 (non-precious metals).

26)
KGB NF 26, 1914-15, p. 167; Deutsche Werkbund Ausstellung, Cöln 1914, Offizieller Katalog, p. 122 "Kollektivausstellung Pforzheim" under "Factory-Produced Jewelry." Among the Pforzheim exhibitors were Ballin, H. Drews, Hepke & Lichtenfels, Moritz Rothgiesser, Karl Lay, Karl Scheufele, Wild & Co., Wimmer & Rieht, Julius Wimmer, Friedrich Zerenner. p. 123; in the main hall Theodor Fahrner exhibited "gold and silver goods (Fahrner Jewelry)."

The Firm's Structure

Marketing Methods, Prices, Advertising. As already noted, Theodor Fahrner's business included the following fields:

1. Plated articles, especially pins, which were sold very successfully in England,

2. Ring manufacture (until 1904),

3. Studio for goldsmithing work,

4. Jewelry and silver goods factory,

5. "Fahrner Jewelry" manufacture.

These branches of the firm formed the financial foundation for the "artist jewelry" experiment.

A far-flung geographical export business with these products — especially to England via the firm of Murrle, Bennett & Co. — guaranteed Fahrner a financial basis which made the constant pursuit of his goal possible. (Further information of the firm of Murrle, Bennett & Co. of London: see pp. 272 ff.)

In 1919 Rücklin mentioned that Fahrner handled the sale of his products at first through a wholesaler and later through direct deliveries to jewelry stores and art houses. The wholesaler was probably Immanuel Saake, who also formed the link to Murrle, Bennett & Co. in London (see p. 272). Fahrner had recognized at the right time that advertising of his artistic jewelry by celebrities had to be done to support his own program. At a later time, this led to direct sales of his artistic jewelry to individual jewelry stores, which were probably visited by salesmen. Only a few names of jewelers are known to us, such as Carl Meyer in Strassburg, Jakob Bender in Wiesbaden and C. Steyl in Königsberg.

Around 1911 the Dresden firm of Stöckig & Co., purveyors to the court of Saxony, offered a special catalog "U" of "modern jewelry", including an entire page of FAHRNER-SCHMUCK to "artist's designs" (#13). It can surely be said that Theodor Fahrner never had the intention of being regarded as one of the producers of low-priced mass products, as V. Becker suggests in her "Art Nouveau Jewellery", p. 218. Of course various new machine

#13.
The mail-order catalog of Stöckig & Co., purveyors to the court, Dresden, circa 1911, includes a reference to "Catalog U" (silver, gold, diamond and pearl jewelry, watches, tableware), p. 7.

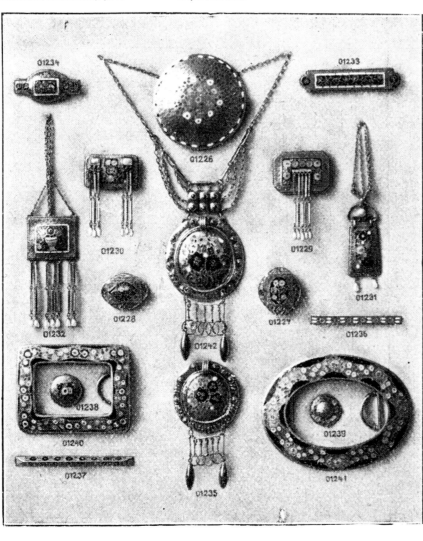

#15. Jewelry piece called "Femme fleure", from the studio of Theodor Fahrner, after a design by Max J. Gradl, ca. 1899-1900.

#14.
Silver brooch to a design by Joseph M. Olbrich, made by Theodor Fahrner. Picture from: Special Winter Number of THE STUDIO, A.D. 1901-1902 (Plate 8).

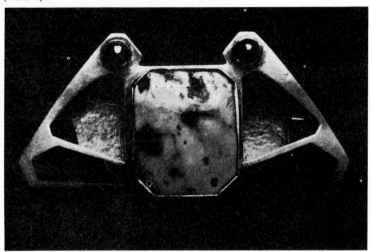

techniques had simplified the production of certain pieces and thus had made those pieces somewhat more affordable, but Fahrner's prices were still far above those of real mass production, such as those made at Gablonz.

Theodor Fahrner: "Studio for Goldsmith Work" Fahrner's approach was that "democratization of luxury" that the French press satirized in connection with the German jewelry industry's exhibit in Paris in 1900: "Well, we shall finally get to see Germany's products; we shall be surprised, really surprised, for that will show us something that amounts to the nicest paradox one could want: la démocratisation du luxe..."[27] Untroubled by the opposition met by other Pforzheim firms which partially imitated French jewelry, Theodor Fahrner followed his course which joined artistic design and

machine production. He had won high acclaim with it and also promoted the reputation of the Pforzheim industry on an international scale (#14). Yet the foundation of the "Studio for Goldsmithing Work" in 1902, or perhaps even slightly earlier, shows that Fahrner was also following a second path. The studio was first mentioned in 1902, in connection with the production of a brooch designed by Eduard von Berlepsch (see p. 82). In 1905, J. Hoffmann, in the publication "Der Moderne Stil", referred to a piece designed by Max J. Gradl and produced in Theodor Fahrner's studio (#15).[28] Later too, we meet the concept again: On a post-1914 letterhead of the Fahrner firm, "Theodor Fahrner Kunstwerkstätten" (see p. 19). There is no reference to the studio here, of course, but a former Fahrner trainee, Konrad Kreutel, recalled the production of a single brooch around 1916, especially

27)
DK I, 1898, pp. 212 ff. Schumacher quotes the French journal "Le Figaro", which mentioned the awaited German exhibit in the World's Fair.

28)
At the 1910 Brussels World's Fair, Theodor Fahrner appeared in the "Official Catalog" in Group 95 as "Theodor Fahrner Kunstgewerbliches Atelier."

#16.
Pendant-brooch by Renè Lalique, 1898-1900, Pforzheim Jewelry Museum, Inventory No. Sch 1736. Picture from "Falk-Schöner, Europäischer Schmuck", 1985, Cat. No. 95, p. 94.

29)
DGZ XXII, 1919, p. 268. See also the St. Louis catalog of 1904, in which Theodor Fahrner is listed as a "jeweler" in Group 37.

30)
Inventory of the Kunstgewerbeschule, No. 1736, 1901.

involving the setting of a gold topaz. It can be assumed that his gold jewelry, such as those by Ferdinand Morawe or E. F. Berner, were produced in this studio.[28] The studio concept permeated Fahrner's life very clearly. After his death it was mentioned that Theodor Fahrner would have loved to limit himself to the production of individual pieces in a studio-like group of workshops.[29] Naturally, it must have been more satisfying for a person of Fahrner's artistic sensibility to devote the greatest attention to a design and the material used in individual work. Gold played an important role therein. The choice of this metal for the production of designs by the "Fahrner artists" von Berlepsch, Benirschke, Berner, Gradl, Matz, Morawe, Kleinhempel and Olbrich, represented quite some expenditure, for

gold was very expensive. We know, for example, that the brooch with the "girl amid the twigs" (Cat. No. 1.23) cost 330 Marks; the "Swallow Brooch" by Lalique (#16) had been bought by the Pforzheim Kunstgewerbeverein for 815 Marks.[30] Silver jewelry cost considerably less. Bürck's brooch (Cat. No. 1.20), for example,

#17.
Six buttons from Theodor Fahrner's silver goods production, circa 1910.

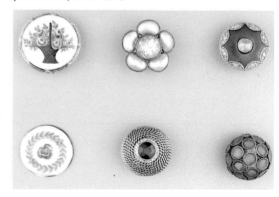

cost 7.50 Marks, Huber's famous belt buckle (Cat. No. 1.49) cost 36 Marks. Considering a jewelry worker's hourly pay of 60 Pfennigs at this time, this price is more than a whole week's pay. Gold was not suitable for series production because of its high price.

To justify his prices and live up to his personal standards, the gold had to be handcrafted by the goldsmith with the greatest finesse. For designs by the aforementioned artists, and later too, exceptions were made in terms of the costly material (#18).

Silver, on the other hand, was much more suitable for machine-working because it was more strongly alloyed. Sometimes gilded, it remained Fahrner's standard material for producing machine-made parts.

These facts also taught Fahrner that, for financial reasons, he would not be able to limit himself to a studio, and that this would be at least a major risk. In addition, an exclusively studio-type business would have conflicted with his series production of "artist jewelry."

It was probably his own dynamism that stood in Fahrner's way. Despite his downright fervent urge to practice pre-industrial workshop methods, he was a very modern man. He turned to advertising early, before other Pforzheim firms had seen its potential. His first advertisement is seen in the catalog of the 1901 Darmstadt Exhibition, in the same year in which he re-

#18, from: DGZ, No. 27-28, 1918, p. 30.

gistered his firm's "TF" monogram as a trade mark (see. p. 263).

In a 1906 advertisement he was already promoting "FAHRNER SCHMUCK after the designs of first-class artists." This advertisement appears, significantly enough, in "Deutsche Kunst und Dekoration", a much-read periodical for all those interested in art and commercial art, and not in one of the trade papers of the goldsmithing organizations, which reached a very different public.

The Silver Goods Factory A sure source of income —according to Rücklin's concept of the "artist-manufacturer" — afforded Fahrner a great advance in the realm of his "artist jewelry." This was his silver goods factory. First listed in the directory in 1903, its products were specified in 1905: "... belt buckles, hatpins, fan chains, glove buttons, blouse and vest buttons, tie pins, knives, candy boxes, cigarette cases, brushes, etc." (#17). At the 1910 Brussels World's Fair Fahrner displayed toilette sets (Cat. No. 1.169) and two table clocks from this branch. In the same year he also donated these or similar silver articles to the Kunstgewerbeschule. It is remarkable that only a few objects have survived, and that scarcely any of them are found in private or museum collections (Cat. No. 1.167). Fahrner had registered numerous samples from this branch of the business (see pp. 73ff): a reversible decorative cover for pocket watches in 1904, a patent for glove buttons in 1906, the "Fahrner Pocket" with reversible bow (see pp. 74, 234) in 1912 and a cigarette box, and a clasp in 1913.

The products of the silver goods factory were thus not only original but also obviously chosen with care. It can be assumed that Fahrner built up this branch of the business in order to make both the ring factory and the manufacturing of plated goods unnecessary. Rings were probably unsuitable as a long-term starting point for large ornamental artistic jewelry — only a single early ring is known, dating from about 1900 (Cat. No. 1.24). And the plated jewelry, most of which was exported, was obviously uninspiring to Fahrner and was probably discontinued at a point in time when the silver goods factory was able to support itself and the artist jewelry. A purse made to a design by Patriz Huber shows that Theodor Fahrner also used artist's designs

31)
Catalog of the Darmstadt Artists' Colony Museum, 1990, Cat. No. 170, p. 118.

32)
See the 1988 Berlin Catalog, Ingeborg Becker, Schmuckkunst in Jugendstil, picture on p. 60.

for silver goods.[31] Later this silver goods factory was also sold to Gustav Braendle.

FAHRNER JEWELRY — Artistic Jewelry

In 1910, as success continued, Theodor Fahrner registered the term "FAHRNER-SCHMUCK" with the Imperial Patent Office in Berlin as a trade mark (see p. 263).

In 1906, in an advertisement in "Deutsche Kunst und Dekoration", this term had already appeared, along with the important information that every piece made by the firm of Theodor Fahrner was stamped with the "TF" monogram. Probably there were a few competitors among the Pforzheim firms whose similar designs occasionally had to be shown not to be Fahrner's. To cite just two examples: Heinrich Levinger (using designs by Kleemann) and Carl Hermann produced stylistically very similar pieces of jewelry.[32] As of about 1906, pictures of Fahrner's jewelry appeared more and more often in the publications of the Kunstgewerbe and the goldsmithing industry without naming the artists.

The term "artist-jewelry" turns up in reference to jewel boxes (see p. 56) as well as in the literature. It seems that Fahrner was using this term to make a first and positive impression. The experiment — involving well-known artists in the jewelry industry — had succeeded. Fahrner had proved it. It was possible to use outstanding and not always originally suitable designs for at least partially machine-production, even if their quality of workmanship and variety of color were achieved only through the talented reworking or further development of qualified goldsmiths. The name of the firm's owner, Theodor Fahrner, now famous among the public as well as in the profession, stood for the success of the experiment, which Fahrner also utilized on a legal level in 1910. With very few exceptions, his jewelry was sold from then on only under the trade mark of "FAHRNER-SCHMUCK", without citing the artist's name. Fahrner had to use a lot of courage, for he had to expect an alienation of the artist from the firm and at the same time rely on the contributions of highly qualified designers within the firm. A residual risk remained, but the economic success of his silver goods factory secured Fahrner's financial foundation. It was not by chance that silver articles made by his firm were displayed at the 1910 World's Fair in Brussels.

Membership in the Deutsche Werkbund
In this respect, Fahrner's membership in the "Deutsche Werkbund" in 1914 can be regarded as a logical consequence, in that the Werkbund proclaimed exactly the goals that Fahrner had already achieved. On the membership lists of May 1, 1914 and June 15, 1919 there appears: "Theodor Fahrner Workshops for Artistic Jewelry, Pforzheim, Luisenstrasse 52." Of the important Pforzheim firms, only Bissinger's is listed in 1919. Fahrner exhibited at two of the Werkbund's exhibitions, in Cologne in 1914 (#19) and Copenhagen in

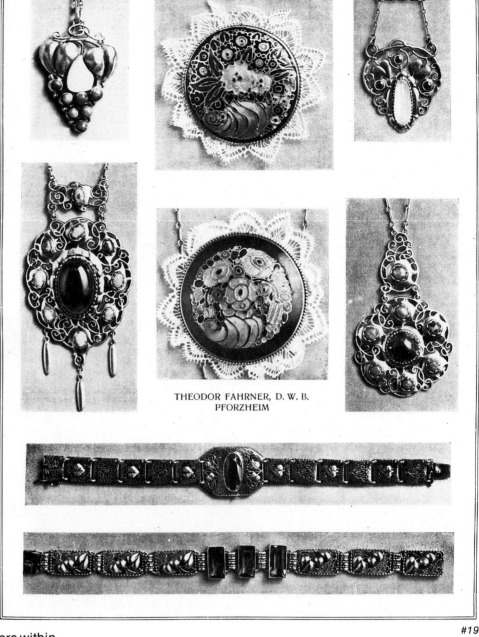

THEODOR FAHRNER, D. W. B.
PFORZHEIM

#19

#19.
From: KGB NF, Vol. 26, 1914-15, No. 9, p. 175.

#20.
Half-finished enamel inlays for brooches.

#21.
Albert Joho's enamel inlay for a brooch, circa 1916.

1918, each time receiving favorable comments from the press.[33]

The Years from 1907 to 1919. It can be presumed (no evidence remains) that the success gained before World War I con-

tinued until its end, although the number of employees declined to some 30 to 40 on account of war service, including that of designer Friedrich Katz. As of 1908 it was particularly the floral type of enameled jewelry, as reintroduced by Hermann

33. KGB NF 26, 1914-15, picture on p. 175.

#21

Häussler, that developed, as well as Neo-Historicism: Ancient (#20), medieval, Renaissance, Baroque, without whose financial support the contemporary jewelry might not have been able to exist. As World War I began, Fahrner introduced an extensive production of patriotic and, later, memorial jewelry on a high level. At the same time, enamel jewelry with, in part, Christian motifs by young Egon Riester and abstract designs by Fahrner's son-in-law Bert Joho (#21) began to appear. In the last war years Fahrner's activities had to be curtailed more and more on account of illness. Until the last days of his life, though, he still drew designs, at first with his right hand, later with his left, using a pencil-holder (#22) that attached to his finger and had been made just for him. An elevator connected his home with the factory,[34] so that, using his strength of will, he could still direct the firm. On July 22, 1919, the life and the suffering of this remarkable man ended.

Looking back to his essay on the "artist-manufacturer", which Rücklin wrote in 1900, Rudolf Rücklin writes in his memoir: "I tried to show in this work how a modern jewelry manufacturer could achieve artistic work, artistically valuable production, profitable collaboration with artists. The model for this imaginary artist-manufacturer was Theodor Fahrner . . . Above all, he strove for artistic freshness and originality. He wanted to obtain that from outside, from the hands of established inventive spirits, while he originally limited himself to the role of the understanding transmitter to the technical and economic requirements of the jewelry industry. This was, if I may say so, an act of boldest self-denial . . ."[35]

#22.
The pencil holder made for Theodor Fahrner.

34)
Friedrich Katz recalled this.

35)
DGZ XXII, 1919, p. 268, see also footnote 4.
Until just a few years ago, Theodor Fahrner's grave was on the middle path of the main cemetery in Pforzheim, at right near the still-remaining grave of Dittler.

Life Style - Family - Travel

#23. Theodor Fahrner in his garden, circa 1910.

36)
Franz Boeres, Wie ich zu meinem Berufe kam, Stuttgart 1937, p. 6. The nail is privately owned.

37)
Fahrner had bought several plots of land on Luisenstrasse. According to the listing in the city directory, the family owned nos. 23, 25, 52, 54 and 56. In 1910 or 1911 the businessman Scheufele bought part of the property at no. 54 (information thanks to his daughter, Dr. Nelly Jancar).

Fahrner was also modern in terms of all technical innovations. He patented numerous technical developments and quickly made use of new devices such as the telephone or the automobile. His driving pleasure is recorded in anecdotes.

Franz Boeres tells that Fahrner was the first resident of Pforzheim to own a car — a nail which sealed the fate of a tire during one of his first drives through Pforzheim still exists, silver-plated and inscribed with the date: "... he looked for me and I received 300 Reichsmark for the first

series of designs, and in his nice car (the first in Pforzheim, in 1905) I went for a ride with his family, which raised the event above the level of the purely material ..."[36] Many sources, even today, have portrayed the deep impression made by the Fahrner family's cultivated feeling for life and home. The family owned one of the loveliest estates in the nicest part of town, and prominent artists had helped to decorate it.[37] In 1902, Max J. Gradl had designed a bedroom that was built by Alfred Bühler of Stuttgart; Fritz Wolber had created a fountain for the garden. The big, parklike garden (#23) was not detracted from by the building of two garages around 1910 — one of them with a bedroom for the chauffeur. This estate became the focal point of an elegant social life that took on a particular significance thanks to the family's love of music.

In 1890 Theodor Fahrner had married Martha Faber, the daughter of a Stuttgart jurist. Their two daughters Vera and Yella, born in 1895 and 1897, were musically and artistically very talented.[38] Of the many foreign trips mentioned by Rücklin, only the Fahrners' great journey to Egypt in 1907 is described in detail. Various photos show the businessman and his wife mounted on camels (#25, see next page) or amid the native population (#24).[39]

These few personal facts from Theodor Fahrner's life may explain why he did not limit himself exclusively to his ideal — the studio. Fahrner's personality was much too expansive and dynamic, too open in many directions, to want to be limited to one workshop with all its financial risks.[40]

38)
See the biography of Vera Joho, née Fahrner (p. 107). Yella Fahrner married the prominent musician, art historian and director Hans Curjel, the son of architect Robert Curjel, who ran a well-known architectural agency in Karlsruhe along with Karl Moser. Hans Curjel (1896 Karlsruhe-1974 Zürich) studied music in Karlsruhe and art history with Vöge, Wölfflin and Jantzen. He wrote a monograph on Hans Baldung Grien, joined the Deutsche Werkbund in 1921, became the musical director at Louise Dumont's Düsseldorfer Schauspielhaus in 1924. Called to Berlin by Klemperer as a dramatist for the Kroll Opera, he later became its managing director, then left to be a theater director and orchestra conductor in Switzerland, and made guest appearances in Paris, Salzburg and Vienna. From 1945 on he was a critic and art writer, known for his studies of Art Nouveau. He directed the Zürich Art Nouveau Exposition in 1952, edited the memoirs of Henry van de Velde, made numerous research trips to the United States, and was a regular contributor to the Swiss journal WERK.

39)
Privately owned.

40)
Theodor Fahrner's ambivalence between being a factory owner and the director of a studio may well be the reason why an exhaustive article about all the major Pforzheim businesses, including photos of workshops and premises, did not mention the firm of Theodor Fahrner. All the same, we still have at least one photo of Fahrner's factory today. Lit.: DGZ IX, 1906, pp. 222 ff.

#24.
Theodor Fahrner on a trip to Egypt, February, 1907.

Life Style - Family - Travel

#25. Martha and Theodor Fahrner on a trip through Egypt in 1907 (first from left: Martha Fahrner, third from left: Theodor Fahrner).

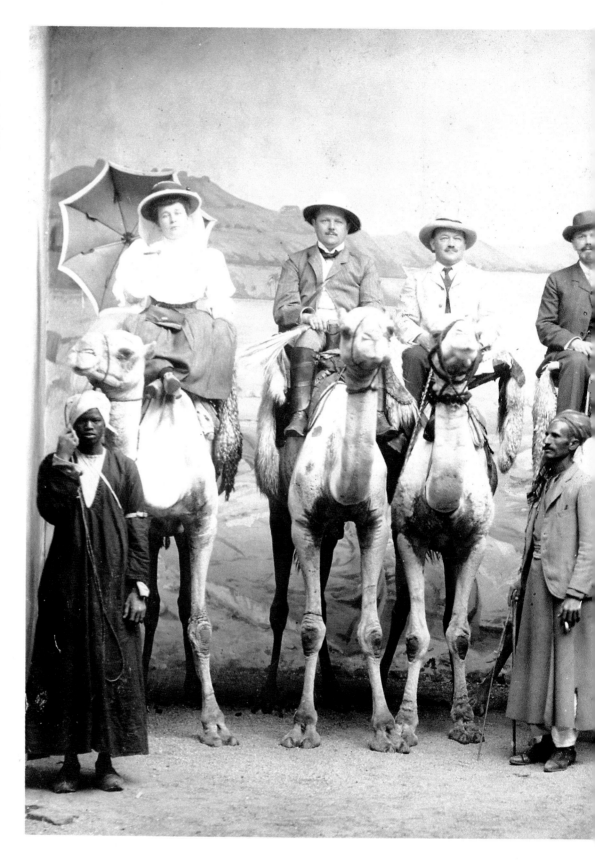

Analysis of Style

#26.

#27. Pin with flower motif, made by Fahrner, circa 1895.

1)
KGB NF 1, 1890, pp. 34 ff.

2)
Journal of the Central German Kunstgewerbeverein, 3, 1888, p. 173 (Frankfurt).

3)
KGB V, 1889, p. 119.

4)
KGB NF IV, 1892-1893, pp. 193 ff.

5)
KGB Pforzheim 1, 1894, pp.3 ff.

6)
Emil Riester, Schmuckentwürfe, Pforzheim 1880.

Historicism. The firm of "Seeger & Fahrner", later "Theodor Fahrner", in the latter half of the 19th Century.

Where there is scarcely any information, we can hardly do more than guess. Practically nothing other than a series of raw models for rings has survived from the first nearly forty years of Theodor Fahrner's company, and some of them were made in the nineties. Just a single decorative ring for a child, engraved with the initials "TF", may date back to the sixties. A small gold-plated ring for a silk scarf, found in Fahrner's effects after his death and made to look like a slim leather band, is characterized by simplicity.

The greater part of the ring collection, as well as two pins with flower motifs (#27), are typical of the manifold styles before the beginning of Art Nouveau, when historical as well as plant motifs were in vogue. These were the years when the German jewelry industry was trying valiantly to get on its feet while leaning on the French industry, which still dominated in terms of both volume and style, as a Pforzheim commentator said: "In fact, the French production is still unequalled in some areas. But one is already watching, with trepidation, the efforts of the German competitors . . ."[1] Thus in Pforzheim the Kunstgewerbeverein and its school were founded in 1877, intended to raise the level of the native industry by funding technical and artistic training. To promote the industry, it was decided in 1888 to gain influence through the fashion journals "Bazar" and "Modewelt", with their high circulation of some 300,000 copies.[2] In the same year the great success of cooperation between commercial art and industry, especially in Pforzheim and Schwäbisch Gmünd, drew praise at a commercial art exhibition in Munich.[3] In the Pforzheimer Kunstgewerbeverein's exhibition of jewelry in 1892,[4] among 270 exhibitors of all kinds of jewelry there were some who, for the first time, cited the names of artists whose works formed a transition to Art Nouveau: Emil Riester, Wilhelm Stöffler, Georg Kolb, Benckiser & Co., Alfred Waag, Georg Kleemann, and in 1884 also Fritz Wolber.[5] It is likely that Fahrner was also one of the exhibitors.

For the first time, names of designers are found here, generally professors at the Kunstgewerbeschule, whose pieces can be identified definitely. Their motifs are generally taken from flora and fauna. As early as 1880, Emil Riester had popularized plants and flowers in stylized forms as models in his beautiful book "Schmuckentwürfe",[6] and thus contributed to the development of this "stylized realism." These pieces, most of them enameled, were suitable in part for machine production, but they also demanded great ability in the realm of enameling.

Two of Fahrner's flower pins (#27) show that he also took part in this "botanization", though perhaps only in the small area of

#28. Raw model of a bird, late 19th Century.

decorative pins. Some finely worked brooches of this type are to be seen at the Pforzheim Jewelry Museum, made by such firms as Meyle & Mayer, Paul Suedes, Wilhelm Feucht and Georg Kolb. Along with plant motifs, realistic animal motifs were also used. The more popular include butterflies, such as those by Meyle & Mayer, and birds, of which examples by the firm of Paul Suedes have been preserved. The series of surviving raw models (#28) from Fahrner's production surely came from these years. We can conclude from them that the Fahrner firm's production in these years, under the direction of Theodor Fahrner, Jr., ranged from realism (sometimes with historic features) to botany.

The Years after 1895. A change began slowly around 1895. It was promoted impatiently by Theodor Fahrner through inventions such as his "stickpin with a sliding decoration on a profiled traverse" (Cat. No. 1.93) or "safety pin as a clothing or bouquet holder in the form of a clef..."[7] Only a few pieces from this period can be traced, as they are difficult to identify

before the introduction of the "TF" trade mark. Then too, no pictures of Fahrner's products, which could have provided points of reference, were published before the 1900 Paris World's Fair. And Fahrner's gifts to the Kunstverein and the Kunstgewerbe School began only in 1900.

First Abstract Art Two sets of three ornamental pins each, made of plated metal, give a clue to this style of the breakthrough years (#29). One of these was registered as a sample in 1897. In jewelry production during these years it was rare for the ornamentation to be reduced boldly to a strong, moving line. This certainly had its beginnings in the styles of the 1870's. But Fahrner's pins, their fluidity having a choreographic effect, are moving and lively, carried by the expectations of the breakthrough style of the years just before 1900. At the same time, they are important forerunners of a

7)
A clef was later mentioned among the assortment of Murrle, Bennett & Co., though without reference to Fahrner's firm. Lit.: V. Becker, Murrle, Bennett & Co., in: Art Collector, 1980, p. 74.

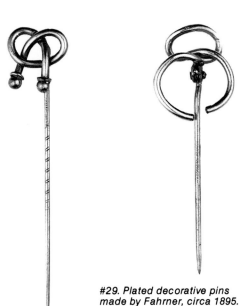

#29. Plated decorative pins made by Fahrner, circa 1895.

decisive basic concept that emerges clearly in Fahrner's work: their ornamentation is abstract, free of the motif-dominated possibilities of association found in symbolism. Thus Fahrner was one of the first jewelry manufacturers to follow, and superbly at that, the ideas of Henry van de Velde, who rejected the literary symbolism of Art Nouveau and promoted only the abstract ornament. But he knew that the pictorial flowing line was originally linked to the provider of motion, such as a wave of water or air, dancing, the growth of plants. According to the will of contemporaries, at the end of the 19th Century these became symbols of energy in motion. Theodor Fahrner recognized that the literary motif could only be portrayed in artistically highly cultivated works, as in the complicated pieces of the French jewelers. Perhaps he also preferred abstraction for the reason that its more or less simple movement could be portrayed better by means of machine production. The six early pins mark the beginning of this determination.

Literary Symbolism Theodor Fahrner was also open to the new literary motifs; until a year or two after the turn of the century, it had an influence on his jewelry production. It did not require the influence of the painter Max J. Gradl, whose motifs formed a large part of the previous production. An extant set of four pins with women's heads (Cat. No. 1.107), dating

from even earlier, shows how strongly Theodor Fahrner still continued to profile his production. But these pins, which followed a very general type that the industry put on the market in great numbers, were soon replaced by better pieces from the Fahrner firm, such as the feminine heads, whose unbound hair formed the wave motion and formed the ornamentation.[8] The first designs by Max J. Gradl appeared contemporaneously with these pieces. His work attracted attention not only because it departed from the contemporary style of French floralism, but also because of the material used: the small brooches, cuff links and pins without pictorial motifs were made of slightly blued steel.

"Here too, Fahrner's esthetic sensitivity is shown, in that he chose the correct material for the artistic design without prejudice, turning to steel where precious metals do not appear appropriate . . ."[9] Fahrner showed great courage in this decision. If one compares Fahrner's jewelry assortment not only with the products of French competitors but also with "prize-winning designs" from German competitions (such as the F. W. Müller and Schmitz Prize of 1900, depicted in the Pforzheim Kunstgewerbeblatt of 1900-01), one can understand the sensation that Fahrner's jewelry created.

A detailed study of the jewelry made by Fahrner to Max J. Gradl's designs is limited by the loss of many early pieces.

8)
Picture in V. Becker, Art Nouveau Jewelry, London 1985, p. 177.

9)
DKD VI, 1900, pp. 528 ff, quote from p. 524.

10)
Pieces from the Gulbenkian Foundation, Lisbon, and the Stoclet collection, Brussels.

11)
Sigrid Canz, Symbolistische Bildvorstellungen im Juweliersschmuck um 1900, dissertation, Munich 1976, particularly pp. 71 ff.

12)
von Hase No. 291 and 422.

13)
See literature on Max J. Gradl (see Cat. No. 1.23).

From publications we know that Gradl's steel jewelry was accompanied by a series of symbolistic portrayals. Motifs of vanity, girls reading, girls under trees, the face in the flower, plants and grapevines — all of these are his early contributions to the theme of symbolism, though modest in their literary relevance. Only Max J. Gradl's "femme fleur" (the "girl's face in the flower"), preserved in pictures (see p. 33), touches the world of the great jewelers such as Lalique, Vever and Wolfers, who also used this subject in jewelry.[10] Thematically the subject had already appeared in literary works such as J.-K. Huysmans' "A. Rebours", Théophile Gautier's "Une nuit de Cléopátre", W. Crane's "Flora's Feast" or Jean Lorrain's "Narkiss (A mon ami Lalique)", which involve the destructive femme fatale as well as the awakening of spring.[11] In Germany, Hugo Schaper (#30) and H. Kreuter created thematically similar pieces,[12] both even more refined than Max J. Gradl's "flower girl." But this piece must have been prized particularly by Fahrner too, for as early as 1905, when the metaphors of Art Nouveau were already being viewed from quite a distance, an illustration appeared in "Der Moderne Stil" by Julius Hoffmann.[13]

The "girl between flower petals" brooch by Max J. Gradl (Cat. No. 1.23) has also been attributed to Ludwig Habich. This is unlikely, though, because of the great stiffness and tension in all the figure motifs of the sculptor Habich. His figured brooches are "small plastics" with partially expressive-manneristic characteristics, such as the extremely spread, overlong fingers of the "Schöne Lau" (see Cat. No. 1.39). On the other hand, the painter Max J. Gradl's pieces are more relaxed. There is a thematically related holder for a silk scarf, "Nixe with ball", which was il-

#30. Hugo Schaper, pendant, "Spring's Awakening", Württemberg State Museum, Stuttgart.

48

lustrated as part of an ensemble which used Gradl's pieces almost exclusively.[14] On December 6, 1900 Fahrner presented the "girl between flower petals" brooch to the Kunstgewerbeverein collection, presumably before his collaboration with Ludwig Habich. The designs of two of Theodor Fahrner's most beautiful pieces made in these years certainly came from Habich. According to Habich's widow, it was a portrayal of the "Schöne Lau" (Cat. No. 1.39) from Eduard Mörike's tale "Das Stuttgarter Hutzelmännlein", with the "Schö'ne Lau" inlaid. "Down below on the ground there once sat a water sprite with long flowing hair. Her body was like that of a beautiful, natural woman, with the one exception that she had webbing between her fingers and toes, pure white and softer than a poppy petal . . . She had crossed her hands over her breast, her face was pale, but her eyes, which were very large, were blue . . ."[15] The picture of the playful sprite, like the "femme fleur" a hybrid creature, was portrayed by Habich in two variations, in which he followed the description in the tale precisely. His portrayals belong to the general theme of "water creatures" found in 19th- and early 20th-Century art. Dvorak's opera "Undine" or Karl Reinicke's "Undine Sonata" are just two examples of the numerous forms in which

we meet the water sprites. The fact that Habich — and perhaps also Gradl — turned to the figure of the Lau in the Swabian Blautopf pool is noteworthy in terms of the internationality of the theme in this era, and surely increased the popularity of these two pieces. The subject of the "Schöne Lau" is otherwise almost never found in jewelry and is thus one of the few unique motifs of Symbolism that were designed for series production from the beginning and not based on the work of other jewelry designers. Also ranking among these pieces is a Fahrner brooch whose central point is a head with closed eyes, carved from ivory (Cat. No. 1.108), a symbol of night or dreams. Here again we find a thematic reference to Lalique, whose pendant with a face carved in crystal and surrounded by poppies (#31) was made around 1900.[16] Fahrner's piece is a simplification of the complex motif of night, sleep or death to which Lalique referred with the blue-violet poppy (from which opium is extracted).[17]

Rings, brooches and pendants made by Fahrner at this time have a rather striking, pictorial character. It is possible that, just after his visit to the Paris World's Fair, at which the works of the great French jewelers were displayed, he gradually reduced production of literarily inspired pieces. His technical facility protected him from the impossibility of transmitting the manifold themes of French Symbolism — which found expression in motifs, materials used and workmanship — to the

14) Ostwald, Moderne deutsche Goldschmiedekunst, in: Westermanns illustrierte deutsche Monatshefte, Vol. 45, March 1901, picture on p. 827.

15) Quote from Eduard Mörike, Selected Works, 2 vol., Munich, no date, Vol. 2, p. 86. Mrs. Habich's information was first published in the 1985 Cologne catalog, No. 275.

16) Gulbenkian Foundation, Lisbon.

17) S. Canz, see note 11, pp. 67 ff.

#32. Max J. Gradl, cast model, "owl between trees", ca. 1900.

level of factory-made jewelry. Any simplification, such as various Pforzheim firms practiced, was against his nature. Perhaps he began at this time to realize his plans for a studio, so as to guarantee the adequate production of individual designs. In 1902 the brooch by E. von Berlepsch, described in detail on page 82, was made in Theodor Fahrner's "Atelier für Goldschmiedearbeiten."

The end of the Symbolistic phase also meant the end of poetic Romanticism in his work. They were not always made only for eye appeal. Gradl's owl (#32) or Kleemann's fat beetles and butterflies take effect through their glowing, usually enameled colors that shine through the gloomy motif of night. Bert Joho's grotesque heads, though they were made somewhat later, also rank in this group (Cat. No. 1.62). Stylized plants, already made by Fahrner to significant though anonymous designs around 1900, also lead up to the transition. In the set of Max J. Gradl's raw models, the development of the plant to an abstract ornament is easy to see. At this time we often find the popular application of flower motifs to abstract tendrils, which probably also goes back to Max J. Gradl (#33). Some of the designs of Ludwig Knupfer, who worked as a designer for Fahrner between 1902 and 1905, suggest caution in trying to ascribe authorship. A close relationship between Gradl's and Knupfer's designs is sometimes obvious in them. A brooch with a fanlike abstract flower motif can be ascribed very definitely to Knupfer on the basis of a stylistic comparison. Various other pieces formerly ascribed to Max J. Gradl can thus be suspected, at least, of being Knupfer's work. The organic abstraction of leaf motifs and bundled blossoms (#34, 35) are typical of him.

A major role in the stylization of vegetable forms was also played by the works of Eugen Friedrich Berner, who

#33. Max J. Gradl, cast model of a flower brooch, ca. 1900.

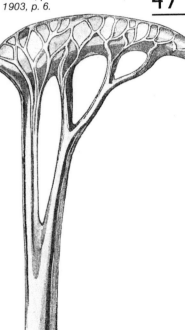

#34. Ludwig Knupfer, design for a woman's umbrella handle; picture from DGS, 1903, p. 6.

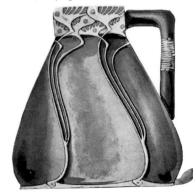

#35. Ludwig Knupfer, from the Kunstgewerbeverein competition for settings on glass, April 1902. Picture from" KGB KGV Pforzheim and Commercial Art Museum, Schwäbisch Gmünd, 1902, No. 2, no page cited.

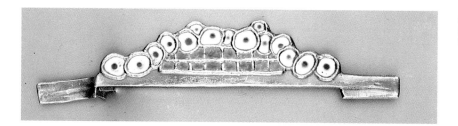

#36. F. E. Berner, test stampings for enameled brooches, ca. 1903 (Private collection, F.N.).

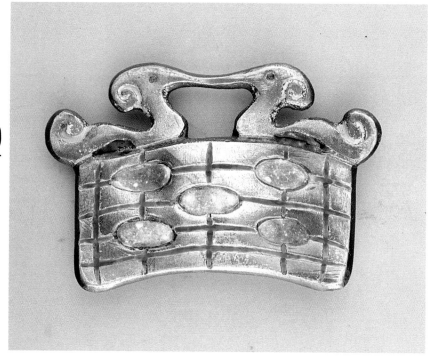

50

enameled jewelry was raised to the level of small plastic art by arching, as were other pieces by being set with jewels.

The Darmstadt Style. Theodor Fahrner's meeting with the artists of the Darmstadt Artists' Colony (see pp. 26 ff) resulted in a great upswing, not to mention the end of the anonymity of his jewelry designs. The following Darmstadt artists collaborated with Theodor Fahrner: Rudolf Bosselt, Paul Bürck, Ludwig Habich, Patriz Huber and J. M. Olbrich. This group of artists will be regarded as a single entity here, for the question arises of whether they essentially influenced the artistic development of his jewelry creation, or whether the success of their pieces lay on another level — the confirmed certainty that collaboration between artists and industry was possible. Habich's brooch, "die schöne Lau", has already been mentioned; unfortunately his other contributions to the 1901 Darmstadt exhibition cannot be separated from the work of the Friedmann firm.

Bosselt's jewelry, as well documented and illustrated in the contemporary literature as it is, has only been identifiable in a few instances.[19] A part of a belt buckle (Cat. No. 1.17) shows only little of the severity which he usually applied to the subject of jewelry. The piece with the striding imaginary bird comes alive through the contrasting effect of the precious-metal colors at various levels. Bürck's pieces, which were made by the

also experimented with stamped and sawed jewelry. But "in general these things are too flat, in many cases they do not rise above the look of stamped or sawed metal ... Berner's small enameled works — flat pit-melted pictures for which a future can be predicted — deserve particular attention." This critical discussion must have hit the artist all the harder as he was also struggling theoretically with the problems of machine production of jewelry: "There is no reason why the machine has to produce artistically tasteless work ..."[18] In his work — test pieces are extant (#36) — he avoided under- and overcutting of ornaments, in which the plant metaphor had its origins. In retrospect it looks as if Fahrner used the technique of flat stamping only rarely. Even the later

[18] Both quotations from: KuH 56, 1905-06, p. 50, the second sentence as a footnote, Mitt. Württ., 1902-03, pp. 243 ff, quote p. 244.

[19] It cannot be ruled out that the pieces shown in DK IV, 1901-02, p. 446, and DKD IX, 1901-02, pp. 110-116, were made by Fahrner.

[20] Koch, 1901, pp. 110 ff.

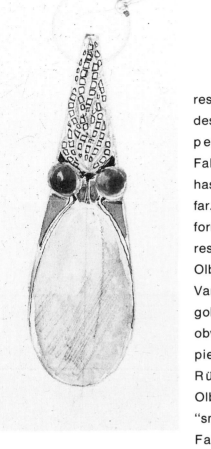

#37. Joseph M. Olbrich, design for a pendant, Berlin Library of Art.

Friedmann firm as well as by Fahrner, are not studied particularly in the literature, and unfortunately, the pieces set with precious stones cannot be found.[20]

The number of designs made by Patriz Huber for Theodor Fahrner is great. We know that Huber designed jewelry exclusively for the Fahrner firm but that some of his designs for silver goods were used by the firm of Martin Mayer in Mainz.

Besides those designs with the spiral motifs so typical of him, very different pieces have also been found. They are stiff motifs, presumably influenced by Aztec designs, counterpoints to his ornaments that feature rotation (Cat. No. 1.60). In them, the element of the flat surface with its soft silver sheen creates the effect. Related pieces, "hanging jewelry", were also created for Fahrner by Ferdinand Morawe.[21] Joseph M. Olbrich also designed series-production jewelry for the firms of Zerenner and Friedmann. A pin by Olbrich, made by Zerenner, bears the artist's stamp "Olbrich." Various pieces, first known from the literature, were also made by Theodor Fahrner, for example, a pendant (#8) that closely resembles a surviving design (#37).[22] A single pendant made by Fahrner (Cat. No. 1.92) has also turned up so far. Its simple, circular form has lost the lively restlessness of many of Olbrich's earlier pieces. Various versions — in gold and silver — of this obviously very popular piece are known. R. Rücklin mentioned Olbrich's and Habich's "small figured work" for Fahrner in 1919, to which at this point only Habich's "Schöne Lau" can be added.

The designs of the Darmstadt artists were of great importance in creating jewelry for Fahrner, for they made Fahrner's daring experiment, the collaboration of artist and manufacturer, a success. And the very variety of their designs expanded and brightened Fahrner's palette. Fahrner's staff designers were only rarely inspired by the artists in terms of motifs,[23] but that had been neither a goal nor a necessity. Certainly, though, the quality of the Darmstadt pieces, as different as they were, strongly marked the phase toward the end of the symbolistic Art Nouveau, between 1901 and 1902, and prepared the firm for a new breakthrough. Many other

21)
DKD VI, 1901-02, pictures on p. 375, and Morawe, KuK V, 1902, pp. 380 ff.

22)
It is not presently known whether the other designs by Olbrich at the Berlin Library of Art were intended for Fahrner.

23)
See von Hase, No. 116.

Pforzheim firms did without this assurance.

Transition and Reaction. Of course the Pforzheim designers had not given up the dreamy themes of Symbolism at one stroke. Fahrner's assortment[24] at the 1904 World's Fair in St. Louis shows that it was the group of professors at the Kunst-

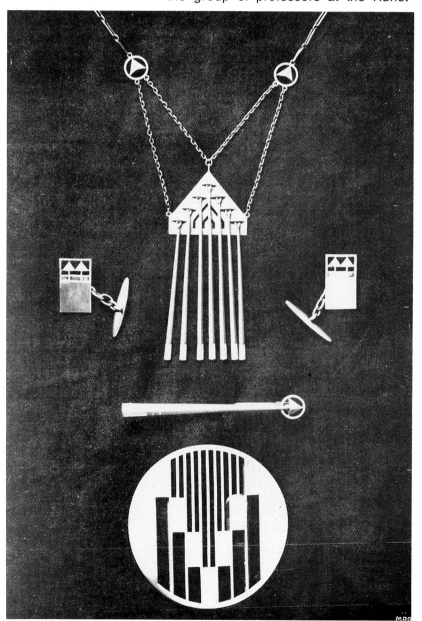

#38. "Franz Böres, jewelry set in silver with blue enamel", picture from: Koch's Monographs IX, Jewelry and Precious Metal Work, Darmstadt, 1906, p. 37.

gewerbe School — Kleemann, Müller-Salem, Wolber — who had sworn off typical ornaments but still clung to a serious, sometimes gloomy symbolism. When one looks at these pieces, one must bear in mind that at least some of them were made just after the turn of the century. Thus we still see symbolic motifs in them: Kleemann's beetle (Cat. No. 1.73) and Wolber's brooches with single- and double-head motifs, Müller-Salem's snake heads (Cat. No. 1.91). Certain pieces by another teacher at the Kunstgewerbe School — Bert Joho, later Fahrner's son-in-law — added a grotesque touch to these types. It is not known whether his pieces were also shown in St. Louis. Forerunners of the new ornamental style did appear at St. Louis, though, such as Müller-Salem's designs for the Pforzheim firm of Söllner.[25] Through the inclusion of circles and ovals, these strictly geometrical works are nevertheless organic. As early as 1900 this new style had appeared in the works of the Pforzheim jewelry artists. With Georg Kleemann's designs in "Moderner Schmuck", published in 1900, this geometrical style began remarkably early and was brought to its fulfillment by Franz Boeres.

Between the 1904 St. Louis World's Fair and 1907, Boeres' disciplined pieces, dominated by the strict discipline of dynamic bundled lines, are known to have been produced by Theodor Fahrner. R. Rücklin wrote of them: "Boeres uses only

German

Fig. A   Fig. B   Fig. C

#39. Chr. Friedrich Morawe,
designs for pendants in gold.
Picture from: Special Winter
Number of THE STUDIO, A.D.
1901-1902 (Plate 7).

geometric forms, but knows how to give his compositions a high degree of organic life. What a long way from sword-lily ornamentation . . . to this ruthless self-limitation!: (#38)[26]

Ferdinand Morawe, an unconventional jewelry designer, had already developed a formal language in 1901 that became fashionable only several decades later (#39). His "hanging jewelry", on the other hand, thrives on the elegance of the material used — shimmering gold or gilded silver, perforated by geometrical screens of dots and set economically with stones.

The years after the end of the symbolistic Art Nouveau were characterized by various reactions and developments, the boldest of which was certainly that of Franz Boeres (Cat. Nos. 1.8 ff). The architect Max Benirschke proceeded similarly strictly, but his designs are always accompanied by details that weaken the proclaimed strength: a big irregular pearl, teardrop pearls of striking additions (Cat. No. 1.3). At this time Theodor Fahrner was able to hire the drawing specialist Alfred

Bernheim as a staff designer. Two other noted artists also designed for Fahrner in this period: Erich Kleinhempel (#40) of Dresden and Louise Matz of Lübeck (see p. 117), who was Kleinhempel's student for a short time. No pieces by her have been found, but the pictures of her Fahrner jewelry show that she also enriched the variety of the firm's products. These were the years of Fahrner's "artist jewelry", which was usually publicized in the press at that time with the names of the artists.

24)
The Pforzheim firms had decided against a combined entry in the exhibition because of the high customs duties.

25)
Shown in KGB NF XVI, 1905, p. 160 bottom.

26)
KGB Pfh. 12, 1905, p. 31.

#40. Erich Kleinhempel, "Necklace
and comb in gilded silver", made by
Theodor Fahrner. Picture from: DKD,
Vol. XVII, 1905-06, no page number
(778).

FAHRNER JEWELRY
and the Neo-Styles

#41. DGZ XII, 1909, p. 313.

27)
DGZ XII, 1909, p. 318; R. Rücklin stressed again in 1914 the collaboration of artists outside the firm, in: DGZ XVII, 1914, p. 126.

28)
DGZ IX, 1906, pp. 110 & 146.

29)
Packeis und Pressglas, Von der Kunstgewerbebewegung zum Deutschen Werkbund, Werkbund Archives, Vol. 16, 1987, p. 345.

the Fahrner staff included such capable artist-artisans as Friedrich Katz, Ludwig Knupfer, Eugen Erhardt and Alfred Bernheim — cannot be answered now. In 1909, Rücklin wrote in the DGZ XII, p. 318, that Fahrner was constantly searching for capable artists to design modern jewelry. In the process, Fahrner is described as an ideal jewelry manufacturer: ". . . to collaborate with independent artists who lead the way in the development of taste . . is remarkably difficult:[27] On the other hand, the thorough training and high artistic skill of his staff goldsmiths was worth the price. Fahrner had always kept both in mind, and as the firm turned to "artist jewelry" he employed not only well-known artists but also in-house designers. The transition took place without incident because the quality remained high. In the "Deutsche Goldschmiedezeitung" of 1906, a report on the Dresden exhibition included pictures of Fahrner's jewelry without reference to the artists.[28] This is particularly surprising because, for the first time, only the designing artists were invited to a Kunstgewerbe exhibition.[29] (In the DKD report on the Dresden show, on the other hand, the artists were named along with the illustrations.) With few exceptions, later publications showing Fahrner jewelry did not name the designers.

Gradually, though, a disassociation from the great artistic names became noticeable; in the literature, the first extensive groups of jewelry appeared, indicating a high degree of artistic designing but remaining anonymous. The answer to the question of whether the designs were made by staff members — over the years,

Filigree Jewelry On November 30, 1908 Theodor Fahrner gave the Pforzheim Kunstgewerbeverein the main pieces of two

#42. Brooch, circa 1906, silver filigree wire, set with amethyst, marked TF; Hans-Peter Callsen collection, Bonn.

assortments of filigree and "wire jewelry", which were depicted in the "Deutsche Goldschmiedezeitung" (#41) in the following year, again without naming the artists who designed them.[30] Fahrner's filigree jewelry was based on an age-old, undying tradition of folk jewelry that came to new life around 1906 as a reaction to the modern approach of Art Nouveau. In his work "Völkerschmuck" of 1906, Haberlandt showed filigree jewelry from the Vierlande, Westphalia, South Germany, Austria, Silesia, the Balkans and the Caucasus, and did much to make "folk jewelry" and "filigree jewelry" synonymous. The question has been raised, though, of whether the filigree designs were made by Fahrner himself — R. Rücklin has reported on his fondness for it and his designs for this type of jewelry.[31] In the following years, many workshops made filigree jewelry, including Ernst Kohlsaat of Heide for C. Greve-Hamburger, Bödewaldt of Tondern, J. Frentzen of Karlsruhe, and M. Duscher of Munich. In Theodor Fahrner's firm, the

laborious working of the soldered or á-jour silver wire, which was granulated, beaded or twisted, was done in masterful style. Of course the expense was also high; a former employee recalled that for a filigree brooch made of five grams of silver, a work time of 35 hours was needed. In retrospect, it is thus not surprising that the production of filigree jewelry once thriving in Schwäbisch Gmünd came to a stop in the 19th century because its production was so expensive. A Fahrner brooch is even worked on the back and shows that the use of machines was scarcely possible in this expensive work process.

Fahrner must have cared very much for this jewelry; this is shown both by the fact that he was not scared off by high production costs and also by his giving a whole set of this filigree jewelry to the Kunstgewerbeverein. The fact that Fahrner's filigree jewelry is scarcely to be found today shows that production of these fragile pieces can only have been very small (#42). In developing the filigree

30)
DGZ XII, 1909, pp. 313, 315-316.

31)
DGZ XXII, 1919, p. 269.

technique, Fahrner also produced a group of gilded silver jewelry with amethysts. Here the rapport of geometrical ornamentation to the theme was stressed, but the effect is not sterile. The rhombus surrounding the oval — a favorite ornament in those days — swings gently inward and thus brings the ornament to life. A pendant from this assortment (Cat. No. 1.122) has survived with its original case, made of leather with gold lettering.

*Lettering on
the case.*

Neo-Biedermeier and Antique Among a further group of jewelry pieces for which no designers can be identified is the enameled work that closely resembles the "Neo-Biedermeier" jewelry designs of the Vienna Workshop. Naturally Fahrner would not have copied their work, but there are certain elements, such as the black-and-white checkered ornamentation, that first appeared in Viennese jewelry. The concentration of a small-format floral motif in the center of a wide, dark enamel background is also typical of Kolo Moser's designs.[32] A pin that Fahrner showed at the Werkbund Exhibition in 1914 (#44, 46) is stylistically based on the Vienna Workshop jewelry and made by

the same cell-enamel technique (#45).[33] Also inspired by the spirit of the Vienna Workshops are the flower-basket pendants, set with precious stones, that were a very popular motif then. They rank among Fahrner's most beautiful pieces (Cat. No. 1.117).

Neo-Empire At the Metal Art Exhibition of 1909 at the State Commercial Museum on Stuttgart, Theodor Fahrner exhibited, in the midst of a large assortment of "the trend of the times", a significant set of jewelry pieces in "Empire character." According to Rücklin's report, this was a finely worked figure relief in gold or silver, in the character of antique cameos, mounted on matte or gloss enamel back-

32)
von Hase No. 720-722.

33)
von Hase No. 775.

34)
R. Rücklin in DGZ XII, 1909,
pp. 354 ff.

35)
R. Rücklin, Die Pforzheimer
Schmuckindustrie, Stuttgart
1911, p. 35, GK 32, 1911, p.
243.

#44. Silver pin, ca. 1910-1914, with green and violet cell enamel, 6 x 50 mm, stamped: TF 935 DEPOSE, exhibited at the Cologne Werkbund Exposition in 1914. Private collection (F.N.).

grounds.[34] In workmanship and motif, these pieces are reminiscent of Cat. No. 1.130a and 1.130b, which are preserved in the Fahrner legacy and in private ownership.

Enamel Jewelry as of 1908. In the years between 1908 and 1910, Fahrner's staff designer Hermann Häussler turned back to the stylistic features of the jewelry inspired by the Wiener Werkstätte. R. Rücklin wrote that he had introduced enameled floral decor "with good luck" (see p. 98). He must have meant a series of pieces with cell enamel, which were first shown in the literature in 1911.[35] At the same time, they form the introduction to a very successful array that begins with the

#45. Vienna Workshops brooch in silver with black, blue and green enamel, 35 mm diameter, stamped with WW monogram; Austrian State Museum, Linz, inventory no. VII 213.

#46. Pictures from: DGZ, No. 43-44, 1915, p. 83.

#47. Catalog Number 1.47 (designed by Hermann Häussler).

breaking up of the surface with filigree wire and proceeds to pictorial surface formation. This pictorial jewelry of cell and pit enamel was very successful until the firm was sold in 1919. Naturally Theodor Fahrner also displayed this work at the Werkbund exhibition in Cologne, remarkably finished with lace, probably inspired by a lace-framed Biedermeier bouquet. From a central floral motif amid a large regularly or irregularly beaten surface (Cat. No. 1.45) to an artistic extension of the motif that now unfolded dynamically and required more and more space was now just a short distance. In the pieces displayed in 1914, the motif had conquered the entire surface. The finely enameled frame design, which usually repeated the colors of the flowers, now gave way to a simple rim (#47). Around 1914 the appearance of Fahrner's enameled jewelry changed; therefore it can be assumed that other designers took over this department.

The "Leaf Motif" A group of pieces that also made use of a Vienna Workshop motif but soon had grown far away from it developed into a long-term success. This was the motif of the small heart-shaped leaf, that appeared in the work of C. O. Czeschka and J. Hoffmann between 1905

and 1910 and immediately attained great popularity, even in German jewelry.[36] It is possible — according to family tradition — that Theodor Fahrner's inspiration to use this motif originated with Friedrich Katz. Invoices with model numbers between 18720 and 31175 date this production between 1910 and World War I. There was actually no other motif used by Fahrner that won so much popularity for so many years, even during the war. In 1917 pieces of this series were still being shown.[37] Such jewelry was still produced in the twenties, for the successor to Theodor Fahrner's firm, Gustav Braendle, made manifold use of the leaf motif. The Kunstgewerbe Schools also played a role, though its importance should not be overrated; their training programs always included studies of plants. In 1926, for example, the results of a typical course of study at the Schwäbisch Gmünd Kunst-

#48. Brooch designed by C. O. Czeschka, ca. 1905, made by the Vienna Workshops. Gold with fire opals; 70 mm high, with WW monogram. Austrian Museum of Applied Art, Vienna, Invantory No. 23110 WI 1928.

36)
For example, Otto Wünsche of Hellerau, in: KGBNF XXV, 1914, picture on p. 101; Paul Pfeiffer, Pforzheim, in: DK XXX, 1914, pictures on pp 43ff., and GK 1917, picture on p. 233; E. Margold of Darmstadt, in: DKD XVII, 1913-14, picture on p. 467.

37)
DGZ XX, 1917, p. 47.

38)
DGK 1926, illustration 2b.

#48. (See text at left.)

#49. Silver brooch with amethyst, ca. 1914, stamped "TF 800"; E. L. collection.

gewerbe School were illustrated in "Deutsche Goldschmiedekunst." One of the designs was produced in almost identical form.[38]

This popularity had several reasons: the leaf motif could be used in countless new variations, with the leaf form in itself being changeable. Early on, it was already combined with pearl bowls, pearls, coral and various semi-precious stones. Coral branches sometimes gave the pieces a symbolic character (Cat. No. 1.148). The lively leaf motif also soon formed a frame for many related types: birds, cherubs making music, foxes (Cat. No. 1.150), and even a unicorn find their places between the leaves, as if in a hedge. But fox and unicorn brooches are particularly reminiscent of Minoan art in form and technique; for example, a "pendant with a wild goat" (#50) of chased gold leaf, ca.

1600 B.C.[39] As often happens in Fahrner's work, a development can be observed here; in the end, it breaks through the closed order of the group and leads to motifs that go farther, in this case into the style of the twenties. The popularity of leaf-motif jewelry also had an economic cause: it was almost always stamped and could be sold at reasonable prices because of the low production costs. This great body of jewelry was, until Fahrner's death, probably the most successful of all, and is the type most often found to this day. We can assume from this that these pieces attained especially high production runs.

Non-European Style Elements. A strange position within the Fahrner firm's production range was taken by a group of jewelry with a "Moorish character", as was recorded in "Die Goldschmiedekunst" in 1910. This was a small group of eccentric pieces that Theodor Fahrner himself may have encouraged. The very fact that the "Moorish" or "exotic" concept turned up in — as far as one can see

#50. Pendant in the form of a wild goat (gold leaf), Minoan, ca. 1600 B.C.; British Museum, London (see Cat. No. 1.150).

39)
London, British Museum; shown in Anderson Black, Die Geschichte des Schmucks, Munich 1976, p. 57. Lalique also took a Minoan "hornet brooch" as a model for his brooch, "four wasps on flowers", 1905-06; see S. Barten, René Lalique, Munich 1977, no. 1175.

#51.
"Moorish jewelry",
picture from: GK,
31, 1919, p. 39.

40)
Compare von Hase
No. A 52.

—three different groups of motifs makes one think that several artists worked on an assigned subject. Perhaps Fahrner had brought back inspiration from his Egyptian trip of 1907.

As early as 1908 the Pforzheim Kunst-gewerbeverein had acquired a necklace from a group that was based on the constantly repeated, almost zoomorphic motif in gilded silver with blue enameling.

Simultaneously with this group, a second group of pieces appeared, this time with pit enamel, and was shown in "Die Gold-schmiedekunst" in 1910 (#51); its motifs are more clearly Arabic. Only one un-finished, not yet enameled piece remains, unfortunately, of this second group, but it still gives an impression of its series production (#52). The half-moon brooches designed and made by A. Hildenbrand

#54. Brooch with enamel
inlays (with cell frames),
made by Theodor Fahrner.

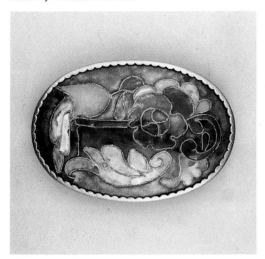

#53. Enamel inlay for a
brooch (glazing technique
without cell frame), as made
by Theodor Fahrner.

#52. Raw model of a brooch
or belt buckle.

(Cat. No. 1.48), the enameling teacher at the Pforzheim Kunstgewerbe School, may have been rarer and more expensive. His recumbent half-moons also follow the Indian and Arabic ornamental styles whose techniques they utilize.[40] A series of pieces, mainly enameled in blue and white, also seems to be based on such models. Among it is a fanciful variation that achieves its effect from the tension between the geometry of the blue and white enamel in combination with inlaid gold paillons (see Cat. Nos. 1.133 and 1.134).

This opposition to European style elements is not unusual for the years after 1907, and can also be seen in works of other artists, such as Ignatius Taschner, Heinrich Vogeler and Ferdinand Hauser. Then too, the "Wiener Werkstätte" (Vienna Workshops) often turned to motifs of so-called "folk jewelry", particularly the Indian. At the same time as the turn to extra-European jewelry forms, Michael

Haberlandt's "Völkerschmuck" had appeared in Vienna in 1906; it was an extraordinary, richly illustrated publication that vividly depicted the awakening interest in foreign styles. This "new discovery" of foreign jewelry and style elements also formed a type of Historicism.

This tendency is also reflected in Fahrner's jewelry: after the gradual turn from architectonic or sharply profiled geometrical forms, the pleasure in the simple and sober was exhausted and was happily replaced by the colorful and exotic.

Enamel Jewelry after 1914. The enameled brooches shown at the 1914 Werkbund Exhibition marked the end of the development of enamelwork in the Fahrner firm. Now the use of this technique within the firm appeared to pass into other hands, perhaps inspired by the many experiments that were also being made elsewhere.[41] It can be assumed that Fahrner had hired enamelers to produce enamelwork within the firm, although it was customary in Pforzheim to have enamelwork produced outside the firm.[42] The traditional technique of cell and pit enamel (#54) was often dispensed with in the following years when the help of the cell frame as a pictorial element could be done without. The resulting pieces were "paintings", with a multitude of color, often in a type of glazing technique.

The background was usually formed by a silver or copper plate, stamped with a pattern than stood out. These pieces were

41)
In Pforzheim, for example: A. Hildenbrand & G. Bastanier; Gebr. Falk (GK 31, 1910, picture on p. 275; enameling competitors in KGB Pforzheim 20, 1913, no page; works by the Nürnberg Kunstgewerbe School students, in: GK 35, 1914, p. 385; M. Flögl for the Vienna Workshops in: DKD XXXIX, 1916-17, p. 112; Eugen Pflaumer, in: GK 33, 1912, picture on p. 750.

42)
Rücklin, see note 35.

WERKSTATT

FÖR KÜNSTLERISCHE

EDELMETALL= UND EMAILARBEITEN

· K · H · EGON · RIESTER ·

usually marked on the reverse with a big grapevine (and sometimes also the year) near the "TF" trade mark (Cat. No. 1.98b). In addition, the traditional technique of cell enameling was still used, with the bridges soldered in place. See pp. 62 ff for more information on pieces with this type of enameling.

Egon Riester Theodor Fahrner's legacy included a series of enameled pieces, most of them with religious motifs, that bear the name of Egon Riester. Obviously the young artist, nephew of the elder Emil Riester, gave new impulses to enamel painting and the firm of Theodor Fahrner in the few years before his early death. His collaboration with Theodor Fahrner is documented by R. Rücklin, though it cannot be determined

for sure that the pieces in Fahrner's legacy were really made by the Fahrner firm. In 1914-15 Riester's "Workshop for Artistic Precious Metal and Enamel Work"#55 in Pforzheim was mentioned. The six surviving pieces are also stamped "IB", and these initials have not yet been identified. These pieces should be shown here, though, not only because Theodor Fahrner obviously considered them important enough to keep, but also as a means of remembering this highly talented artist. Perhaps it was both the fascinating enameling technique and the subject matter that attracted the attention of Fahrner, who was now seriously ill, to Egon Riester. The motifs include the Virgin Mary and crosses (Cat. Nos. 1.97 and 1.100) plus symbols of hope. Cross pendants of other types also appear now in Fahrner's work, inspired too by the shattering events of World War I (#56). Another group of four nearly three-dimensional pendants, that portray figures of saints as if in tabernacles, originated with Egon Riester (Cat. No. 1.97). They too are overlaid with enamel. Various unmounted enamel plates and raw forms, privately owned, also show the touch of Riester's hand. Other Christian motifs are also seen on "glazed" brooches. The "Angel of Peace" so fervently awaited during World War I, the "St. George" or the "Pietà", are only a few examples from an extensive production.

New Trends in Enamel Jewelry''
Enameled jewelry did not bear only religious motifs. Rather the technique of enameling gave rise to experiments that were obviously performed by Fahrner's daughter Vera and her husband Bert Joho as well. An unmounted enameled plate can be traced back definitely to a design by Vera (Cat. No. 1.68). An enameled plate with abstract decor, after a design by Bert Joho, anticipated the formal trends of the twenties (Cat. No. 1.65). Other pieces, donated to the Pforzheim Kunstgewerbe School by Martha Fahrner in 1921, also use antique or medieval motifs that might have been done better in other techniques. At the same time, though, they give evidence of the many uses of enamel.

War and Mourning Jewelry. War jewelry is understood to mean material "emblems"

#57. War and mourning jewelry by Theodor Fahrner; picture from: DGZ, No. 11-12, 1915, p. 19.

43)
DGZ XXI, 1918, pp. 75 ff.

Kriegs- und Trauerschmuck

Theodor Fahrner Pforzheim

worn to show agreement with the political authorities and the fighting forces: "An expression of the spirit involved in the war's events, in the form of jewelry, was requested by many."[43] It ranged from tastefully enameled warrior saints (St. George, St. Michael, St. Barbara) and versions of the Iron Cross[44] to decorative settings for shell fragments,[45] to name only

44)
For example, by Wilhelm Lucas von Cranach, in: DGZ XVII, 1914, p. 378

45)
DGZ XVIII, 1915, p. 1.

#58. Iron jewelry with hematite, 1914, made by Theodor Fahrner.

46)
These swastika designs came on the market around 1908 as "good-luck symbols." Such "swastika lucky charms" by Theodor Fahrner have also survived (privately owned). JGK 29, 1908, pp. 55 ff; DGZ XVII, 1914, p. 379.

47)
Heimat und Handwerk, included in the Badische Gewerbe- und Handwerkerzeitung, No. 1-2, 1918.

48)
DGZ XVIII, 1915, picture on p. 19.

49)
See articles by Max Platen and Georg Pazaurek in: KGB NF XXVII, 1915, p. 210 ff, and KGB NF XVIII, 1916, pp. 57 ff.

50)
Mode für alle, V, 1912, no page.

51)
Communicated by granddaughter Traudl Hauck.

52)
DKD XLIII 1918-19, picture on p. 263. In 1915 the GK also advertised "invalid jewelry", though this was not made by Fahrner.

a few possibilities. As early as November of 1914 the "Deutsche Goldschmiede-zeitung" announced its first competition on these. What turned up again were swastika crosses, "...a symbol of German confidence and power."[46] Theodor Fahrner's production was considerably limited to clearly formed iron jewelry, set with stones appropriate to the material, such as bloodstone or opal. The use of these stones in jewelry designs by the artists Morawe, Benirschke or Boeres, whose puritanical strength returned to life (#57). War jewelry — even cuff links or brooches — was marked with the year 1914 or 1915 (#58), the years of the German Army's first strategic successes.[47] Fahrner also produced oak-leaf settings for the Iron Cross as a medal of bravery. It is also interesting to note the individual use of the German eagle emblem in war jewelry.[48] Finally, pieces are also found which express "thanks from the Father-land" — brooches whose inscriptions, proclaiming "My gold to the Fatherland" or "I gave gold for iron"(#59), record contributions of precious-metal jewelry to help pay the cost of the war. These pieces follow a tradition of the Wars of Liberation against Napoleon and became popular again during World War I.[49]

The need for mourning jewelry became obvious all too soon. This was not based on a long tradition. In 1912, though, the journal "Mode für Alle" had already taken up this subject in anticipation.[50] It was probably Friedrich Katz, Fahrner's designer for many years, who expressed the theme of mourning jewelry so well

that, even in the twenties and thirties, the firm produced it in only slightly changed form. This genre includes leaflike round, oval or rectangular silver pieces with gridlike veins, covered by matte black material and set with small irregular pearls (#60). Also in connection with the subject of mourning and loss, we find pieces with symbolic expressions: pearls as a symbol of tears.[51] This unpathetic, soundless cry is directed at the end of the unfortunate war. Theodor Heuss, as a journalist at the Werkbund Exhibition in 1918, included such a piece, made by Theodor Fahrner, in the illustrations for his article, surely not by chance.[52]

#59. Iron jewelry, 1914-15, by Theodor Fahrner.

#60. Mourning jewelry with pearls, 1914, design attributed to Friedrich Katz, silver with black enamel; private collection.

Historical Variations

#61. Cameo, privately owned (F.N.).

Antique. It is certainly not surprising that jewelry in classical antique forms was made by Fahrner during the war. A cameo cut from two layers of onyx was found in Fahrner's legacy; it may be an individual piece (#61). But the greater part of the piece follows the laws of economic reproductability: The motif is chased from silver or copper plate and enameled white over a light blue, brown or blue-green background, not imitating the layer but recalling it. In Fahrner's pieces too, the subject matter — Diana, wagon drivers, the head of Pallas Athena — follows the classical model. This backward reach is not alone in the history of art. Neo-classicism and Neo-Antique were reawakened around 1906 and followed strict reactionary styles, finding expression particularly in the growing popularity of lapidary jewelry, publications on which increased in the journals. Again Fahrner found a way to use this art form not as a copy, but

rather to make it suit the material at hand, whether silver, gold or copper. It seems that he made very little use of the lapidary work that was done by machine in, for example, Idar-Oberstein. Among Fahrner's effects a box was found, addressed: "Empire (Modelle)-Pressungen von Rettatet, Paris."

Neo-Biedermeier. Another inclination toward classic themes and techniques was begun in 1915 by Theodor Fahrner's older daughter Vera Joho. Her silhouettes are also very closely related to the Neo-Biedermeier trend of the time.[53] Vera Fahrner scarcely adhered to the classic canon of Biedermeier motifs; the unclad woman amid flowering plants (#62) may have been based on the goddess Venus, but the Wilhelmine warrior wearing a Pickelhaube and riding a horse (#63) is diametrically opposed to the sentimental

53)
For example, E. M. Engert, Walter Kampmann, Johanna von Schäfer, in: DKD XX, 1917, pp. 88 ff.; DKD XXI, 1917, pp. 353 ff.; DKD XXIII, 1919, pp. 152 ff.; DK XXXII, 1915, pp. 151 ff., 316 ff.

#62. Vera Joho, silhouette jewelry, 1916.

#63. Vera Joho, silhouette jewelry, 1916.

#64. Vera Fahrner, circa 1914.

patterns of the late 17th Century.[56] Fahrner jewelry with a "Renaissance character" was mentioned in 1918. "Along with his modern artist jewelry, one also had many opportunities to meet him in this realm . . ."[57] (#18).

54) Similar portrayals of fighting men are also found in Heinrich Vogeler, for example, in "Am Heidrand", ca. 1900; picture in H. Vogeler, Berlin, 1895, p. 19, and among his Stollwerk Chocolate pictures of 1902.

55) Blätter des Kunstgewerbevereins Pforzheim, NF, 23, 1921-22, pictures on pp. 9-11.

56) Compare a bodice ornament, shown by Anderson Black, p. 199.

57) DGZ XXI, 1918, pp. 136 ff.

58) KGB NF XXVI, 1914-15, p. 162.

59) R. Rücklin II, p. 43, no. 1; Georg Hirth, Formenschatz 1906; KuH 59, 1909, picture on p. 112; Ernst Bassermann-Jordan, Der Schmuck, Leipzig 1909, picture on p. 76; Max Greutz, Geschichte der edlen Metalle, Stuttgart 1909, picture on p. 433, KuH 62, 1912, picture on p. 116; Otto von Falke, Der Mainzer Goldschmuck aus dem Hausschatze der Kaiserin Gisela, Berlin 1913; Gertrud Thiry, Die Vogelfibeln der germanischen Völkerwanderungszeit, Bonn 1939.

silhouettes of the Biedermeier era.[54] A woman's head is also reminiscent of the Biedermeier, as is an almost grotesque couple (Cat. No. 1.69). Of Vera Fahrner herself we have a photo taken around 1914, which shows her in a Biedermeier dress and hair style, sitting on a Biedermeier sofa (#64). The lady on an unmounted enameled plate that can be ascribed to Vera Fahrner is also typically Biedermeier. But her fashion drawings that included jewelry, dating from 1920-21 (see p. 245), were completely detached from the historic model.[55]

Neo-Rococo and - Renaissance. Up to this point, one could always speak of a timely reworking of historical themes. Yet individual pieces exist that lead one to conclude that they were wanted by a conservative public and were an economic necessity for the firm during the war. Among these pieces are a pendant with a leaflike flamed rocaille frame, a brooch (Cat. No. 1.162) whose heavy ornamentation is reminiscent of jewelry

"Frankish and Merovingian Jewelry" and its provable prototypes. The use of early medieval motifs in the jewelry creations of Theodor Fahrner's firm was already noted at the Werkbund Exhibition in 1918.[58] In 1917 pictures of these pieces, some of them splendidly worked, appeared (Cat. No. 1.163). Here we are dealing with an exception, for direct prototypes can be found, on which these pieces made by similar techniques were based. In what is now the Mainz State Museum, there were then two eagle clasps of the "bird with outspread wings" type, on which brooches by Fahrner were based. In the literature of the time, one of these clasps (#65), dating from circa 1030 and owned by Empress Gisela, was depicted several times, including in Rücklin's "Schmuckbuch" of 1901 and Hirth's "Formenschatz" of 1906.[59] Fahrner's pieces correspond quite closely to the prototypes in form and technique, if one disregards the colors of individual stones or the — perhaps unintentional — variations of the enamel tones. Both of the

Mainz pieces are also direct prototypes in terms of their varying frames with their settings of filigree wire, or the ovals of the sapphires. But there is one surprising difference: The eagle decorated with sapphire has his head turned to the left, while the medieval original faces right.

A third bird clasp made by Fahrner also indicates a precise knowledge of the Mainz items, although the type with an open frame was widespread.[60] But only the clothing pin from the latter half of the 6th Century, shown by Thiry as number 75, corresponds to the brooch made by Fahrner. The prototype with cloisonné enamel in a round central piece was changed to an oval by Fahrner. It is possible to find further prototypes for this series. Rücklin shows a Merovingian clasp that was reproduced by Fahrner, and Haberlandt's "Völkerschmuck"[61] shows a fabulous creature of pre-Columbian origin. It seems to lead a lone existence amid the medieval complex, for a number of extraordinary pieces from this group have survived (Cat. No. 1.157). Cross pendants with cloverleaf ends, inlaid garnets or chased decoration based on medieval types can also be included here (Cat. No. 1.161).

Since the end of the 19th Century, a traditionalistic movement had urged the recovery of Germanic types of art and life.

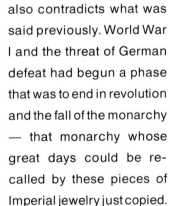

#65

In the realm of art this revival of folk art had come as a reaction to the "modern." Fahrner's filigree jewelry had also, to some extent, been a part of this trend, although he had been trying to modernize ornamentation and techniques. "Folk jewelry" certainly did not apply to the pieces he made that were copied from old Imperial possessions. But it was not a desire to "democratize luxury" alone that led to the reproduction of these medieval pieces that had never been copied before. The fact that here, with Fahrner's blessing, historical models were copied by his firm for the first time needs to be explained in another way. The cause is connected only indirectly with the creation of jewelry, and also contradicts what was said previously. World War I and the threat of German defeat had begun a phase that was to end in revolution and the fall of the monarchy — that monarchy whose great days could be recalled by these pieces of Imperial jewelry just copied.

In this respect they were years of saying farewell — politically and, tragically, also for Theodor Fahrner personally.

#65. Eagle clasp from the golden treasures of Empress Gisela, circa 1030, Mainz State Museum.

60)
Gertrud Thiry, Die Vogelfibeln der germanischen Völkerwanderungszeit, Bonn 1939. Thiry lists 527 pieces of this type.

61)
Haberlandt, Michael, Völkerschmuck, Vienna 1906.

Trade Marks and Emblems of Theodor Fahrner

The "TF" Trade Mark. As for its origin (see also pp. 262 ff), the "TF" trade mark was registered only on July 22, 1901 and entered in the "Warenzeichenblatt" on August 25, 1902. In comparison, the other better-known Pforzheim firms had registered theirs earlier: Zerenner, Fiessler and D. F. Weber in 1886, Lutz & Weiss and Knoll & Preziger in 1887, H. Drews, O. Stoeckle Benckiser in 1888; F. Speidel in 1893, Kollmar & Jourdan, Rodi & Wienberger in 1894, A. Daub in 1896 and W. Frey in 1901.

Thus the "TF" trade mark appeared in 1902, one of the few firms' symbols entered in the "Warenzeichenblatt" to be based stylistically in Art Nouveau.[1] For a firm that was founded in 1855 and had been so successful, this registration came remarkably late, and this has not been explained satisfactorily. But it seems as though Fahrner had decided to do it only after his success at the 1900 Paris World's Fair, although this success was already a result of his new strategy. The signet with the "TF" initials first appeared, to my knowledge, in an advertisement on page 136 of J. M. Olbich's "Die Ausstellung der Künstler-Kolonie 1901 in Darmstadt Mathildenhöhe." The trade mark specifically designated as such in this advertisement — strongly influenced by Japanese calligraphy — did not appear on any piece of jewelry and was not identical to the symbol shown in the "Waarenzeichenblatt" in 1902. Between the short time in which the

catalog was printed for the Darmstadt exhibition, which opened on May 15, 1901, and the registration for the "Waarenzeichenblatt" on July 22, 1901 there were only a few months, during which the final form of the initials "TF" in a circle was created, never to be essentially changed.

The question arises as to who actually designed the symbol. The person could be sought in that circle of young Darmstadt artists who provided designs for Fahrner in that period. Some of the pieces they designed were marked with their names. It is not unthinkable that Patriz Huber had a hand in making the new design of Fahrner's monogram.

Other than Ferdinand Morawe, who was not a member of the artists' colony, Huber was the only one whose monogram, rather than his signature, was put on Fahrner's jewelry. Identifying the originator of an object was certainly an intention of the Darmstadt artists. Joseph M. Olbrich placed his monogram, as a form of decoration, even on the flower boxes that decorated the street side of his home in Darmstadt (see Ein Dokument Deutscher Kunst, Darmstadt 1901, p. 89).

Max J. Gradl, whose various contributions to technical and "small art" designs betray a tendency to devise monograms, and whose typology shows a close kinship with that of the TF monogram, appears to be a likelier creator. In the book "Bunte Verglasungen" (Stuttgart, 1903), the monograms of the participating

1)
Waarenzeichenblatt Vol. IX, 1902, Class 17, No. 55308, F. 3819-17. TF also appears with the same number in Class 19, "hand and travel implements."

designers are included, some of them presumably designed by Max J. Gradl (#66). The typography of the written names of the participating artists is more interesting; they were drawn by Max J. Gradl and very much resemble the TF monogram in detail. The close friendship between Fahrner and Gradl, who also designed furniture for Fahrner's house, encourage one to draw conclusions, although actual evidence is lacking. On the basis of a comparison of types, it can be said with assurance that the text of a Fahrner advertisement in an insert in "Deutsche Kunst und Dekoration" of November 1906 was drawn by Max J. Gradl (see p. 263, no. 4).

Use of the "TF" Trade Mark. One can assume that Fahrner's jewelry was marked with his monogram as of 1901. For that year, though, there is doubt as to the stamping. In the Cologne Kunstgewerbe Museum Jewelry Catalog for 1985, for example, Habich's brooch "Die Schöne Lau" is cited as an example of the problems involved in different stampings. Different types of stampings are found on the following items:

Type I:
TF 935 DEPOSE (Pforzheim, Inv. No. Sch 3192/57)
DEPOSE 900 (Cologne, Kunstgewerbe Museum)

Type II:
HABICH DEPOSE 900 (Pforzheim, Inv. No. Sch 3192/58)
DEPOSE 900 (Pforzheim, Inv. No. Sch 3192/58a, smaller example)
DEPOSE 900 (private collection, smaller example)
DEPOSE 900 (Darmstadt, Hessian State Museum, Inv. No. Lg 1, No. 9; this item was a gift to the Christiansen family by Habich)

Even if one assumes that the artists signed various types of contracts with Fahrner, the example just above offers no satisfactory explanation for the variety of stampings. It is possible that the "TF" monogram was already borne by pieces exhibited at Darmstadt in 1901, although the monogram was not registered until July of that year. But this does not rule out the possibility that the first pieces of jewelry designed by the Darmstadt artists were made without the manufacturer's and designer's monograms. These stampings could have been added to later issues.

Marking the pieces leaving Theodor Fahrner's firm after 1901 with the "TF" trade mark was done very reliably. Exceptions are found in pieces from Fahrner's legacy or those donated to the Kunstgewerbe School's collection by Fahrner himself (for example, Emil Riester, Sch. 2425, Habich, Sch. 3192/58). Pieces from the Fahrner legacy may, of course, have been bought and sold over the years too.

In the aforementioned advertisement of 1906, Fahrner guaranteed to apply the "TF" monogram. At the same time, he first used the term "FAHRNER-SCHMUCK", which to the best of my knowledge is found only in the literature, in advertisements and on letterheads and was not

 R·BACARD

 R·BEAUCLAIR

 G.M.ELLWOOD

 R.GEYLING

 J.GOLLER

 M·J.GRADL

 P.LANG

 R·ROCHGA

 A.WALDRAFF

#66. Picture from: Bunte Verglasungen, Stuttgart (undated) 1903.

69

Paul Bürck (see p. 90), see Cat. No. 1.20 (1901).

Max J. Gradl (see p. 93), see Cat. No. 1.28 (1901-03).

Max J. Gradl (see p. 95), see Cat. No. 1.31c (1901-03).

Max J. Gradl (see p. 96), see Cat. No. 1.36 (1902-03).

used on the jewelry itself.

Great care and imagination, appropriate to the material used, were devoted to applying the trade mark. The so-called "leaf jewelry", made of thin stamped sheet silver on the reverse of which nothing could be punched in, was usually equipped with small silver plates soldered to the back to carry the monogram and the stamp of silver content. Pieces from the blue and white enameled series sometimes bore a blue monogram of cell enamel. Various enameled pieces bore both the monogram and a grapevine (Cat. No. 1.98).

Artists' Monograms and Names. Theodor Fahrner's innovative business policy of giving contracts to free-lance artists as well as hiring staff designers in the years around 1900, thus breaking away from the hitherto customary practice in the jewelry business, also required new legal principles.

As early as January 11, 1876 the "Fashion Sample Law" had become a kind of protection for the inventor: Paragraph 1 stated: "The right to copy a commercial sample or model wholly or in part belongs exclusively to the inventor.

Only new and independent products can be regarded as samples or models in the sense of this law." Paragraph 2: "In the case of such samples and models as are made by designers, painters, sculptors, etc. employed within a German business establishment under contract or for the profit of the proprietor of the business establishment, the latter is to be regarded as the inventor of the samples and models as long as nothing else is specified by contract."[2] Thus it is possible that there were special contracts between Theodor Fahrner and those artists who were not employees of the firm. The majority of their works were marked with the name or monogram, while jewelry made to designs by staff designers was never so marked. Samples or models had to be registered with the legal authorities — at the district court in Pforzheim — at a firm's main location. No more than fifty models or samples could be contained in one parcel. They were protected for three years, and the fee per sample or parcel was one Mark a year for the first three years, two Marks a year through the tenth year, and three Marks a year through the fifteenth year. For fashion samples too, there was no positive definition to recognize them as

2)
Reichsgesetzblatt 1876.

Max J. Gradl (see p. 96),
see Cat. No. 1.35
(1902-03).

Ludwig Habich (see p. 97),
see Cat. No. 1.40 (1901).

The use of the "TF"
trade mark, pp. 262
ff.

Patriz Huber (see p. 103),
see Cat. No. 1.57
(1901-02).

Bert (Albert) Joho (see p.
106), see Cat. No. 1.65
(1916-19).

such, meaning that a protective designation was left to the manufacturer's
imagination. Thus "ges.gesch."
(gesetzlich geschützt: protected by law)
could refer to a utensil or fashion sample
protection or even to a patent, although
the latter were usually marked more
precisely.

The frequently used French marking
"modèle déposé", or just "déposé" (#67)
was not strictly regulated either. For
obvious reasons, the French designations
disappeared about at the beginning of
World War I. But the same Fashion Sample
Law includes in Paragraph 1 a regulation
for designers from outside a firm, which is
particularly important in view of the artists'
monograms and names on Fahrner's
jewelry. Obviously there were both
designs for products to which the artist
could insist on having his name attached
and applied, and on the other hand,
designs that were sold with all rights,
could be changed, and could be sold
without naming the artist. Naturally,
naming the artists was not so much a
problem as a necessity for Theodor
Fahrner, who was using the names of the
famous designers as a form of advertising.

Chr. Ferdinand Morawe
(see p. 120), see Cat. No.
1.88b (ca. 1903).

KH EGON RIESTER

Egon Riester (see p. 125),
see Cat. No. 1.95 (ca.
1915).

#67.

Yet some things are not clear when we look at the list of stamped names and monograms known to us. Bürck, Habich and Egon Riester "signed" their names, while Max J. Gradl (his monogram varied), Huber and Morawe used monograms. The question of whether a name or monogram was used was probably decided by the artist himself. Artists' markings appeared between 1901 and 1904, with the exception of Gradl's, exclusively on pieces designed by the Darmstadt artists. During World War I, Egon Riester's pieces were also marked; he had already become known and opened his own workshop by that time (see p. 125). It is much more surprising that Bosselt and Olbrich did not have their pieces of jewelry marked. Yet caution is advised, for jewelry marked with their names may still turn up. We know that the pins designed by Olbrich and made by Zerenner bore Olbrich's name. In addition, the part of a belt buckle illustrated here, designed by Bosselt and found among Fahrner's effects, was not intended for sale. It is known that Benirschke and Boeres, plus the Pforzheim professors Hildenbrand, Joho, Kleemann, Müller-Salem, Emil Riester and Wolber did not use such markings. Finding marked pieces by Berlepsch, Kleinhempel or Louise Matz would change the picture presented here only slightly. There is thus no legal principle concerning the identification of artists on jewelry. This is most regrettable in the case of Max J. Gradl and Ludwig Knupfer, for they provided very similar designs and this makes ascribing their work difficult. The already noted difference in the stamping of Habich's brooch "Die schöne Lau" shows that the same piece came on the market in two sizes, both marked and unmarked.

Länder	üblicher od. gesetzlicher Feingehalt (in Tausendstel)			Punzierung obligatorisch fakultativ
	Platin	Gold	Silber	
Belgien . . .	—	min 750 800	min 800 900	fakult.
Dänemark .	—	min 585	826 in Praxis 830	fakult.
Deutschland	900 950	333 585 750	800 835 900 925	fakult.
Finnland . .	—	min 585 750 833 875 969	min 813 875 916	obligat.
Frankreich .	950	583 für Export 840 750 920	800 950	obligat.
Groß- britannien. .	—	375 500 625 750 833 916	925 958	obligat., fakult. nur Schmuck
Italien	—	500 750 900	min 800 900 950	fakult.
Norwegen .	—	min 585	min 830	fakult.
Oesterreich	950	585 750 900 986	800 900 935	obligat.
Polen	—	585 750 960	800 875 940	obligat.
Portugal . .	—	min 800 916³/₃	916³/₃ 833	obligat.
Schweden .	950	min 760	min 830	obligat.
Schweiz. . .	950	585 750	800 875	obligat.¹)
Spanien . . .	—	750	916³/₃	fakult.
Tschecho- slowakei . .	950	585 750 900 986	800 835 900 925 959	obligat.

Indications of Quality. In working with the products of Theodor Fahrner, it became necessary to consider the various legal measures concerning patent rights, sample and model protection. Without these specifications, certain stampings and markings would remain unclear. But unfortunately, no "right" of exact marking exists for the observer. This situation regarding quality markings is somewhat simpler, as they are usually given as 800, 835, 900, 935 and sometimes also 925. The often-cited "Die schöne Lau" was made of 900 and 935 silver. On that subject, the following must be noted: the definitions of quality were set at various levels in the European countries. An overview of the Pforzheim Board of Trade, published in 1934 and reproduced here (at left), shows this.[3]

This regulation explains the differing quality markings on the Fahrner firm's jewelry, and thus it can be understood that the silver content of 935 was gradually chosen. This quality allowed problem-free exporting to almost all countries — except Poland.

Patent and Sample Protection Registration by the Theodor Fahrner Firm. The records of samples that have been registered for protection show entries for improvements to both jewelry and silver goods such as purses, watch cases, belt buckles or cigarette cases. Scarcely any of these objects have survived, as they were seldom collected as systematically as jewelry. A few "patented" pieces have survived, though, and it is quite possible that they were made for private use in the Fahrner house: napkin rings, a page holder for a book, and finally the pencil holder with whose help the ailing Fahrner could still write and draw (see p. 39). In a considerable series of original registrations there is a patent for a "cuff lock", registered on September 3, 1904 and published as a patent with a drawing in 1906. Fortunately, cuff links of this type have survived (Cat. No. 1.165) — their excellent working makes us regret that they are not still manufactured today.

The Role of Patent and Sample Protection in the Theodor Fahrner Firm. The publication of the patent sheet with its listing of patents and sample protections lead us on a trail that has not been followed before in connection with the products of Theodor Fahrner's firm. In the period from 1895 to 1913 there are some 13 numbers that show Theodor Fahrner to be an inventor of small new techniques. The high value that he placed on them is shown by an unusual entry of his name in the Pforzheim directory of 1895: "Patent on a safety pin and a brooch." Both pieces are actually found in the 1895 patent sheet, though listed not under the patent numbers but rather the sample numbers: "No. 35968. Safety pin in the form of a clef, usable as a clothing or bouquet holder . . . F.1633." "No.36635. Stickpin with movable and changeable decorations on a profiled traverse, F. 1634." The protection of the

3)
From: Fritz Burkard, Die deutsche Edelmetall- und Schmuckwarenindustrie, Dissertation, Cologne 1934, p. 148.

clef pin was extended in 1898. In Fahrner's effects a specimen of the last type is preserved, bearing the — actually incorrect — stamp "DRPa." The fact that this brooch was made several years after its principle was protected suggests the lasting success of this invention. In 1895 too, Theodor Fahrner's third sample protection registration, No. 49321, was made, and turns out to be an exception: "No. 49321. Rollers with parallel-running, variously spaced fashioned longitudinal grooves F. 2271." Here, then, it is a matter of a new technique in the realm of machine production. In the following years, to 1913, numerous inventions appear, which attest to Fahrner's tireless striving for improvement as well as his inventive talent.

The following **Pattern Protection Registrations and one Patent (of 1906)** are listed:

1895: Nos. 35368 and 36635.

1896: No. 54520. Pin-point holder for pins, brooches . . . and the like with self-securing, of one piece . . . F.2533.

1897: No. 72045. Decorative pin with elliptical or circular spangle . . . F.3280.

1898: No. 35968. Safety pin usable as clothing or bouquet holder, etc. . . . F.1633 (Protection extended until 1895).

No. 96446. Belt buckle with slit and step located on one side of the traverses and closing staffs sliding inside the buckle frame . . . F.4623. No. 106281. Earrings with spring-operated attaching apparatus . . . F.5223.

1900: No. 72045. Decorative pin etc. . . . F.3280 (protection extended from 1897).

1903: No. 198713. Flexible, self-closing ring bracelet, ending on one end in a decorative addition which serves to lead and lock the opposite end . . . F.9405.

1904: No. 223409. Changeable decorative cover for pocket watches in the form of a pocket-watch case . . . F.10357. No. 225279. Belt-buckle frame with changeable decorative addition . . . F.10770.

1906: Patent number 174273, Fahrner No. 19255. Cuff link (published in Group 44a, 1906).

1912: No. 508772. Portable purse with a stiff bow enclosing its side panels . . . F.25864. There is a design drawing of this purse in repeated advertisements in "Die Goldschmiedekunst" 34, 1913 (see p. 243).

No. 506672. Case for cigarettes or parallel-lying objects, with self-activating forward movement of the individual pieces into the removing position . . . F.26080. No. 517043. Purse with bow and cross-hinge on the top for the purpose of attaching a covering lid, under which various utensils can be arranged . . . F.27092.

1913: No. 552552. Clasp for fastening bows or ties (F.29007) (Note: F = Fahrner number).

But the number of **Model Protection Registrations** on pieces by Fahrner not only throws light on the inventive spirit of Fahrner the manufacturer, but also gives important data for dating his jewelry. With care, the "Fahrner" factory numbers published along with the samples can be used to set up a chronology by which the sequential model numbers can more or less limit the pieces in time. This system is the only means of dating the models and model drawings now that all of the model books that existed as of Fahrner's death have been lost.

Year of publication by Patent Office	Fahrner Model Number (perhaps only for silver goods)	
1895	1633, 1634	Both registered 1/22/1895
1896	2271	Registered 11/9/1895
1897	2533	Registered 3/11/1896
1898	3280	Registered 2/18/1897
–	1633	(Renewal)
–	4623	Registered 5/5/1898
–	5223	Registered 11/18/1898
1899	–	
1900	3280	Renewal
1901	–	
1902	–	
1903	9405	Registered 12/22/1903
1904	10 357	Registered 9/26/1903
–	10 770	Registered 1/29/1904
1905	–	
1906	19 255	Patent, Registered 9/3/1904
1907	–	
1908	–	
1909	–	
1910	–	
1911	–	
1912	25 864	Registered 11/24/1911
–	26 080	Registered 1/2/1912
–	27 092	Registered 6/18/1912
1913	29 007	Registered 4/11/1913
1914	–	

In some cases the Fahrner numbers have been preserved on invoices or inventories. A congruence is, unfortunately, not always given.

Fahrner Model Numbers

Fahrner Model Numbers for jewelry in the inventories of the Kunstgewerbeverein and Kunstgewerbe School of Pforzheim from the years 1901, 1902 and 1908. The inventories are incomplete.

1901		1902		1908	
1901	338	**1902**	112	**1908**	15550
	339		11814		15736
	342		11847		15776
	345		11867		15792
	11 115		11897		
	11 455		11904		
	11 476		11907		
	11 487		11910		
	11 502		11917		
	11 698		11918		
	11920		11936		

The three-digit numbers are all those of brooches. But other brooches appear with five-digit numbers.

Jewelry pieces from Theodor Fahrner's effects:

	Model Number
Antique style jewelry with walking women (circa 1908)	18,159
Leaf style jewelry (1910-1919)	18,725
	18,725 and 31,200
	281 and 31,175
	3720 and 18,703
	17,531
	1475 and 18,720
Memorial (1914-1919)	31,850

Theodor Fahrner with his daughters Vera and Yella (ca. 1910).

About the Factory Catalog

For a better overview, we have divided the factory catalog into two parts:
Catalog Part 1: Era of Theodor Fahrner (to 1919); **Catalog Part 2:** Era of Gustav Braendle, Theodor Fahrner's Successor (1919-1979).
Each catalog number is preceded by the number of the catalog part for example, 1.87 or 2.127).

Catalog Part 1 (to 1919): Arranged by designers alphabetically

Catalog Part I (pp. 80-155) is organized alphabetically according to the name of the designer and begins with a brief biography of each. References to the literature concern only the jewelry creation of the artist in question. Pieces of jewelry whose designers cannot be identified follow in chronological order; the order corresponds to that of the text "Analysis of Style (pp. 44 ff). Stylistic groups are combined under one catalog number.

The pieces of jewelry coming from Theodor Fahrner's effects are marked "F.N." (Fahrner-Nachlass) to indicate ownership. If mention of markings and trade marks is lacking in the catalog descriptions, then these pieces are unmarked; most of these are objects from Fahrner's effects.

Until 1919 the "TF" trade mark was always in ligature form; thus the notation was omitted from the description of the item.

In the rediscovered inventories of the Kunstgewerbe School of Pforzheim (KGS Pfh. Inv.), the sale prices of the pieces at the time are listed, even when they were gifts from firms or goldsmiths; these prices, when available, are given as the "sale prices" in the catalog descriptions. The prices stated in the inventory for the "Fahrner Endowment" (F.St.), which was donated by Martha Fahrner in 1921, are not identical to the sale prices.

Catalog Part 2 (1919-1979): Arranged by designs chronologically

For the pieces of jewelry from the production of the firm of Gustav Braendle, Theodor Fahrner's Successor, the designers can hardly ever be identified, and for that reason this catalog (pp. 185-233) is organized according to subject and motif groups and arranged chronologically within each group.

Dating the pieces could be done very exactly as long as designs were found in the pattern books. An indication of size was omitted for the designs, since the piece of jewelry was usually drawn in 1:1 scale, and thus its dimensions are identical to those of the finished product.

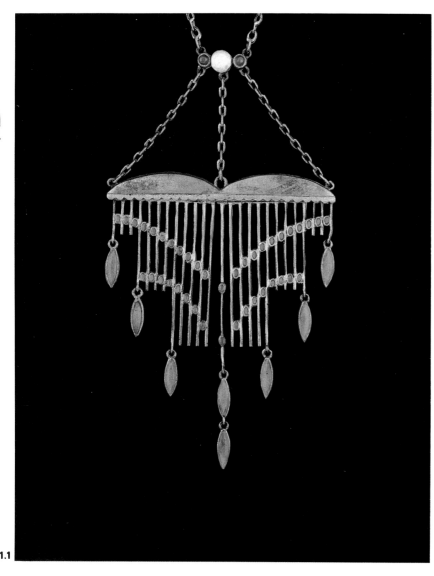

1.1

*B*enirschke, Max
Architect and Designer
May 7, 1880, Vienna †*September 28, 1961,* Düsseldorf

1895-1897 Weaving Trade School, Mährisch-Schönberg
1897-1902 Kunstgewerbe School, Vienna
1897-1899 Attended the preparatory class
1899-1902 Attended Josef Hoffmann's class
1903-1919 Teacher at the Kunstgewerbe School, Düsseldorf
1903-1904 Assistant in the Architecture class of Peter Behrens
1904 Teacher of Preparatory Class A
1919-1936 Teacher at the School for Handiwork and Industry, Düsseldorf. Member of the Deutsche Werkbund. Collaboration with Theodor Fahrner documented between **1905** and **1907.**

Lit.: Georg Howe, Neue Arbeiten von Max Benirschke, in: DK XVIII, 1907-08, pp. 355 ff, picture, p. 360.

1.1 NECKLACE 1905-1907 Designed by Max Benirschke.
Silver, gilded, green agates, pearls, green enamel.
Height 69, width 38 mm.
Jewelry Museum, Pforzheim.
Inv. No. Sch 3192/51 (F.St.)
Lit.: KGS Pfh. Inventory, Dec. 25, 1921, value 100 Marks. The added comment "design by Olbrich" must be based on an error, as the piece has no stylistic relation to Olbrich's work, whereas its authorship is reliably ascribed to Benirschke in Georg Howe's article in "Die Kunst"; DK XVIII, 1907-08, picture on p. 360; Irene von Treskow, Die Jugendstil-Porzellane der KPM, Munich 1971, Picture No. 254; von Hase 33; Falk 1985 No. 185; I. Becker, Kat. Berlin 1988, No. 167.

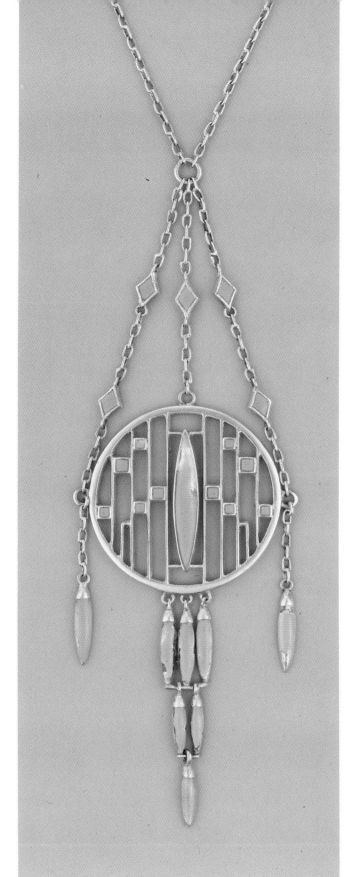

1.2

1.2 NECKLACE 1905-1907
Designed by Max
Benirschke.
Silver, gilded, green enamel.
Height 84, width 29 mm.
Jewelry Museum, Pforzheim,
Inv. No. Sch 3192/50 (F.St.)
Lit.: KGS Pfh. Inventory, Dec.
25, 1921, value 50 Marks. As
for the added comment "by
Olbrich", see Cat. No. 1.1.
DK XVIII, 1907-08, picture on
p. 360 (with out the teardrop-
shaped pendants); von Hase
34; I. Becker, Kat. Berlin 1988,
No. 165.

1.3 NECKLACE 1905-1907
Designed by Max
Benirschke.
Silver, river pearls, blue opal
enamel.
Length 90 mm (pendant).
Stamped TF (ligature), plus
quality.
City Museum, Düsseldorf, Inv.
No. 1988/34.
Lit.: DK XVIII, 1907-08, picture
on p. 360; Galerie Torsten
Bröhan, Düsseldorf 1986,
picture on p. 14; I. Becker,
Kat. Berlin 1988, No. 166.

1.3

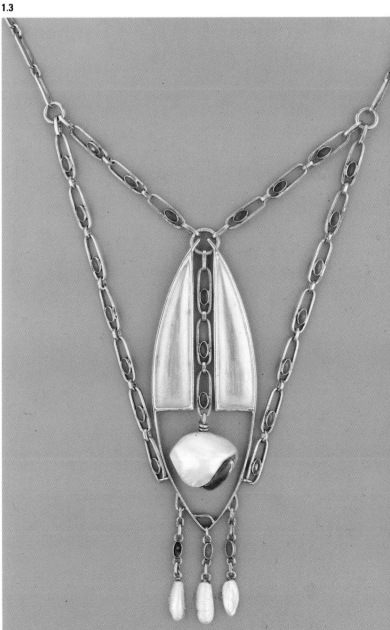

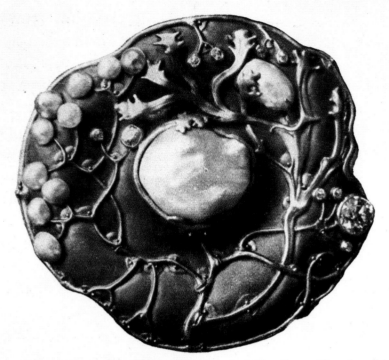

442. Bruſtſchmuck; nach Entwurf von H. E. v. Berlepſch. Planegg-München, ausgeführt von Th. Fahrner, Atelier für Goldſchmiedearbeiten, Pforzheim. Material: grünliches Gold mit dunkelviolettem Email, großer Mittelperle, kleineren Perlen und Brillanten.

Picture from: Kunst und Handwerk, Vol. 53, 1903, p. 255.

Berlepsch-Valendas, Hans Eduard von

Painter, architect, designer.

*__December 31, 1849__, St. Gallen †__August 17, 1921__, Planegg near Munich.

__1868-1871__ Studied architecture and art history at the Polytechnikum in Zürich.

__1877-1879__ Studied landscape painting at the Academy in Munich (with Löfftz and Lindenschmit). Free-lance artistic work in Munich.

__1902__ Founded a small "School for Architecture and Applied Art" in his home at Planegg.

Designed for Fahrner in 1902.

"It should be noted above all that certain available diamonds and pearls had to be used in this piece of jewelry; the client always wore simple, long, very dark clothing with a wide band around the hips, and the piece of jewelry had to be suitable as a 'Devant de corsage' there."

The one-of-a-kind piece was certainly made at the "Theodor Fahrner Studio for Goldsmithing Work"; it is a "pectoral ornament" of greenish gold with dark violet enamel, a large central pearl, smaller pearls and diamonds.

Lit.: KuH 53, 1902-03, p. 258, picture on p. 255. Literature on the pieces that were made by Karl Rothmüller and Paul Merk in Munich: DKD III, 1898-99, pictures on pp. 13, 14 and 34; KuH 54, 1903-04, p. 291, pictures on pp. 276 and 277; DGZ VIII, 1905, picture on p. 129; von Hase, p. 171.

B

Berner, Friedrich Eugen, painter, designer, probably also metalworker
***May 8, 1865,** Bruchsal †**1948**

1884-1889 Studied at the Academy, Stuttgart.

1902 Lived in Munich, Lachnerstrasse 26; worked at the "United Workshops" in Munich.

post-1902 Substitute teacher and

post-1903 Director of the metal workshop at the Instructional and Experimental Workshops in Stuttgart. Collaborated with Theodor Fahrner during these years.

post-1905 Lived in Bavaria as a free-lance artist.

1913 Lived in Hechendorf, Upper Bavaria.

Lit.: E. F. Berner, Ueber Feinmetallindustrie als Kunstindustrie, in: Mitt. Württ. II, 1903-04, pp. 243 ff; Mitt. Württ. II, 1903-04, picture on p. 211; KuH 56, 1905-06, p. 50, picture on p. 28; First Exhibition of the Munich Society of Applied Art, Kat. Munich 1905, p. 35, nos. 44-46 (work with gold and precious stones).

E. F. Berner.
Gold and silver jewelry with enamel and stones, made at the Instructional and Experimental Workshops, Stuttgart. Picture from: Mitt. des Württ. Kunstgewerbevereins Stuttgart, Vol. II, 1903-04, No. 4, p. 211.

1.4 BROOCH 1905-1906
Designed by Albert
Bernheim.
Silver, one amethyst, wing
pearls.
Height 43, width 34 mm.
Stamped: TF 935 DEPOSE.
Antiker Schmuck-Gutachter
Firma Röder,
Bergisch-Gladbach.
Note: Made at Theodor
fahrner's studio.
Lit.: compare similar pieces,
also chains, in DGZ IX, 1906,
picture on p. 146, and DKD
XVIII, 1906, picture on p. 780,
citing name; displayed at the
1906 Deutsche
Kunstgewerbe Exhibition in
Dresden.

1.5 BROOCH ca. 1906
Design attributed to Alfred
Bernheim.
Silver, lightly beaten, 1 lapis
lazuli.
Height 39, width 26 mm.
Stamped: TF 935 DEPOSE.
Wiener Interieur, Vienna
Compare a related piece
displayed at the 1906
Dresden exhibition, shown in:
DGZ IX, 1906, p. 152.

1.6 PENDANT in Empire
style, ca. 1906
Design attributed to Alfred
Bernheim.
Gold, reddish composition
stone, pearl shells.
Height 67, width 36 mm.
Stamped: TF 585.
Antiker Schmuck-Gutachter
Firma Röder,
Bergisch-Gladbach.
Note: Presumably made in
Theodor Fahrner's studio.
Compare similarly structured
brooches by Bernheim in:
DKD XVIII, 1906, picture on p.
780; compare the laurel-
wreath motif later in pieces
"with Renaissance
character" in: DGZ XXI, 1918,
pictures on pp. 30-31.

1.7 BROOCH 1906-1907
Design attributed to Alfred
Bernheim.
Silver, partly sulfured,
amethysts.
Height 65, width 35 mm.
Stamped: TF 935 DEPOSE.
Jewelry Museum, Pforzheim,
Inv. No. Sch 2321.
Lit.: A very similar jewelry
design by A. Bernheim,
shown in: DGZ 1907, p. 117,
No. 5; von Hase 126.

1.6

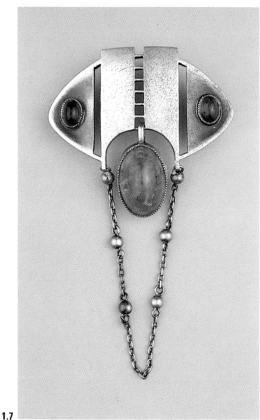

1.7

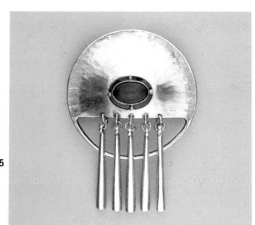

1.5

B

ernheim, Alfred,

in the literature by R. Rücklin 1919, Max
Bernheim Designer

Date of birth, unknown.
1905-1908 employed in the firm of
Theodor Fahrner.

Lit.: KGB Pfh. 11, 1904 (Müller Konkurrenz 1904) with
photos: DKD XVIII, 1906, photo page 146; DGZ X.
1907, page 117; DGZ XXII, 1919, page 268.

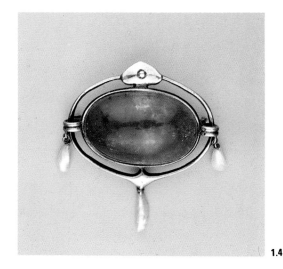

1.4

*A. Bernheim (Atelier Fahrner). From Theodor
Fahrner Pforzheim, Photo from: DKD, book XVII,
1905/06, page 780.*

B oeres, Franz

Painter, sculptor, designer

*September 4, 1872, Seligenstadt **†May 25, 1956,** Winnental

1886-1891 Drawing Academy, Hanau (with Prof. Andorf, August Ofterdinger, Prof. Schulz, Max Wiese).

1892-1900 Modeller in the Paul Stotz Brass Foundry, Stuttgart; also free-lance activity as a designer.

post-1903-04 Designs for Theodor Fahrner.

1905 Special show of his designs at the Art Society, Stuttgart.

post-1910 Furnished the villa and country houses of Robert Bosch.

post-1918 Numerous war memorials, monuments, fountains, medals, landscapes and still lifes.

First Pieces by Theodor Fahrner to designs by Franz Boeres were shown and publicized at the 1904 World's Fair in St. Louis, although Boeres himself, in retrospect, set the beginning of their collaboration at 1905: "Then when the Pforzheim jeweler Theodor Fahrner, seeing my exhibition in the State Museum of Commerce (in 1905 — ed.), considered me suitable for his "Fahrner Jewelry", he looked me up and I received RM 300 for the first series of designs and was allowed to go on pleasure drives with his family in his nice car (in 1905 it was the first car in Pforzheim), which raised the situation above the purely material . . ." (from: Wie ich zu meinem Berufe kam, Stuttgart 1937,

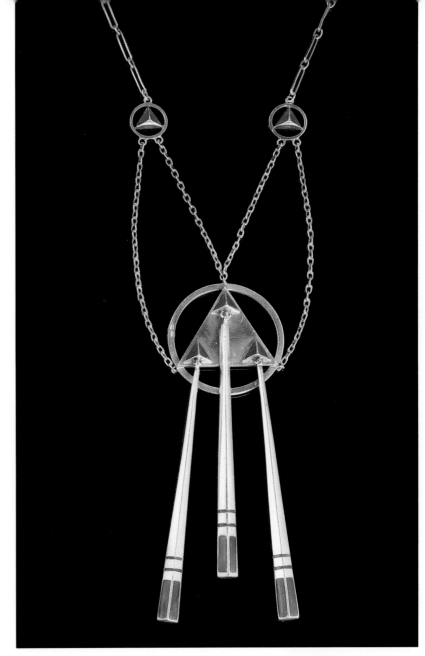

1.8

p. 6).

1948 Boeres wrote: ". . . and until Theodor Fahrner's death I made designs in Pforzheim for the 'Fahrner Jewelry' named after him. I also modeled the portrait of his children and a bust for his relatives . . ." (from: Erinnerungen aus meinem Leben, Stuttgart 1948. Thanks to Mr. Achim Zöller of Seligenstadt for the quotations.)

The portrait of the children and the bust for his relatives have not yet been traced.

1.8 PENDANT with chain, 1904-1905
Designed by Franz Boeres. Silver, blue opaque enamel. Height 118 mm (central section), width 25 mm, length 316 mm.
Stamped: TF 935 DEPOSE plus French import stamp for silver goods with countermark.
E. L. collection.

Compare a pendant with chain in: Zöller, 1983, picture on p. 54. A similarly worked pendant with chain is found in the Museum for Glass and Jewelry at Gablonz on the Neisse, Inv. No. P 286/G 157, shown in von Hase, picture no. 271 (incorrectly included in Georg Kleemann's work). Characteristic of Boeres' work is the repeatedly occurring small "pyramidal corner motif" (Cologne Catalog) as a decorative and attachment element.

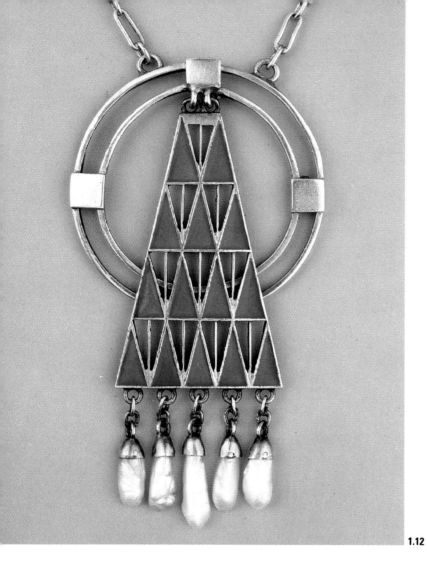

1.9

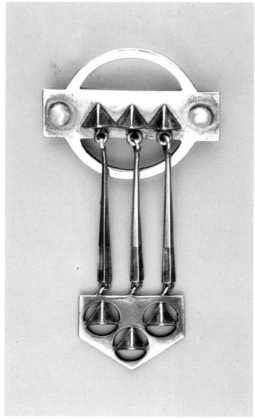

1.10

Literature on Franz Boeres: Zöller, Boeres, Documentation, Seligenstadt District Museum, 1983, particularly pp. 20, 53 ff.; Pforzheimer Feinmetallarbeiten auf der Weltausstellung St. Louis, in: DKD XIV, 1904, p. 506, with picture; Velhagen & Klasings Monatshefte XIX, 1904-05, Vol. 1, pictures on pp. 552, 553; KGB Pforzheim 12, 1905, p.31; Robert Forrer, Geschichte des Gold- und Silberschmucks nach Originalen der Strassburger historischen Schmuck-Ausstellung von 1904, Strassburg 1905, picture on p. 55 (dated 1901, questionable); Hoffmann, 1905, T. 57; Koch 1906, pictures on pp. 37, 40; Mitt. Württ. 1907-08, p. 40, picture on p. 33; Die Stuttgarter Kunst der Gegenwart, Stuttgart 1913, pp. 207 ff.; DGZ XXII, 1919, p. 268; Stuttgarter Zeitung 25, April 1950; von Hase, pp. 174 ff, 41-46.

1.12

1.9 BROOCH 1904-1905
Design by Franz Boeres.
Silver, one lapis lazuli, one wing pearl, blue enamel.
Height 33, width 43 mm.
Stamped: TF 935 DEPOSE.
Privately owned, Munich.
Note: At about the same time, Hans Ofner created structurally related but less striking jewelry in Vienna; see DKD XVII, 1905-06, picture on p. 332.
Lit.: Hoffmann 1905, picture T.57, von Hase 43.

1.10 BROOCH 1904-1905
Designed by Franz Boeres.
Silver, small pearls, violet translucent enamel.
Height 50, width 27 mm.
Stamped: TF 935 DEPOSE
Museum of Applied Art, Cologne, Inv. No. G 1351.
Lit: Cologne Catalog 1985 I, No. 278.

1.11 NECKLACE (dog-collar), ca. 1904.
Designed by Franz Boeres.
Silver, gilded, blue cell enamel.
Length 340, height 26 mm.
Stamped: TF 935 DEPOSE.
Ursel Gronert collection, Berlin.

1.12 PENDANT with chain, 1904-1905
Designed by Franz Boeres.
Silver, wing pearls, blue enamel.
Height 45, width 28 mm.
Stamped: TF 935 DEPOSE.
Galerie Torsten Bröhan, Düsseldorf.
Lit.: Koch 1906, picture on p. 40, Zöller 1983, picture on p. 55 (chain replaced).

1.11

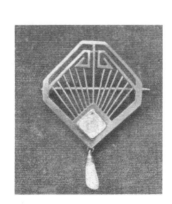

*Jewelry to designs by
Franz Boeres.
Original photos, Boeres
Archives, Seligenstadt.*

1.14 a

1.14 b

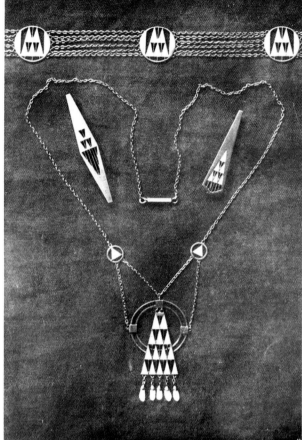

F. Boeres, jewelry in silver with blue enamel, made by Th. Fahrner. Picture from: Kochs Monographien IX, Schmuck und Edelmetall-Arbeiten, Darmstadt, 1906, p. 40.

1.13 BROOCHES ca. 1905
Designed by Franz Boeres.
1.13a Silver, wing pearls, blue cell enamel.
Height 93, width 44 mm.
Stamped: TF 935 DEPOSE.
Privately owned.
Note: The central section, as a brooch with wing pearls, is shown in photos at the Boeres Archives, picture on p. 87, also in Hoffmann 1905, T. 57.
1.13b Silver, one wing pearl, blue cell enamel.
Height 37, width 41 mm.
Stamped: TF 935 DEPOSE.
Antiquarius, Gromotka-Dr. Westermeier, Munich.
Compare similar jewelry designs by Boeres that are extant as photos, picture on p. 87.

1.14 LAPEL PINS ca. 1905
Designed by Franz Boeres.
1.14a Silver, blue cell enamel.
Height 85, width 10 mm.
Stamped: TF 935 DEPOSE
Württemberg State Museum, Stuttgart, Inv. No. G 60, 529.
Lit.: see Koch 1906, picture on p. 40; Mitt. Württ. 1907, p. 33; von Hase 45; Zöller, 1989 picture on p. 55.
1.14b Silver, violet cell enamel.
Height 43, width 10 mm.
Stamped: TF 935 DEPOSE.
E. L. collection.
Lit.: Koch 1906, picture on p. 40; Mitt. Württ. 1907, p. 33; von Hase 45.

1.15 DRESS PIN ca. 1905
Designed by Franz Boeres.
Silver, blue cell enamel.
20 x 20 mm (central section), height 96 mm.
Stamped TF 935 DEPOSE.
G. Silzer collection.

1.16 NECKLACE (dog-collar) ca. 1905
Designed by Franz Boeres.
Silver, blue cell enamel.
Length 310 mm (upper rim), height 22 mm.
Stamped: TF 935 DEPOSE.
Hans Peter Callsen, Bonn.
Compare similar necklaces, Cat. No. 1.11; in Koch 1906, picture on p. 40; Mitt. Württ. 1907-08, p. 40, picture on p. 33 (with reference to the Kunstgenossenschaft Exhibition, Stuttgart 1906).

88

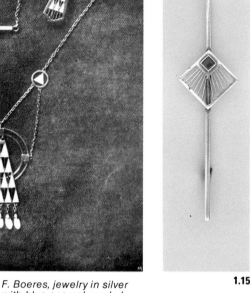

1.16

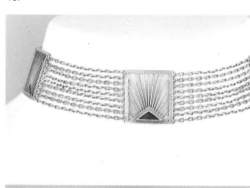

1.15

1.13a

1.13b

Bosselt, Rudolf

Sculptor, metal artist, chaser, designer

*June 29, 1871, Perleberg near Potsdam

†January 2, 1938, Berlin

post-1885 Study and collaboration as a chaser at the Berlin Bronzeware Factory of Otto Schulz.

1891-1897 Kunstgewerbe School, Frankfurt (sculpture with Wiedemann, medal work from chaser J. Korwazik).

1897-1899 Académie Julien, Paris (sculpture from D. P. Puech).

1899-1903 Member of the Darmstadt Artists' Colony, collaboration with Theodor Fahrner at this time.

1901 Special exhibit at the colony's first exhibition.

1903-1911 Teacher at the Düsseldorf Kunstgewerbe School.

1911-1925 Director of the Commercial Art und Handicraft School in Magdeburg.

1928-1931 Director of the Braunschweig Kunstgewerbe School. In Berlin as of 1931.

His collaboration with Theodor Fahrner can be documented to date only for a belt buckle (Cat. 1.17) and a comb (Lit.: Hoffmann 1901, T. 92, Nos. 13, 14). Yet it is possible that the many pieces shown in the literature without a manufacturer's name listed were also made by Theodor Fahrner. Bosselt designed other pieces for F. Friedmann's Successors D. & M. Loewenthal (for example, DK IV, 1901-02, picture on p. 446), perhaps also for Wilhelm Krieger in Pforzheim (von Hase no. 50).

1.17

1.19

1.18

Lit.: DKD VII, 1900-01, picture on p. 134; Koch 1901, pp. 285 ff; Olbrich Catalog 1901, p. 40; Hoffmann 1901, Plate 92; W. Fred, Die Darmstädter Künstlerkolonie, in: KuK IV, 1901, p. 451, pictures on pp. 450-451; F. Commichau; Rudolf Bosselt, in: DKD IX, 1901-02, pp. 93 ff, pictures on pp. 110-116; Von der Darmstädter Künstlerkolonie, in: DK IV, 1901-02, p. 289, picture on p. 296; R. Bosselt, Aufgaben und Ziele der Künstler-Kolonie in Darmstadt, in: DK IV, 1901-02, pp. 432 ff, pictures on pp. 446, 447, 449; DGZ 6, 1903, p. 81 with picture; R. Bosselt, Zur Wiederbelebung der Medaillenkunst in Deutschland, in: DKD XIII, 1903-04, p. 37 with picture; Koch 1906, picture on p. 6; J. Geller, Arbeiten von Rudolf Bosselt, in: KGB NF 23, 1912, picture on p. 81; Darmstadt Catalog 1976 IV, pp. 20ff; von Hase, p. 175.

1.17 BELT BUCKLE
1900-1901
Designed by Rudolf Bosselt
Part of a two-piece belt buckle.
Silver, chased, flowers gilded.
Height 56, width 45 mm.
Unmarked.
Privately owned (F.N.)
Lit.: J. Hoffmann, Der moderne Schmuck, Stuttgart 1901, Plate 92, No. 13; von Hase 48.

1.18 BROOCH with eagle's head 1901
Designed by Rudolf Bosselt or his group.
Silver, one amethyst, in feathers of ivory and violet enamel.
Height 38, width 31 mm.
Stamped: 935 TF DEPOSE.
B. M. collection.
Note: Probably same designer as Cat. 1.19. Compare a pendant with two eagle heads, shown in V. Becker 1895, picture 215; V. Becker sees, probably correctly, a relation to Rudolf Bosselt's style.

1.19 BROOCH with oval pendant, ca. 1901
Designed by Rudolf Bosselt or his group.
Silver, one pearl, green and blue-violet enamel.
Height 29, width 34 mm.
Stamped: TF 935 DEPOSE.
Wiener Interieur, Vienna.
Note: Probably same designer as Cat. No. 1.18.

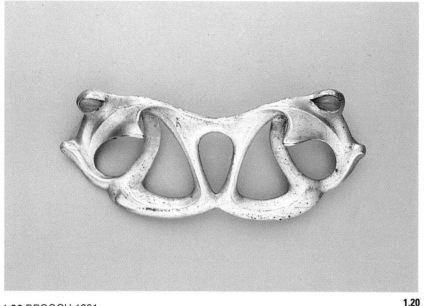

1.20 BROOCH 1901
Designed by Paul Bürck
Silver, colored agates.
Height 23, width 55 mm.
Stamped: BURCK TF
DEPOSE 900.
Pforzheim Jewelry Museum,
Inv. No. Sch 1771.
Note: Presumably displayed
at the exhibition of the
Darmstadt Artists' Colony in
1901.
Lit.: Inv. KGS Pfh., Nov. 30,
1901. Fahrner No. 11455,
sale price 7.50 Marks; von
Hase 54; Darmstadt Catalog
1976 IV, No. 48.

1.20

*B*ürck, Paul

Painter graphic artist, designer
*September 3, 1878, Strassburg **†April 18, 1947,** Munich

1894-1897 Training as decoration painter in Munich, while also attending the Kunstgewerbe School.

1899-1902 Member of the Darmstadt Artists' Colony; collaborated with Theodor Fahrner during this time.

1902-1903 Teacher at the Commercial Art und Handicraft School in Magdeburg.

1905-1906 In Rome, then in Munich; graphic art work, oil paintings, frescoes.

1921 Lived in Neulustheim (near Munich), designed jewelry for J. Friedmann's Successors D. & M. Loewenthal, Frankfurt.

Lit.: Koch 1901, pp. 110 ff; Olbrich Catalog, p. 41; R. Rücklin, Die Resultate der Ausstellung der Darmstädter Künstlerkolonie (Lecture at the KGS in Pforzheim on Nov. 4, 1901), in: KGB Pfh. 8, 1901, no page (disturbing in Bürck is the "oracular mania for symbolism which . . . affords understanding only for the chosen few"); DKD VIII, 1901, pp. 506 ff; Darmstadt Catalog 1976, pp. 24 ff; von Hase, p. 176.

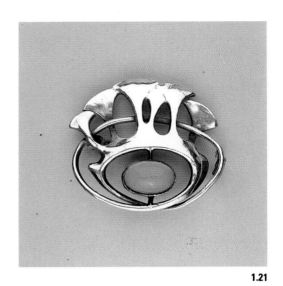

1.21

E

rhardt, Karl Eugen

Landscape painter, steel engraver, medal-maker

*Nov. 6, 1889, Feuerbach †**1972,** Stockholm

Trained as a steel engraver by his uncle Wilhelm Müller in the firm of W. Kucher in Gmünd. Attended the Commercial and Trade Schools in Gmünd, there a student of Holl, Stadelmaier, Weingand and Fürst.

About 1906 Studied at the Kunstgewerbe School, Pforzheim, with Georg Kleemann, Julius Müller-Salem; preference for metal techniques

August 1, 1919 Hired by the firm of Theodor Fahrner.

Twenties Probably worked as a free-lance artist in Paris.

Pre-1924 Settled in Malmo.

1931 Steel engraver at the Royal Mint in Stockholm. ". . . Erhardt, who had been a free-lance and sometime staff colleague of Fahrner's for some years, and had shown his ability in many successes in artistic life in Pforzheim and at artistic competitions, tried in more recent years to introduce figured motifs into jewelry, with much success." (Rücklin XXII, 1919, p. 268).

Lit.: DGZ IX, 1906, p. 212, pictures on pp. 214, 236, 240; DGZ X, 1907, p. 35, pictures on pp. 5, 44; KGB Pfh. 14, 1907, picture beside p. 30; DGZ XI, 1908, p. 315, pictures on pp. 43 and 311; PKG Pfh. 19, 1912, pictures on pp. 39, 41; KGB Pfh. XX, 1913, picture on p. 40; DGZ XVIII, 1915, pictures on pp. 26, 32 ff, 36; DGZ XXII, 1919, p. 268; Walter Klein, Gmünder Kunst der Gegenwart, Stuttgart 1924, p. 133, pictures on pp. 106-108; Albert Deibele, Eugen Erhardt zu seinem 75. Geburtstag, in: Gmünder Heimatblätter 25, 1964, pp. 73 ff; von Hase, p. 187.

1.22

Eugen Erhardt: Jewelry designs. Pictures from: KGB Pfh., Vol. 12, 1905, no page (31).

1.21 BROOCH ca. 1908
Designed by Eugen Erhardt (or his group).
Silver, one chrysoprase.
Height 26, width 28 mm.
Stamped: TF 950 REGD MBCo
E. L. collection.
Compare a pendant with related motif by Eugen Erhardt in: DGZ XI, 1908, p. 43, picture no. 3.

1.22 PENDANT with cherub, ca. 1915
Designed by Eugen Erhardt (or his group).
Silver, lapis lazuli.
Height 49, width 43 mm.
Stamped: TF 800.
Pforzheim Jewelry Museum, Inv. No. Sch 3192/26 (F.St.)
Compare a cherub with horn on a coin, by Erhardt in: Klein, 1924, picture on p. 136.
Note: Rücklin notes in his remembrance of Theodor Fahrner, 1919, about Eugen Erhardt "In recent years he was very successful in introducing figured motifs to jewelry." It is thus quite possible that this is a design by Erhardt.
Lit.: KGS Pfh. inventory, Dec. 25, 1921, value 150 Marks; von Hase 150.

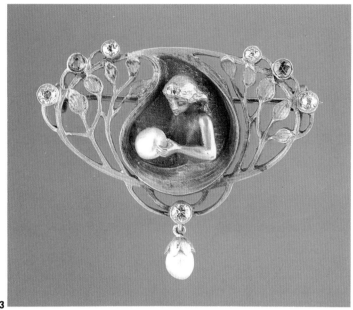

1.23

1.24

1.23 BROOCH 1899-1900
"Girl among twigs"
Designed by Max J. Gradl.
Gold, olivine, diamonds,
pearls.
Height 36, width 42 mm.
Pforzheim Jewelry Museum,
Inv. No. KV 1416.
Note: Displayed at the 1900
Paris World's Fair. The piece
is not stamped, since it was
made before the trade mark
was introduced; for motif see
p. 47.
Compare a silk scarf holder
with the same motif (girl with
ball) in: Ostwald, p. 827, and
DKD VI, 1900, p. 525.
Lit.: KGV Pfh. inventory, Dec.
6, 1900, sale price 330.48
Marks. (Lalique's "swallow
brooch" had cost 815 Marks
in Pforzheim in the same
year); KGB Pfh. 9, 1902,
picture on p. 8; von Hase 112;
Falk 1895, No. 178, I. Becker,
Berlin Catalog 1988, No. 9.

1.24 RING with woman's
head, 1898-1900
Probably designed by Max J.
Gradl.
Gold, green enamel.
Diameter 23 mm.
Stamped: 750.
Pforzheim Jewelry Museum,
Inv. No. KV 1417.
Note: Displayed at the 1900
Paris World's Fair.
Lit.: KGV Pfh. inventory, Dec.
6, 1900, sale price 72.90
Marks; KGB Pfh. 9, 1902,
picture on p. 8; Ostwald, p.
826; von Hase 113.

G

radl, Max Joseph
Architect, painter, graphic artist, designer
*September 10, 1873, Dillingen on the
Danube †**February 10, 1934,** Landsberg
on the Lech.

1888-1892 Kunstgewerbe School, Munich
(especially with Theodor Spiess).
to 1901 Lived in Munich, then moved to
Stuttgart in 1901.
1903 Displayed numerous works at the
Fine Metal Exhibition in Stuttgart.
1910 Moved to the house he built in
Schondorf on the Ammersee.
Designs for pattern books for commercial
art, bindings, title pages of journals
("Deutsche Kunst und Dekoration",
"Tapetenzeitung", "Innendekoration", etc.),
collaborated with the firm of Alexander
Koch in Darmstadt, industrial design,
designs for "Dekorative Vorbilder" and
"Der Moderne Stil" for Julius Hoffmann
Publishing, Stuttgart. His collaboration as
an "artistic consultant" to Theodor
Fahrner probably began in 1899 and
lasted at least to 1910. Many of his early
designs are thus marked neither with his
own "MiG" punch nor with the "TF" trade
mark, which were first used in 1901. It is
not impossible that the design of the "TF"
trade mark was made by Gradl (see p. 68).

Lit.: Reto Niggl, Hermann d. A: Gradl — Max Joseph
Gradl — Hermann d.J. Gradl, in: An-
tiquitäten-Zeitung No. 16, 1984, pp. 1 ff; R. Rücklin,
Das Schmuckbuch I, picture on p. 249; anon.,
Moderner deutscher Schmuck, in: DKD VI, 1900, pp.

1.26

1.25 CUFF LINKS 1900
Designed by Max J. Gradl.
Blued steel, hematite.
Stamped: TF DEPOSE.
Height 20, width 12 mm.
Privately owned (F.N.)
Note: See p. 46 re Gradl's
steel jewelry.
Lit.: See Gradl's steel jewelry
at the 1900 Paris World's Fair
in DKD VI, 1900, picture on p.
524; Ostwald, p. 823.

1.26 BROOCH ca. 1900
Designed by Max J. Gradl.
Silver, gilded, gold
background, one sapphire,
pearls, green, light blue
translucent enamel.
Height 25, width 30 mm.
Stamped: MiG, 585.
Pforzheim Jewelry Museum,
Inv. No. Sch 1775.
Lit.: KGS Pfh. Inv. No. 1775,
Nov. 30, 1901. Fahrner No.
11115. Sale price 68.50
Marks; DGZ IV, 1901, picture
on p. 5, No. 8; Rücklin I,
picture on p. 249; Ostwald,
picture on p. 822; Falk 1985,
No. 180; von Hase 179; Niggl
1984, picture 102, V. Becker
1985, picture 214, I. Becker,
Berlin Cat., No. 81.

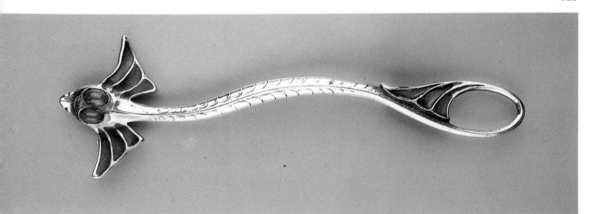

1.27

1.27 DRESS PIN 1901-1903
Probably designed by Max J.
Gradl.
Silver, translucent enamel,
eyes of green colored
chalcedony, copper pin
(replacement?).
Width 96 mm.
Stamped: TF 950 REGD MB
& Co.
Private German collection.

1.28 BELT BUCKLE, two-
piece, 1901-1903
Designed by Max J. Gradl.
Silver, hematite.
Height 46, width 67 mm.
Stamped: TF DEPOSE 900
MiG.
Galerie Urlass, Frankfurt on
the Main.
Lit.: Mitt. Württ. II, 1903-04,
picture on p. 204; Niggl 1984,
picture 106.

518 ff, mentioned on p. 524, picture on p. 525; KuH 50,
1900, p. 402 (bronze metal as designer in class 97,
metalwork); DGZ IV, 1901, pictures on p. 5, nos. 8-11;
Ostwald, Moderne deutsche Goldschmiedekunst, in:
Westermanns Monatshefte 45, 1901, pp. 822 ff, with
picture; KGB Pfh. Vol 9, 1902, p. 8; DGZ VI, 1903,
pictures on pp. 119 and 166 ff, continued on p. 167,
picture on p. 158; Mitt Württ. II, 1903-04, pictures on
pp. 203-205, 244, 245, continued on p. 357; Hoffmann
1905, Plate 9; KGB NF XXI, 1910, picture on p. 176;
DGZ XXII, 1919, P. 268; von Hase, p. 202; V. Becker
1980, pp. 74 ff, with picture; V. Becker 1985, pp. 108,
129 ff, 222, 235, with pictures; V. Becker 1987, pp. 158
ff, with picture.

1.28

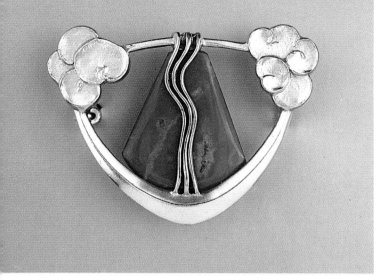

1.29   1.30

1.31a

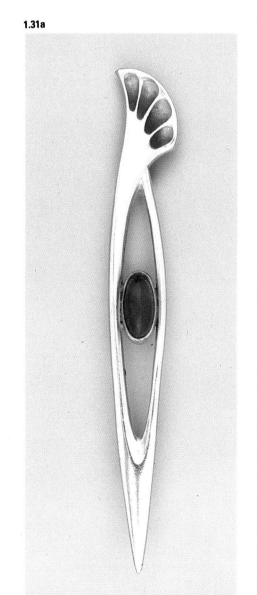

1.31b

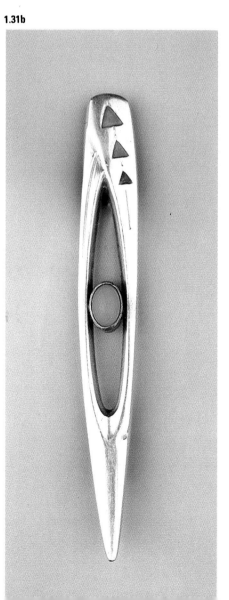

1.31c

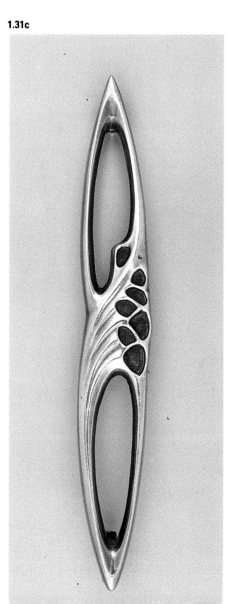

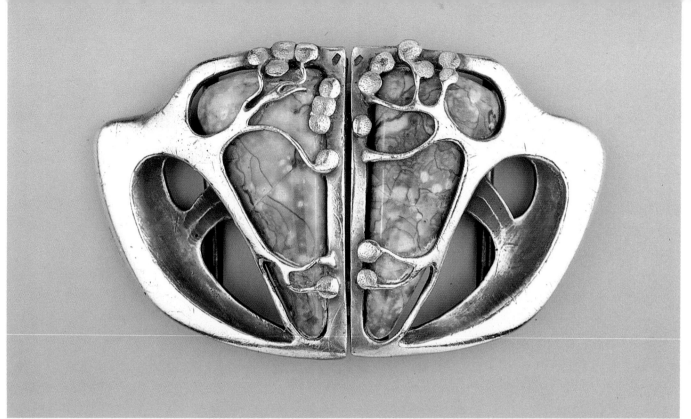

1.32

1.29 BROOCH 1901-1902
Design attributed to Max J. Gradl.
Silver, partly gilded, lapis lazuli.
Height 26, width 35 mm.
Stamped: STERLING TF 935 DEPOSE.
Pforzheim Jewelry Museum, Inv. No. Sch 2057.
Note: The ornamental structure appears in 1901 on a design by J. M. Olbrich; compare the design of a brooch in J. M. Olbrich Exhibition Catalog, Darmstadt 1967, no. 163.
Lit.: Shown in an advertisement of the firm of Murrle, Bennett & Co. in "The Studio", shown in: Adrian Tilbrook, The designs of Archibald Knox for Liberty & Co., London 1976; von Hase 114; Niggl 1988, picture 8.

1.30 CUFF LINKS 1901-1903
Design attributed to Max J. Gradl.
Silver, turquoise, amethyst 13 x 13 mm.
Stamped: TF 950 REG:D MBCo.
On top: F (= foreign), striding lion, silver 11 ounces. B. M. collection.
Lit.: V. Becker 1985, picture 210, I. Becker, Berlin Cat. 1988, No. 142.

1.31 DRESS PINS 1901-1903
Designed by Max J. Gradl.
1.31a Silver, one lapis lazuli, blue enamel.
Length 83 mm.
Stamped: TF 935 DEPOSE.
Udo Thomale collection.
1.31b silver, one chrysoprase, green enamel.
Length 69 mm.
Stamped: TF 935 DEPOSE.
Antiquarius, Gromotka-Dr. Westermeier, Munich.
1.31c silver, black enamel.
Length 80 mm.
Stamped: TF 950 REDD MBCo. MiG.
G. Silzer collection, Hannover.

1.32 BELT BUCKLE (2-piece) ca. 1902
Designed by Max J. Gradl or Ludwig Knupfer.
Silver, German lapis lazuli.
Height 40, width 64 mm.
Stamped: TF 900 DEPOSE.
Dr. Karl Kreuzer.
Compare: Knupfer's designs, see pp. 114 ff.
Lit.: von Hase 184 (attributed to Gradl); Karl Kreuzer, Gürtelschliessen des Jugendstils, Munich 1990, in preparation.

1.33 BROOCH ca. 1902
Designed by Max J. Gradl.
Silver, hematite.
Height 29, width 44 mm.
Stamped: TF 900 DEPOSE MiG.
Pforzheim Jewelry Museum, Inv. No. Sch 3192/67 (F.St.)
Lit.: KGS Pfh. inventory, Dec. 25, 1921, value 50 Marks; DGZ VI, 1903, picture on p. 158; Mitt. Württ. II, 1903-04, picture on p. 244; Niggl 1984, picture 104; von Hase 181; V. Becker 1985, picture 208, V. Becker 1987, picture on p. 258; I. Becker, Berlin Cat. 1988, no. 128.

1.33

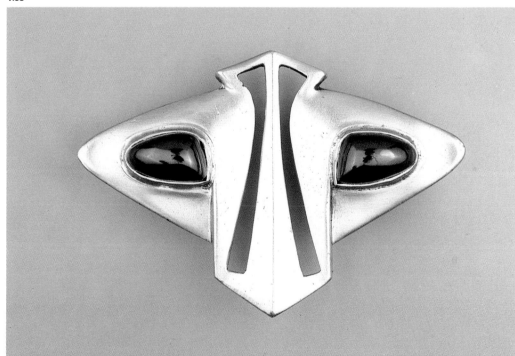

1.34

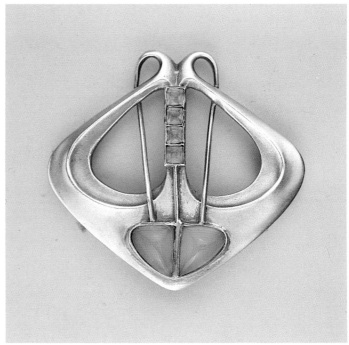

1.35   1.36

1.37   1.38

1.34 BROOCH with leaf
motif, ca. 1902
Designed by Max J. Gradl.
Silver, green colored
chalcedony, translucent
enamel.
Height 26, width 41 mm.
Stamped: TF 900 MiG
DEPOSE
Privately owned, Darmstadt.

1.35 BROOCH 1902-1903
Designed by Max J. Gradl.
Silver, chrysoprase.
Height 20, width 46 mm.
Stamped: TF 900 DEPOSE
MiG.
E. L. collection.
Lit.: DGZ VI, 1903, pictures
pp. 150 and 16; Mitt. Württ. II,
1903-04, picture on p. 244
("stamped work"); Niggl 1984,
picture No. 104; I. Becker,
Berlin Cat. 1988, No. 127.

1.36 BROOCH, 1902-1903
Designed by Max J. Gradl
Silver, chrysoprase
Height 38, width 39 mm.
Stamped: TF 900 DEPOSE
MiG. On the pin, French
import stamp. Galerie Urlass,
Frankfurt on the Main.
Lit.: DGZ VI, 1903, picture on
p. 158; Mitt. Württ. II, 1903-04,
picture on p. 245 ("stamped
work"); von Hase 180; Niggl
1984, picture no. 105.

1.37 BROOCH, ginko leaves
ca. 1903
Design attributed to Max J.
Gradl.
Silver, chrysoprase.
Height 25, width 25 mm.
Stamped: TF DEPOSE 900.
Galerie Urlass, Frankfurt on
the Main.

1.38 BROOCH, ca. 1909
Designed by Max J. Gradl.
Silver, green and black
enamel, green stone
(chrysoprase?).

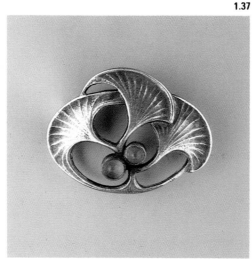

Length 47, diameter 24 mm.
Stamped: TF (ligature) 935
DEPOSE.
Note: This piece was bought
from Ed. Schöpflich in
Munich (exact date
unknown).
City Museum in the Prediger,
Schwäbisch Gmünd, Inv. No.
1959/G 1342.
Lit.: KGB XXI, 1910, picture
on p. 176 (with pendants in
different order); Niggl 1984,
picture 110.

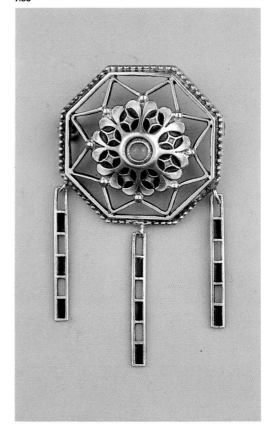

Habich, Ludwig

Sculptor, interior decorator, designer

*April 2, 1872, Darmstadt †January 20, 1949, Jugenheim (Bergstrasse).

Städel Art Institute, Frankfurt, with sculptor G. Kaupert.

1890-1892 Karlsruhe Academy, with sculptor H. Volz.

1892-1899 Munich Academy, with W. von Ruemann.

1899-1906 Member of the Darmstadt Artists' Colony.

post-1901 Director of courses in sculpture at the Adolf Beyer School of Art in Darmstadt.

1906-1910 Professor of Decorative Plastic Art at the Technical College in Stuttgart.

1912 Member of the Deutsche Werkbund.

1910-1937 Professor at the Academy of Art, Stuttgart.

1937 Returned to Darmstadt.

At the exhibition of the Darmstadt Artists' Colony in 1901, jewelry to designs by Ludwig Habich, made by Theodor Fahrner and by the firm of J. Friedemann's Successors D. & M. Loewenthal in Frankfurt, was displayed and mentioned in various publications. Of these pieces, only the two variations of "Die schöne Lau" have survived (Cat. Nos. 1.39 and 1.40). Further work for Theodor Fahrner in later years has not been provable, though it is possible that among the pieces shown in the literature for 1901, additional pieces were made by Theodor Fahrner.

Lit.: Olbrich Cat. 1901, pp. 103, 108; Koch 1901, picture on p. 195; DKD IX, 1901-02, p. 7, picture on p. 33; KuK IV, 1901, p. 451, picture on p. 449; DGZ XXII, 1919, p. 268; Darmstadt Cat. 1976 IV, pp. 78 ff; von Hase, p. 205.

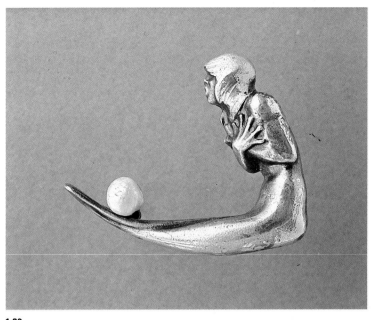

1.39

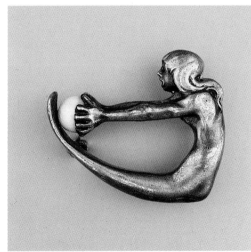

1.40

1.39 BROOCH (or tiepin) "Die schöne Lau" 1901 Designed by Ludwig Habich.
Silver (pressed), partly gilded, one pearl, the hair originally enameled green (traces).
Height 30, width 34 mm.
Stamped: TF 935 DEPOSE.
Pforzheim Jewelry Museum, Inv. No. Sch 3192/57 (F.St.)
Note: See also pp. 47 ff.
Displayed at the exhibition of the Darmstadt Artists' Colony in 1901. The brooch was made in large numbers and different sizes (for example, height 25, width 28 mm).
Lit.: KGS Pfh. inventory, Dec. 25, 1921, with note "Design by Habich", value 50 Marks; Koch 1901, picture on p. 221; DKD IX, 1901-02, picture on p. 33; KuK IV, 1901, picture on p. 449; Darmstadt Cat. 1976 IV, No. 284; von Hase (1985) 194; Niggl 1978, p. 11; Cologne Cat. 1985, No. 275 (very thorough, with exhaustive description of the motif); Falk 1985, No. 179; I. Becker, Berlin Cat. 1988, No. 10.

1.40 BROOCH (or tiepin), "Die schöne Lau", second version, 1901
Designed by Ludwig Habich.
Silver (pressed), hair gilded, ivory ball.
Height 25, width 29 mm.
Stamped: HABICH DEPOSE 900.
Pforzheim Jewelry Museum, Inv. No. 3192/58 (F.St.)
Compare mote to Cat. No. 1.39.
Lit.: KGS Pfh. inventory, Dec. 25, 1921, value 50 Marks; Koch 1901, picture on p. 221; DKD IX, 1901-02, picture on p. 33; Darmstadt Cat. 1976 IV, No. 286; von Hase (1985) 195; I. Becker, Berlin Cat. 1988, No. 11.

1.41

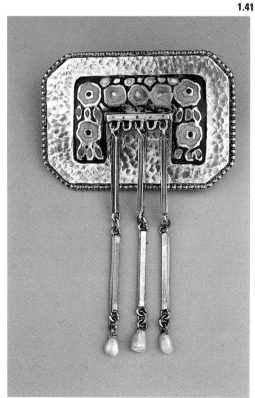

1.42

1.43

Häussler, Hermann
Designer
Birth and death dates unknown.

1908-1911 Staff designer (probably also enameler) in Theodor Fahrner's firm. Rücklin reports that Häussler introduced "enameled flower decor with good luck" (DGZ XXII, 1919, p. 268). The enameled brooches shown in the catalog were all made while he worked for Theodor Fahrner. On the basis of Rücklin's statement, it seems plausible to attribute works to him.

Lit.: DGZ XVIII, 1915, picture on p. 6 ("War Memorial Jewelry" competition); DGZ XXII, 1919, p. 268.

1.41 NECKLACE 1908-1910
Design attributed to Hermann Häussler.
Silver, citrine, black, yellow, blue and green cell enamel.
Height 62, width 25 mm.
Stamped: 935 DEPOSE TF ANTIK OFFICE, R. & S. Diehl, Frankfurt on the Main.
Compare Cat. No. 1.42 and similar versions in catalog of Stöckig & Co. mail-order house, Dresden (ca. 1911), No. 01242 and 01235.

1.42 BROOCH with flowers 1908-1910
Design attributed to Hermann Häussler.
Silver, beaten, blue, green, white and violet cell enamel.
Height 49, width 32 mm.
Stamped: TF 935 DEPOSE.
Pforzheim Jewelry Muesum, Inv. No. Sch 3192/44 (F.St.)
Compare note on Cat. No. 1.41; identical brooch shown in catalog of Stöckig & Co. mail-order house, Dresden, stock delivered by Fahrner: right side of advertisement, No. o1229; compare a similar brooch in: GK 32, 1911, picture on p. 243.
Lit.: KGS Pfh. inventory, Dec. 25, 1921, value 100 Marks; von Hase 129.

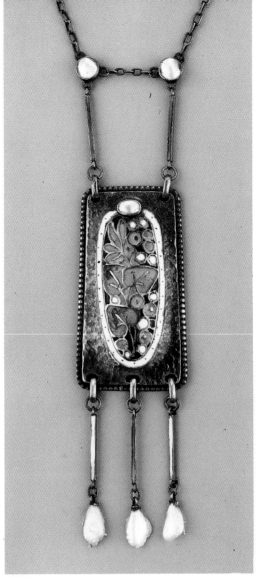

1.44

1.46

1.45 a   **1.45 b**

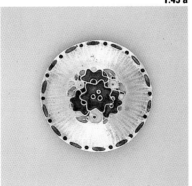

1.47 a   **1.47 b**

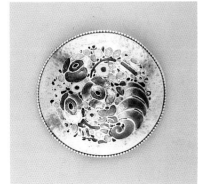

1.45 BROOCHES 1908-1910
Designs attributed to
Hermann Häussler.
1.45a Silver, finely beaten,
green, violet, yellow and pink
cell enamel.
Diameter 35 mm.
Stamped: TF 935.
Udo Thomale collection.
1.45b Silver, finely beaten,
blue, green and yellow
enamel.
Height 48, width 48 mm.
Stamped: 935 TF DEPOSE.
Ursel Gronert collection,
Berlin.
Lit.: Compare a similar
brooch in: R. Rücklin,
Stuttgart 1911, picture on p.
35; GK XXXII, 1911,
picture on p. 243.

1.46 NECKLACE 1908-1910
Design attributed to Hermann
Häussler.
Silver, central piece blue,
green, yellow, black and
gray-green cell enamel,
hematite on the mounting.
Height 93, width 47 mm
(without chain).
Stamped: 935 TF DEPOSE
G. Silzer collection,
Hannover.
Lit.: Compare picture in
catalog of Stöckig & Co.
mail-order house, Dresden
(ca. 1911), No. 01242 GK
XXXII, 1911, picture on p.
243 (central piece as
brooch).

1.47 BROOCHES 1910-1914
Designs attributed to
Hermann Häussler.
1.47a Silver, violet, green and
yellow cell enamel, rim of
black cell enamel.
Diameter 45 mm.
Stamped: TF 935 (on round
silver plate).
Udo Thomale collection.
Note: In this version, set on a
lace background, the brooch
was displayed at the 1914
Werkbund Exhibition in
Cologne.
1.47b Silver, beaten, violet,
black, green and gold cell
enamel.
Diameter 49 mm.
Stamped: 935 TF DEPOSE.
Privately owned.
Note: The flower motif with
the fanlike leaves was used
in many variations:
miniaturized, with various rim
widths, oval forms.
Lit.: Yearbook of the
Deutsche Werkbund 1915,
Munich 1915, picture on p.
105; KGB NF XXVI, 1914-15,
mentioned on p. 162, picture
on p. 175.

1.43 BROOCH 1908-1910
Design attributed to Hermann
Häussler.
Silver, beaten, yellow, green,
violet and white cell enamel,
one pearl.
Height 48, width 24 mm.
Stamped: 935 DEPOSE TF
plus cast-in B/460 Cns/w
NA/W.
Udo Thomale collection.

1.44 NECKLACE 1908-1910
Design attributed to Hermann
Häussler.
Silver, beaten, wing pearls,
mother-of-pearl, green, blue,
violet and black cell enamel.
Height 85, width 20, length
455 mm (chain).
Stamped: TF (ligature)
DEPOSE
Museum of Applied Art,
Cologne.
Lit.: Compare picture in
catalog of Stöckig & Co.
mail-order house, Dresden
(ca. 1911), Model No. 01231;
Cologne Cat. 1985, I, No. 25.

1.48a

1.48 BROOCHES, half-moon shaped, 1908-1910
Designed by Adolf Hildenbrand.

1.48a Silver, gilded, amethyst, light green, light blue and wine-red cell enamel, light blue counterenamel.
Height 52, width 42 mm.
Stamped: TF 935 (on the pin).
Pforzheim Jewelry Museum, Inv. No. Sch 3192/49.
Lit.: KGS Pfh. inventory, Dec. 25, 1921, value 50 Marks; von Hase 145.
1.48b Silver, gilded, green, gray, black and ivory enamel, light blue counterenamel.
Height 52, width 42 mm.
Stamped: TF 935 (on the pin).

Pforzheim Jewelry Museum, Inv. No. 3192/48.
Note: The identical diamond motif is used on the pendant of Cat. No. 1.122. The pit-enamel works by Hildenbrand shown at the 1910 Brussels World's Fair are reminiscent of Indian work.
Lit.: KGS Pfh. inventory, Dec. 25, 1921, value 50 Marks.

1.48b

Hildenbrand, Adolf
Painter, graphic artist, enameler.
*September 14, 1881, Löffingen, Black Forest †December 12, 1944, Pforzheim.

post-1898 Kunstgewerbe School, Karlsruhe (graphic techniques, painting, enameling).

1902 Assistant drawing teacher, director and founder of the enameling class at the Kunstgewerbe School, Pforzheim.

1908 Professor; in the following years he traveled to Rome, Paris, Colmar, Basel.

1913 Declined a professorship at the Art Academy in Berlin.

post-1919 Long stays in high valley of Bernau.

1920 Declined a professorship at the Kunstgewerbe School, Karlsruhe.

1933 Suspended from his professorship in Pforzheim. Special exhibits in Darmstadt, Freiburg, Konstanz, Pforzheim, Waldshut, Zürich.

The introduction of the enameling class at the KGS in Pforzheim certainly influenced production at the Fahrner firm. Hildenbrand's collaboration with Theodor Fahrner can be documented, though, only for two pieces made in 1908-10.

Lit.: Adolf Hildenbrand 1881-1944, Exhibition Cat., Pforzheim, 1981.

1.49

Huber, Patriz

Architect, interior decorator, designer

***March 19, 1878,** Stuttgart †**September 20, 1902,** Berlin

Attended the Kunstgewerbe School in Mainz (studied with his father Anton Huber), and studied in Munich with the painter L. von Langenmantel; subsequently studied architecture, interior architecture and design.

1899-1902 Member of the Darmstadt Artists' Colony.

1902 Moved to Berlin, founded the "Patriz Huber Studio", which was continued by his brother Anton Huber after his death, in part using the designs of Patriz Huber.

Collaboration with Theodor Fahrner 1901-02. As the evidence and results of research show, Huber's jewelry designs were made exclusively by Theodor Fahrner, his numerous designs for silver articles mainly by Martin Mayer of Mainz. Huber's jewelry was produced in large quantities: "Some of his brooches ... were sold by the thousands, not only in Germany, but also in Paris and elsewhere outside Germany ..." (DKD XIII, 1903-04, p. 40).

1.50

1.49 BELT BUCKLE (two-piece) 1901
Designed by Patriz Huber.
Silver, partly sulfured, green colored agates.
Height 48, width 87 mm.
Stamped: TF DEPOSE 900 PH
Pforzheim Jewelry Museum, Inv. No. Sch 1768.
Note: Displayed at the Darmstadt Artists' Colony Exhibition in 1901.
Lit.: KGS Pfh inventory no. 1768, Nov. 30, 1901. Fahrner No. 11476. Sale price 36 Marks; Koch 1901, picture on p. 181; J. Hoffmann, Der moderne Stil, Stuttgart 1901, T. 92; DK VIII, 1901, picture on p. 577; Darmstadt Catalog 1976, IV No. 364; von Hase 236; Niggl 1978, p. 11; Falk 1985, No. 181; Ulmer pp. 65 ff, Cat. No. 10;l. Becker, Berlin Catalog 1988, No. 186; W. Pieper, Geschichte der Pforzheimer Schmuckindustrie, Gernsbach 1989, picture on p. 176.

1.50 BELT BUCKLE (two-piece) 1900-1901
Designed by Patriz Huber.
Silver, partly inlaid with gold, green colored agates.
Height 48, width 72 mm.
Stamped: TF 900 DEPOSE.
Baden State Museum, Karlsruhe, Inv. No. 77/21.
Note: Designed for the Darmstadt Artists' Colony Exhibition in 1901. Made in two different variations and sizes.
Lit.: Koch 1901, picture on p. 181; J. Hoffmann, Der moderne Stil, Stuttgart 1901. T. 92; DK VIII, 1901, picture on p.463, DKD VII, 1901., picture on p. 577; Alfred Mohrbutter, Das Kleid der Frau, Darmstadt 1904. (The lady in the black chiffon dress, p. 44, wears the clasp as an ornament); Darmstadt Catalog 1976, IV No. 363; Ulmer pp. 65 ff, Cat. No. 11; Erwerbungsbericht Vol. 15, 1978, p. 176, picture no. 23 (Karlsruhe); Kandinsky in München, Munich Exhibition Catalog 1982, No. 162; Irmela Franzke, Jugendstil, Catalog of the Baden State Museum, Karlsruhe 1987.

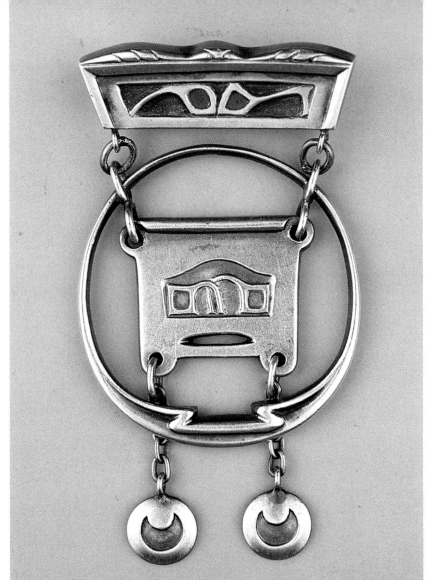

1.51

1.52

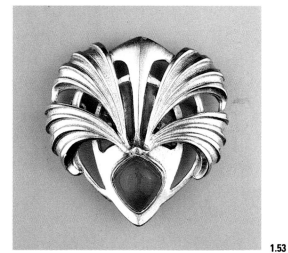

1.53

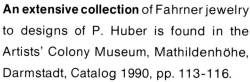

1.54

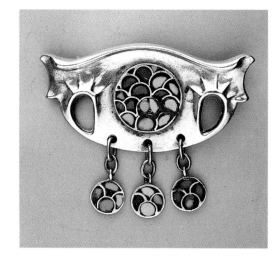

1.55

An extensive collection of Fahrner jewelry to designs of P. Huber is found in the Artists' Colony Museum, Mathildenhöhe, Darmstadt, Catalog 1990, pp. 113-116.

Lit.: Renate Ulmer, Patriz Huber, master's thesis, Heidelberg 1982; also Koch 1901, pictures pp. 180 ff; Olbrich Catalog, 1901, pp. 44, 47; Hoffmann 1901, T. 92 (1-12); E. W. Bredt, Patriz Huber's Arbeiten auf der Ausstellung der Künstlerkolonie in Darmstadt, in: DK VIII, 1901, pp. 457 ff, picture on p. 462; DKD VII, 1901, pp. 545 ff, pictures on pp. 576 ff; Mitt. Württ. I, 1902, p. 119, picture on p. 109; anon., Schmuck- und Leder-arbeiten von Patriz Huber, in: DKD XIII, 1903-04, pp. 39 ff, pictures on pp. 40, 42; Velhagen & Klasings Monatshefte XIX 1904-05, Vol. 1, picture on p. 552; Koch 1906, picture on p. 5; DGZ XXII, 1919, p. 268; Adrian Tilbrook, The designs of Archibald Knox for Liberty & Co. (picture no. 164 attributed); Darmstadt Catalog 1976, pp. 116 ff; von Hase, pp. 85 ff, 214 ff; V. Becker 1980, pp. 74 ff; V. Becker 1985, pp. 108 ff, with picture; V. Becker 1987, pp. 258 ff with picture.

1.56

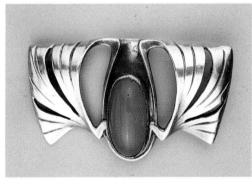

1.57

1.51 BROOCH 1901
Designed by Patriz Huber.
Silver, red and blue enamel.
Height 48, width 26 mm.
Stamped: PH TF (ligature)
935 DEPOSE.
Privately owned (F.N.).
Lit.: V. Becker 1987, pictures
pp. 258 ff; I. Becker, Berlin
Catalog 1988, No. 187.

1.52 BROOCH 1901-02
Designed by Patriz Huber
and Max J. Gradl.
Silver, red and blue enamel,
gilded silver panels.
Height 39, width 26 mm.
Stamped: TF DEPOSE 900.
Galerie Urlass, Frankfurt on
the Main.
Note: This brooch is certainly
a rare mixture of designs by
P. Huber and Max J. Gradl;
the central piece, originally
designed by Huber and
shown in Cat. No. 1.51, is
now replaced by a medallion
designed by M. J. Gradl in
1900. This medallion, with a
young lady looking in a
mirror, decorated a slim-
rimmed brooch that Max J.
Gradl designed for Theodor
Fahrner for the 1900 Paris
World's Fair.
Lit.: On Gradl's brooch:
Rücklin I, Das Schmuckbuch,
1901, picture on p. 241.

1.53 BROOCH 1900-1901
Designed by Patriz Huber.
Silver, sulfured, green
colored agates, blue enamel.
Height 33, width 32 mm.
Stamped: PH TF 900.
Pforzheim Jewelry Museum,
Inv. No. Sch 1930.
Lit.: von Hase 233; Ulmer,
Cat. No. 19.

1.54 BROOCH 1901
Designed by Patriz Huber.
Silver, partly gilded.
Height 39, width 30 mm.
Stamped: PH TF DEPOSE
900.
E. L. collection, identical
model in the Pforzheim
Jewelry Museum, Inv. No.
Sch 1791.
Note: The brooch was made
in at least four versions:
1. with agate trim,
2. with bright-flecked enamel,
3. without side pendants,
4. partly gilded.
The size also varies.
Lit.: KGS Pfh. Inventory, Dec.
14, 1901. Fahrner No. 11487.
Gift of Theodor Fahrner;
Hoffmannm T. 92; Darmstadt
Catalog 1976, No. 362; V.
Becker 1985, picture 205; von
Hase 232 a; Ulmer p. 65, Cat.
No. 12.

1.55 BROOCH ca. 1901
Designed by Patriz Huber.
Silver, with small turquoises
and green colored stones set
in glass paste.
Height 35, width 43 mm.
Stamped: TF 900 DEPOSE
PH
Dr. Karl Kreuzer
Note: Also made with lapis
and enamel, the pendants
with half-moon motifs.
Lit.: Koch 1901, picture on p.
181; DK VIII, 1901, picture on
p. 462; Darmstadt Catalog
1976, IV No. 367; Ulmer No.
15; Silber des Jugendstils
Catalog, Munich 1979, No.
149; Bruckmann's
Silberlexikon, Munich 1982,
picture on p. 249.

1.56 BELT BUCKLE two-
piece 1901-1902
Designed by Patriz Huber
Silver, 4 chrysoprases.
Height 42, width 69 mm.
Stamped: PH TF 935
DEPOSE STERLING.
Privately owned.
Note: A variation with three
chrysoprases also exists.
Lit.: DKD XIII, 1903-04,
picture on p. 42; V. Becker
1987, picture on p. 258.

1.57 BROOCH 1901-9102
Designed by Patriz Huber.
Silver, one chrysoprase,
violet enamel.
Height 26, width 42 mm.
Stamped: PH TF 900
DEPOSE.
Galerie Urlass, Frankfurt on
the Main.
Note: "Some of his brooches,
such as that at the upper left
on page 42, were sold by the
thousands, not only in
Germany, but also in Paris
and elsewhere outside
Germany . . ." (from: DKD XIII,
1903-04, see Lit.).
Lit.: DKD XIII, 1903-04,
picture on p. 42 (upper left);
Koch 1906, picture on p. 5;
von Hase 234; Ulmer pp. 65
ff, Cat. No. 20.

1.58

1.58 pair of CUFF LINKS
1901-1902
Designed by Patriz Huber.
Silver, one amethyst each.
Diameter 12 mm.
Stamped: TF 950 REG:D
MBCo PH
Galerie Urlass, Frankfurt on
the Main.

1.59 NECKLACE 1901-1902
Designed by Patriz Huber.
Silver, chrysoprase.
Height 53, width 26 mm
(without chain).
Stamped: TF 935 DEPOSE
PH.
Galerie Urlass, Frankfurt on
the Main.
Note: The motif was slightly
varied and produced as a
brooch, see Koch, p. 5, lower
left.
Lit.: DKD XIII, 1903-04,
picture on p. 42 (slightly
changed, brooch); Koch
1906, picture on p. 5 (slightly
changed, brooch); Armin
Zweite, Kandinsky und
München, Exhibition Catalog,
Munich 1982, p. 241, No. 166;
Ulmer Catalog, No. 18.

1.60 BROOCH 1901-1902
Designed by Patriz Huber.
Silver, one turquoise.
Height 25, width 34 mm.
Stamped: PH TF 935
DEPOSE.
Privately owned, Düsseldorf.
Note: The 1985 Cologne
catalog correctly refers to
motifs of Aztec art, which
may well have been models
for Huber here. Compare, for
example, the reverse of a
stone sculpture in San
Vincente Tancuayalab (San
Luis Potosi), Huactec culture,
in: Ferdinand Anton, Alt-
Mexiko und seine Kunst,
Leipzig 1965, picture 180.
Lit.: Ulmer Cat. No. 22a; Cat. I,
Cologne 1985, No. 276; I.
Becker, Berlin Catalog 1988,
No. 121.

1.61 BROOCH 1901-1902
Designed by Patriz Huber.
Silver, one lapis lazuli, blue
enamel.
Height 32, width 25 mm.
Stamped: TF 935 DEPOSE
PH.
Privately owned, Düsseldorf.
Lit.: I. Becker, Berlin Cat.
1988, No. 120.

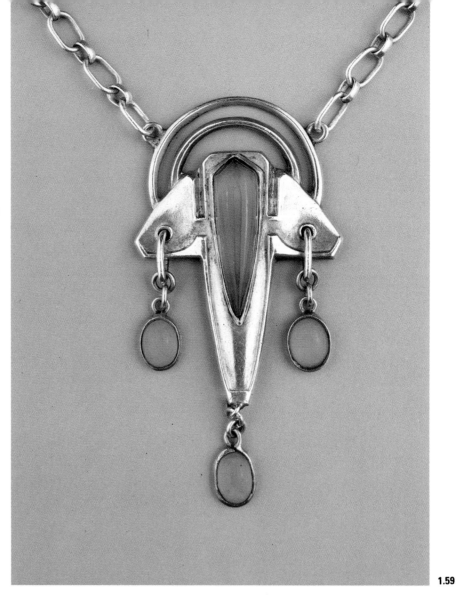

1.59

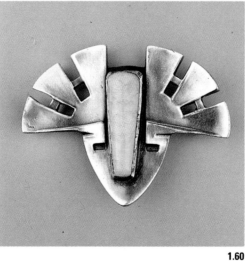

1.60

1.61

J oho, Bert (Albert)

Painter, designer

*February 23, 1877, Bruchsal †**October 6, 1963,** Zürich

1895-1899 Kunstgewerbe School and Academy in Karlsruhe (painting).

1904 Taught at the Kunstgewerbe School in Pforzheim; class: "Evaluating nature studies for simple flat patterns."

1916 Married Vera Fahrner, the elder of Theodor Fahrner's two daughters.

1921 Professor at the Pforzheim Kunstgewerbe School.

1942 Banned from his profession by the National Socialists.

1945 Destruction of his studio by bombs; loss of numerous pictures.

Numerous circus and show-business pictures. Designs for stage settings and choreographies, festival decorations. He and his wife traveled in Switzerland, Italy, France, Holland, with longer stays in Mexico, Guatemala, Cuba and the USA.

Little is known of Joho's close collaboration with Theodor Fahrner. All the pieces of jewelry designed by him that are shown in the catalog are from Fahrner's effects. All are unsigned. They may be one-of-a-kind pieces.

Lit.: R. Rücklin, Die Weihnachtsausstellung des Pforzheimer Kunstgewerbevereins, 1905, in: KGB Pfh. 12, 1905, pp. 49 ff, mentioned on p. 50, pictures on pp. 54, 56 (hatpins); Dressler, Kunstjahrbuch 1907, p. 403; Memorial to the Grand Ducal Kunstgewerbe School in Pforzheim, in: DGZ XIV, 1911, p. 341, mentioned on p. 347; DGZ XXII, 1919, p. 268; Bert Joho-Vera Joho, Exhibition Catalog, Pforzheim 1962.

1.62

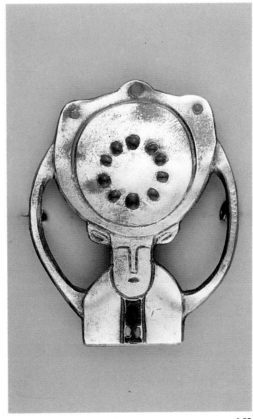

1.63

1.62 PENDANT CA. 1905
Designed by Bert Joho
Silver, imitation stones, green enamel.
Height 42, width 30 mm.
Pforzheim Jewelry Museum, Inv. No. 1979/13, from Bert Joho's ownership.
Compare similar designs in KGB Pfh. 12, 1905, pictures after p. 30.

1.63 BROOCH ca. 1905
Designed by Bert Joho.
Silver alloy, chased, orange-colored glass stones, blue enamel.
Height 45, width 35 mm.
Privately owned, from Bert Joho's ownership.
Compare hatpins in: KGB Pfh. 12, 1905, pictures on pp. 54, 56.

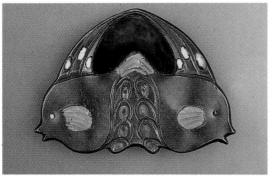

1.64

1.64 BROOCH ca. 1905
Designed by Bert Joho.
Silver, green, blue and white
enamel (stamped).
Height 29, width 40 mm.
Pforzheim Jewelry Museum,
Inv. No. 1979/12, from Bert
Joho's possession.

1.65 ENAMELED PLATE
1916-1919
Unset, with abstract motif.
Designed by Bert Joho.
Copper, enamel in green, red,
olive and blue on a mother-
of-pearl-colored
background.
Height 52, width 40 mm.
Adhesive label on the back:
Professor Joho. Accepted for
D.G.S. Pforzheim (D.G.S.
probably means "German
model protection").
Pforzheim Jewelry Museum,
Inv. No. Sch 3192/39 (F.St.);
identical specimen owned by
Bert Joho.
Compare the pattern on a fan
designed by Vera Joho in:
Blätter des
Kunstgewerbevereins Pfh.
NF, 23, 1921-22, picture on p.
9.
Lit.: Inv. KGS Pfh, Dec. 25,
1921, value 50 Marks.

1.66 ENAMELED PLATE
1916-1919
Unset, with abstract motif.
Designed by Bert Joho.
Copper, enamel in blue,
green, yellow, gold in
mother-of-pearl-colored
background.
Height 45, width 36 mm.
Privately owned, previously
by Bert Joho.

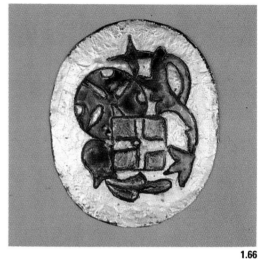

1.65   **1.66**

1.68

Joho, Vera, née Fahrner
(Theodor Fahrner's daughter)
Painter, jewelry and fashion designer
*****January 23, 1895,** Pforzheim †**September
19, 1987,** Mexico

Studied painting in Paris, Karlsruhe,
Dresden, many foreign trips. As well as
portraits, flower painting and still lifes, she
also made designes for clothing, stage
settings for masquerades and ballets,
fashion and jewelry designs.
1916 Marriage to Bert Joho.
The participation of Theodor Fahrner's
daughter, highly talented in the realms of
painting and music, in the creation of
jewelry for her father's firm can only be
documented in a few cases. Aside from a
very early gold brooch (Cat. No. 1.67),
which her father had produced from a
childhood design, the literature shows
silhouettes (ca. 1917) as well as an
enameled plate intended to be set.

Lit.: DGZ XX, 1917, picture on p. 46; DGZ XXII, 1919, p.
268; Vera Joho-Fahrner: Mode und Schmuck, in:
Blätter des Kunstgewerbevereins Pfh. NF 23, 1921,
pp. 1 ff; Vera Joho-Fahrner, Zu den Modebildern, in:
Blätter des Kunstgewerbevereins Pfh. NF 23, 1921,
p. 12, pictures 9-11; Bert Joho — Vera Joho, Exhibition Catalog, Pforzheim 1962; Blumenbilder von
Anmut und Schönheit, in: Pforzheimer Kurier 235,
10/9/1976.

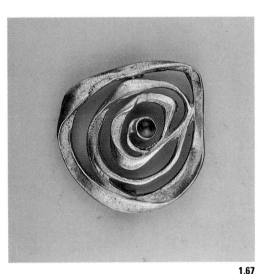

1.67

1.69

1.67 BROOCH "The Little
Ear" ca. 1900
Designed by Vera Joho.
Silver, gilded, one sapphire.
Height 25, width 26 mm.
Privately owned (F.N.)
Note: Vera Fahrner drew her
"little ear" as a child. Her
father had this single piece
made for her to her design.

1.68 ENAMELED PLATE ca.
1916
Young woman with
Biedermeier bouquet.
Designed by Vera Joho.
Copper, blue, brown and
white cell enamel.
Diameter: 43 mm.
Privately owned, previously
by Vera Joho.
Note: Pieces with related
motifs were being produced
at the Vienna Workshops at
the same time.
Compare brooch no. 818 in
Ketterer auction catalog no.
148, 1990.

1.69 PENDANT ca. 1916
Silhouette of a Biedermeier
couple.
Designed by Vera Joho.
Silver, partially gilded,
silhouette enameled in black.
Height 56, width 45 mm.
Privately owned (F.N.)
Compare picture on p. 151: a
head as silhouette on a white
background, in: DGZ XX,
1917, picture on p. 46.

1.70

1.71

1.70 BROOCH 1910-1914
Designed by Friedrich Katz.
Silver, gilded, one pearl shell,
lapis lazuli.
Height 30, width 35 mm.
Stamped: TF 935.
Privately owned (F.N.)
Note: A stylistically related
piece with a large pearl shell
was displayed at the 1914
Werkbund Exhibition in
Cologne. See DGZ XVIII,
1915, picture on p. 83.

1.71 BROOCH 1910-1914
Designed by Friedrich Katz.
Silver, one pearl shell, citrine.
Height 36, width 40 mm.
Privately owned (Katz
effects).
Note: The flowers are fully
three-dimensional on both
sides. See note on Cat. No.
1.70.

1.72 BROOCHES 1914-1919
Mourning jewelry
Design attributed to Friedrich
Katz.
1.72a Silver, gilded, black
matte enamel, small irregular
pearls.
Diameter 39 mm.
Stamped: TF 935.
Privately owned (F.N.)
1.72b Silver, gilded, black
matte enamel, large pearl
shells.
Diameter: 42 mm.
Stamped: TF 935.
Pforzheim Jewelry Museum,
Inv. No. Sch 3192/9 (F.St.)
Lit.: KGS Pfh. inventory, Dec.
25, 1921, value 100 Marks.
1.72c Silver, gilded, black
matte enamel, two pearl
shells.
Height 29, width 48 mm.
Stamped: TF EX 935 (on
silver plate).
Private collection (F.N.)
Lit.: Similar pieces were
displayed at the Werkbund
Exhibitions in Cologne in
1914 and Copenhagen in
1919, see DGZ XVIII, 1915,
picture on p. 83, and DKD
XLIII, 1918-19, picture on p.
263.

Katz, Friedrich
Goldsmith, pattern designer
*September 1873 †July 16, 1941

1888-1893 Studied at the Carl Rau Jewelry
Factory in Pforzheim; then military service.
1896-1899 Again worked as a jeweler for
Carl Rau.
1900 Worked for F. Weeber, Pforzheim.
Oct. 15, 1900 to Theodor Fahrner's death:
worked as a mounter and first pattern
designer, intermediate certificate on July
4, 1913, when Katz obviously intended to
leave the firm, then 4 years of military
service. After Theodor Fahrner's death he
continued to work for Gustav Braendle as
cabinetmaster. In this position, which he
may already have held for several months
before Braendle bought the firm, he
remained until 1938. Traveled with Gustav
Braendle to Paris, Madrid and Barcelona.
The designs from his entire career with
the Fahrner firm were burned in Pforzheim
in 1945. According to information from his
granddaughter, the designs for the "leaf
style" were made by Friedrich Katz, and
the black-enameled mourning jewelry may
also have been his work. After 1920 Katz
turned to Egyptian jewelry, among others.
See also page 59.
(Many thanks to Frau Traudl Hauck for
much information.)

Lit.: KGB Pfh 19, 1912, p. 21; KGB Pfh. 20, 1913, p. 29
(gift of various pieces of jewelry to the Kunstgewerbe
Museum), DGZ XXII, 1919, p. 269.

1.72a

1.72b

1.72c

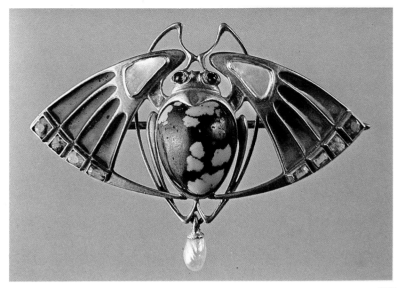

1.73

K
leemann, Georg

Designer

*December 8, 1863, Oberwurmbach, Middle Franconia †**1932**

Kunstgewerbe School in Munich, then training at the Spiess Gallery (designs for ceramics, wallpaper, bookbindings, etc.).
1887 Professor at the Pforzheim Kunstgewerbe School (designing classes).
1900 Published his book "Moderner Schmuck" (100 pages of designs for jewelry of modern character), published by Birkner & Brecht, Pforzheim.

Collaboration with Theodor Fahrner probably since 1901. Kleemann provided numerous jewelry designs to various Pforzheim firms, as far as can be determined, to Carl Herrmann, Lauer & Wiedmann, Victor Mayer, Rodi & Wienenberger, Söllner, Zerenner.

1.73 BROOCH with beetle
1902
Designed by Georg Kleemann.
Gold, one turquoise, emeralds, rubies, pearl shells, blue translucent enamel.
Height 28, width 46 mm.
Stamped: TF 585.
Pforzheim Jewelry Museum, Inv. No. Sch 1934.
Note: Displayed at the 1904 World's Fair in St. Louis. Compare similar designs in: G. Kleemann, Schmuckentwürfe, pp. 1 and 85.
Lit.: KGS Pfh inventory, 12/6/1902, Fahrner No. 11910, selling price 116 Marks; DGZ VI, 1903, picture on p. 117; DKD XIV, 1904, p. 500; KuH 55, 1904-05, picture on p. 109, KGB NF XVI 1905, picture on p. 158 KGB Pfh. 12, 1905, picture on p. 98; Koch p. 7; Falk 1985 No. 197, picture no. 196; von Hase 262; I. Becker, Berlin Catalog 1988, no. 23.

1.74a

1.74 BROOCHES 1901
Designed by Georg
Kleemann
1.74a Silver, opals, blue and
green enamel.
Height 25, width 36 mm.
Stamped: TF 935.
Reverse side worked.
E. L. collection.
1.74b Silver, gilded,
almandine garnet.
Height 36, width 36 mm.
Stamped: TF DEPOSE
STERLING 935
E. L. collection.
Note: Examples of variations
of a basic form. Similar
designs were made by the H.
Levinger firm2Lit.: von Hase
258 (this example was given
to the Pforzheim KGS by
Theodor Fahrner at the end
of 1901.

1.75 BROOCH 1900-1902
Designed by Georg
Kleemann.
Silver, gilded, turquoise
matrix, pearls.
Height 24, width 33 mm.
Pforzheim Jewelry Museum,
Inv. No. Sch 1861.
Lit.: DGZ VI, 1903, pictures on
pp. 9, 117; von Hase 264.

1.76 BROOCH 1902
Designed by Georg
Kleemann.
Silver, gilded, green colored
agates, one pearl shell.
Height 29, width 34 mm.
Stamped: TF 900.
Pforzheim Jewelry Museum,
Inv. No. Sch 1862.
Lit.: KGS Pfh. Inventory, Nov.
11, 1902, Fahrner no. 11917.
Sale price 27.50 Marks; DGZ
VI 1903, pictures on pp. 9,
117; von Hase 266.

1.74b

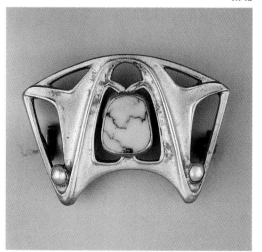

1.75

1.76

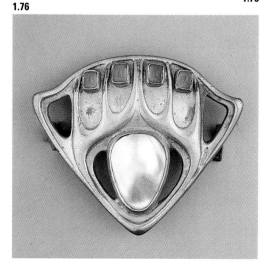

Lit. on Georg Kleemann: Das Kunstgewerbe
(Dresden) 3, 1892, pp. 149 ff, 169; R. Rücklin, Die
Fachausstellung für Bijouterie des Pforzheimer
Kunstgewerbevereins, in: KGB Pfh. 1, 1894, pp. 3 ff;
Georg Kleemann, Moderner Schmuck, Pforzheim
1900; Anniversary Art Exhibition Catalog, Karlsruhe
1902, p. 58; DGZ VI, 1903, p. 91, pictures on pp.
91-92; DGZ VI, 1903, p. 24, pictures on pp. 25, 117,
240; KGB Pfh. 10, 1903, picture without page number;
Pforzheimer Fein- und Metallarbeiten auf der
Weltausstellung St. Louis, in: DKD XIV, 1904, pp. 500
ff, picture on p. 503; DKD XV, 1904-05, picture on p.
130; F. von Thiersch, Architektur und Kunstgewerbe
auf der Weltausstellung in St. Louis, in: KuH 55,
1904-05, picture on p. 109; R. Rücklin, Die moderne
Schmuckkunst im Lichte der Weltausstellung zu St.
Louis, in: KGB NF 16, 1905, picture on p. 158; Koch, p.
7; KGB Pfh. 13, 1906, picture on p. 54; K. Widmer, Die
Karlsruher Jubiläumsausstellung, in: DKD XIX 1906-
07, pp. 125 ff, pictures on pp. 126-127; DKD XX, 1907,
picture on p. 346; DK XVIII, 1907-08, picture on p.
315; KuH 58, 1907-08, pictures on pp. 220-221;
Velhagen & Klasings Monatshefte XIX 1907-08, Vol.
1, p. 159, picture on p. 160; F. Sales Meyer, Kunst-
gewerbliches aus dem Grossherzogtum Baden, in:
KGB NF 19, 1908, p. 27, picture on p. 38; KGB Pfh. 15,
1908, pictures on pp. 13, 17-18; DGZ XXII, 1919, p.
268; von Hase pp. 94, 97, 224 ff; V. Becker 1985, p.
130.

*Georg Kleemann,
Moderner Schmuck, 1900, no
page.*

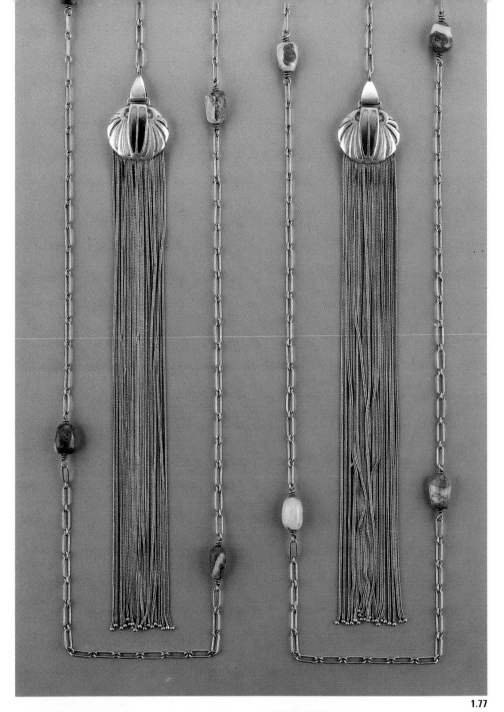

1.77

1.77 CHAIN with silver tassels 1902-1903 Designed by Georg Kleemann.
Silver, blue-green cell enamel, nine opal matrices in the chain, fine silver tassels with silver pearls.
Length: 218 mm.
Stamped: TF 950 MBCo REG.D.
Ludwig Kuttner collection.
Note: The chain was wrapped around the neck several times, with the decorative parts and tassels to the front.
Compare a similar design with round parts (without tassels): G. Kleemann, Schmuckentwurfe, no. 76.
See nearly identical designs by Kleemann in: DGZ VI, 1903, pictures on p. 117 (see below), above the signature: "Design for a modern tablet with artistically arranged jewelry..

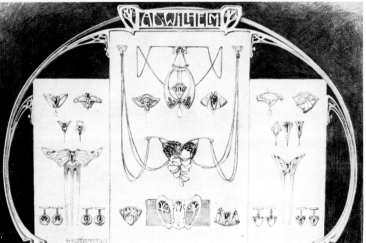

Jewelry designs by G. Kleemann, pictures from: DGZ VI, 1903, p. 117.

1.78 NECKLACES 1906-1908
Designed by Erich
Kleinhempel.
1.78a Silver, amethysts, wing
pearls.
Height 70, width 28 mm.
Pforzheim Jewelry Museum,
Inv. No. Sch 3192/1.
Lit.: KGS Pfh. Inventory, Dec.
12, 1921, value 100 Marks;
von Hase 137; compare a
similar pendant in JGK 30,
1909, picture on p. 160, plus
a cuff link by Erich
Kleinhempel in DKD XVIII,
1906, pictures on p. 779, see
p. 113 (upper right).

1.78 a

Kleinhempel, Erich
Painter, architect, designer
***January 9, 1874,** Leipzig †1947

1890-1893 Training at the Kunstgewerbe
School, Dresden.
1906-1912 Teacher at the Kunstgewerbe
School, Dresden. He and his siblings
Gertrud and Fritz directed a private school
for commercial art in Dresden. Director of
the State Commercial Museum of the
Kunstgewerbe School in Bremen. Member
of the Deutsche Werkbund.
Collaboration with Theodor Fahrner for
the "Deutsche Kunstgewerbe 1906"
Exhibition in Dresden. The pieces displayed there have not been found. Other
designs were given to goldsmiths Arthur
Berger, H. Ehrenlechner and the Saxon
Agate Industry in Dresden-Briesnitz: the
firm of Rimatei & Co.

Lit. for collaboration with Theodor Fahrner:
Das deutsche Kunstgewerbe 1906, Exhibition
Catalog, Dresden, p. 252 (piece in gold); DKD XVIII,
1906, pictures pp. 778 ff; DGZ IX, 1906, picture on p.
146 (designer not named); KGB NF 17, 1906, p. 211;
DKD XXII, 1908, picture on p. 280; P. Schumann, Von
angewandter Kunst in Dresden, in: DK XXIV, 1910-
11, picture on p. 474 (above) Additional lit.: F. Sch.:
Die dekorative Kunst auf der Dresdner Ausst. 1901,
p. 396, pictures pp. 402 ff; J. Kleinpaul, Das Kunstgewerbe auf der internationalen Kunstausst.
Dresden 1901, in" KGB NF 13, 1902, p. 33, picture pp.
21, 26; Moderner Schmuck, in DK VIII, 1902-03, p.
181, picture on p. 187; A. L. Plehn, 1. Internationale

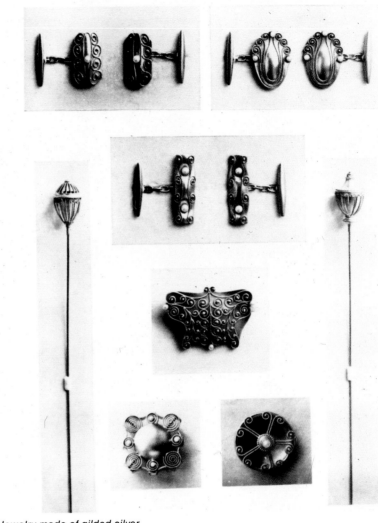

Jewelry made of gilded silver by Theodor Fahrner, pictures from: DKD XVIII, 1906, p. 779.

1.78b

1.78b Silver, amethysts. Height 92, width 24 mm. Pforzheim Jewelry Museum, Inv. No. Stadt 1969/141.
Note: A similar necklace was given to the Kunstgewerbeverein by Theodor Fahrner on November 30, 1908. Fahrner No. 15550.
Lit.: (see Cat. No. 1.78a) von Hase 138.
At the 3rd Kunstgewerbe Exhibition in Dresden, Fahrner displayed jewelry designed by Erich Kleinhempel and set in folk-style filigree. The same motif as that of the two necklaces appeared on a pair of cuff links: filigree spirals around a plain surface or a faceted stone. Both necklaces have almost the same motif in their added decorative parts.

Ausst. für moderne dekorative Kunst in Turin, in: KGB NF 14, 1903, picture on p. 20; J. Kleinpaul, Die Dresdner Ausst. 1903, in: KGB NF 14, 1903, p. 221, pictures pp. 217, 220; Württ. Mitt. 1903-04, picture on p. 247; E. Haenel, Von Dresdner Architektur und Kunstgewerbe von der Ausst., in: DK XIV, 1905-06, p. 240, picture on p. 241; Das Deutsche Kunstgewerbe Exhibition Cat. 1906, Dresden 1906, pictures pp. 247, 252; von Hase, pp. 102, 106, 110, 225.

L. Knupfer, silver pendant (below) made by Theodor Fahrner.
Picture from: DGZ VI, 1903, p. 119.

1.79 CHATELAINE
1901-1903
Attributed to Ludwig Knupfer.
Silver, chrysoprase.
Height 136, width 26 mm.
Stamped: TF DEPOSE 900.
Hans-Peter Callsen, Bonn.

K

nupfer, Ludwig

1902-1905 Designer employed by Theodor Fahrner's firm.

1898, 1900 & 1905 Listed as "artist" in the Pforzheim Directory.

1903 Listed in the "Address- and Hand-book for the German Goldsmithing Profession", Leipzig, as "Chaser and artist" under the "commercial art workshops."

Two brooches by Knupfer can be identified definitely on a basis of style (Cat. No. 1.82a & b); he is thought to have designed many other pieces, in which a stylistic closeness between Knupfer and Gradl can be seen.

Lit.: Der Wettbewerb um den IV. C. A. Schmitz-Jubelpreis 1902, in: KGB Pfh. 9, 1902, no page; DGZ VI, 1903, p. 131, picture on p. 119 (showing a pendant made by Fahrner); KGB Pfh. 13, 1906, picture on p. 15 (belt buckle); DGZ XXII, 1919, p. 268.

1.79

1.80

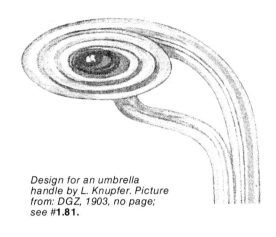

*Design for an umbrella handle by L. Knupfer. Picture from: DGZ, 1903, no page; see #**1.81.***

1.80 PENDANT with chain
1901-1902
Design attributed to Ludwig Knupfer.
Silver, one chrysoprase, green translucent enamel.
Height 34, width 34 mm.
Stamped: TF 950 REGD MB & Co.
ANTIK OFFICE, R + S. Diehl, Frankfurt on the Main.
Note: Compare von Hase 125; necklace with pendant on Gablonz on the Neisse, Museum for Jewelry and Decoration, Inv. No. B 3958; this piece, probably dated too late, is by the same designer.
Lit.: V. Becker 1987, picture on p. 259.

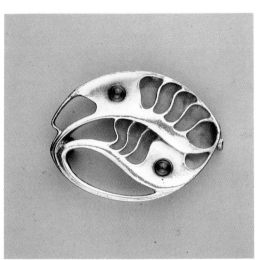

1.82b

1.81

1.81 BROOCH ca, 1903
Design attributed to Ludwig Knupfer.
Silver, red·glass stones, violet enamel.
Height 28, width 30 mm.
Stamped: TF.
Pforzheim Jewelry Museum, Inv. No. Sch 1933.
Note: As to attribution, see an umbrella-handle design by L. Knupfer with identical decoration in: DGZ XI, 1903, no page (see above).
Lit.: von Hase 116.

1.82 BROOCHES 1902-1903
Designed by Ludwig Knupfer
1.82a Silver, green colored chalcedony.
Height 50, width 63 mm.
Stamped: TF 950 MBCo REG.D, on top MB & Co. F (' foreign), plus marks for London 1902.
Galerie Telkamp, Munich.
1.82b Silver, translucent enamel, two red stones.
Width 28, height 22 mm.
Stamped: TF (ligature) 950, REG.D M B Co.
Marianne Geitel collection, Berlin.

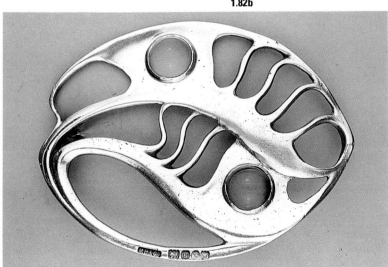

1.82a

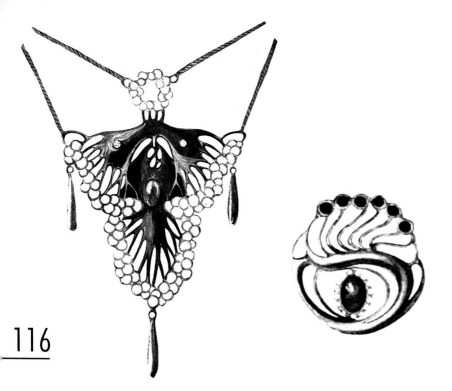

Jewelry designs by L. Knupfer. Pictures from: KGB Pfh. 1902, no page.

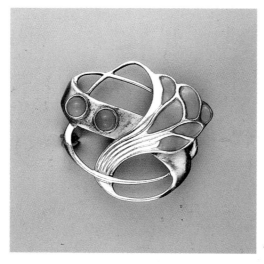

1.82c

1.82c Silver, chrysoprase, blue-green translucent enamel.
Height 27, width 30 mm.
Stamped: TF 900 DEPOSE.
Dr Karl Kreuzer.
Note: It is possible that Cat. No. 1.82a, unusually large for a brooch, was also used as a belt buckle; see the smaller form of Cat. No. 1.82b.
Lit.: V. Becker 1980, picture on p. 75; V. Becker 1987, picture on p. 259.

1.83 BELT BUCKLE, two-piece ca. 1905
Designed by Ludwig Knupfer or Max J. Gradl.
Silver, red-brown transparent pit and turquoise cell enamel (the turquoise section polished).
Height 46, width 71 mm.
Pforzheim Jewelry Museum, Inv. No. Sch 3192/56 (F.St.).
Lit.: KGS Pfh. inv. Dec. 25, 1921, value 50 Marks.

1.83

Jewelry designed by Louise Matz, made by Theodor Fahrner. Picture from: KuH 56, 1905-06, p. 173.

M
atz, Louise, née Mayer

Designer (chiefly of textiles and jewelry)

*May 30, 1857, Reutlingen †**June 5, 1938,** Lübeck

Lübeck Art School (training in drawing from Prof. von Lütgendorf), short practice in commercial art studio of Erich Kleinhempel in Dresden (see also pp. 112 ff).

pre-1908 Founded the "Werkstätte für künstlerische Frauenarbeit" in Lübeck, listed in the directory from 1910 to 1917; the studio was at Breitenstrasse 14, in the same building as the "Magasin von Tapeten Decorations-Artikeln, Teppichen etc. Papier-Lager en gros & en détail" (founded 1908) of Carl Johannes Matz, Louise Matz's husband; designs for textiles, jewelry, porcelain, ceramics, tinware, wallpaper.

Collaboration with Theodor Fahrner 1905-1906.

Lit.: KuH 56, 1905-06, picture on p. 173, see above. Other works, particularly with filigree and pearls, were made by goldsmith Arthur Berger of Stuttgart. (For biographical notes and a family tree, our thanks to the Archives of the Hanseatic City of Lübeck.)

Lit.: Neue Perlarbeiten, in DK XVI, 1906-07, p. 262, pictures pp. 260 ff; Mitt. Württ. 1906-07. pictures pp. 107 ff; Otto Kofahl, Werkstätte für künstlerische Frauenarbeit, in: KGB NF XIX, 1908, pp. 73 ff, pictures pp. 74 ff.

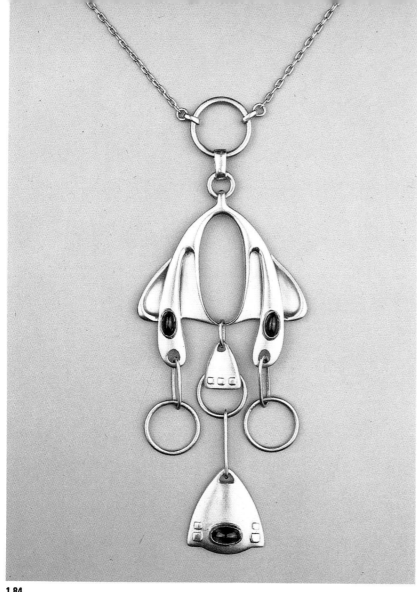

1.84

1.85

1.84 PENDANT with chain
1902-1903
Designed by Ferdinand
Morawe.
Silver, gilded, sapphires.
Height 85, width 35 mm.
Unsigned.
Galerie Torsten Bröhan,
Düsseldorf.
Compare a similar pendant in
DK VIII, 1902-03, picture on
p. 190. The piece shown
there, in beaten gold and with
rubies, may have been made
singly.

1.85 PENDANT with chain
1902-1903
Design attributed to
Ferdinand Morawe.
Silver, one turquoise.
Height 54, width 34 mm
(without chain).
Stamped: DEPOSE 935 TF.
Ludwig Kuttner collection.
Compare similar pendant in
DK VIII, 1902-03, p. 190, in
beaten gold with opals,
rubies and platinum. These
may have been made singly.

M

orawe, Christian Ferdinand
Writer, painter, designer
*February 27, 1865, Breslau †**August 8,
1931,** Berlin-Zehlendorf

Studied at the Breslau Art School.
1893 Married Claire Thum, who married
Joseph Maria Olbrich (see p. 123) in 1903.
1896 Active as an "art dealer, painter and
art writer" in Munich.
March 1900 Moved to Darmstadt.
March 10, 1902 Moved to Berlin.
to 1910 Teacher at the art school, then
director of the state manual training
courses.
Early thirties Teacher at the State Art
School in Berlin.
Collaboration with Theodor Fahrner from
1901 to 1909, documented.

Lit.: Karl Scheffler, Unterricht im Kunstgewerbe, in:
DK VI, 1901-02, pp. 365 ff, pictures pp. 374 ff; Holme,
German Section, Plate 7; Moderner Schmuck, in: DK
VIII, 1902-03, p. 181, pictures pp. 190 ff; KuK V, 1902,
pp. 380 ff; DGZ VII, 1904, p. 14, pictures pp. 12, 16, 21;
JGK 27, 1906, picture on p. 3 (mirror); Velhagen &
Klasings Monatshefte XXI, 1906-07, Vol. 1, pictures
pp. 646 ff; DGZ XII, 1909, p. 318, picture on p. 311; von
Hase, pp. 77, 94, 107, 236; Reto Niggl, Eine Jugend
und ihr Stil, in: Antiquitäten-Zeitung 21, 1983, pp. 523
ff, re Fahrner p. 525.

Jewelry designs by C. F. Morawe made by Th. Fahrner, pictures from: DK VIII, 1903, p. 190.

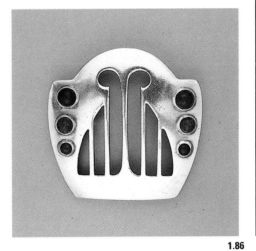

1.86

Jewelry designs by C. F. Morawe made by Th. Fahrner, pictures from: DGZ Vol. XII, 1909, p. 311.

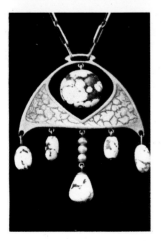

1.86 BROOCH
1902-1904
Designed by
Ferdinand Morawe.
Silver, blue stones.
Height 30, width 30
mm.
Monogram FM.
Privately owned.

1.87

1.87 PENDANT with chain
ca. 1903
Designed by Ferdinand
Morawe.
Silver, amethyst balls, violet
enamel.
Height 62, width 33 mm.
Overall length 290 mm.
Stamped: TF 935 DEPOSE.
Schneidewind/Wilksen
collection, Freiburg.
Compare similar pendant in
DK VI, 1901-02, picture on p.
375. The piece shown there,
in gold with pearls and
emeralds, may have been
made singly. Compare also a
picture in: Velhagen &
Klasings Monatshefte XXI,
1906-07, p. 646. Felix
Poppenberg refers to pieces
by Morawe in "Berliner
dekorative Chronik" in KuKH
V, 1902, pp. 78 ff: ". . . these
linked golden pieces with
pearls as heads look like a
Japanese glockenspiel . . . At
every movement they will
swing and ring together . . ."

1.88 BROOCHES ca. 1903
Designed by Ferdinand
Morawe.
1.88a Silver, amethysts, violet
enamel.
Height 34, width 42 mm.
Stamped: TF 935 DEPOSE,
FM monogram.
G. Silzer collection,
Hannover.
Lit.: DGZ VI, 1903, drawing on
p. 16 (as a pendant for a belt
buckle).
1.88b Silver, amethysts.
Height 42, width 42 mm.
Stamped: TF 900 DEPOSE,
FM monogram.
Galerie Urlass, Frankfurt on
the Main.

1.89 PENDANT 1904-1905
Designed by Ferdinand
Morawe's group.
Gold, sapphires, wing pearls.
Height 54, width 30 mm.
Stamped: TF 750, Austrian
stamp for foreign gold and
silver. Privately owned (F.N.)

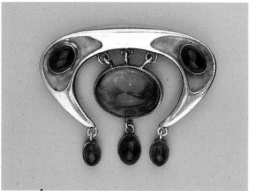

1.88a

1.88b

1.89

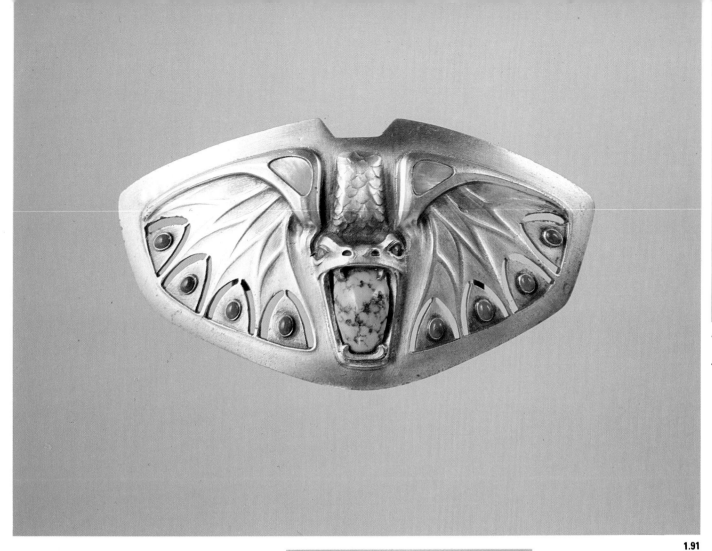

1.91

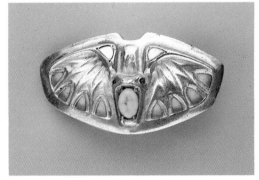

1.91b

M

üller-Salem, Julius

Painter, architect, designer

*February 9, 1865, Salem **†November 20, 1946,** Eutingen

Studied at the Kunstgewerbe School in Karlsruhe and with Prof. Schmid-Reutte in Munich.

1899 Called to the Pforzheim Kunstgewerbe School to teach action and figure drawing; Professor at the Pforzheim Kunstgewerbe School in 1906.

Collaboration with Theodor Fahrner since ca. 1901 and continuing for many years. Designs for the firms of Söllner and Lauer & Wiedmann have been documented.

Lit.: Mitt. Württ. I, 1902, picture on p. 108 (with correction on p. 204); Jubiläumskunstausst. Kat. Karlsruhe 1902, p. 58; DGZ VII, 1903, picture on p. 6; DGZ VII, 1904, p. 111, picture on p. 106; Pforzheimer Fein-Metallarbeiten auf der Weltausstellung St. Louis, in: DKD XIV, 1904, p. 506, pictures pp. 504 ff; R. Rücklin, Die moderne Schmuckkunst im Lichte der Weltausstellung zu St. Louis, in: KGB NF XVI, 1905, pictures pp. 158 ff; Koch 1906, pictures pp. 8-9; DGZ XXII, 1919, p. 268; von Hase, pp. 28, 237; Lothar Müller in: Blickpunkt 1986-87, pp. 16 ff. Pfh.

1.91 BELT BUCKLE with snake's head 1901-1902 Designed by Julius Müller-Salem.
1.91a Silver, sulfured, lapis lazuli, turquoise, pearl shells. Height 43, width 77 mm. Stamped: DEPOSE 935 TF. Pforzheim Jewelry Museum, Inv. No. Sch 1864.
Lit.: KGS Pfh. Inv. of Nov. 11, 1902. Fahrner No. 11927, sale price 45 Marks.
1.91b Silver, turquoise, turquoise-colored cell enamel.
Height 23, width 41 mm. Stamped: TF 950 REGD MBCo.
Galerie Urlass, Frankfurt on the Main.
Note: Displayed at the 1904 World's fair in St. Louis. Shown is a snake of the Dasypeltis genus, holding the egg in its mouth (von Hase p. 28).
Lit.: Mitt. Württ. I, 1902-03, picture on p. 108 (there attributed to J. Schmid, report on p. 204); DGZ VI, 1903, picture on p. 6; DKD XIV, 1904, picture on p. 504; KGB NF XVI, 1905, picture on p. 159; Koch, picture on p. 9; von Hase 335; V. Becker 1985, picture 167; I. Becker, Berlin Cat. 1988, no. 33.

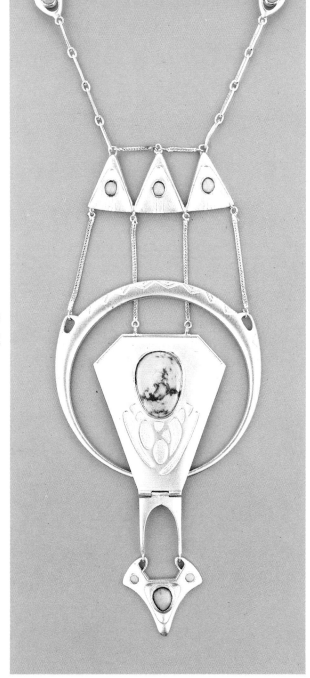

1.90

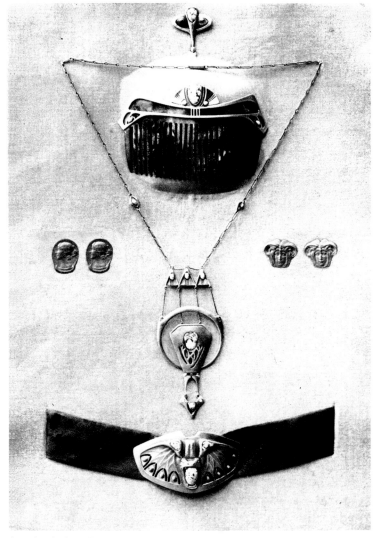

1.90 NECKLACE with pendant 1901-1902 Designed by Julius Müller-Salem.
Silver, sulfured, turquoises.
Height 109, width 46 mm.
Stamped: DEPOSE 935 TF.
Pforzheim Jewelry Museum, Inv. No. Sch 1866.
Note: Displayed at the 1904 World's Fair in St. Louis.
Lit.: KGS Pfh. Inventory, Nov. 11, 1902. Fahrner No. 11920, sale price 59 Marks; Mitt. Württ. I, 1902-03, picture on p. 108 (attributed to J. Schmid, description p. 204); DGZ VI, 1903, picture on p. 6; DKD XIV, 1904, picture on p. 504; KGB NF XVI, 1905, picture on p. 159; Koch, picture on p. 9; von Hase 333.

Jewelry designs by Prof. Julius Müller-Salem, illustration from: Kochs Monographien IX, Schmuck und Edelmetall-Arbeiten, Darmstadt 1906, p. 9.

O

lbrich, Joseph Maria

Architect, interior decorator, designer

*December 22, 1867, Troppau †**August 8, 1908**, Düsseldorf

1882-1886 State Trade School, Vienna.

1890-1893 Academy in Vienna (architecture with C. von Hasenauer).

1893-1894 Traveled to Italy and North Africa.

1894-1899 Colleague of Otto Wagner in Vienna.

1897 A founder of the "Secession" in Vienna.

post-1899 Member of the artist colony in Darmstadt.

1907 Founding member of German Werkbundes.

During his years in Darmstadt, he collaborated with Theodor Fahrner; other designs were made by the firms of Joseph Siess' Sons in Vienna and J. Friedmann's Successors D. & M. Loewenthal in Frankfurt.

Jewelry designs by Olbrich are found in the Berlin Art Library, but only one of them has been related to a piece made by Fahrner (Schreyl, No. 12066; von Hase, #358).

Lit.: Joseph Maria Olbrich, Ideen, Vienna 1899, pictures pp. 12, 58; Holme, German Sect. pp. 2 ff, Plates 1, 2, 3 and 8 (Fahrner); DGZ VI, 1903, p. 23; R. Forrer, Die Strassburg historische Schmuckausstellung von 1904, in: Das Kunstgewerbe in Elsass-Lothringen, V, 1904-05, picture on p. 134;

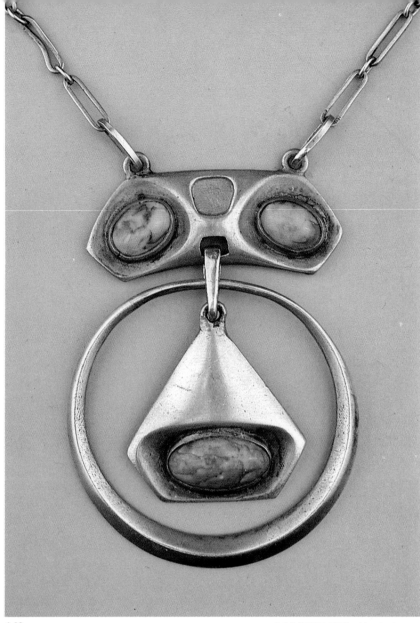

1.92

Aus der Geschichte des Gold- und Silberschmucks, in: JGK 26, 1905, p. 173, picture p. 167; R. Forrer, Geschichte des Gold- und Silberschmucks, Strassburg 1905, p. 54, with picture; DGZ XXII, 1919, p. 268; Joseph M. Olbrich 1867-1908, Kat. Ausst. Darmstadt, Vienna, Berlin 1967, No. 154 ff; Karl Heinz Schreyl & D. Neumeister, Joseph Maria Olbrich, Die Zeichnungen in der Kunstbibliothek Berlin, Berlin 1972; Kat. Darmstadt 1976 No. 509; von Hase pp. 241 ff; V. Becker 1985, p. 218.

1.92 PENDANT with chain
ca. 1902
Designed by Joseph Maria Olbrich.
Silver, partly gilded, agates.
Length 310, diameter 31 mm.
Stamped: TF 935 DEPOSE FM
E. L. collection.
Note: The displayed pendant is stamped "FM" (Ferdinand Morawe), but the contemporary literature confirms Olbrich's authorship several times. The example in the Mathildenhöhe Museum in Darmstadt bears only the TF stamp. Presumably the FM stamp was applied by accident. A version in gold with turquoise is privately owned in England.
Lit.: DGZ VI, 1903, p. 54 (as a brooch); Das Kunstgewerbe in Elsass-Lothringen V, 1904-05, picture on p. 134; JGK 26, 1905, picture on p. 167; R. Forrer, Geschichte des Gold- und Silberschmucks, Strassburg 1905, picture on p. 54; Umelecka / Kolonie Darmstadt 1899-1914, Kat. Ausst. 1989, No. 320; Kat. Museum Künstlerkolonie Darmstadt, 1990, p. 202, No. 308.

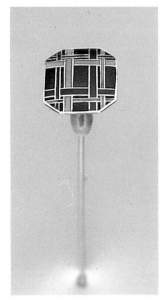

1.93a

1.93 PIN and SLIDING CLIP ca. 1902
Designed in the style of J. M. Olbrich.
1.93a Pin: Silver, black, green and blue enamel.
Decorative plate height 20, width 17 mm.
Stamped: 935 TF.
1.93b Brooch: black, green, white and blue enamel.
Stamped: TF DEPOSE 935 DRPa.
Privately owned (F.N.)
Note: Decorative plate of the slide and head of the pin are adjustable or removable. Both decorative pieces are chased on the underside. The plate of the slide clip sits on a raised bar that allows a piece of cloth to be pulled through it. Under number 36635   the pin was entered in the "Patentblatt" in 1895 as sample protection. Obviously the design was a great success and was still being made many years after its registration, presumably with other decorative plates.
J. M. Olbrich's "Design for a muff chain" is based on a similarly clearly structured surface geometry that was rare at that time. Thus it is not impossible the design originated with Olbrich or in his group.
Lit. on Olbrich's muff chain: Joseph M. Olbrich 1867-1908, Kat. Darmstadt 1967, No. 155.

1.94 BROOCH ca. 1902
Design from J. M. Olbrich's group.
Silver, moss agate, wing pearls, green translucent enamel.
Height 41, width 29 mm.
Stamped: TF 935 DEPOSE.
Antiker Schmuck/Gutachter Firma Röder, Bergisch-Gladbach.
Compare V. Becker, 1985, Picture 213 shows a similarly structured brooch ascribed to Olbrich.
Note: The fine twiglike wire setting of the moss agate suggests that it was made in Fahrner's studio.

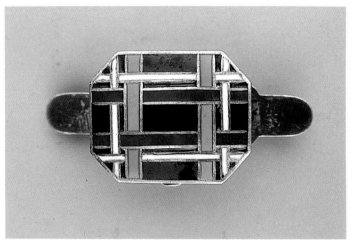

1.93b

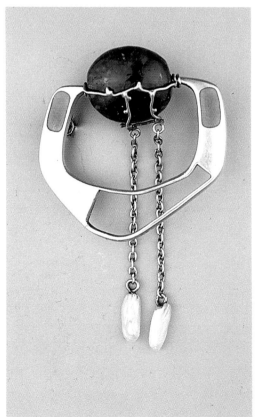

1.94

1.95

Riester, Egon

"Jewelry artist", goldsmith, enameler, illustrator

(Emil Riester's nephew) fell in action late in 1917.

Studied at the Pforzheim Kunstgewerbe School (enamel painting with A. Hildenbrand) and in Berlin with Pfeiffer (Paul Pfeiffer?, who became a teacher at the Goldsmithing School in Pforzheim in 1910). After 1910 founded the "Werkstatt für künstlerische Edelmetall- und Emailarbeiten K. H. Egon Riester" in Pforzheim. In the last years he designed embroidered cushions and covers, title pages and illustrations.

Collaboration with Theodor Fahrner probably began in 1914 and also includes numerous works with a religious character.

Lit.: Velhagen & Klasings Monatshefte XXIX, 1914-15, Vol. 3, mentioned on p. 566, picture on p. 568; DGZ XX, 1917, p. 217, pictures pp. 58 ff (about the workshop); DGZ XXI, 1918, p. 8 (memorial tablet for the dead); DGZ XXII, 1919, pp. 268 and 354.

1.96

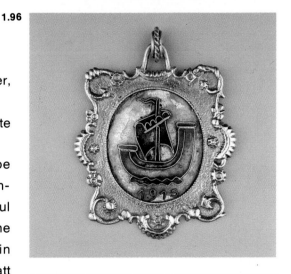

1.97

1.95 BROOCH ca. 1915
Woman riding a dolphin.
Designed by Egon Riester.
Silver, the framed plate with blue-green dolphin, gold woman, red cloth over silver-blue background of transparent enamel.
Height 39, width 42 mm.
Stamped: K H
EGON/RIESTER 800 IB (lig.); stamp of IB not identified.
Privately owned (F.N.)

1.96 PENDANT with ship 1915
Designed by Egon Riester
Silver, gilded, the framed plate with a brown ship over yellow-brown background of translucent cell enamel.
Height 51, width 40 mm.
Stamped: K.H.EGON
RIESTER 800, label with Fahrner no. 18652.
Privately owned (F.N.)

1.97 PENDANT with figure of saint ca. 1915
Design attributed to Egon Riester.
Silver, lightly gilded, two chrysoprases over the spiral pillars, saint's figure on gold cell enamel before green leaves and blue sky with gold stars.
Height 34, width 34 mm.
Privately owned (F.N.)

1.98a   **1.98b**

1.98 BROOCH with St. Mark's Lion ca. 1915
Design attributed to Egon Riester.
1.98a Silver, the copper plate with light relief, brown, blue, yellowish and white enamel.
Height 48, width 43 mm.
Stamped: TF 800 plus grapevine (see Cat. No. 1.98b).
Privately owned (F.N.)
1.98b Reverse side of a brooch 1915
Silver, gilded, stamped grapevine.
Height 46, width 41 mm.
Privately owned (F.N.)

Note: The grapevine motif with the TF trade mark appears on various enameled pieces made around 1915. They are usually pieces with Christian motifs (saints, dove of peace, apostles).

1.99 BROOCH 1915-1919
Dove of Peace
Design attributed to Egon Riester.
Silver, the framed copper plate with light relief, gold-green and green-blue enamel.
Height 46, width 40 mm.
Stamped: TF 800 Rs, stamped grapevine.
Privately owned (F.N.)

1.100 ENAMELED PLATE (unset) Pietà 1915-1919
Design attributed to Egon Riester.
Copper with light relief, brown and blue enamel.
Height 50, width 46 mm.
Privately owned (F.N.)

1.101 PENDANT with Quadriga 1915-1919
Design attributed to Egon Riester.
Silver, copper plate with light relief, green translucent enamel.
Height 50, width 40 mm.
Stamped: TF 800.
Pforzheim Jewelry Museum, Inv. No. Sch 3192/41.
Lit.: KGS Pfh. inventory, Dec. 25, 1921, value 50 Marks.

1.99

1.100

1.101

R iester, Emil

Goldsmith, designer, painter

*1885, Hausen in the Kirchtal †**1920?**

Attended the Kunstgewerbe School.
Professor of Jewelry at the Pforzheim
Kunstgewerbe School.
Three designs for Theodor Fahrner in
1908 can be documented. Other designs
were made for the firms of Bohnenberger
& Böhmler, Wilhelm Feucht, A. Hauber,
Julius Wimmer and O. Zahn, all in Pforz-
heim.

Lit.: Emil Riester, Schmuckentwürfe, Pforzheim 1880
(20 plates); Emil Riester, Moderner Schmuck und
Ziergeräte nach Pflanzen und Tierformen, Pforzheim
1897-98; Emil Riester, Schmuckmotive, Pforzheim
1913; KGB NF IV, 1892-93, pp. 193 ff; Der Bazar 43,
1897, picture on p. 474; DKD IV, 1899, picture on p.
483; Rücklin I, p. 254, II, plate 179; KGB Pfh. 13, 1906,
picture on p. 47; F. Sales-Meyer, Kunstgewerbliches
aus dem Grossherzogtum Baden, in: KGB NF XIX,
1908, p. 27, picture on p. 39; August Beringer,
Badische Malerei 1770-1920, 1922, p. 105; von Hase

1.102 PENDANT 1908-1909
Designed by Emil Riester.
Silver, gilded, amethysts,
pearls, wing pearls, green
stones.
Height 51, width 28 mm.
Profzheim Jewelry Museum,
Inv. No. Sch 2425.
Lit.: KGS Pfh. Inventory, June
18, 1909, sale price 13 Marks;
von Hase 403; Falk 1985, No.
194.

1.103 BROOCH 1908-1909
Designed by Emil Riester.
Silver, gilded, pearls, lapis
lazuli, agates, small
turquoises, green translucent
enamel.
Height 29, width 24 mm.
Pforzheim Jewelry Museum,
Inv. No. Sch 2424.
Lit.: KGS Pfh. Inventory, June
18, 1909, sale price 9 Marks.

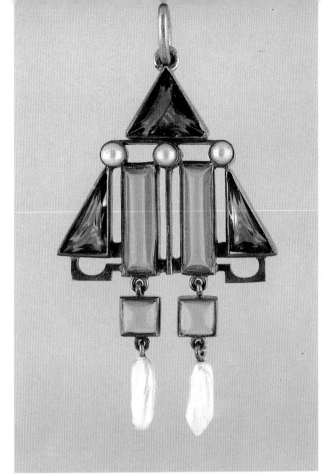

1.102

1.103

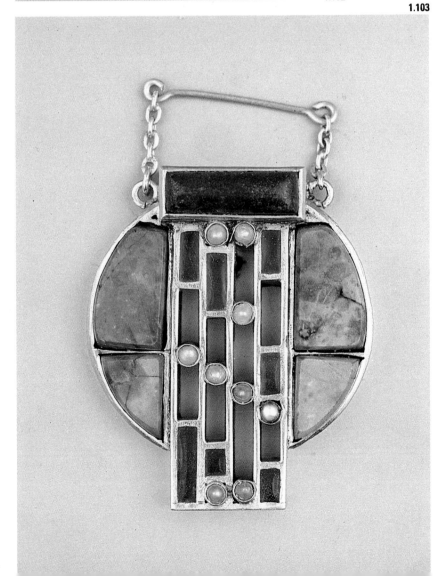

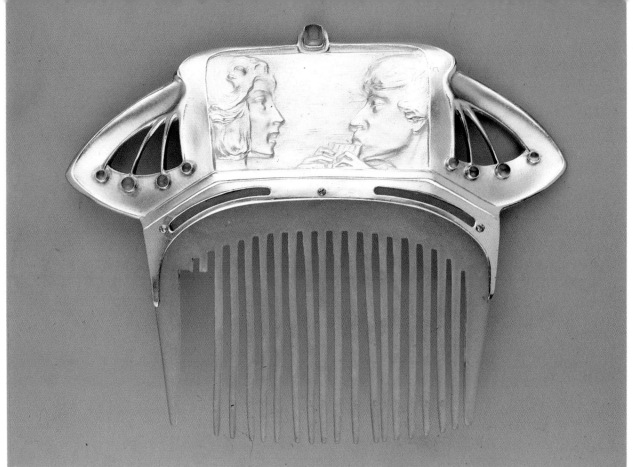

1.104

1.104 ORNAMENTAL COMB
1901-1902
Designed by Fritz Wolber.
Silver, partly gilded, colored
agates, tortoiseshell.
Height 102, width 121 mm.
Stamped: TF 900.
Pforzheim Jewelry Museum,
Inv. No. Sch 1863.
Lit.: KGS Pfh. Inventory, Nov.
11, 1902. Fahrner No. 11867,
sale price 89.50 Marks; DGZ
VI, 1903, picture on p. 9; von
Hase 584.

1.105 BROOCH with two
heads 1901-1902
Designed by Fritz Wolber.
Silver, gilded, pearls, one
imitation teardrop pearl,
green enamel.
Height 41, width 35 mm.
Stamped: TF 935 DEPOSE.
Pforzheim Jewelry Museum,
Inv. No. Sch 1869 (not
identical to KGS inventory
number).
Note: Displayed at 1904 St.
Louis World's Fair.
Lit.: DGZ VI, 1903, picture on
p. 9; DKD XIV, 1904-05,
picture on p. 504; KGB NF
XVI, 1905, picture on p. 160
(as a chain); von Hase 585.

1.105

Wolber, Fritz

Sculptor
*1867, Schiltach †1952, Pforzheim

1884-1888 Studied at the Karlsruhe
Kunstgewerbe School, then at the Académie Julién, Paris.
1892-1933 Teacher and professor at the
Pforzheim Kunstgewerbe School.
Collaboration with Theodor Fahrner probably began in 1901. A fountain designed
by Wolber for the garden of the Fahrner
house was destroyed in 1945, as were
Wolber's archives.

Lit.: KGB Pfh. 1894, pp. 3 ff; Jubiläumskunstausst.
Kat. Karlsruhe, 1902, p. 58; DGZ VI, 1903, picture on
p. 9; Pforzheimer Fein-Metalarbeiten auf der Weltausstellung St. Louis, in: DKD XIV, 1904, p. 506,
pictures pp. 503 ff; R. Rücklin, Die moderne
Schmuckkunst im Lichte der Weltausstellung in St.
Louis, in: KGB NF XVI, 1905, pictures pp. 158 ff; Koch
1906, picture on p. 8; DGZ XXII, 1919, p. 268; von
Hase p. 294.

Unknown Designers

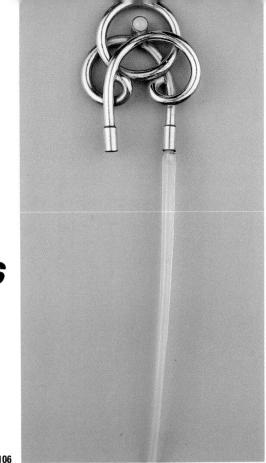

1.106

1.107

1.106 HAIRPIN 1860-1870
Gold-plated wire, turquoise.
Height 120, width 27 mm.
Privately owned (F.N.)
Compare similar pin in KGB
Pfh. 9, 1902, picture on p. 1
(Pforzheim
Kunstgewerbeverein
Anniversary Issue).

1.107 PIN with woman's head
1897-1900
Gold-plated.
Stamped: . . . GOLDA . . .
(damaged). Re stamp, see pp.
272 ff.
Length 60 mm.
Privately owned (F.N.)

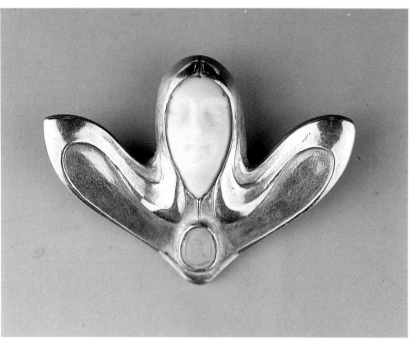

1.108

1.109a

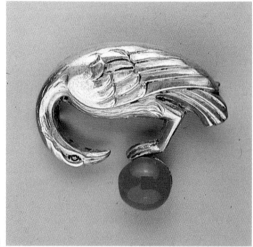

1.109b

1.108 BROOCH "Night" ca.
1901
Silver, one turquoise, head of
carved ivory.
Stamped: TF DEPOSE 900
Height 29, width 37 mm.
ANTIK OFFICE, R. + S. Diehl,
Frankfurt on the Main.
Note: Another brooch with
carved ivory in Cat. No. 1.124.
The carving may have been
done at a workshop in
Erbach in the Odenwald.

1.109 BROOCHES in the
form of birds ca. 1900
1.109a Model for bird
Brass.
Height 19, width 32 mm.
Privately owned (F.N.)
Note: The model is the
original form of a model
produced for decades, see
Cat. No. 1.109c. A bird
brooch with a similar motif
was made by Georg Jensen
of Copenhagen; this piece
was also owned by Theodor
Fahrner.
1.109b Brooch or hat
ornament ca. 1900
Silver, gilded, coral.
Height 23, width 32 mm.
Stamped: TF 935.
Galerie Urlass, Frankfurt on
the Main.

1.109c Brooch or hat
ornament 1926
Silver (thin, stamped), gilded,
marcasite, coral.
Height 23, width 36 mm.
Stamped: FAHRNER TF 925.
G. Silzer collection.
Note: The bird motif was
produced and varied by the
Fahrner firm for decades; see
also p. 182. Cat. No. 1.109c
was made in the Braendle
era; on Nov. 24, 1926 a
design numbered 20321 was
entered in the design books,
showing a new setting of the
motif set with marcasite; in a
Fahrner firm catalog of 1931-
32 there is shown, under No.
20321, corresponding to that
of the design, an offer of
"popular pins (usable as
clasps or hat decorations)
with real coral. Gilded silver,
RM 8. — , with real coral,
oxidized silver, RM 7. — :.
Along with the bird motif, as
far as can be told from extant
pattern books and catalogs,
only the "mourning jewelry"
of the Braendle era,
produced until about 1970,
carried on the theme.

1.109c

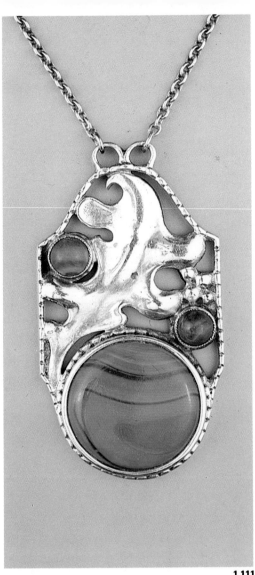

1.111

1.112

1.110

1.110 PENDANT 1900-1902
Design: M. J. Gradl's or
Müller-Salem's group.
Silver, gilded, small rubies,
inset medallion with girl's
head.
Height 36, width 28 mm.
Stamped: TF DEPOSE 900.
Pforzheim Jewelry Museum,
Inv. No. Sch 2044.
Lit.: von Hase 115.

1.111 PENDANT 1902-1905
Silver, malachite.
Height 59, length 260 mm
(with chain)
Stamped: 935 TF.
Antiker Schmuck/Gutachter
Firma Röder,
Bergisch-Gladbach.
Note: There is a stylistic
relationship with the works of
the Dresden designers
around Erich Kleinhempel.

1.112 BROOCH ca. 1904
Silver, green colored agates,
green enamel.
Height 72, width 33 mm.
Stamped: TF 935 DEPOSE.
Pforzheim Jewelry Museum,
Inv. No. Sch 2249.
Lit.: von Hase 127.

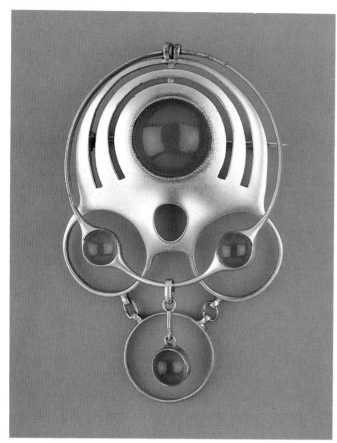

132

1.113 BROOCH ca. 1906-07
Silver, green colored agates.
Height 56, width 34 mm.
Stamped: TF 935 DEPOSE
Pforzheim Jewelry Museum,
Inv. No. Sch 2250.
Note: Same designer as Cat.
No. 1.112. The motif of the
circles is also found in a
design for jewelry by Eugen
Erhardt in: DGZ IX, 1906,
picture on p. 214.
Lit.: von Hase 124; V. Becker,
1985, picture 206; I. Becker,
Berlin kat. 1988, No. 191.

1.114 NECKLACE (dog
collar) 1905-1906
Silver, gilded, white opaque
enamel.
Height 27, width 340 mm.
Stamped: TF 935 DEPOSE.
Pforzheim Jewelry Museum,
Inv. No. KV 1634.
Note: There is a stylistic
relation to Franz Boeres'
necklaces, though they are
more severe, and to designs
by Kleemann.
Lit.: KGV Pfh. inv. Nov. 10,
1906, sale price 50 Marks;
von Hase 135; Falk 1985, No.
186.

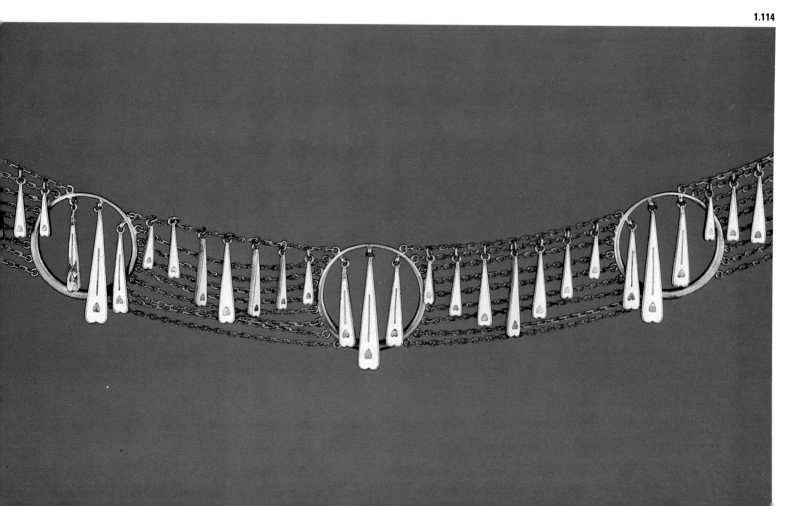

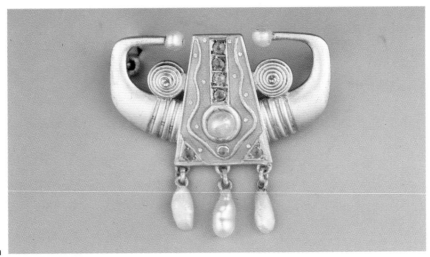

1.115a

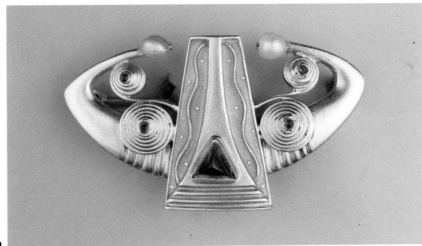

1.115b

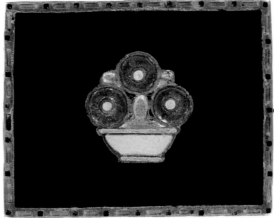

1.116a

1.116b

1.115 BROOCHES
1905-1906
1.115a Silver, pearls, rubies,
light blue enamel.
Height 21, width 36 mm.
Stamped: TF 935 DEPOSE
Pforzheim Jewelry Museum,
Inv. No. Sch 2322.
Lit.: DGZ IX, 1906, picture on
p. 110.
1.115b Silver, gilded, rubies,
pearls, blue enamel.
Height 24, width 26 mm.
Stamped: TF 935 DEPOSE.
Pforzheim Jewelry Museum,
Inv. No. KV 1633.
Note: The stylistic relation to
Max Strobl's work is striking,
yet his collaboration with
Theodor Fahrner has not
been documented to date.
See DKD XVIII, 1906,
picture on p. 779.
Lit.: KGB Pfh. Inventory, Nov.
10, 1906, sale price 12 Marks;
von Hase 132.

1.116 BROOCHES with
flower basket ca. 1906
Silver, black, yellow, blue and
green cell enamel.
1.116a Height 32, width 36
mm.
Stamped: TF 935.
Pforzheim Jewelry Museum,
Inv. No. 1979/11.
Lit.: Falk 1985, No. 182; I.
Becker, Berlin Kat. 1988, No.
172.
1.116b Height 30, width 30
mm.
Pforzheim Jewelry Museum,
Inv. No. 3192/52.
Lit.: KGS Pfh. Inventory, Dec.
25, 1921, value 50 Marks;
Falk 1985, No. 183; I. Becker,
Berlin Kat. 1988, No. 172.

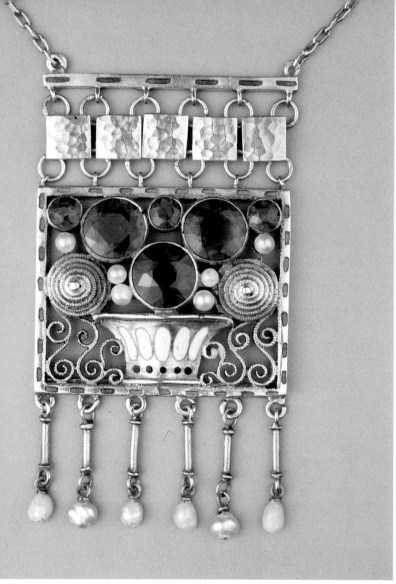

1.117

1.117 NECKLACE 1906-1908
Silver, rubies, small pearls,
white and green enamel.
Height 51, width 29 mm.
Stamped: 935 TF DEPOSE.
Privately owned.
Compare a pectoral
ornament by Emanuel
Margold, von Hase 673, with
free flower-basket motif.

1.118a BROOCH 1906-1908
Silver, laips lazuli, pearls,
green, violet and white cell
enamel.
Diameter 35 mm.
Pforzheim Jewelry Museum,
Inv. No. Sch 3192/4 (F.St.)
Note: The flower-basket motif
was put back into production
at the beginning of the
twenties; for the same motif,
see Cat. No. 1.118b.
Lit.: KGS Pfh. Inventory, Dec.
25, 1921, value 150 marks;
von Hase 149.

1.118b PENDANT post-1932
Silver, gilded, turquoise,
marcasite, synthetic
aquamarine.
Diameter 35 mm.
Stamped: TF 935.
German private collection.
Lit.: Musterbuch VI (see p.
165), Model No. 3180.

1.119 NECKLACE 1906-1910
Silver, lightly gilded,
amethysts, pearls, green,
white and black cell enamel.
Height 60, width 33 mm
(without rosette).
Stamped: TF 935 (damaged).
Udo Thomale collection.

1.120 CHAIN (watch chain)
1906-1910
Links of plain translucent
enamel with fine gold spots
melted in, gold intermediate
links with small pearls.
Length 600 mm.
Unsigned.
Privately owned (F.N.)
Note: A small bag with the
pearls of the intermediate
links came with the chain.
Similar chains were also sold
by the firm of Cartier in Paris.

1.121 CHAIN with pendant
set with pearls 1906-1910
Links of green translucent
enamel, intermediate links of
gold with small pearls, pearl
and diamonds on pendant.
Length 550 mm.
Unsigned.
Privately owned (F.N.)
Note: Nearly identical in
technique is a watch-chain
made by Cartier of Paris,
dated 1909. See "The Art of
Cartier" exhibition catalog,
Paris 1989, pictures pp. 57,
120, No. 92.

1.118a   **1.118b**

1.119   1.121

1.120

1.122

1.122 NECKLACE 1906-1908
Silver, gilded, amethysts.
Length 70, width 27 mm.
Stamped: TF 935 DEPOSE.
In original leather case with
gold lettering:
FAHRNER/KUNSTLER/
SCHMUCK.
Stamped inside by retailer:
Jakob Bender/Juewlier/Wiesbaden.
Galerie Urlass, Frankfurt on
the Main.
Note: A similar piece with
Fahrner No. 15776 was given
to the Kunstgewerbeverein
by Fahrner on Nov. 30, 1908.
The identical diamond motif
also appears on a design by
Adolf Hildenbrand, see Cat.
No. 1.48a.
Lit.: DGZ XIII, 1910, picture on
p. 170 (as a brooch); see a
group in DGZ XII, 1909,
picture on p. 315, and KGB
NF XX, 1909, picture 9.83.

*Gilded silver jewelry with
amethysts and pearls, made
by Th. Fahrner;
Picture from: DGZ Vol. XII,
1909, p. 315.*

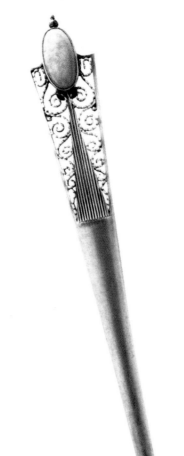

1.125

1.123

1.124

1.123 BROOCH 1906-1908
Silver, amethysts, silver cord.
Height 67, width 40 mm.
Stamped: TF 935 DEPOSE.
Hans-Peter Callsen, Bonn.
Note: The filigree wire is also
worked on the reverse.
Compare a brooch in: DGZ
XI, 1909, picture on p. 315,
and KGB NF XX, 1909,
picture on p. 83. A very
opulent brooch of the
"filigree group", with Fahrner
No. 15792 (sale price 24.50
Marks) was given to the
Kunstgewerbeverein by
Theodor Fahrner on
November 30, 1908.

1.124 BROOCH with dancing
girls 1908-1909
Filigree silver, gilded, four
amethysts, ivory plate with
carved relief in the center.
Height 38, width 42 mm.
Stamped: TF 935.
German private collection.
Compare: Filigree jewelry in
DGZ XI, 1909, picture on p.
315, and KGB NF XX, 1909,
picture on p. 83. The
somewhat playful variant was
probably to have been set
originally with a large central
stone, presumably an
amethyst. The ivory relief was
added later. It was made
around 1900, probably at
Erbach in the Odenwald.

1.125 DRESS PIN 1908
Silver, amazonite.
Length 101, width 13 mm.
Württemberg State Museum,
Stuttgart.
Inv. No. G 9, 349.
Compare two similar dress
pins in: KGB NF XX, 1909,
picture on p. 85.
Lit.: State Commercial
Museum, Stuttgart, 1909
Report, p. 15; JGK 30, 1909,
picture on p. 161; von Hase
142.

1.126

No. 3.
Pendants.
Set with moonstones.
£1 7 6

1.126 NECKLACE 1907-1909
Silver, amazonite, baroque
pearl.
Length 250 mm, diameter (of
pendant) 35 mm.
Stamped: TF 935 DEPOSE.
German private collection.
Lit.: For the same form, but
worked as a brooch or
pendant, see KGB NF XX,
1909, picture on p. 82; DGZ
XIII, 1910, pictures on pp.
169, 170.
Note: In the Liberty & Co.
sales catalog (probably ca.
1900), No. 3 on p. 38 is
shown a very similar pendant
with moonstone (upper right).
Victor Arwas, Liberty Style,
London, Tokyo 1983, pictures
pp. 22 and 87. It is possible
that the designer of our piece
was inspired by that one.

1.127 SET OF JEWELRY
1906-1910
1.127a Brooch: Silver,
hematite.
Height 56, width 56 mm.
Stamped: TF 935 DEPOSE.
Gabriela Arnold collection.
1.127b Pin: Silver, hematite.
Height 7, width 78 mm.
Stamped: TF 935.
Privately owned (F.N.)
1.127c Cuff links
Silver, hematite.
Diameter 17 mm.
Stamped: TF 935.
Privately owned (F.N.)

1.127a

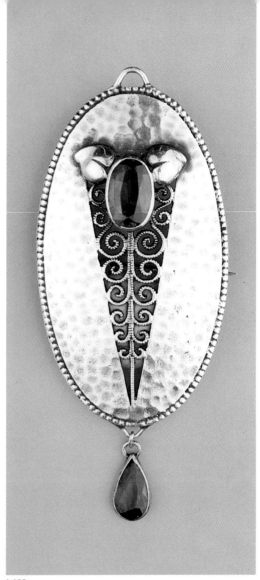

1.128

1.129

1.127c

1.127b

1.128 PENDANT 1908-1910
Silver, beaten, pink
tourmaline, filigree wire.
Height 52, width 22 mm.
Stamped: TF 935 REG.D MB
& Co.
German private collection.
Compare similar pieces in:
GK XXXII, 1911, picture 243,
and R. Rücklin, 1911, picture
on p. 35.

1.129 NECKLACE 1908-1910
Silver, spinels, two pearls on
the chains, filigree wire.
Height 41, width 27 mm.
Stamped: REG.D TF 935 MB
Co.
ANTIK OFFICE, R + S Diehl,
Frankfurt on the Main.
Re lit. and dating, see Cat.
No. 1.128.

1.130a

1.130b

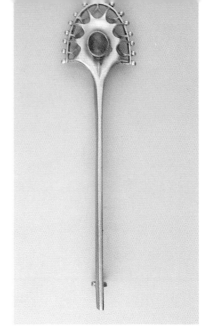

1.131b

1.131a

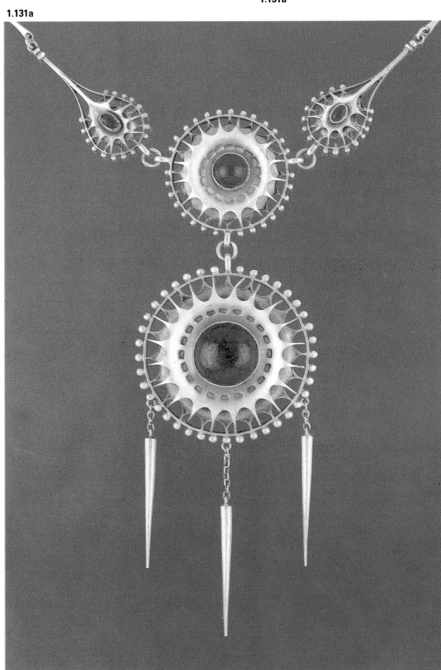

1.130 NECKLACE and
PENDANT ca. 1908
Walking women in chitons.
1.130a Necklace: Silver,
gilded, blue enameled
background, two pearls.
Length 290 mm.
Stamped: DEPOSE TF 935.
Schneidewind-Wilkens
collection, Freiburg.
1.130b Pendant Silver, black
enameled background.
Height 28, width 26 mm.
Privately owned (F.N.)
Label: Fahrner No. 18159.
Lit.: DGZ XII, 1909, pp. 345 ff.
". . . The present trend brings
a lot of jewelry in Empire
style. But it is something
different from the rest of
modern Empire jewelry:
There are very delicately and
finely worked figured reliefs
in the nature of antique
cameos, laid out on matte or
gloss enamel backgrounds
and made of gold or silver."
The motif with the "walking
women" was used in many
forms — as necklaces,
pendants or brooches — and
in a variety of enamel tones
and different sizes, see p. 56.

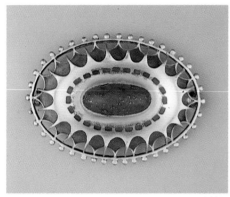

1.131c

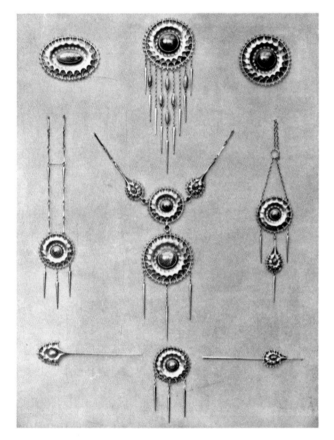

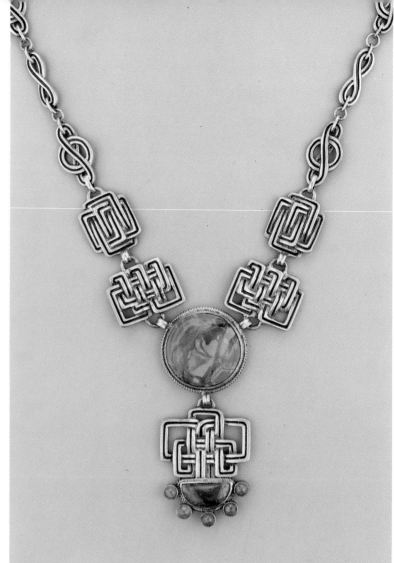

1.132

1.131 SET OF JEWELRY
1907-1908
Silver, gilded, real and
imitation lapis lazuli, blue
enamel.
1.131a Necklace, length 119
mm (without chain).

*Gilded silver jewelry with
delicate enamel tones and
blue jasper, made by
Theodor Fahrner, picture
from: GK 31, 1910, p. 36.*

1.131b Dress pin: Height 65,
width 16 mm.
Stamped: TF 935 DEPOSE.
1.131c Brooch: Length 28,
width 37 mm.
Stamped: TF 935 DEPOSE.
Pforzheim Jewelry Museum,
Inv. No. KV 1687, Sch
3192/54 & 53.
Lit.: KGB Pfh. Inventory, Nov.
30, 1908; KGS Pfh. Inventory,
Dec. 25, 1921, value 50
Marks and 100 Marks
(necklace); GK 31, 1910, p.
37, picture on p. 36, as
jewelry with a "Moorish
character"; von Hase Nos.
139, 140 (example in
Stuttgart), 141.

1.132 NECKLACE ca. 1910
Silver, gilded, black enamel
in weave, malachite, lapis
lazuli; reverse engraved
before gilding.
Stamp obliterated.
Length 226 mm.
Pforzheim Jewelry Museum,
Inv. No. Sch 3192/63 (F.St.)
Lit.: Bracelet with same
weave: DGZ XIII, 1910,
picture on p. 170; KGS Pfh.
Inv. Dec. 25, 1921, value 200
Marks.

1.133a

1.133b

1.133 BRACELET and
pendant 1910-1913
Silver, partly gilded, white,
blue and green cell enamel,
gold paillons.
1.133a Bracelet: Length 197,
width 13 mm.
Stamped: 935 TF DEPOSE.
Pforzheim Jewelry Museum,
Inv. No. Sch 3192/45 (F.St.)
1.133b Pendant: Height 23,
width 27 mm.
Stamped: TF (silver inlay in
blue enamel)
Pforzheim Jewelry Museum,
Inv. No. Sch 3912/42 (F.St.)
Lit.: KGS Pfh. Inventory, Dec.
25, 1921, bracelet value 150
Marks, pendant value 50
Marks; von Hase 147
(pendant).

1.134 PENDANTS 1910-1913
1.134a Silver, chrysoprase,
small blue stones, blue and
white cell enamel, gold
paillons.
Diameter 25 mm.
Stamped: TF (silver inlay in
blue enamel).
Privately owned (F.N.)

1.134a

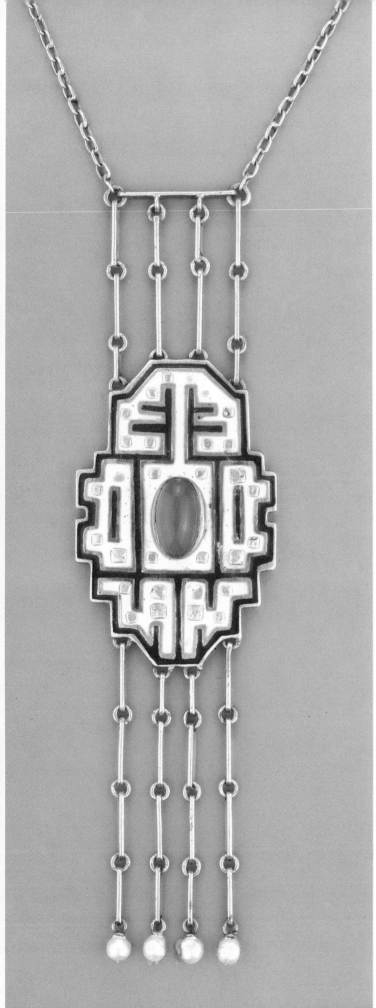

1.134b

1.135

1.134b Silver, chrysoprase, pearls, blue and white cell enamel, gold paillons.
Height 85, length 300 mm (chain).
Stamped: TF (silver inlay in blue enamel), 935.
Pforzheim Jewelry Museum, Inv. No. Sch 3192/43 (F.St.)
Lit.: KGS Pfh. Inventory, Dec. 25, 1921, value 100 Marks.

1.135 PENDANT with lily
1910-1913
Silver, almandine garnet, small pearls, white cell enamel with inlaid gold stars.
Diameter 35 mm.
Stamped: 935 TF (in silver inlay) DEPOSE.
Pforzheim Jewelry Museum, Inv. No. Sch 3192/59 (F.St.)
Note: The lily motif, uncommon in jewelry at that time, suggests that this piece was made for export to France.
Lit.: Compare a piece with similar motif and workmanship in: GK 34, 1913, picture on p. 394; KGS Inventory, Dec. 25, 1921, value 200 Marks; von Hase 146.

1.136a   1.136b

1.136 PENDANTS 1910-1914
1.136a Silver, amethysts, white enamel with black dots.
Height 48, width 26 mm.
1.136b Silver, amethysts, one wing pearl, white enamel with small black dots.
Height 47, width 25 mm.
Stamped: TF 935.
Pforzheim Jewelry Museum, Inv. No. Sch 3192/47 and 3192/38 (F.St.)
Lit.: KGS Pfh. Inventory, Dec. 25, 1921, value 100 Marks.

1.137 PENDANT and BROOCH 1910-1914
1.137a Pendant: Silver, blue enamel, pearl shells.
Height 30, width 23 mm.
Stamped: TF 935 EX; Fahrner No. 17792 on label.
Privately owned (F.N.)
1.137b Brooch: Silver, black enamel, pearl shells.
Height 28, width 35 mm.
Stamped: TF 935.
Privately owned (F.N.)
Lit.: DGZ XIII, 1914, pictures pp. 49-50, with the designation "Fahrnerschmuck."

1.138 PENDANT 1910-1914
Silver, small chrysoprases.
Height 43, width 36 mm.
Fahrner No. 18720 on label.
Privately owned (F.N.)

1.139 BROOCH and PENDANT 1910-1914
1.139a Brooch: Silver, lapis lazuli.
Height 29, width 41 mm.
Stamped: TF 935.
Privately owned (F.N.)
Fahrner Nos. 31200 and 18631.
1.139b Pendant Silver, topaz.
Height 70, width 40 mm.
Stamped: TF 935.
Pforzheim Jewelry Museum, Inv. No. Sch 3192/15.
Note: Displayed at the 1914 Werkbund Exhibition, Cologne.
Lit.: KGS Pfh. Inventory, Dec. 25, 1921, value 150 Marks; KGB NF 26, 1914-15, p. 175.

1.137a

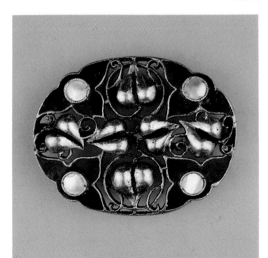

1.137b

1.138

1.139b

1.139a

1.141 **1.142**

1.140a

1.140b

1.140 BROOCHES
1910-1914
1.140a with bird.
Silver, sulfured, lapis lazuli,
mother-of-pearl bird, red
glass stone as eye.
Height 32, width 37 mm.
Stamped: TF 800.
Pforzheim Jewelry Museum,
Inv. No. Sch 3192/11 (F.St.)
1.140b with flower
Silver, sulfured, baroque
pearls, three golden topaz.
Height 32, width 35 mm.
Pforzheim Jewelry Museum,
Inv. No. Sch 3192/10 (F.St.)
Lit.: KGS Pfh. Inventory, Dec
25, 1921, value 150 Marks
each.

1.141 PENDANT with chain
ca. 1914
Silver, chrysoprase and
amazonite.
Height 45, width 31 mm.
Stamped: TF 800.
Gabriela Arnold collection.

1.142 PENDANT ca. 1914
Silver, crenated, lapis lazuli.
Height 54, width 38 mm.
Stamped: TF 935.
Udo Thomale collection.

1.143 BROOCH ca. 1914
Silver, citrine.
Height 37, width 51 mm.
Stamped: TF 935.
E. L. collection.

1.144 BROOCH ca. 1914
Silver, citrine.
Height 47, width 45 mm.
Stamped: TF 800.
Galerie Urlass, Frankfurt on
the Main.

1.145 BROOCH, leaf motif ca.
1914
Silver, one hematite, green
colored chalcedony, leaves
lacquered black on the
reverse.
Height 35, width 63 mm.
Stamped: TF 935.
Privately owned, Darmstadt.

1.146 BROOCHES ca.
1912-1914
1.146a Silver, amethysts,
pearl shells.
Height 33, width 45 mm
1.146b Silver, chalcedony.
Height 33, width 45 mm.
Stamped: TF 935.
Galerie Urlass, Frankfurt on
the Main.

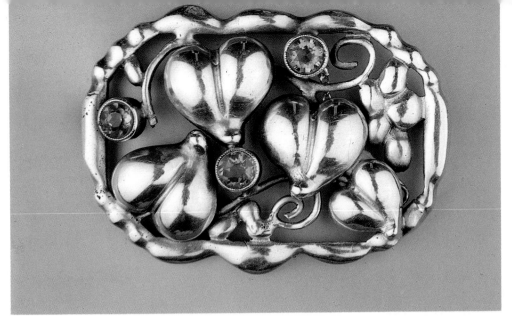

1.143

1.145

1.144

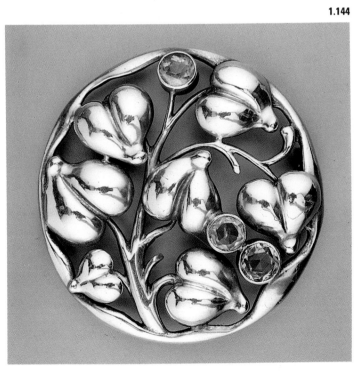

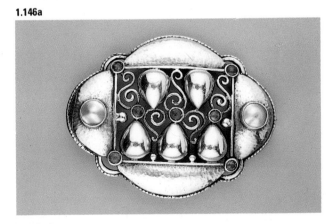

1.146a

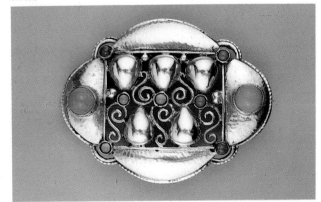

1.146b

1.147

1.148

1.147 BROOCH ca.
1915-1919
Silver, grained
Diameter: 40 mm.
Stamped: TF FAHRNER
SCHMUCK TF 935
ANTIK OFFICE, R. + S. Diehl,
Frankfurt on the Main.

1.148 BROOCH with coral
branch 1912-1914
Silver, sulfured, one coral
branch, lapis lazuli.
Height 35, width 80 mm.
Stamped: TF 800.
Pforzheim Jewelry Museum,
Inv. No. Sch 3192/13 (F.St.)
Lit.: KGS Pfh. Inventory, Dec.
25, 1921, value 150 Marks.

1.149 PENDANT with chain
pre-1914
Silver, background of central
piece in dark blue enamel,
piece of mother-of-pearl in
the middle, surrounded by
four dark-blue enameled
flowers plus white glass
stones, pendant of blue
enamel.
Height 54, width 27, length
235 mm (chain).
Stamped: TF 935 MB Co REG
D F, on the clasp: STERLING.
German private collection.

1.150 BROOCHES
1915-1918
1.150a with unicorn.
Silver, sulfured, blue-green
transparent enamel, reverse
blue counterenamel.
Height 53, width 63 mm.
Stamped: TF 935 (on a silver
plate on the reverse).
Pforzheim Jewelry Museum,
Inv. No. Sch 3192/12 (F.St.)
Lit.: KGS Pfh. Inventory, Dec.
25, 1921, value 100 Marks;
von Hase 154.
1.150b with fox.
Silver, sulfured, blue-green
enamel below, reverse with
blue counterenamel below.
Height 55, width 55 mm.
Privately owned (F.N.)

Note: Minoan motifs may
have served as models.
Compare a pendant in the
form of a wild goat of beaten
gold leaf (see p. 59).

1.149

1.150a

1.150b

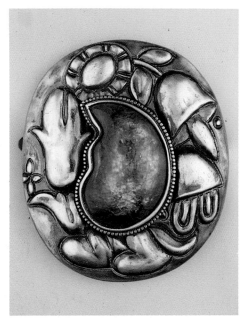

1.151

1.151 BROOCH 1915-1918
Silver, blue-green enamel.
Height 55, width 47 mm.
Stamped: TF 935.
Pforzheim Jewelry Museum,
Inv. No. Sch 3192/21 (F.St.)
Note: A raw model of this
piece was found in Fahrner's
effects.
Lit.: KGS Pfh. Inv. Dec. 25,
1921, value 100 Marks.

1.152 BELT BUCKLE with
hoopoe 1914-1919
Silver, green, red, yellow and
black cell enamel.
Diameter: 65 mm.
Stamped: TF 935 DEPOSE.
Privately owned (F.N.)

1.152

1.153

1.154a

1.154b

1.153 PENDANT ca. 1919
Silver, lapis lazuli.
Height 73, width 32 mm.
Stamped: TF 800.
Pforzheim Jewelry Museum,
Inv. No. Sch 3192/14.
Lit.: KGS Pfh. Inv. Dec. 25,
1921, value 200 Marks.

1.154 PENDANT War jewelry
1914
Iron, lightly beaten, hematite.
1.154a height 79, width 40
mm.
1.154b Height 66, width 40
mm.
Stamped: WELT-KRIEG 1914.
Pforzheim Jewelry Museum,
Inv. No. KV 4011, 4012.
Note: Stylistic similarity to
work of Ferdinand Morawe,
and slightly to Franz Boeres,
cannot be missed.
Lit.: DGZ XVIII, 1915, pictures
pp. 18-19; W. Pieper,
Geschichte der Pforzheimer
Schmuckindustrie,
Gernsbach 1989.

1.155 Plates for BROOCHES
ca. 1915
Copper, white enamel,
reverse blue-green
counterenamel.
1.155a "antique head"
Height 39, width 32 mm.
Pforzheim Jewelry Museum,
Inv. No. Sch 3192/30 (F.St.)
1.155b "Diana with stag"
Height 51, width 36 mm.
Pforzheim Jewelry Museum
(F.St.)
Lit.: KGS Pfh. Inventory, Dec.
25, 1921, value 50 Marks (a);
DGZ XX, 1917, p. 180, picture
on p. 46 (head in octagonal
setting on blue-green
background).

1.156 BROOCHES ca. 1915
Copper, white enamel,
setting silver, reverse gray
counterenamel.
Diameter 35 mm.
1.156a with female figure
1.156b with chariot
Pforzheim Jewelry Museum,
Inv. No. (a) Sch 3192/32, (b)
Sch 3192/31 (F.St.)
Lit.: KGS Pfh. Inventory, Dec.
25, 1921, value 50 Marks
each; von Hase 143.

1.155a

1.155b

1.156a

1.156b

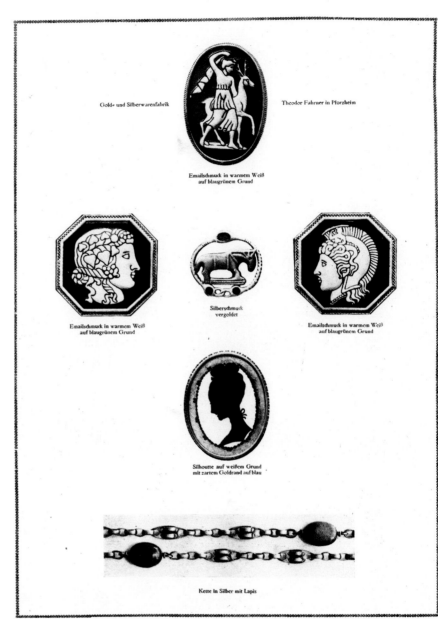

Enameled jewelry made by
Th. Fahrner. Picture from:
DGZ XX, 1917, p. 46.

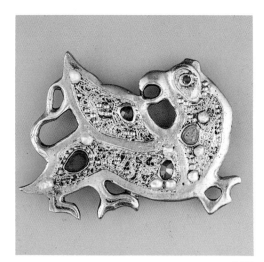

1.157   **1.158**

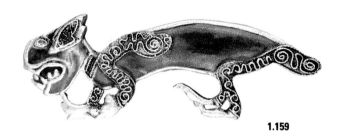

1.159

1.160

1.157 GRIFFIN BROOCH
1915-1919
Merovingian style.
Silver, gilded, garnets, small
pearls.
Height 37, width 45 mm.
Stamped: TF 935.
Privately owned (F.N.)
Note: An exact copy, on a
clasp, in a museum at Arras,
is shown by R. Rücklin in Vol.
II, p. 41, No. 10.

1.158 CLASP with two lions
1915-1919
Early medieval style.
Silver, gilded, garnets.
Height 49, width 44 mm.
Stamped: TF 800.
Privately owned (F.N.)
Note: Flat sword-sheath
ornaments may have served
as models; see illustrations in
Bernard Salin, Die
altgermanische
Thierornamentik, Stockholm
1935, No. 530.

1.159 BROOCH (mustical
creature) ca. 1917
Silver, gilded, olive enamel.
Height 14, width 57 mm.
Stamped: TF 800.
Privately owned (F.N.)
Note: The model was a
"dragon" shown as
"Columbian" in Haberlandt,
Plates 99, 26. Presumably it
is a "pre-Columbian" piece.
This is the only piece with a
South American model.

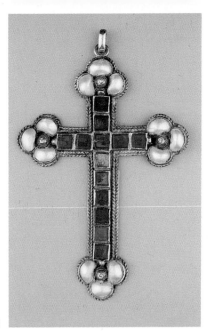

1.161

1.162

1.163a

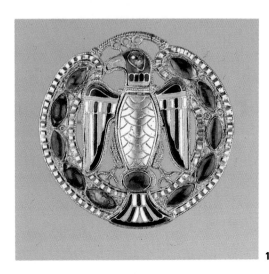

1.163b

1.160 CHAIN with carnelian
1915-1919
Intermediate links of silver with fluted leaf designs, five unpolished carnelians.
Length 660 mm.
Stamped: TF (obliterated) 800.
Privately owned (F.N.)
Compare DGZ XX, 1917, picture on p. 45 (chain); a similar though simpler chain was shown in KuKH on the Upper Rhine, 1925, Vol. I, p. 93 (Gustav Braendle, Th. Fahrners Nachf.)

1.161 CRUCIFIX PENDANT
1915-1919
Silver, gilded, garnets, pearls.
Height 64, width 44 mm.
Stamped: TF 935 EX.
Privately owned (F.N.)
Note: Fahrner's crosses go back to the cloverleaf cross type, especially popular as triumphal crosses in the 13th Century, but also used subsequently as pendants. Compare a cross from Silesia, first half of the 15th Century, Museum of Handicrafts, Frankfurt. In the Fabergé studio the cloverleaf cross was also made as a pectoral shortly before the turn of the century. Fabergé Cat., Munich 1987, No. 574.

1.162 BROOCH 1916-1919
Renaissance style.
Silver, gilded, topaz, pearls.
Height 49, width 45 mm.
Stamped: TF 935 EX.
Dr. Brigitte Marquardt collection.
Lit.: Pieces in Renaissance style are mentioned in: DGZ XXI, 1918, p. 136.

1.163 EAGLE CLASPS
1915-1919
1.163a Version I: Silver, gilded, imitation filigree, blue, turquoise, white and yellow opaque cell enamel, amethysts. The enameled parts (wings, head and tail) are individually inset and attached.
Height 53, width 51 mm.
Stamped: TF 935.
Privately owned (F.N.)
Note: Mounted as a brooch. The eagle clasp is a very precise, though partly machine-made, copy of an eagle clasp from the golden treasures of Empress Gisela, ca. 1030. It is now at the Middle Rhenish State Museum in Mainz, see pp. 66 ff.
1.163b Version II
Silver, gilded, blue stones (glass?), blue, turquoise and white opaque cell enamel.
Height 55, width 53 mm.
Stamped: TF 935.
Private collection, Pforzheim.
Note: Mounted as a brooch. Altered copy of a second eagle clasp from the same source (see Version I). At that time it was also in the Middle Rhenish State Museum in Mainz, now it is at the Berlin Museum of Commercial Art, Köpenick Castle. On the medieval clasp the eagle's head was turned to the right. The original eagle clasp was published in: Ernst Bassermann-Jordan, Der Schmuck, Leipzig 1909, p. 77.

Silver Goods

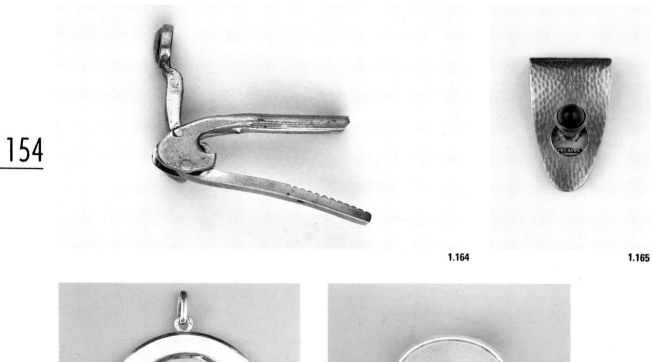

1.164

1.165

1.167

1.168

1.166

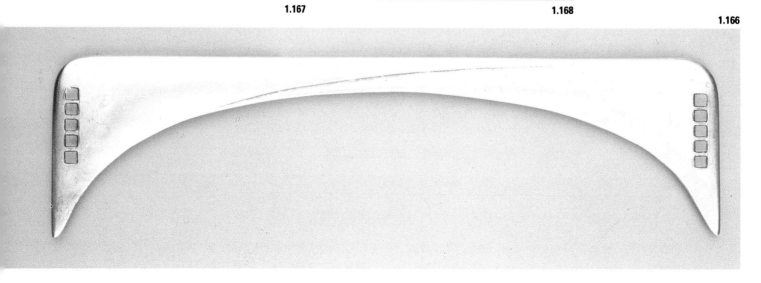

1.169

1.164 CLAMP ca. 1900 (?)
to fasten a silk kerchief
Silver, partly gilded,
openable, with fluted
handhold.
Width 31 mm.
Privately owned (F.N.)

1.165 CUFF LINK 1904
Silver, beaten, one amethyst.
Height 25, width 10 mm.
Stamped: PAT APPL 950 TF.
Privately owned (F.N.)
Note: The cuff link was
registered at the Imperial
Patent Office on September
3, 1904, with patent number
174723, and published in
Patent Group 44a in 1906.

1.166 COMB HOLDER
1904-1905
Attributed to Georg
Kleemann.
Silver, green enamel.
Height 32, width 123 mm.
Stamped: 935 TF DEPOSE.
Fahrner No. 12904 on
adhesive label.
Privately owned (F.N.)
Lit.: Compare design for a
purse, G. Kleemann,
Moderner Schmuck, 1900, no
page.

1.167 POWDER BOX ca.
1908
Silver, gilded inside, lid and
back green, rim around lid
white, translucent enamel
over guilloched background.
Diameter 40 mm.
Stamped inside: 935 TF
DEPOSE, on the ring
Austrian import stamp for
silver goods.
Privately owned (F.N.)

1.168 PILLBOX ca. 1908
Silver, gilded inside, light
blue translucent enamel over
guilloched background with
white rim.
Height 11, diameter 27 mm.
Stamped inside: 935.
Privately owned (F.N.)
Note: Cartier of Paris sold
very similar pieces made by
the guilloche technique,
which was very popular at
this time, see "The Art of
Cartier" Exhibition Cat., Paris
1989. In the German journals
the technique was explained
repeatedly, for example, in
JGK 27, 1906, picture on p.
367.

1.169 HAND MIRROR
1909-1910
designed by Franz Boeres
(see p. 85 f.)
Silver, enamel, decorative
stones.
Length 258, diameter 115
mm., ca. 230 mm.
Württemberg State Museum,
Stuttgart, Inv. No. G 10,524.
Lit.: DK XXII, 1909-10, picture
on p. 583; Royal State
Commercial Museum,
Stuttgart, 1910 Report, p. 40.

1.170 WINE COASTER ca.
1910 (no photo)
Silver.
Diameter 130 mm.
Stamped: TF and
CONTRAETZ HEPP.
Privately owned.

Advertising placard, late twenties, Wiener Interieur, Vienna.

History of the Jewelry Factory
Gustav Braendle, Theodor Fahrner Nachfolge,
1919-1979
Christianne Weber

1919 Purchase of Theodor Fahrner's jewelry factory by the Esslingen jeweler Gustav Braendle, the closing taking place late in the year. Signatories were Mrs. Martha Fahrner and Mr. Gustav Braendle. The new proprietor was required to keep all previous employees. The firm was now called "Gustav Braendle — Theodor Fahrner Nachf."[1]

1920 Gustav Braendle exhibited at the Jewelry Wholesalers' Fair in Stuttgart from June 28 to July 3.[2] By a publicity stunt, the publication of a telegram in the "Deutsche

Fabrik· GB Marke

DGZ No. 16, 1920, p. 58a.

1)
The exact date of the closing on the purchase of Theodor Fahrner's jewelry factory by Gustav Braendle has not been determined. According to oral information, Mrs. Martha Fahrner concluded the sale.

Goldschmiedezeitung", Gustav Braendle drew attention to himself as the firm's new proprietor.[3] Full-page advertisements in the "Deutsche Goldschmiedezeitung" followed. The trade mark of "GB" in an octagon was introduced.[4] Some fifty employees worked for the firm of Gustav Braendle.

1921 January: new advertisements in the "Deutsche Goldschmiedezeitung" with

„Fahrnerſchmuck"

1. "Fahrnerschmuck" Als Warenzeichen angemeldet am 15.7.1921 beim Deutschen Patentamt in Berlin. Eingetragen am 28.10.1921 unter Nr. 274300, Gruppe 17 (B. 41164). Veröffentlich in..

the "GM" octagon trade mark.[5] **July 15:** Extension by "Gustav Braendle, Theodor Fahrner Nachf., in Pforzheim" at the Imperial Patent Office, of the registration of the "TF" trade mark registered by Theodor Fahrner in 1901 (first registered on July 22, 1901). The business was described as "jewelry manufacturing." The production program listed "genuine and imitation jewelry, gold, silver, plated and alloy wares."[6] **October 28:** renewed extension of the firm's title, "FAHRNER SCHMUCK", at the Imperial Patent Office.[7]

1921-22 In the pocket address book of the Pforzheim jewelry industry, the firm of Gustav Braendle, Theodor Fahrner Nachf. was listed. The production program was listed as "excellent marcasite and silver jewelry in connection with enamel and semi-precious stones, necklaces, pendants, brooches, pins, pendeloques (teardrop earrings and pendants), belts etc."[8]

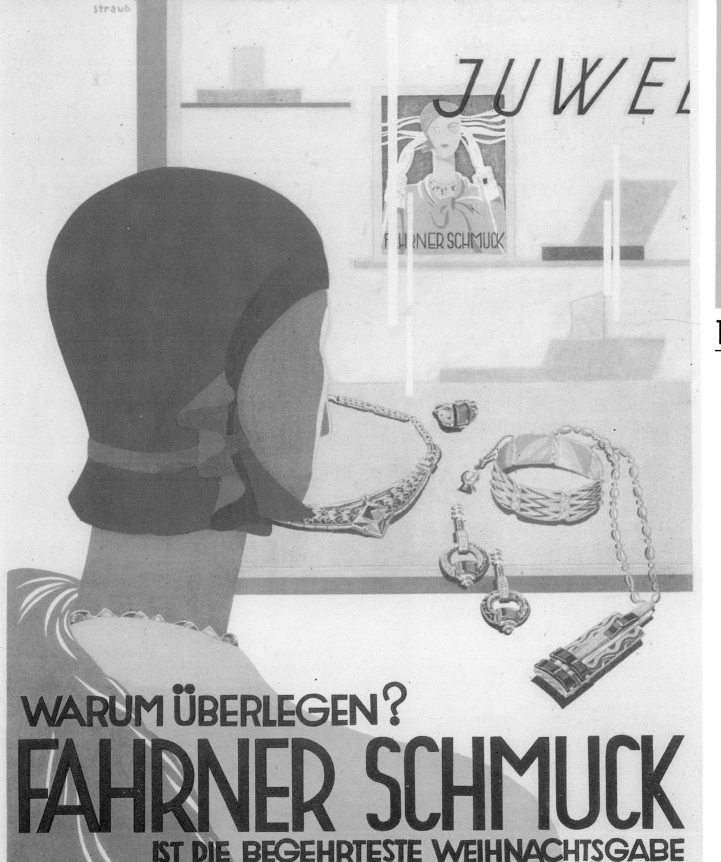

The Gustav Braendle firm's premises on Luitgardstrasse.

The information on the firm's history are based extensively on statements of family members and former employees. Documents from the prewar era were lost when the firm's archives were destroyed on February 28, 1945, and documents on the years from 1945 to 1979 were either lost or destroyed when the firm went out of business in 1979. A few pattern books (see pp. 164 ff) and catalogs were preserved.

2)
DGZ No. 12, 1920, p. 52.

3)
DGZ No. 16, 1920, p. 58a.

4)
Ibid.

5)
See note 2.

6)
Excerpt from the German Patent Office's continuation of the role of the Imperial Patent Office, Number 273516. The period of protection for the "TF" (in a circle) trade mark was renewed on July 15, 1931. Every ten years another extension was made, the last on July 15, 1971, with the note: "The mark can only be made applicable in the Federal Republic to genuine and imitation jewelry, gold and silver goods, plated German silver goods as articles similar to jewelry, and plated goods." On December 30, 1981 it was stated: "This mark can no longer be made applicable in the Federal Republic." Neither sales literature nor advertisements can be found that indicate production of gold and silver goods (mass goods) or plated goods after 1919. It cannot be ruled out, though, that such may prove to exist in private ownership, but nothing can be found of them in public institutions.

7)
Only a few days after the entry cited above, on October 28, 1921, the firm's title of "Fahrner Schmuck" was entered at the Imperial Patent Office under number 274300. For this term too, protection expired in 1981 (see note 6).

8)
Taschenadressbuch für die Bijouteriebranche Pforzheim 1921/22, Verlag J. Balweg, Pforzheim, no page (The firms are listed in alphabetical order).

1925-1930 The jewelry business of Gustav Braendle employed 250 to 300 employees.

1928 Registration of the "Fahrner Plombe" trade name at the Imperial Patent Office, entry on February 14, 1929.[9]

1928 Move into the modern business premises at Luitgardstrasse 11. The firm maintained its own manufacturing premises with sales departments in Berlin and Düsseldorf. At the end of the twenties a large-scale advertising campaign for "Original Fahrner Jewelry" began in fashion magazines such as "Die Dame", "Neue Linie" and "Der Querschnitt."

1930-1939 In the spring and fall, new assortments of jewelry were displayed at the Leipzig Fair at Speckshof. Business contracts with customers, especially in Britain, Holland, Switzerland, Italy, Austria, Spain and the USA. At fashion shows in Hotel Adlon in Berlin and the Palasthotel in Dresden, film actresses modeled the newest "Fahrner Jewelry."

1931-1932 The firm of Gustav Braendle, Theodor Fahrner Nachfolge, instituted prize competitions.[10]

1932 At the end of March the jewelry assortment was expanded with a new series, the "DEA Jewelry."[11] A new sales strategy was begun. Instead of using multicolor, sometimes full-page advertisements in magazines, small-format black-and-white advertisements were used. At the same time, production of a new line of so-called "Filigree Jewelry" began. Advertisements were replaced by sales brochures with catchy slogans.

1933 Designs of swastika jewelry have been found in pattern books.[12]

1934 The economic crisis resulted in short working hours at Gustav Braendle's firm.

1934-1939 Only some 70 to 80 employees worked for Gustav Braendle. **On March 30, 1935** Gustav Braendle registered a new sales slogan with the Imperial Patent Office in Berlin: "FAHRNER SCHMUCK ENTZÜCKT BEGLÜCKT."[13]

1938 Cabinetmaster Friedrich Katz left the firm voluntarily, his position being taken over by Mr. Hermann.

1939-1945 During World War II, some production was adapted so that valuable specialists could be retained for jewelry production and the export trade. The business was able to continue during the war, with limitations.

1941 Several employees had to be discharged.

1942 On August 25 Gustav Braendle, Jr.

died in action.

1944 In February, the second son, Hans, died in action.

1945 On February 23, the firm's premises and archives were destroyed by a bomb attack on the city of Pforzheim.

Post-1945 Gustav Braendle and his son Herbert worked to rebuild the firm and resume jewelry production. Extensive exports to the USA are documented by numerous sales brochures in English.

1952 Gustav Braendle planned to extend his jewelry production with a series of modern gold jewelry. At the end of January, Gustav Braendle died in Pforzheim. Remembrance in the "Deutsche Goldschmiedezeitung": "After a long illness, manufacturer Gustav Braendle died at the end of January, at the age of 69 years. After World War I he purchased the firm founded by Theodor Fahrner over 100 years ago and gained worldwide acclaim for it with then-new types of jewelry, along with enamel. With his three sons, manufacturer Gustav Braendle had come through the economic crises of 1923 to 1934 successfully and brought the firm to a new high point until its destruction in 1945.

World War II, in addition to material losses,

took the lives of two of his sons. But together with his son Herbert, who returned home from military service, the late Mr. Braendle energetically undertook the rebuilding of the firm."[14]

1952 Continuation of the firm by son Herbert Braendle, with some 160 employees.

1954 After an oral announcement, the work force was reduced to 70 employees on account of the decreasing demand for fashion jewelry.

1955 The firm moved to Habsburger Strasse 31.

1960 Production of modern silver jewelry with decorative stones in the style of the times.

Sixties-seventies The assortment was expanded by the "Antique Art" series, gold and silver jewelry with Roman or Egyptian motifs.

1971 Production of gold jewelry with precious stones.

1972 The Braendle firm employed some 25 employees.

1979 February 27: Death of the firm's proprietor, Herbert Braendle. Dissolution of the firm of "Gustav Braendle, Theodor Fahrner Nachf." in Pforzheim. Most of the firm's records were destroyed.

9)
Imperial Patent Office, February 14, 1929; as goods for which the term is intended, gold, silver, nickel and aluminum goods made of German silver, Britannia and similar metallic alloys, genuine and imitation jewelry, cuff links of precious and base metals, watches, watch cases and watch parts were named. The term was registered until 1979.

10)
Christmas 1931 brochure, see also p. 170, note 13.

11)
The journal "Der Querschnitt", ca. 1931, p. 415, "Der Querschnitt", No. 3, late March 1932, p. 210. DEA = (Latin) goddess. Re "DEA" jewelry, see p. 173.

12)
Swastika = Indian cross symbol; Pattern Book IV, ca. 1933, No.s 1181 to 1185, see pp. 164 ff.

13)
Imperial Patent Office, No. 476215, entered on May 31, 1935. The term of protection was extended several times; on December 3, 1975 it was stated: "This mark can no longer be made valid in the Federal Republic" (see note 7).

14)
DGZ No. 2, 1952, p. 45.

Gustav Braendle (center) and his employees, 1932-33.

Braendle Style

From Fahrner Style to Braendle Style

After Gustav Braendle came home from the war in 1918, he was supposed to take over his father's jewelry business in Esslingen. But the young businessman saw better conditions for the success of a jewelry business in Pforzheim. Buying the established and well-known jewelry firm of Theodor Fahrner was thus a welcome opportunity to him. At first the new proprietor set out to maintain the tradition of the established "Fahrner Jewelry", as is shown especially clearly by his keeping the name of the original owner. Gustav Braendle also kept most of Theodor Fahrner's former employees. One who deserves mention is the cabinetmaster Friedrich Katz, who served as the firm's technical director and designer, but was also (along with their father) an important teacher for the sons, Gustav and Herbert Braendle.[1] Gustav Braendle also brought employees with him, as the business in Esslingen was closed in January of 1920.[2] It is also known that a brother, Hermann Braendle, was active as a sales consultant to the firm until 1932. Whether he moved to Pforzheim at the very beginning is not

known. Many Pforzheim firms were compelled by the 1923 economic crisis to stop production. The firms that could work with less costly raw materials (silver or plate and decorative stones) were luckier. The lower and medium price ranges had a better chance of succeeding on the market, and that included Gustav Braendle's products. It is understandable that the new proprietor at first continued the well-known and popular "Fahrner Style" characterized by silver commercial-art jewelry and semi-precious stones, ivory or pearls. Jewelry with floral

1)
Re Friedrich Katz, see notes in his biography, p. 108.

2)
Information from the Esslingen State Archives.

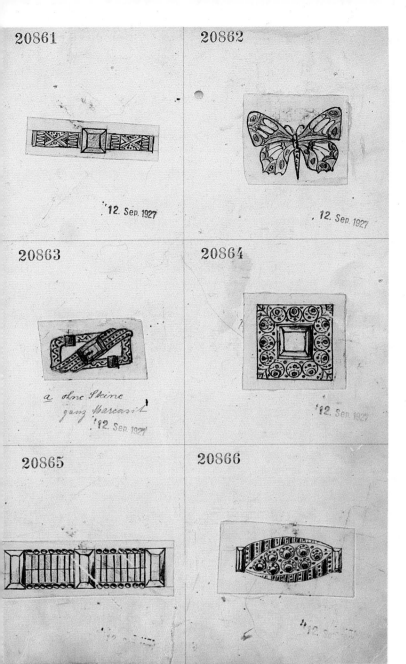

20861

20862

"12. Sep. 1927

. 12. Sep. 1927

20863

20864

a. ohne Steine
ganz Marcasit
'12. Sep. 1927

'12. Sep. 1927

20865

20866

Double page from Pattern Book I, 719 models, August 1926 to September 1927.

No. 2.8). An advertisement of 1922 shows that this was not a single piece, but that several variations in a style reminiscent of Biedermeier were produced.[3] From this early phase there is also a pendant that attracts attention by its size, the material used, and the work required to make it (Cat. No. 2.1). A typical piece is a round one of aventurine quartz enhanced with pearl shells and synthetic rubies. Special care was devoted to forming the reverse side of the silver setting. The use of green-colored stones

or leaf motifs (or stylized floral patters) was produced most of all. War-related shortages of materials such as gold and silver, plus the necessity of keeping a moderately priced assortment on the market, resulted in the use of "non-precious" metals. Dark wood was combined with silver, citrine quartz and enamel to make a pendant (Cat. No. 2.2). As a further example of production in 1921-22, a silver pendant may be cited which was made in floral decor with enamel, marcasite, turquoise and pearl shells and was closely related to the floral motifs of the prewar years (Cat.

was very fashionable around 1920: "The fashion color of green. Just a few years before, a Parisienne would have rejected a green fan, green parasol or green jewelry as a gift, politely but firmly. Green was generally regarded as an unlucky color. Now, though, a different viewpoint had developed, and the newest fashion color that competes with the splendor of young nature in all its nuances this spring is green..."[4] Around 1922 Gustav Braendle put a new assortment of jewelry on the market, in order to break away gradually from the Fahrner style of the years before

3)
Illustriertes Jahrbuch und Führer durch die deutsche Schmuckwarenindustrie, Pforzheim 1922. The piece shown here has a faceted colored stone in the center. Two other pieces, identically made, are shown. In the DGZ 12, 1920, p. 52, reference is made to "unusual silver commercial-art jewelry in connection with semi-precious stones, ivory, pearl shells and marcasite." Semi-precious stones was originally used to mean colored stones that were not precious stones; today it has been replaced by the term "decorative stone" (Schmuckstein." Marcasite (pyrite) is gray-green and opaque, with a metallic luster; the use of marcasite in Germany began around 1910.

4)
DGZ No. 7, 1921, p. 99.

1918. At this time Eugen Erhardt probably left his position as a designer (see p. 91). Ludwig Segmiller mentioned the Braendle firm in his report on the permanent sample display in Pforzheim, saying: "Now as before, silver commercial-art jewelry is produced, plus recently a specialty, enamel-marcasite jewelry along with semi-precious stones. The latter type has made a very favorable impression because of its unique character, which is attained through the use of enamel . . ."[5]

Sample Books (Twenties to Seventies)
Rediscovered pattern books allow concrete statements as to the creation and dating of the Braendle firm's jewelry. The materials from the twenties and early thirties prove that numerous stylistically different series were created by different designers at the same time. Many drawings are labeled with the exact date. The productivity of the Braendle firm in its first years can be determined thanks to the pattern book of a Spanish jeweler who, on his yearly buying trip to Pforzheim, visited the firm of Braendle-Theodor Fahrner Nachf. In the 1921 pattern book at least three pendants made by Braendle are shown (with production numbers); the 1923 pattern book also shows a piece of Braendle jewelry with its exact production number. This shows that between 1921 and 1923 approximately 450 designs were put into production.[6]

By the mid-twenties the number of available models was growing steadily. In a pattern book, 720 designs for brooches, bracelets, pendants, necklaces, etc., from the period between August 1926 and September 1927 can be authenticated. 486 designs for rings alone (Pattern Book II) were created from February 13, 1927 to June 25, 1930. On the other hand, the model policy in the thirties, affected by the Great Depression and a "national style" for the German woman, was just the opposite. From November 3, 1931 to August 14, 1936 "only" 1055 designs for brooches, bracelets, pendants and necklaces were produced (Sample Book IV). It can thus be seen clearly that the best years of the Braendle firm were between 1925 and the beginning of the Thirties. In the following years, a limitation to a certain assortment of models was announced. On the basis of Pattern Book I of 1926-27, another interesting fact can be determined. From April to September of that year, a stylized flower-tendril design was used on four different pieces of jewelry: on two different pendants, a bracelet and a chatelaine (Cat. No. 2.78). Thus they did not plan one set of jewelry from the start, but rather waited to see if a certain decor sold well and then expanded on it.

Rediscovered pattern books have made possible an exact dating of many pieces of jewelry:

5)
Professor Ludwig Segmiller, Die ständige Musterausstellung der deutschen Schmuckwarenindustrie im Hansahaus in Pforzheim, 1922, p. 182.

6)
Two pattern books, 1921-1935, of the jeweler Jorge Colom Farré, Artesania en Plata y oro, Barcelona.

Pattern Book I No. 20225 (August 1926) to No. 20944 (September 1927).
Pattern Book II (Rings) No. 5000 (first dated model No. 5234, Feb. 13, 1927) to No. 5719 (June 25, 1930).
Pattern Book IIa (Rings) No. 6440 (Dec.6, 1935) to No. 7168 (no date).
Pattern Book IIIa (Rings) No. 201 (1932) to No. 304 (April 13, 1932) = DEA Jewelry; **IIIb** (gold rings): No. 101 (sixties) to No. 458 (July 1973) See also Book VIII.
Pattern Book IV No. 1078 (Nov. 3, 1931) to No. 2222 (last dated model No. 2136, July 31, 1936).
Pattern Book Va World War I jewelry; **Vb** No. 2235 to No. 2378 (not dated).
Pattern Book VI (photo album) No. 1501 to No. 3228 (not dated); also pictures for Book V.
Pattern Book VII No. 4957 to No. 05754 (not dated).
Pattern Book VIII No. 05104 to No. 05793 (not dated).
Pattern Book IX "GOLDBUCH/RINGE" (photo album) No. 101 to No. 260. See also Book III.
Pattern Book X (gold jewelry) No. 10001 (March 5, 1960) to No. 10516, plus photo album: No. 10001 to No. 10300.
Pattern Book XI "cuff links" No. M 01 to No. M 151 (not dated).
Account Book XII Account of pattern maker Artur Klingel (August 16, 1948 to December 11, 1973).
Price Index I (with photos) No. 61 to No. 05073 (not dated).

Note: Pattern books, price index and account book are privately owned; we thank Mr. Hering and Mr. Arnold.

New Esthetics of "FAHRNER JEWELRY" —Designs by "Leading Artists." To be able to create such an extensive palette of jewelry, a foundation has to be built in a firm that can deal with these demands from a standpoint of personnel and technology. In a jewelry manufacturing company, the work can be done almost exclusively by skilled workers. Along with the high-quality technical production, the artistic creation, the designing was essential to the success of a piece of jewelry. Even before 1910, Theodor Fahrner had avoided the use of artists' monograms on individual pieces. Yet the concept of "artist jewelry" was maintained in the Braendle firm's advertising until well into the fifties. Who were these "leading artists"? Gustav Braendle himself possessed artistic talent and designed — perhaps in collaboration with Rudolf Rücklin, then the director of the Goldsmithing School — numerous pieces of jewelry in the early years.[7] Until about 1922 Eugen Erhardt, already a long-time Fahrner employee, can be documented as a designer (see p. 91). Decisive impulses and artistic cooperation were also provided after 1930 by the two sons, Hans and Gustav. Beginning in 1929, the firm's style was influenced significantly by Gustav Braendle, Jr. On the basis of preserved original drawings and letters it

can be documented that, even during the time he spent in Paris in 1930, he made a large number of designs for jewelry that was made by the firm a few months later. The painter and commercial artist Anton Kling designed a bracelet (Cat. No. 2.13) for the firm.[8] The already-mentioned cabinetmaster (person responsible for supervising production) Friedrich Katz, who had been providing designs since 1900 and worked for the firm until 1938, is also worthy of mention (see p. 108). In addition, designs were purchased from free-lance artists.[9] Knowledge of dealing with various materials and technical processes was expected of a designer. As a first step, a design was made into a model of tombac or brass. After the various steps of the formative phase of creation came the "decorative work"; the pieces were cut, pre-polished or gilded. Then the setter added the stones, the engraver decorated the surface, the enameler provided the coloring of the piece. The firm of Gustav Braendle had its own enameling department which produced the effective matte-enamel components.

Styles of the Twenties and Thirties
One of the earliest pieces that can be dated as a design in Pattern Book I of 1926 is a brooch made of a matte-cut rock

7)
The information on Rücklin comes from statements by Mr. Friedrich Brüwer in 1978.

8)
See E. Schmuttermeier Catalog, Schmuck von 1900 bis 1925, Vienna 1986, p. 13, no. 25, picture 29; original photo at the Pforzheim Fachhochschule, no inventory number; thanks to Mrs. Leitz for her assistance.

9)
According to information from Hans Niemann (Gustav Braendle's son-in-law), who worked for the firm until 1952.

20723

20724

26. Aug. 1927

26. Aug. 1927

20725

20726

/a

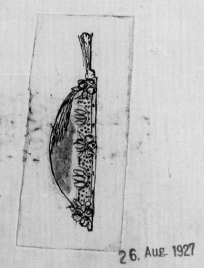

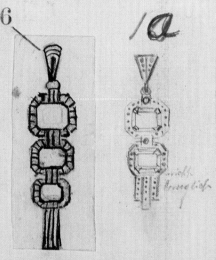

26. Aug. 1927

26. Aug. 1927

20727

20728

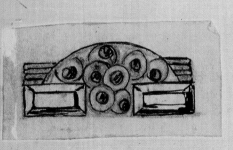

26. Aug. 1

20729

26. Aug. 1927

20730

26. Aug. 1927

20731

26. Aug. 1927

20732

26. Aug. 1927

20733

26. Aug. 1927

20734

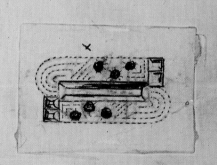

26. Aug. 1927

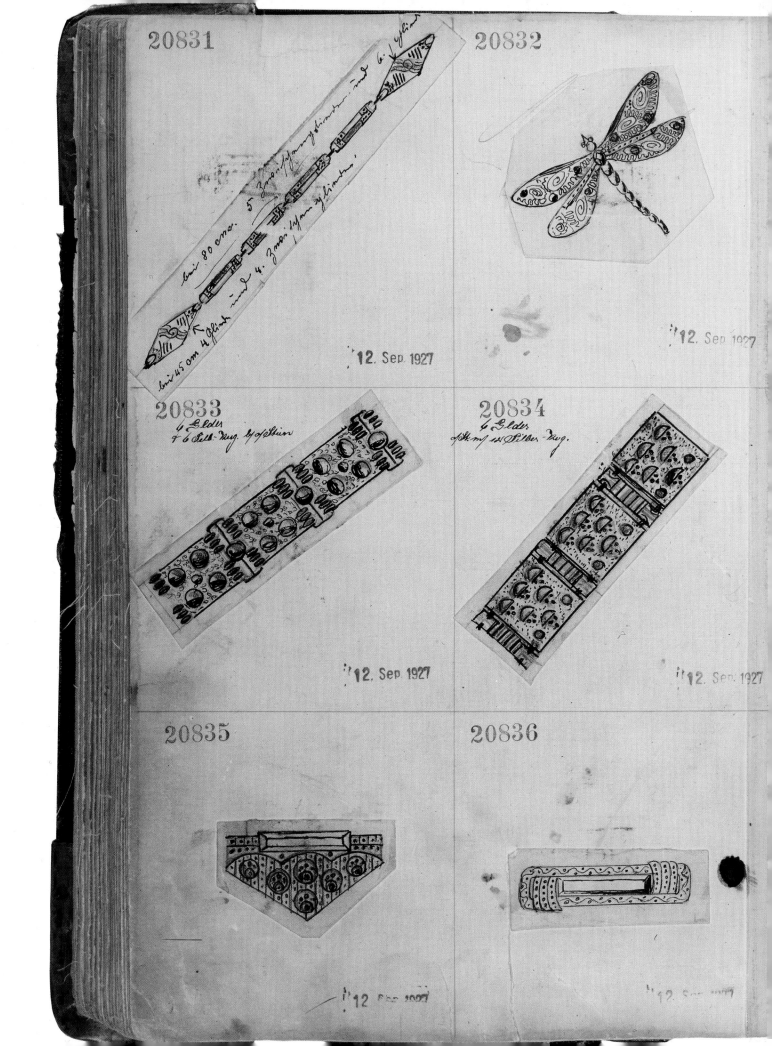

20831

20832

12. Sep. 1927

12. Sep. 1927

20833

12. Sep. 1927

20834

12. Sep. 1927

20835

20836

12. Sep. 1927

12. Sep. 1927

20837

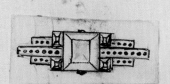

12. Sep. 1927

20838

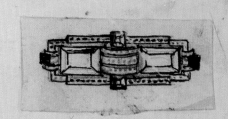

12. Sep. 1927

20839/a

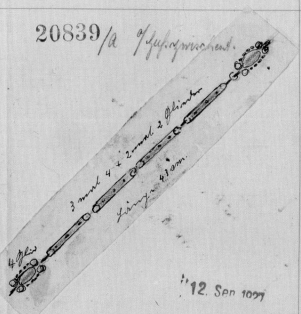

12. Sep. 1927

20840

12. Sep. 1927

20841

12. Sep. 1927

20842

12. Sep. 1927

10)
Pattern Book I, design for Model No. 20225. The design is made to actual size by pencil and drawing ink, but not dated. A design two pages further is dated 8/30/26, so a date in August of 1926 can also be presumed for the piece in question. A variation of the brooch is shown under number 20852, dated September 12, 1927.

11)
See a brooch with matte rock crystal plus enamel, diamonds and rubies, presumably made by Gerard Sandoz (1902-), shown in V. Becker, Antique . . . 1987, pp. 272-273.

12)
Catalog "I gioielli degli anni 20-40. Cartier e i grandi del Deco", Milano 1986, p. 29, No. 7.

13)
Christmas sales brochure, 1931.

14)
Die Fouquet 1860-1960, Schmuckkünstler in Paris Catalog, Paris 1984, p. 108, two pendants.

15)
Quoted in Sylvie Raulet, Schmuck Art Déco, Munich 1985, p. 328.

crystal frame, with marcasite in vegetable forms set in silver at the sides, enhanced by the attachment of corals (Cat. No. 2.15).[10] The type of matte-cut rock crystal in frame form can also be documented in the French jewelry art of the twenties.[11] The large quartz crystal of a pendant is worked from two entwined rosebuds and much resembles a cut tourmaline pendant from the House of Cartier in Paris (Cat. No. 2.14).[12]

Rock crystal was also worked in strictly geometric forms (Cat. No. 2.22). Rectangular or circular forms of matte quartz were enhanced with marcasite and onyx (Cat. No. 2.25).[13] One could almost speak of a copy of a pendant with onyx and diamonds designed in 1925 by Eric Bagge (1890-1978).[14] As of 1926 the first designs for enameled jewelry using genuine and synthetic colored stones and enhanced with filigree wire can be found in the

pattern books. On close examination of this series it can be seen that the formal development up to shortly after 1930 became more and more laborious, but the coloring remained subdued. From a standpoint of form, there were definite parallels to French art-deco jewelry in the latter half of the twenties. But Braendle's situation was very different; he produced high-quality industrially produced fashion jewelry of pleasing esthetics and excellent workmanship. Braendle could do without the costly materials — such as were used by the famous Parisian jewelers; he made his "creations" of silver and enhanced them with decorative stones, marcasite and enamel. The excellence of artistic design and the use of simple materials (as later urged by the Werkbund and still later by the Bauhaus) — which was the Theodor Fahrner firm's policy into the fifties — was proclaimed in France by the likes of Emile Sedeyn only in the thirties: "It is not necessarily the costly creations that will last, but rather those where the metal is combined with a decorative stone whose price is modest in comparison to its beauty, such as aquamarine, topaz, amethyst, tourmaline, moonstone, turquoise, jade, lapis lazuli or coral. The eternally young art will lengthen the careers of these semi-precious stones and display their true character. They will not be removed so the materials can be used for other purposes. They are primarily works of art, and only then valuable objects." (La bijouterie, la

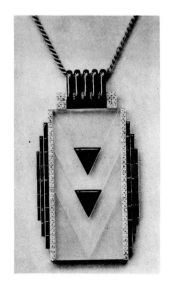

BIJOUX ET ORFEVRERIE, 1930, Plate 9 (G. Fouquet).

BIJOUX ET ORFEVRERIE, 1930, Plate 16 (E. Bagge).

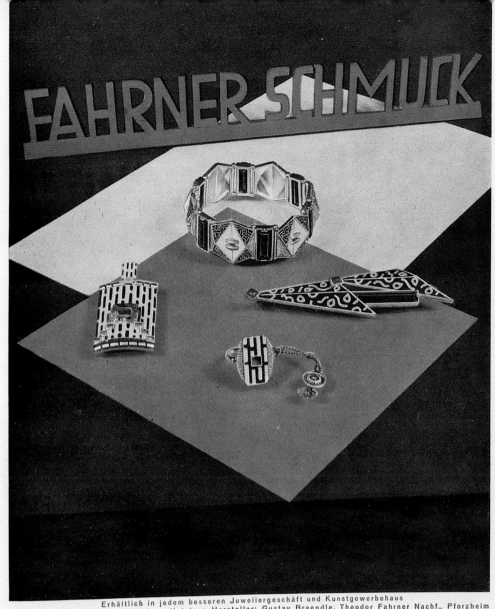

FAHRNER SCHMUCK

Erhältlich in jedem besseren Juweliergeschäft und Kunstgewerbehaus
Bezugsquellennachweis durch den alleinigen Hersteller: Gustav Braendle, Theodor Fahrner Nachf., Pforzheim

DIE DAME,
1929, No. 26, p. 45.

joallerie, la bijouterie de fantasie au XXe siècle, 1934, p. 151).[15] From 1932 on, an interesting change in the use of filigree wire can be seen, as it was gradually limited to corded wire (as a surface-covering formative material). The design of Model No. 20809 in Pattern Book I is drawn exactly to size in pencil with black drawing ink and red and blue colored pencils, and dated December 5, 1927. The surface of the oval pendant has circles of filigree wire soldered on, broken by waves and flowers that are filled in with colored matte enamel (turquoise, blue and red-brown; Cat. No. 2.68). The same pattern, in another combination of enamel colors, covers a pendant earring (Cat. No. 2.69). This combination of colored matte enamel surfaces and filigree wire circles is varied in numerous earrings and pendants. The striking quality of this series is the use of filigree wire circles; for particular accenting, square colored stones were added, and the enameled fields were made in Y shapes, as spots or segments of an arc as well as in angles. The same shaping of the enamel fields was retained in another group, but instead of filigree wire, a rough granulation of the surface was used to fill the surfaces (Cat. No.

172

2.120). What prevails in these models is the constant play with geometrical elements such as circles, rectangles and segment forms (Cat. No. 2.121). On a crossette band (this type of jewelry was seldom found at the end of the twenties), the surface was made in a very striking manner. Matte enamel in black and white was inset to cover the surface, and the white circles were surrounded by corded wire. The granulation extends like branches over the surface, corals and lapis-lazuli carrées provide colorful accents (Cat. No. 2.116). The inspiration and model for the designer of this piece might have been a bracelet by Cartier.[16]

A further possible use of corded wire is seen in a group of pendants and brooches. Fine filigree wires are arranged in parallels and form enclosed areas, in contrast to the semi-precious stones used (Cat. No. 2.88). Yet another use of filigree wire is seen in a pendant, a bracelet and a

brooch in which the wire forms small flower petals and lends the piece an Oriental air (Cat. No. 2.110). Purely geometrical forms are found in large pendants and brooches in which the corded wire is used only very sparingly, only enclosing the enamel fields used on all the pieces. The stones used are hematite, smoky quartz, carnelian, lapis lazuli and matte rock crystal, as well as onyx. The outlines on these pendants form rectangles, partly arranged as steps. The formative style of French Art-Déco jewelry is represented here in all its variations, made of simple but effective materials. A brooch and a ring are accentuated in unusual form, a three-dimensional hematite ball is set on the surface (Cat. No. 2.136). The designs for these pieces could not be found in the sample books, but the advertisements in the magazine "Die Dame" in the Christmas season of 1929 show that they were in production in that year.[17] These regularly appearing advertisements, in excellent graphic form, appear again and again in the following years. Drawings of elegant ladies, adding a chic aura to pictures of "Fahrner Jewelry", stand in the centers of these advertisements. Brief advertising texts draw attention to the products. "Why think it over? Fahrner Jewelry is the most desired Christmas gift", or "Fahrner Jewelry with the seal, the mark of the well-dressed lady of 1930."[18] In the late twenties an exclusive series of striking pieces of jewelry were developed by Braendle; they

16)
See Catalog Note 12, p. 40, No. 23.

17)
"Die Dame" Magazine, H. 6, 1929-30, p. 32.

18)
The full-page advertisements in the fashion magazine "Die Dame" are created in outstanding graphic style and superbly communicate the spirit of the twenties. Most of the advertisements are signed with the name of Straub, but it could not be determined whether it was an employee of the Braendle firm or an advertising agency that created this advertisement.

were lavishly set with marcasite. Pendants, brooches and earrings show a touch of Egyptian pyramid structure and lotus blossoms. The "Egyptian fashion" had enjoyed a great comeback since the discovery of Tutankhamun's tomb in 1922 and certainly had not failed to make an impression on the Braendle firm's designers.[19] Sets of jewelry enjoyed particular popularity; they generally consisted of a necklace, pendant, earrings and a ring. An ensemble of silver with large onyx stones, plenty of marcasite and coral carrées were found in the assortment of evening jewelry (see upper left). In the magazine "Die Dame", a full-page advertisement showed a couple in evening dress. "Evening jewelry is no longer a problem for the modern woman. Whatever the color and cut of her clothes, she will find her choice among the many splendid new models of valuable FAHRNER JEWELRY."[20]

With the creation of "costly evening jewelry" it was possible now for high-society ladies to wear fashion jewelry in the evening too. This development can be seen as an innovation in the jewelry and fashion consciousness of the twenties. Through the used of decorative stones in subdued colors along with marcasite, these pieces were afforded a particular elegance. The striking artistry in form often makes one forget that it was achieved here only with marcasite and decorative stones, not with costly jewels. This spectacular and expensive assortment probably found its appropriate customers mainly in America and England. Gustav Braendle must soon have realized that the economic situation in Germany offered no assurance that this comparatively expensive jewelry would sell.

As of 1932 the manufacturer produced another series, the "DEA Jewelry", in addition to his marcasite assortment.[21] An advertisement in the magazine 'Der Querschnitt" asks the reader: "Why DEA Jewelry?" The firm adds the explanation: "To complete my world-famous Fahrner Jewelry. Creation of economical, ideal jewelry for the broadest circles. Series production, thus unusual economy. Genuine stones, 935 silver. The new great values at new

Warum
DEA
SCHMUCK?

Ergänzung meines welt-berühmten Fahrner-Schmucks. Schaffung eines billigen idealen Zeitschmucks für wei-teste Kreise. Serien-mäßige Herstellung, daher ungewöhnliche Preiswürdigkeit. Echte Steine, 935 Silber. Der neue große Wert zu neuen kleinen Preisen.

Der blau-schwarze Ring

ist das Kennzeichen des DEA-Schmucks

DEA-SCHMUCK

Erhältlich in den einschlägigen Geschäften. Bezugsquellen-Nachweis durch den alleinigen Hersteller: Gustav Braendle, Theod. Fahrner Nachf., Pforzheim

19)
Cabinetmaster Friedrich Katz is said to have gotten involved with Egyptian motifs around 1925, using models from books. These designs may perhaps be ascribed to him.

20)
"Die Dame", 1930-31, no page.

21)
"Der Querschnitt" Magazine, No. 3, March 1932, p. 210.

modest prices. The blue-black ring is the identifying mark of DEA Jewelry."[22] Around 1930 Braendle advertised with the slogan "more beautiful necklaces, refined in form and color. The new fashion calls for neck jewelry. Therefore Fahrner necklaces have been made with special care, still differentiated and individual, noble in form and material —primitive jewelry is passé." Silver necklaces with a large central piece or several individual links in the center are now in style. The links are made of circles, rectangles or segments of arc and usually combined with dark stones such as onyx, smoky quartz or hematite, sometimes enhanced by modest strips of material (Cat. No. 2.158).

Astrological Jewelry. In 1932 jewelry with astrological motifs came into style. Braendle followed this trend immediately and presented, for example, astrological good-luck rings of silver with matte

enamel and colored stones. The rings bore the various signs of the zodiac in figured and symbolic forms, as well as portrayals of the planets (above and lower left). In the same year, an article by Prof. Ludwig Segmiller on "Astrology and Jewelry" appeared in the "Deutsche Goldschmiedezeitung." It is noted there that a strong tendency toward astrological jewelry was evident in commercial art. Goldsmiths' workshops and large firms took up this subject, for example Max Kolb in Munich, Otto Hahn in Bielefeld and Romula Wagner in Berlin, as well as the firm of Bruckmann and Sons in Heilbronn.[23]

Sport Jewelry. With increasing interest in sporting activities and sport clothes, an appropriate line of jewelry had to be created. "The style of sport clothes requires simple, clear, objective lines. These charming new creations, as necessary enhancements for the clothing of the modern sport-loving woman, are new, charming and economical."[24] These popular sporting motifs reached their high point in 1936, when the Olympic Games took place in Berlin. But in the assortment of the forties too, a brooch in the form of a tennis racket appeared, made of silver

22)
The "blue-black ring" mentioned has not been found as yet on any piece of jewelry. The jewelry itself was stamped with "DEA" (see Cat. No. 2.151). The "blue-black ring" and the "Fahrner seal" also mentioned were fastened to the piece of jewelry and removed before wearing.

23)
DGZ No. 41, 1932, pp. 404-406.

24)
"Der Querschnitt" Magazine, 1930-31, no page.

DGZ No. 13, 1932, p. 135.

with filigree wire, its handle set with marcasite and the tennis ball, a small cultured pearl, set on the head of the racket.

Swastika. The firm of Gustav Braendle also took up, as of the spring of 1933, the design and manufacture of pendants and brooches with swastika motifs.[25]

Filigree Jewelry. A second tendency (along with the simple, somewhat heavy-looking silver jewelry) was the filigree jewelry offered as of 1932 in a wide variety of motifs.[26] Originally regarded as folk and peasant-dress jewelry, it was suitable for stressing a typically German, even Germanic style. The small spirals of corded wire covered the surfaces of pendants, brooches and rings, whole sets of jewelry. To a great variety of patterns, models of brass or tombac were made by hand. The pieces were cast in sand after these models (in the thirties). In filigree jewelry production in the forties, and especially after World War II, the so-called centrifugal casting process was used.[27] As a technical specialty, these pieces made of silver were given a special greenish gilding. Gustav Braendle had his own personal secret formula for this patina, which he patented.[28] The production of filigree jewelry was likewise accompanied by expensive advertising. Hundreds of thousands of sales brochures were printed, in both English and German. The repertoire of this trend in jewelry was immeasurably large and included all areas of jewelry.

Copies and Imitations. The worldwide success of "Fahrner Jewelry" inspired competitors to imitate it. For that reason Gustav Braendle had already registered the "Fahrner seal" with the Reich Patent Office in 1929 as an unmistakable way to protect his products. An advertisement in the magazine "Der Querschnitt" in 1931 shows that Gustav Braendle had to protect himself against copiers of his jewelry, and naturally he refers, not without pride, to the popularity of his products. "The most wonderful recognition for me is the fact that all over the world, attempts are made to imitate Fahrner Jewelry and copy whole series of my models. As the only creator

FAHRNER SCHMUCK

IST NUR ECHT MIT DIESER PLOMBE ACHTEN SIE BEIM EINKAUF DA= RAUF, WENN SIE SICH VOR MINDERWERTIGEN NACH= AHMUNGEN HÜTEN WOLLEN

straub

and manufacturer of Fahrner Jewelry in anything even approaching his style and his quality, I consider it my moral duty to warn you of the many imitations! Every

25)
Pattern Book IV, ca. 1933. Model No. 1181 to No. 1185: designs for brooches, pendants and rings with swastika motifs.

26)
Filigree (Filum granum = string and knot): Filigree wire is knotted or corded wire that is placed on the background metal and attached by means of solder. In the Braendle firm, every filigree wire was soldered on by hand. According to an employee, filigree jewelry production began with Model No. 1514 in 1932 and ended with production number 05566 in 1974. (see Pattern Book IV, pp. 164 ff).

27)
Sandcasting: in sandcasting the molding material is sand which is prepared with water. The form frame consists of light metal. The casting form is made with a handmade model of brass which is removed when the sand solidifies. The sand mold is unusable after being used once, but the advantage of sandcasting is that there is less loss of material. Centrifugal casting: A wax model is surrounded by an non-flammable mass and warmed until the wax flows out the later casting channel, and the hollow mold is filled with metal. In modern centrifugal casting, a rubber mold is vulcanized. In hand centrifugal casting a single wax model is used.

28)
According to an employee, the patina for the gold alloy was developed before 1939 by a Mrs. Fahrner who was not connected with the firm of Theodor Fahrner. Just when Gustav Braendle used this green-gilding, or whether two gilding processes were used at the same time, is not known.

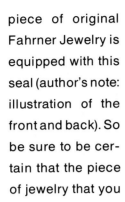

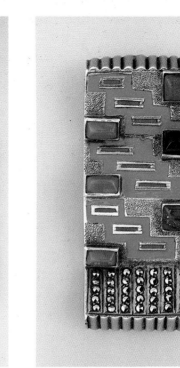

piece of original Fahrner Jewelry is equipped with this seal (author's note: illustration of the front and back). So be sure to be certain that the piece of jewelry that you buy is equipped with a seal. Then you have the safe assurance of owning original Fahrner Jewelry, the leading fashion jewelry . . ."[29]

Copy or Model? If one takes a look at the jewelry production of other Pforzheim firms, one can understand the measures taken to protect models. On the other hand, one may wonder what inspiration came to the designers in Gustav Braendle's firm; the relation of some pieces to the French "Haute Joaillerie" has already been noted. The strict geometric decor of Fahrner Jewelry has also been seen in the work of Paul Brandt's studio in Paris, and his work was popular in Germany. There pendants of platinum were decorated with stones and brightened with enamel.[30]

The use of colored enamel as surface-covering decor in combination with stones was popular in many forms of jewelry and suited the style of the time. The pendant made by an unknown artist shows stylized leaf decor that was typical of the thirties, as well as the very popular segment forms

(upper left). A very close relation to Braendle's products is seen in those of Karl Karst's commercial art studio in Pforzheim, but a possible collaboration between the two firms cannot be documented. In Karst's case too the pieces were made of silver and partly gilded. In a bracelet the links form a geometrical pattern covered with green, blue and black matte enamel, enhanced with triangles set with marcasite. A brooch was made as a three-dimensional zigzag band, its form also made up of surface decor (upper right). An exact dating of the Karst pieces is not possible, so it cannot be said whether they were inspired by Braendle's or appeared earlier. Graphically structured enamel decor also played an important role in the production of the Pforzheim firm of Louis Kuppenheim, as a golden bracelet from the twenties shows. The same is true of the jewelry produced by the firm of Rodi and Wienenberger. Here jewelry appeared in various color combinations of matte enamel, mainly in floral patterns. Three examples of chains show elements similar to those of Braendle's assortment, in the structure of the chain links and the

29)
"Der Querschnitt" Magazine, No. 6, March 1931, p. 415, showing the front and back of the "TF Seal."

30)
"Die Schaulade" Magazine, Vol. 7, 1930, pp. 608-609.

arrangement of the corded wire decor (below). Two of the cited examples are unstamped but can be attributed, on the basis of their stylistic agreement with the third, stamped piece, as having been made by the firm of Rodi & Wienenberger. Another necklace, made of crownlike links of green and black matte enamel, belongs to the same series. The firm of H. Zwernemann, founded at Hanau in 1873, advertised "Hazet Jewelry" in the magazine "Die Dame" around 1930: "Through the sensitive harmony of the tender enamel colors with the tones of the synthetic gemstones, small wonderworks are created, suitable for every atmosphere, every opportunity, and easy to buy because of their current prices." The strict decor of the illustrated pieces shows a clear relationship to the Braendle assortment. With the formation of his laboriously worked marcasite pieces too, Gustav Braendle was not the only manufacturer on the jewelry market. The firms

of Bruno Baader and of Lutz & Weiss in Pforzheim also offered, in addition to gold and gems, marcasite jewelry of 935 silver with cut decorative stones. But these pieces cannot be compared in any way with the imaginative brooches and pendants in the Braendle assortment, which rose far above the cited comparison pieces in terms of decor. Very closely related to Braendle's work in structural terms is a brooch by an unknown manufacturer; it is striking because of its color combination of blue and black and its strict use of marcasite decor (upper right). The spectrum of comparison pieces could be extended at will. The outstanding designs of the Braendle assortment in the twenties and thirties clearly lift themselves above the usual trend.

Export. Success in the export trade was clearly a part of increased business. Calculating it, though, was made difficult by two factors: to suit the newest fashion trends, separate designs had to be drawn for every country. The varying percentages of purity prevailing in various countries compelled the manufacturers to produce goods with a different percentage for each country (see p. 72). But in the economically difficult years between the wars, the expansion of the export trade took on great significance. The "permanent sample display" in Pforzheim, a presentation opportunity for the German firms, provided an important contact point with foreign customers. . Beyond that, there were wholesalers in different countries

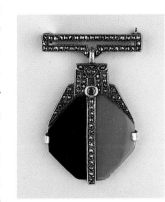

who distributed Fahrner Jewelry in their countries; for example, the jewelry firm of Gathmann, founded in Pforzheim in 1853, had a representative in Caracas that handled Fahrner Jewelry in Venezuela.[31]

The Firm's Philosophy and Advertising Strategy — the Success of Gustav Braendle. When Pieper says: "The personality of the entrepreneur, his capability in the choice of patterns, in the search for new markets and dealing with customers hat a great importance to the success of the undertaking", this is particularly true of the Braendle firm. The manufacturer knew best how to handle developments in fashion and the new consciousness of the woman. The success of this business strategy and the esteem in which he was held at the end of the twenties are shown by his inclusion in the Reichshandbuch der deutschen Gesellschaft in 1930.[32] Here the five hundred most important personalities in business and public life in Germany were listed. It may be regarded as a very special honor that Gustav Braendle was listed there.

In his book on the advertising strategy of the Pforzheim jewelry industry, Pieper observes: "The sales literature such as catalogs, circulars and slogans, on the other hand, was less striking", but this does not apply to the Braendle firm.[33] In all the well-known fashion magazines such as "Die Dame", "Die elegante Welt", "Der Querschnitt" or "Die deutsche Elite" we find full-color and sometimes full-page advertisements of the highest artistic quality. Free-lance graphic artists, such as HW (not identified, 1921), Marlice Hinz (1927), Walter Biedermann of Stuttgart (1927), as well as Straub, were responsible for their creation. No opportunity was missed to bring the jewelry to the woman, or the man either, for the "man aware of jewelry" was also spoken to. Movie actresses and other personalities displayed the Fahrner products in large-scale advertisements. The texts of these advertisements show clearly for what type of woman Fahrner Jewelry was intended. "Fahrner Jewelry is frankly not meant to satisfy the whole world's taste. It is individual jewelry. It harmonizes with the taste of the time, but at the same time it characterizes the wearer." Or: "The society lady does not want to have what everybody has; she prefers what is special and striking."[34] With these advertisements the Braendle firm put special emphasis on their customers; the "well-dressed lady" was to be addressed. In their 1931 Christmas brochure, a bracelet in strict

178

31)
A kind contribution from Mr. Erich Bahnmuller of Pforzheim; from 1928 to 1974 he was a managing colleague in the jeweler firm of Gathmann Hermanos in Caracas, Venezuela, and also bought Fahrner Jewelry for his firm.

32)
Reichshandbuch der deutschen Gesellschaft. Das Handbuch der Persönlichkeiten in Wort und Bild, Berlin 1930, p. 195; photo and short biography of the person and firm.

33)
Wolfgang Pieper, Geschichte der Pforzheimer Schmuckindustrie, p. 213.

geometric style, of rock crystal with marcasite, was offered at a price of 182 Reichs-Marks. This is a clear indication that this assortment was meant for the well-to-do bourgeois class.[35] To serve as broad a spectrum of customers as possible, though, more reasonably priced jewelry also had to be offered. In the series of filigree jewelry are pieces in the price range between 10 and 80 Reichs-Marks. The particularly understated pieces of silver with genuine onyx or lapis lazuli were also priced at 40 Reichs-Marks or less. In another clever bit of market strategy, Braendle used fashion shows to make his jewelry known. At the Hotel Adlon in Berlin and the Palasthotel in Dresden, film actresses presented the renowned Fahrner Jewelry.[36] According to a former employee, the Braendle firm also undertook joint advertising campaigns with Henkel Sekt

and made an advertising film with the UFA Filmgesellschaft of Berlin.[37] It can certainly be said that Gustav Braendle spared no expense to offer his jewelry assortment to his customers. Ten per cent of the firm's income was regularly invested in advertising, an unusually high amount that only a few firms could afford.

A striking change in advertising strategy appeared after 1932. Smaller advertisements in black and white, no more than half a page in size, refer to Fahrner rings.[38] Three small examples of rings are accompanied by a simple sales text: "Special care in designing and production has always been devoted to the Fahrner ring, because as a piece of jewelry, the ring characterizes the wearer. The new times require understatement and simplicity. This requirement is met by the creation of simple, refined forms through which surprising effects are achieved, and that yet are reasonably priced . . ." "The new times require understatement and simplicity", the main theme of the thirties; the German woman did not need to wear luxurious jewelry, she was supposed to be primarily a housewife and mother. Extravagance was reserved for the stars of film and theater, the women of the world. On account of the economic situation, "low-priced" jewelry had to be offered now. Jewelry had to be not reasonably priced, but low-priced. It was made mainly of silver with simple colored stones, in many sturdy forms that had nothing more to do with the elegant, colorful

Die Dame, Vol. 56, 1929, No. 20, p. 60.

34)
"Die Schaulade" Magazine, Vol. 7, No. 2, 1931, p. 117.

35)
1931 Christmas brochure. To evaluate the price ranges in the thirties, it might be noted that a Studienrat (a representative of the good bourgeois class) earned about 450 Reichs-Marks a month circa 1935.

36)
"Die Dame", Vol. 34, 1927, No. 26, p. 46.

37)
According to Mrs. Thekla Baader, an employee for many years.

38)
"Die Dame", No. 1, 1932-33, p. 45.

Post-War Times

Gustav Braendle, portrait by the painter Hahnle, 1946.

39)
In 1936-37 Jean Lambert Rucki designed beaten silver bracelets that could have been godparents to the Braendle assortment in terms of basic characteristics. They do, though, go far beyond the Pforzheim products in detail. Picture in "Die Fouquet, 1860-1960", Paris 1984, p. 123.

jewelry that featured enamel and marcasite.[39] The "Deutsche Goldschmiedezeitung" expressed praise for this simple jewelry in a commentary on the 1932 Leipzig Autumn Fair.[40] In the thirties too, the suggestive sales slogans in the brochures spoke to the woman very personally and appealed to her individuality, her uniqueness when she wore Fahrner Jewelry. "Do you love a personal touch? Would you like to unveil a very personal charm in the way you dress? Then choose the magical Fahrner Jewelry. It completes your stylish appearance and stresses your beauty."[41]

Post-war Times. For the Braendle firm, the war years of 1939 to 1945 meant a decided limitation of their production. Yet exports to foreign lands, especially to the USA, could be maintained to a great extent. On February 23, 1945 the firm's building was destroyed in a bombing attack. For Gustav Braendle, this meant the destruction of his life's work and his material security. An even more painful loss was the death of his sons Hans and Gustav, who fell in the war. Both had played important roles in designing the important Fahrner assortment of the thirties. But shortly after the war ended, this energetic man had applied himself to rebuilding his firm. A painting made in 1946 shows Gustav Braendle at his desk with one of his now-important filigree assortments before him. This portrait of the manufacturer expresses the unbroken energy of Gustav Braendle that, after the complete destruction of his firm, did not hesitate to set out to rebuild it, along with his son Herbert.[42]

DGZ No. 47, 1932, p. 466.

Style of the Fifties. Around 1950 one could already read in an advertisement: "In close cooperation of experienced staff members with talented artists, today again an inexhaustible array of all kinds of this choice, timeless jewelry is being created."[43] At the beginning of the fifties Gustav Braendle wanted to expand his assortment with gold jewelry. This capable man surely would have made a fine success of it, but a serious illness soon brought his creative activities to an end. After his father's death in 1952, Herbert Braendle had to assume control of the business. The production of filigree jewelry with marcasite and colored stones was continued by him in grand style, originally retaining the motifs of the pre-war years. But gradually new jewelry designs and creations were added to the existing assortment. Business outside Germany was intensified by Herbert Braendle. In a post-1952 sales brochure it was said: "Fahrner Jewelry products are exported to all the world again, Fahrner Jewelry enchants, delights." This slogan, already registered by Gustav Braendle in 1935, was used again here. In general, the sales texts reflect the spirit of the fifties and the new advertising terminology.[44] Foreign-language brochures were enhanced with wordplay, the former sales pitch was changed.

In the times around 1955, production of filigree jewelry was changed; not only do exact filigree spirals cover the surfaces of pieces of jewelry, but unequal, wavelike lines also decorate the surfaces. An old formative means from Fahrner Jewelry production in the twenties was used again in changed form: Enamel in various color combinations, but no longer in the matte-enamel technique, but in translucent, glittering form. A jewelry set of chain, bracelet,

F or the lady with discriminating taste

A selection of the finest Jewellery

H undreds of different designs

R are beautiful genuine or synthetic stones set in sterling silver

N ew, unique and artistic

E very one true to the tradition of the German goldsmith

R ight for every occasion that is:

FAHRNER JEWELLERY

earrings and ring is entitled "good-mood jewelry" in an advertisement. In a further sales text, the old tradition of enameling is mentioned: "Millenia watch over it, for two thousand years before modern times the

Title page of a sales brochure from the fifties.

40)
DGZ No. 37, 1932, p. 361. The commercial art at the 1932 Leipzig Autumn Fair: "In a class by themselves are the products of the firm of Gustav Braendle, Theodor Fahrner Nachfolge, Prforzheim, that extract all the beauty from the material and, avoiding hints of the Baroque, once again presents new jewelry that simply must be described as excellent and tasteful. With the simplest elements of form, flat panels with recessed hemispheres or leaf-like motifs in matte and beaten silver with onyx or malachite, decorative effects are attained here that are often amazing. But unceasing efforts lead to success."

41)
Sales brochure.

42)
Oil painting by the painter Hahnle, made in 1946. Mr. Hahnle was supported by the Braendle family during the war. He painted manufacturer Gustav Braendle to express his thanks.

43)
Several sales brochures from the fifties have been preserved, though they are not dated. When the firm's address is stated, one can keep in mind that brochures with the Habsburger Strasse address can be dated after 1955, since the firm moved at that time. The designer of the new assortment was Adam Fenz, who worked for the Braendle firm as a jewelry designer from 1946 to 1961.

44)
Sales brochure, with the name of Hofranz cited as the graphic artist.

Sc-4685/S-45 v

STIL

Fahrner-Schmuck atmet nich
den flüchtigen Augenblick
der Zeit. Fahrner-Schmuc
überdauert modische Strö
mungen und begeistert im
mer. Das zeigen Ihnen die
anmutigen Modelle. Sie sin
beschwingt wie eine frö
liche Melodie und schenke
Ihnen den Zauber des frei
digen Besitzes... für heu
und für viele Jahre.

45)
Bird of paradise in silver with colorful enamel, set with marcasite. Auction catalog of Dr. Fritz Nagel, 325th auction, December 1-3, 1988, No. 325.

Egyptians practiced the art of making colorful enamel. We still admire their splendid creations today." The repertoire of this jewelry assortment takes on the new style of the fifties; swinging lines are used along with accents of color. The use of floral and plant forms is clear to see. The surface formation of the individual chains, pendants and brooches varies between filigree soldering in spiral form and free wavelike movements, accentuated or completed by glowing enamel and strict, more subdued areas that are achieved through the so-called millegriff technique (in that the surface is very grained or beaded, for example, Cat. No. 2.180). Some pieces are made only in millegriff technique with marcasite or enamel highlights. Through the inclusion of symbolic features, the brooches, chains and pendants take on a new meaning. Thus it is said in a sales slogan: "Symphony of Beauty" — This piece of

jewelry from the House of Fahrner with its seal refers in meaning and form to the eternal life-force of the sun. The center glows with bright stones and colorful enamel. The wavy rim is sown with shimmering marcasite that is sparklingly alive. Thus Fahrner Jewelry, made of fine sterling silver, possesses its own, very special style."

The Bird Motif in Fahrner Jewelry. A "special" group is made up of many animal

brooches. We find snails, dogs and birds in filigree wire (left), partly set with marcasite. But there are also very effectively made large. very stylized birds set with marcasite.[45] It was this same bird motif that had already been found in Theodor Fahrner's jewelry production. The bird is offered in many variations, a small animal with its head tilted far downward, holding a ball in its claws, that was made of either a pearl or coral (see Cat. No. 1.109b). The creature itself was available in silver or gilded silver and, in another variation, gilded silver set with marcasite.[46] In these portrayals of animals too, Fahrner was not alone; in the forties and fifties in particular, such figures can be found in the products of the great French jewelry manufacturers. One example is a clip-on brooch in the form of a flamingo, made in 1940. This fine piece is made of platinum enhanced with diamonds, rubies and sapphires.[47]

The Last Two Decades. In the sixties and seventies it became clearer and clearer that the products of the Gustav Braendle firm matched the general trends; "Original Fahrner Jewelry" in its true sense no longer existed. First there came a large assortment of silver jewelry no better than

46)
Re the motifs of animal
brooches, see p. 130.

47)
Hans Nadelhoffer, "Cartier",
Herrsching 1984, p. 293.

the usual factory-made jewelry. One example is a set of jewelry consisting of a chain, bracelet and pendant decorated with small rounded squares and rectangles. It was available in various types, sometimes enhanced with pearls or colored stones (Cat. No. 2.186). A special feature now was jewelry with antique, i.e. Roman, Etruscan and Egyptian motifs in silver and 14- or 18-karat gold, called "Antique Art." One pendant portrays the tombstone of Upwatmose, dating to 1400 B.C. The back of this pendant is covered with hieroglyphics (lower right). Among the "Antique Art" there was also a bracelet showing, in a field of raised rectangles, the head of a woman; she was the wife of Akhnaton, from 1370 B.C. (Cat. No. 2.196). As a single motif, this portrayal is also used on a pendant from the same as-

sortment. The design for this piece, No. 10317 in Pattern Book X, is accompanied by the comment "ten links including lock." The extension of gold jewelry production began at the beginning of the seventies. In the 1970 Christmas assortment, small golden brooches, resembling fir branches and enhanced with cultured pearls or rubies, were offered (Cat. No. 2.192). The use of time-honored old jewelry motifs in new products was not avoided. But expanding the program with large-scale gold jewelry production came too late, and now the firm of Gustav Braendle could no longer be saved from its final dissolution. On February 18, 1979, with the death of the firm's last proprietor, Herbert Braendle, the era of world-famous "Fahrner Jewelry" came to an end.

FAHRNER-SCHMUCK

Erhältlich in jedem besseren Juweliergeschäft und Kunstgewerbehaus — Bezugsquellennachweis durch den alleinigen Hersteller:
Gustav Braendle, Theodor Fahrner Nachf., Pforzheim

Braendle, Hans, merchant, *11/6/1909, Esslingen †February 1944, fell in action. Mercantile training in his father's firm. Spent time in France and England. Brief service as volunteer in a Berlin jewelry business. Then in charge of export trade in his father's business.

Braendle, Herbert, goldsmith, designer, *5/26/1913, Esslingen †2/27/1979, Pforzheim. Trained at the Goldsmithing School and the Baden Kunstgewerbe School, both in Pforzheim. Active in the thirties as a jewelry designer in his father's firm. After World War II Herbert Braendle became part-owner of the firm of Gustav Braendle Theodor Fahrner Nachf. After his father's death in 1952 he directed the firm until his death. The firm was dissolved in 1979.

Braendle, Gustav, Jr., goldsmith, designer, merchant, *10/30/1910, Esslingen †8/25/1942, fell in action. Mercantile training in his father's business. 1925-27: Attended toe Goldsmithing School in Pforzheim. 1927-29: Training at the Baden Kunstgewerbe School, Pforzheim. 1930: Language study in Paris. Active as a jewelry designer in his father's firm as of 1929.

Braendle, Gustav Hermann Adam Heinrich, merchant, entrepreneur, jewelry designer and artist.

*May 30, 1883, Esslingen †late January 1952, Pforzheim. Son of Heinrich Adam Braendle, goldsmith and jeweler in Esslingen on the Neckar.[1] Mercantile training at the jewelry factory of Albert Huttenlocher in Esslingen. Then volunteer for one year in the gold goods factory of Friedrich Pfälzer and Sons in Stuttgart.

Spent time in Berlin and worked for the jewelry business of Sy & Wagner, then worked two years for the firm of Louis Fiesseler & Co. in Pforzheim. Then in his father's jewelry business in Esslingen.

Built up production of silver jewelry. Married Johanna Luise Heinz of Pforzheim on September 24, 1908. Returning from war service, he bought the firm of Theodor Fahrner in Pforzheim at the end of 1919 and did business as "Gustav Braendle Theodor Fahrner Nachf." In 1920 the business in Esslingen was dissolved.[2]

1)
According to an entry in the registry of business changes, Adam Braendle took over the goldsmithing business of his mother, Adam Braendle's widow, on Nov. 22, 1880.

2)
According to an entry in the registry of business changes, Nov. 24, 1920.

1919-1925

2.1 PENDANT 1919-1920
Silver, aventurine quartz,
synthetic rubies or garnets,
pearl shells.
Height 104, width 50 mm.
Stamped: TF (linked) 935.
Laborious metalwork on the
reverse.
Privately owned, U. Thomale.

2.2 PENDANT 1919-1920
Balsa wood, stained black,
silver, gilded, white and black
matte enamel, dark citrine.
Height 72, width 22 mm.
Stamped: TF (linked) 935.
Wiener Interieur, Vienna.

2.3 PENDANT ca. 1920
Silver, white enamel,
carnelian (?), marcasite.
Height 65, width 35 mm.
Stamped: TF (linked), 935 (5
illegible).
German private collection.

2.4 PENDANT ca. 1920
Silver, black enamel, two
pearl shells, marcasite.
Height 35, width 18 mm.
Stamped: TF (linked) 800.
Gabriela Arnold collection.

2.5 PENDANT ca. 1920
Pierced work in silver, pearl
shells, marcasite.
Height 45, width 25/15 mm
Stamped: TF (linked) 800.
Gabriela Arnold collection.

2.1

2.2

2.3

2.4

2.5

2.7

2.8

2.6 PENDANT with chain ca. 1920 with extending section of the chain.
Silver, five turquoise cabochons of varying sizes, six turquoise balls worked into the chain, pearl shells, the extending section includes two turquoise balls.
Height 75, length 130 mm, chain length 310 mm (with extension).
Stamped: TF (linked) 935 STERLING.
Ursel Gronert collection, Berlin.

2.7 PENDANT 1920-1921
Silver, translucent lilac (flowers), green (stalk) and black (frame) enamel, marcasite (flower stamp).
Height 40, width 32 mm.
Stamped: TF (linked) 800.
A variant is numbered 18898.
German private collection.
Lit.: Ill. Jb. Pfh., 1922. Model No. 18898, an oval brooch with the same decor, is illustrated.

2.8 PENDANT 1920-1921
Silver, black enamel, turquoise, marcasite.
Height 46, width 30 mm.
Stamped: TF (linked) 800.
Model No. 18887.
ANTIK-OFFICE, R. + S. Diehl, Frankfurt on the Main.
Lit.: Ill. Jb. Pfh., 1922, the illustrated piece has a faceted stone in the middle instead of turquoise.

2.9 BROOCH 1920-1921
Silver, black enamel, light green enameled flowers, mother-of-pearl shell.
Height 37, width 50 mm.
Stamped FAHRNER (?) illegible.
German private collection.
Lit.: Ill. Jb. Pfh., 1922, Model No. 18862/10.

2.6

2.9

2.10

2.10 PENDANT 1920-1921
Silver, black enamel, green
colored agate, marcasite.
Height 50, width 33 mm.
Stamped: GERMANY
STERLING (in rectangle), TF
(linked).
German private collection.
Lit.: Ill. Jb. Phh., 1922, under
Model No. 18939/17 a
variation of the pendant is
illustrated, its central floral
design like that of the piece
shown here.

2.11 PENDANT 1922
Silver, three green agate
rings, onyx, one large and
three small cut hematite,
marcasite.
Height 80, width 35 mm.
Stamped: GERMANY (in
rectangle), TF (linked),
STERLING (in rectangle).
German private collection.

2.12 EARRINGS ca. 1922
Silver, two onyx rings,
marcasite.
Height 65 mm.
Stamped: TF (linked)
STERLING GERMANY.
Beatrice Ost collection.

2.11

2.12

Kling, Anton

Painter, designer

*Nov. 26, 1881, Vienna †Sept. 21, 1963, Karlsruhe

Attended the Imperial and Royal Kunstgewerbe School, Vienna (with Josef Hoffmann, among others).

1908-1923 Worked at the Kunstgewerbe School, Hamburg. Member of the Deutsche Werkbund.

post-1923 Director of the Kunstgewerbe School, Pforzheim, collaborated with Gustav Braendle, Theodor Fahrner Nachf., at this time; as of 1927 active as a freelance artist in Karlsruhe.

1930-1940 Taught as the State Technical Institute, Karlsruhe.

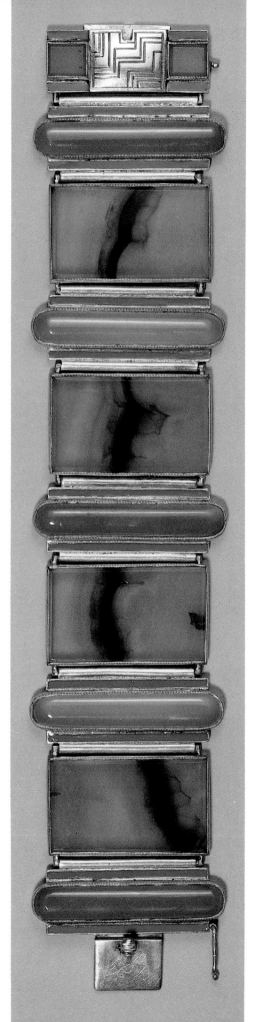

2.13 BRACELET post-1923
Designed by Anton Kling.
Of his collaboration with Gustav Braendle, only this bracelet could be documented.
Silver, banded agate, blue enamel.
Height 40, length 193 mm.
Stamped: 945 TF.
Austrian Museum of Applied Art, Vienna, Inv. No. Bi 1531.
Lit.: Vienna Catalog, 1986, p. 13, no. 25, picture on p. 19; photo album, Fachhochschule Pforzheim, no inv. no.

Rock Crystal

2.15

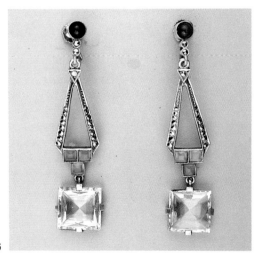

2.16

2.17

2.14

2.14 PENDANT twenties
Silver (setting), matte rock
crystal cut in form of two
rosebuds, set with marcasite,
gold topaz.
Height 100, width 45 mm.
Unsigned (bought directly
from the Fahrner firm in the
early twenties).
May have been inspired by a
French piece from Cartier.
Flesser collection, Hof.
Lit.: Cat. "I gioielli . . .", 1986,
p. 29, no. 7.

2.15 BROOCH 1926
Silver,e rock crystal.
Height 30, width 60 mm.
Stamped: TF (linked) 925.
Private collection, Pforzheim.
2.15a Design in Sample Book
I, Model No. 20225.
Pencil, black drawing ink;
without exact date but can be
dated as 1926, since the next
page of the book is dated
8/30/26. Drawn full-size.

2.16 EARRINGS 1926-1927
Silver, rock crystal, light blue
cabochons, marcasite.
Height 60 mm.
Stamped: TF (linked) 935
STERLING GBM (= Gustav
Braendle Model?).
Privately owned, E. L.
2.16a Design, Pattern Book I,
Model No. 20379. Pencil,
marking ink. Dated "January
1, 1927." Drawn full-size.

2.17 BROOCH 1927
Silver, marcasite, coral, matte
rock crystal.
Height 35, width 25 mm.
Unsigned.
May have been inspired by a
brooch by the Frenchman
Georges Sandoz (born 1902).
B. M. collection.
2.17a Design, Pattern Book I,
Model No. 20852. Pencil,
drawing ink, green and red
colored pencils. Dated "Sept.
12, 1927."
Height 40, width 35 mm.
Picture in Vivienne Becker,
**Antique and Twentieth
Century Jewellery**, Essex
1987, pp. 272-273, Plate 52.

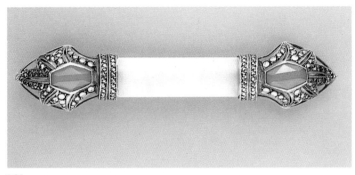

2.21

2.18

2.19

2.20

2.22

2.18 BROOCH late twenties
Silver, marcasite, synthetic aquamarine, matte rock crystal.
Height 35, width 50 mm.
Stamped: TF 925.
Private collection, Pforzheim.
2.18a Photo in Pattern Book VI, Model No. 3045, no date.

2.19 BROOCH late twenties
Silver, matte rock crystal, eight small turquoises, marcasite.
Height 28, width 40 mm.
Stamped: TF (linked) 925.
The flower-basket motif revives a typical decor used earlier, in Theodor Fahrner's time (see Cat. No. 1.128 ff).
Here in stylized floral form.
German private collection.
2.19a Photo, Pattern Book VI, Model No. 3123, no date.
This piece is numbered 3123/2 in a sales brochure of the fifties.

2.20 BROOCH late twenties
Silver, marcasite, synthetic aquamarine, matte rock crystal.
Height 25, width 55 mm.
Unsigned.
Gabriela Arnold collection.
2.20a Photo, Pattern Book VI, Model No. 3039, slight variations as actually made.

2.21 BROOCH ca. 1930
Silver, matte rock crystal, green colored agate (?), marcasite.
Height 20, width 80 mm.
Stamped: TF (linked) 935.
Beatrice Ost collection.

2.22 PENDANT with chain 1931
Designed by Gustav Braendle, Jr.
Silver, matte rock crystal, onyx, marcasite.
Height 65 (48), width 18, length 420 mm (chain).
Stamped: FAHRNER 935 (pendant).
B. M. collection.
Lit.: The 1931 Christmas brochure shows a similar earring, numbered "23058 earring, richly set with genuine marcasite, oxidized silver, matte rock crystal and onyx, RM 90.-"

2.23

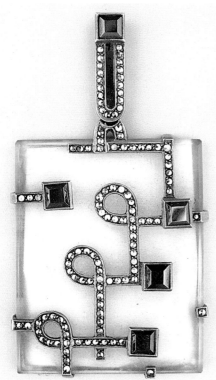

2.24

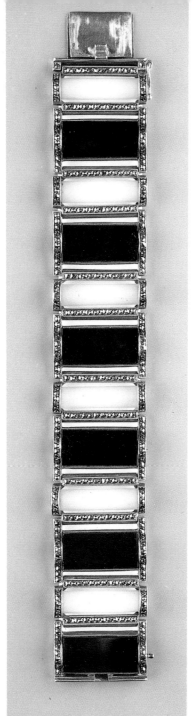

2.25

2.23 PENDANT 1930
Designed by Gustav
Braendle, Jr.
(similar design to original
drawing 5, No. 40.
Silver, oxidized, matte rock
crystal, hematite, marcasite.
Height 75 (45), width 36 mm.
Stamped: TF (linked) 935.
B. M. collection.

2.24 PENDANT ca. 1931
Silver, oxidized, matte rock
crystal, coral ball, marcasite.
Height 50 (35), width 25 mm.
Unsigned.
Beatrice Ost collection.

2.25 BRACELET 1930
Designed by Gustav
Braendle, Jr.
Silver, oxidized, matte rock
crystal (cylindrical form),
onyx, marcasite.
Length 185, width 28 mm.
Stamped" TF (linked)
STERLING GERMANY
B.M. collection.
Lit.: 1931 Christmas sales
brochure shows similar
bracelet, No. 23089, RM 182.-
2.25a Design, suitable for
necklace. Original drawing
7a + b, No. 60, and photo in
Pattern Book VI, Model No.
3127, detailed drawing
without date.

Marcasite Jewelry

2.26

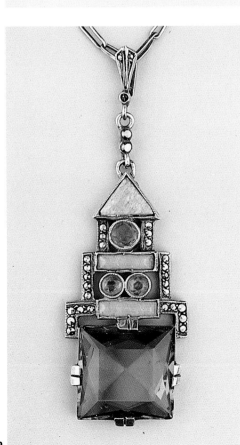

2.29

2.28

2.26 EARRINGS 1926
Silver, black enamel,
amazonite, marcasite.
Height 60, width 10 mm.
Stamped: TF (linked) 935.
Beatrice Ost collection.

2.27 BRACELET 1926
Silver, black enamel, orange-
brown glass stones (?).
marcasite.
Length 180, width 18 mm.
Stamped: TF (linked), 935.
B. M. collection.
The case has also been
preserved; it is marked "Merk
City Magazin" (The firm of
Merk in Pforzheim supplied
the cases for the Braendle
firm).
2.27a Design, Pattern Book I,
Model No. 20286.
Pencil, drawing ink, dated
"10/15/1926", some links
shown.
Comment: "5 links."

2.28 BROOCH 1927
Silver, onyx, coral,
chalcedony.
Height 23, width 45 mm.
Stamped: TF (linked)
STERLING GERMANY.
German private collection.
2.28a Design, Sample Book I,
Model No. 20594.
Pencil, drawing ink, dated
July 12, 1927, drawn life-size.
Lit.: S. Raulet, Schmuck Art
Deco, p. 258, showing
brooch made of different
materials.

2.29 PENDANT 1927
Silver, smoky quartz, gold
topaz, amazonite, marcasite.
Height 60, width 20 mm.
Stamped: TF (linked) 935.
Ursel Gronert collection,
Berlin.
2.29a Design, Sample Book I,
Model No. 20599.
Pencil, drawing ink, dated
"July 12, 1927", drawn
full-size.

2.30 BROOCH 1927
Silver, light blue matte
enamel, amazonite,
marcasite, pearls, the flower
is three-dimensional.
Height 40, width 40 mm.
Stamped: GERMANY
STERLING.
Beatrice Ost collection.
2.30a Design, Pattern Book I,
Model No. 20662.
Pencil, drawing ink, dated
"Aug. 9, 1927", drawn
full-size.

2.27

2.30

2.31 EARRINGS 1927
Silver, onyx, chrysoprase,
marcasite.
Height 65, width 12 mm.
Stamped: TF (linked) 935.
Variant as a brooch.
Pattern Book I, Model No.
20837. (Sept. 1927)
Beatrice Ost collection.

2.32 RING 1928
Silver, onyx, amazonite,
marcasite.
Height 35, width 12 mm (at
head).
Stamped: TF (linked) 935.
Beatrice Ost collection.
2.32a Drawing, Pattern Book
II, Model No. 5429.
Pencil, drawing ink, red and
blue colored pencils, dated
"Nov. 26, 1928", drawn
full-size.

2.33 BROOCH 1928
Silver, smoky quartz,
amazonite, marcasite.
Height 20 (middle), width 65
mm.
Stamped: TF (linked) 935.
Beatrice Ost collection,
Berlin.

2.34 BROOCH ca. 1928
Silver, black matte enamel,
hematite, marcasite.
Height 24, width 65 mm.
Stamped: TF (linked) 935.
Beatrice Ost collection.

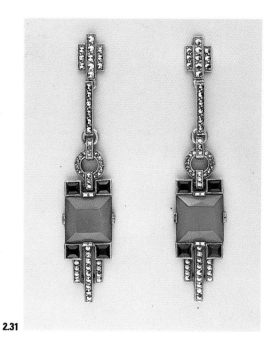

2.31

2.34

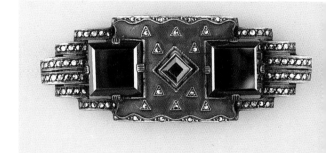

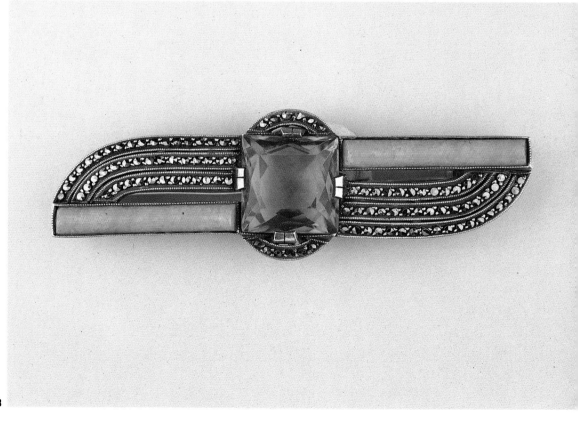

2.32

2.33

2.35

2.37

2.38

2.35 NECKLACE 1930
Silver, onyx, marcasite.
Height 40, width 40 mm
(pendant), half-length 210
mm (chain).
Stamped: TF (linked) 935.
Private collection, Pforzheim.
Lit.: Die Dame, 1930-31, No.
22, inside front cover
(advertisement), photograph
of Mrs. von Stetten wearing
the necklace shown above
(see p. 256).

2.36 CLIP (clothing clip) 1930
Silver, black matte enamel,
onyx, marcasite.
Height 30, width 20 mm.
Stamped: FAHRNER 935.
Private collection, Pforzheim.

2.37 BRACELET ca. 1930
Silver, amazonite (cabochon),
gray-brown agate rings,
marcasite.
Length 200, width 18 mm.
Stamped: TF (linked)
STERLING GERMANY.
German private collection.

2.38 BRACELET ca. 1930
Silver, three-dimensional cut
rose quartz, moonstone,
amazonite, marcasite.
Length 180, width 16 mm.
Stamped: TF (linked) 935.
German private collection.

2.39 TWO CLIPS (clothing
clips) 1931
Silver, marcasite.
Height 30, width 25 mm.
Stamped: TF (linked) Sterling
GERMANY.
Beatrice Ost collection.
2.39a Photo (variation),
Pattern Book VI, Model No.
2662, no date.

2.36

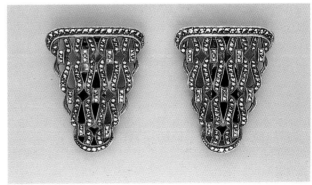

2.39

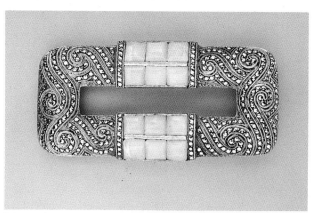

2.41

2.45

2.40 BRACELET ca. 1931
Silver, opals, marcasite.
Length 180, height 15 mm
(link with stones).
Stamped: TF (linked) 935
FAHRNER.
Private collection, Pforzheim.
2.40a Photo, Pattern Book VI,
Model No. 2800, no date.
Lit.: Shown in a sales
brochure of the fifties,
Production Number 2800/2,
"bracelet, genuine opals and
marcasite."

2.41 BROOCH ca. 1930
Designed by Gustav
Braendle, Jr.
Silver, opals, marcasite.
Height 25, width 55 mm.
Stamped: TF (Linked) 925
ORIGINAL FAHRNER (in
octagon).
Private collection, Pforzheim.
2.41a Photo, Pattern Book VI,
Model No. 2834, no date.

2.42 BRACELET 1931
Silver, acid-etched,
amethysts, marcasite.
Length 17.5, width 15 mm.
Stamped: TF (linked) 935
FAHRNER.
Private collection, Pforzheim.
Lit.: A fifties advertisement
shows it as part of a set
consisting of necklace,
earrings, bracelet and ring.
The bracelet is numbered
2730/2 and has the notation
"genuine amethysts and
marcasite."

2.43 TWO CLIPS
(clothing clips) ca.
1931
Silver, pearls,
marcasite.
Height 40, width 25
mm.
Stamped: TF
(linked) 925.
Privately owned,
Stuttgart.

2.44 BROOCH 1932
Silver, cut gold topaz,
marcasite.
Height 15 (middle), width 60
mm.
Stamped: TF (linked) 935.
Private collection, Pforzheim.
2.44a Photo (line drawing),
Pattern Book VI, Model No.
3220, no date.
Lit.: The brooch is shown in a
contemporary photo with
Model No. 23529.

2.45 EARRINGS ca. 1932
Silver, onyx, marcasite.
Height 55, width 10 mm.
Stamped: TF (linked) Sterling
GERMANY.
Beatrice Ost collection.
2.45a Photo, Pattern Book VI,
Model No. 3152, no date.
Lit.: Die Dame, No. 5, 1932-
33, p. 51. The earrings are
part of a set which consists
of a chain, two rings and the
earrings.

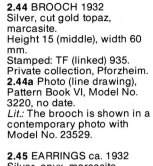

2.44

2.40

2.43

2.42

Evening Jewelry

2.46 NECKLACE ca. 1929
Silver, gilded, soldered
corded wire, matte enamel in
beige, brown and orange-
red, cut smoky quartz.
Length 420 mm.
Stamped: TF (linked) 935.
Private collection, Pforzheim.
Lit.: Die Dame, No. 6, 1929-
30, p. 32 (photo) and
advertisement.

198

2.48 PENDANT 1929
Silver, gilded, soldered with
corded wire; matte enamel in
red, brown, light green, light
blue, three cut smoky quartz.
Height 60, width 27 mm.
Stamped: TF (linked) 935.
Marianne Geitel, Berlin.
Lit.: Die Dame, No. 18, 1929,
p. 54 (advertisement).

2.48

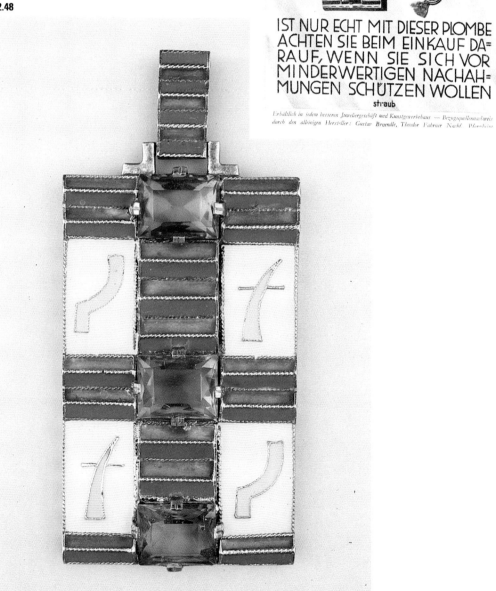

2.47

2.47 BRACELET ca. 1929
Silver, gilded, soldered with
corded wire in zigzag wave
form; matte enamel in ocher,
beige and orange-red, cut
gold topaz, five enameled
rectangular links alternating
with raised rectangular
stones.
Length 200, height 18, width
20 mm (one link).
Stamped: TF (linked) 935.
Marianne Geitel, Berlin.
Lit.: Die Dame, No. 6, 1929-
30, p. 32. The picture of a
bracelet showing the
crosswise enameled links as
raised rectangles.

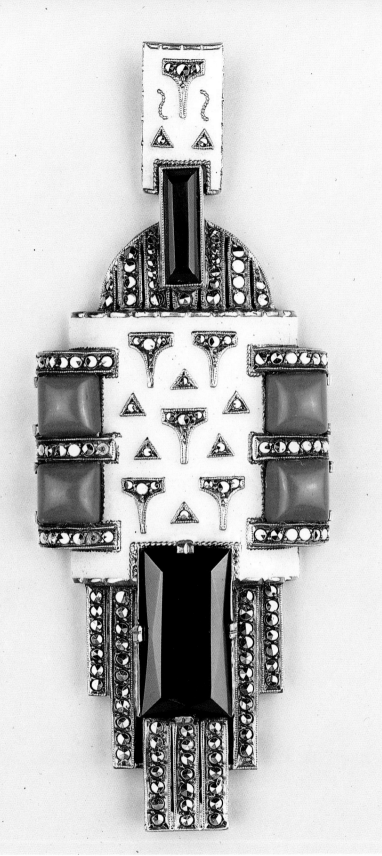

2.50

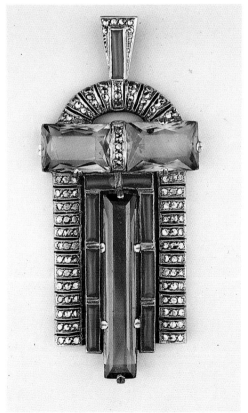

2.51

2.49

2.49 PENDANT ca. 1929
Silver, matte enamel in light
gray, onyx, coral (?),
marcasite.
Height 90, width 10-35 mm.
Stamped: TF (linked) 935.
Marianne Geitel, Berlin.

2.50 PENDANT with chain
ca. 1930
Silver, cut smoky quartz,
amazonite (one stone
replaced by glass), marcasite
Height 80, width 32, length
300 mm (chain).
Stamped: TF (linked)
STERLING GERMANY.
Galerie Torsten Bröhan,
Düsseldorf.

2.51 PENDANT ca. 1930
Silver, smoky quartz, coral,
marcasite.
Height 70, width 45 mm.
Stamped: TF (linked) 935.
Wiener Interieur, Vienna.

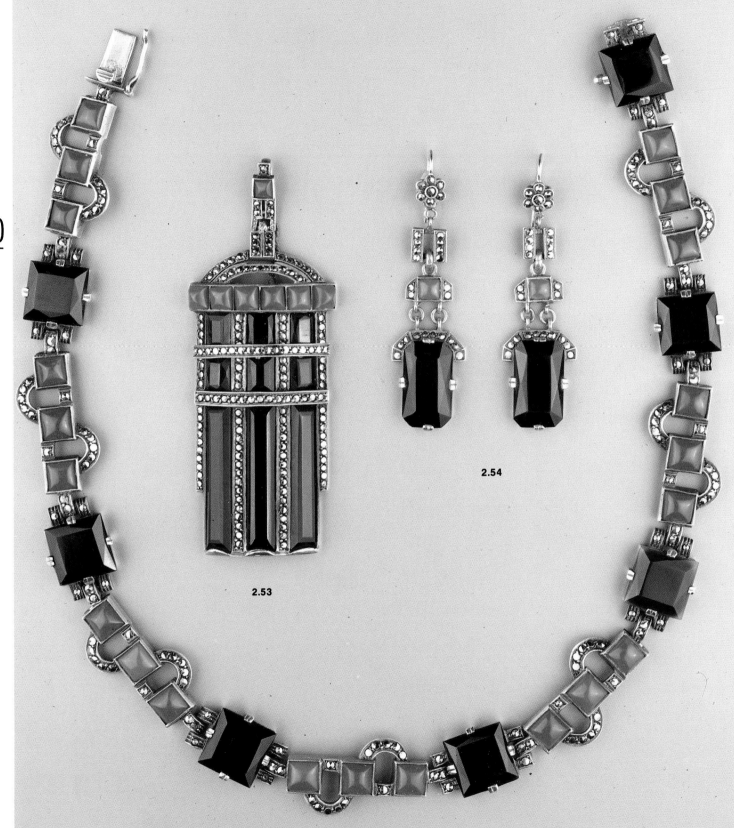

2.53

2.54

2.52

2.55

2.56

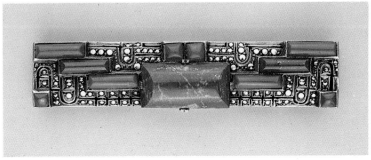

2.58

2.57

2.52 CHAIN ca. 1929
Silver, cut onyx stones, coral
marcasite.
Length 380, width 12 mm.
Stamped: TF (linked) 935,
seal,
"FAHRNER-SCHMUCK."
B. M. Collection.

2.53 PENDANT ca. 1929
Silver, onyx, coral, marcasite.
Height 80 (60), width 28 mm.
Stamped: TF (linked) 935,
seal,
B. M. collection.
Lit.: Die Dame, No. 6, 1929-
30, p. 32, picture with text:
"Silver pendant with genuine
stones and marcasite."

2.54 EARRINGS ca. 1929
Silver, onyx, coral, marcasite.
Height 50, width 10 mm.
Stamped: TF (linked) 935.
B. M. collection.

2.55 PENDANT with chain
ca. 1930
Designed by Gustav
Braendle, Jr.
(similar design, original
drawing 3, No. 22)
Silver, matte rock crystal,
hematite, marcasite.
Height 65, width 5 to 35 mm
(pendant), length 440 mm
(chain).
Stamped: TF (linked) 935.
B. M. collection.

2.56 EARRINGS ca. 1930
Silver, matte rock crystal,
hematite, marcasite.
Height 55, width 10 mm.
Stamped: TF (linked) 935.
Beatrice Ost collection.

2.57 BRACELET ca. 1930
Silver, matte gray enamel,
lapis lazuli, coral, marcasite.
Length 210, width 13 mm.
Stamped: TF (linked) 935.
Beatrice Ost collection.

2.58 BROOCH ca. 1930
Designed by Gustav
Braendle, Jr.
Silver, lapis lazuli, coral,
marcasite.
Height 15, width 67 mm.
Stamped: TF (linked) 935.
Beatrice Ost collection.
2.58a Design, original
drawing 8, variation.

2.59

2.63

2.59 NECKLACE ca. 1930
Silver, lapis lazuli, marcasite.
Height 55, width 25 mm
(center).
Stamped: STERLING TF
(linked) GERMANY.
German private collection.

2.60 BRACELET ca. 1930
Silver, onyx, marcasite.
Length 185, width 15 mm.
Stamped: Sterling GERMANY
FAHRNER TF (linked) 925,
also F. German private
collection.

2.61 RING ca. 1930
Silver, onyx, marcasite.
Height 25, width 15 mm (head
of ring).
Stamped: TF (linked) 333 9
CT (bar replaced).
Beatrice Ost collection.

2.62 RING ca. 1930
Silver, carnelian, onyx,
marcasite.
Height 32, width 13 mm (head
of ring).
Stamped: TF (linked) 935.
B. M. collection.

2.63 NECKLACE 1930
Designed by Gustav
Braendle, Jr.
Silver, hematite, marcasite.
Height 70, width 18 to 35 mm.
Stamped: TF (linked) 935 TF
(linked) STERLING
GERMANY.
Flesser collection, Hof.
2.63a Design, original
drawing 7a + b, No. 60,
variations.

2.60

2.65

2.64

2.66

2.67

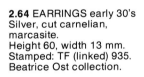

2.64 EARRINGS early 30's
Silver, cut carnelian,
marcasite.
Height 60, width 13 mm.
Stamped: TF (linked) 935.
Beatrice Ost collection.

2.65 NECKLACE early 30's
Silver, cut carnelian,
marcasite.
Height 38 (center), diameter
135 mm.
Stamped: TF (linked)
STERLING GERMANY.
German private collection.

2.66 BRACELET early 30's
Silver, cut carnelian,
marcasite.
Length 180, width 20 mm.
Stamped: TF (linked)
STERLING GERMANY.
German private collection.

2.67 BROOCH 1927
Silver, cut carnelian,
marcasite.
Height 40, width 50 mm.
Stamped: TF (linked)
STERLING GERMANY.
German private collection.
2.67a Design, Pattern Book I,
Model No. 20557.
Pencil, drawing ink, dated
"June 2, 1927", drawn
full-size.

2.61

2.62

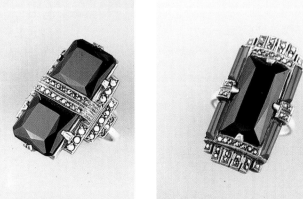

Matte Enamel Without Stones

2.68 PENDANT 1927
Silver, gilded, soldered with corded and smooth wire in circles and lines; matte enamel in blue, green, red-brown, enameled flowers and waves.
Height 60, width 18 mm.
Stamped: TF (linked) 935.
Marianne Geitel, Berlin.
2.68a Design
Pattern Book I, Model No. 20809.
Pencil, drawing ink, blue and red colored pencils.
Dated "Sept. 5, 1927", drawn full-size.

2.69 EARRINGS 1927
Silver, gilded, soldered with corded and smooth wire in circles and lines; flowers and waves in matte enamel, golden brown, blue, turquoise.
Height 60, width 18 mm.
Stamped: TF (linked) 935.
The decor of the earrings matches the 2.68 pendant; the matte enamel surfaces are made in other colors.
Beatrice Ost collection.
2.69a Design
Pattern book I, Model No. 20809.
Pencil, drawing ink, blue and red colored pencil.
Dated "Sept. 5, 1927", drawn full-size.

2.70 EARRINGS 1927
Silver, gilded, soldered with corded wire circles, matte enamel in red and beige (dots, stripes, segment arcs).
Height 55, width 18 mm.
Stamped: TF (linked) STERLING GERMANY.
The form of the earrings matches Cat. No. 2.69.
Beatrice Ost collection.
2.70a Design, Pattern Book I, Model No. 20826.
Pencil, drawing ink, blue and red colored pencils.
Dated "Sept. 12, 1927", drawn full-size.

2.71 EARRINGS ca. 1927
Silver, gilded, soldered with corded wire in circles and as frames for the enamel fields, matte enamel in blue, brown and turquoise in V-shape, turquoise pearls.
Height 43 mm.
Stamped: TF (linked) 935.
Marianne Geitel, Berlin.

2.72 CHAIN late 20's
Silver, gilded, soldered with corded wire in parallel lines, matte enamel in beige (rectangle) and brown (square).
19 square links linked by wire loops.
Length 380 mm.
Stamped" TF (linked) 935.
Marianne Geitel, Berlin.

2.73 CHAIN late 20's
Silver, gilded, soldered with corded wires in parallel lines, matte enamel in green (rectangle) and black (square).
Seven square links in the middle, the other links of flat oval metal.
See Cat. No. 2.72.
Marianne Geitel, Berlin.

2.68

2.69

2.70

2.74

2.76

2.71

2.77

2.75

2.74 CHAIN late 20's
Silver, gilded, coarse graining, soldered with corded wire, matte enamel in red and beige. The chain consists of slim rectangular links, with seven horseshoe-shaped links in front, hung by wire rings.
Height 50 mm (one link).
Stamped: TF (obliterated).
Marianne Geitel, Berlin.

2.75 BRACELET late 20's.
Form and material match Cat. No. 2.74.
Matte enamel in black and light green.
Length 180, height 50 mm (one link).
Stamped: TF (linked), STERLING (?)
Antiquarius Gromotka/Dr. Westermeier, Munich.

2.76 EARRINGS late 20's
Material as Cat. No. 2.74.
Matte enamel in black and red.
Height 50, width 15 mm.
Stamped: TF (linked) STERLING.
B. M. collection.

2.77 BROOCH ca. 1930
Silver, five diagonal silver crossbars, soldered with corded wire, matte enamel in light blue, gray and red.
Height 8, width 60 mm.
Stamped: TF (linked) 935.
Marianne Geitel, Berlin.

Matte Enamel With Stones

2.78 BRACELET 1927
Silver, soldered with corded wire, black matte enamel, marcasite, red corals.
Length 210, width 17 mm.
Stamped: STERLING TF (linked).
Privately owned.
2.78a Design, Pattern Book I, Model No. 20503.
Pencil, black drawing ink. Dated "May 2, 1927" (cutout).

2.79 BROOCH 1927
Silver, gilded, soldered with corded wire, black matte enamel, marcasite, amazonite.
Height 20 (center), width 60 mm.
Stamped: TF (linked) 935.
Private collection, Pforzheim.
2.79a Design, Pattern Book I, Model No. 20512.
Pencil, drawing ink. Dated "May 2, 1927", drawn full-size.

2.80 BROOCH 1927
Silver, soldered with corded wire, light blue matte enamel, marcasite, amazonite.
Height 22 (middle), width 45 mm.
Stamped: TF (linked) 935.
G. Silzer collection, Hannover.
2.80a Design, Pattern Book I, Model No. 20499.
Pencil, black drawing ink. Dated "May 2, 1927."
Drawn full-size.

2.81 BROOCH 1927
Silver, gilded, soldered with corded wire, red matte enamel, hematite, turquoise.
Height 16, width 55 mm.
Stamped: STERLING GERMANY.
Antiquarius Gromotka/Dr. Westermeier, Munich.
2.81a Design, Pattern Book I, Model No. 20717.
Pencil, drawing ink, colored pencil. Dated "Aug. 26, 1927." Drawn full-size.

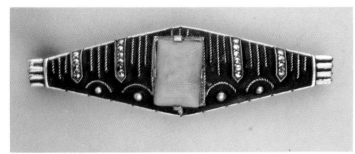

2.79

2.80

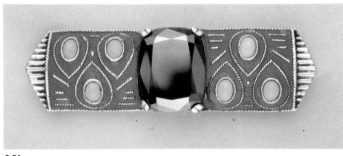

2.81

2.82

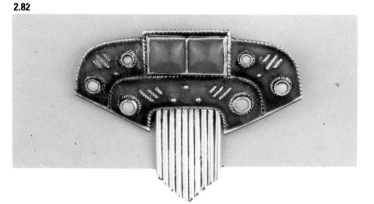

2.89

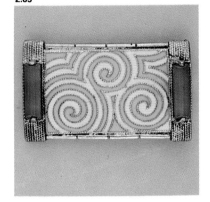

2.83

2.84

2.87

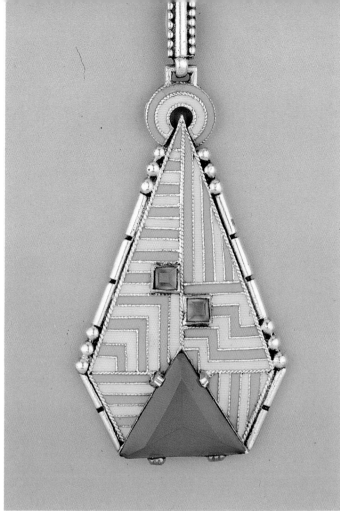

2.85

2.88

2.86

2.82 BROOCH 1927
Silver, gilded, turquoise, brown matte enamel.
Height 30 (middle), width 40 mm.
Stamped: TF (linked) 935 and "Original Fahrner" seal.
Gift of Gustav Braendle, 1931.
City Museum in the Prediger, Schwäbisch Gmünd, Inv. No. 1959 / G 2407.
2.82a Design, Pattern Book I, Model No. 20750.
Pencil, black drawing ink. Dated "Aug. 26, 1927." Drawn full-size.

2.83 RING ca. 1927
Silver, gilded, soldered with corded wire, smoky quartz, turquoise, brown matte enamel.
Height 25, width 20 mm.
Stamped: TF (linked) 935 and "Original Fahrner" seal.
Gift of Gustav Braendle, 1931.
City Museum in the Prediger, Schwäbisch Gmünd, Inv. No. 1959 / G 2402.

2.84 RING 1928
Silver, soldered with corded wire, matte enamel in black, yellow and white, two chalcedony (?)
Height 28, width 10 mm (head of ring).
Unsigned (the bar was replaced).
Marianne Geitel, Berlin.
2.84a Design, Pattern Book II, Model No. 5404.
Pencil, drawing ink, blue and red colored pencils.
No date (ca. October 1928), drawn full-size.

2.85 PENDANT ca. 1928
Silver, soldered with corded wire, matte enamel in light green, light blue, green glass stones.
Height 50, width 27 mm.
Stamped: TF (linked) 935.
Marianne Geitel, Berlin.

2.86 BRACELET 1928
Silver, soldered with corded wire in parallel lines, coral and lapis lazuli bars, 8 square links.
Length 180, link 18 x 18 mm.
Stamped: TF (linked) 935.
Marianne Geitel, Berlin.

2.87 RING 1928
Silver, corded wire, red enamel, hematite.
Height 25, width 13 mm.
Stamped: TF (obliterated) 835. (935?)
Astrid and Rainer Schill, Heilbronn.
2.87a Design, Pattern Book II, Model No. 5421.
Pencil, drawing ink, red, yellow and blue colored pencils.
Dated "Nov. 22, 1928." Drawn full-size.

2.88 BROOCH ca. 1928
Silver, gilded, soldered with corded wire in parallel lines, black (gloss, originally matte) enamel, marcasite triangles, three cut onyx stones. The brooch consists of two rectangles linked together, slightly displaced.
Height 25 (middle), width 55 mm.
Stamped: TF (linked) 935.
B. M. collection.

2.89 BROOCH ca. 1929
Silver, gilded, soldered with corded wire in spirals and parallel lines, matte enamel in light green and light blue, two green stones (colored agate?).
Height 25, width 40 mm.
Stamped: TF (linked) 935.
Marianne Geitel, Berlin.

2.90

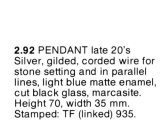

2.91

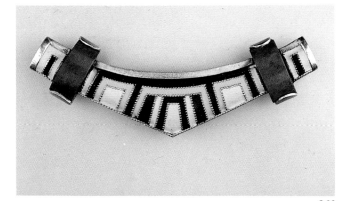

2.96

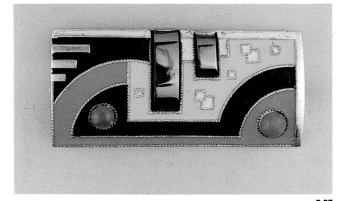

2.97

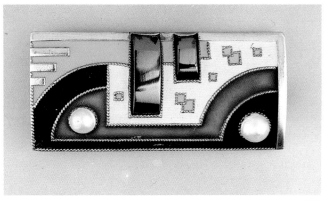

2.98

2.90 BRACELET ca. 1929
Silver, gilded, soldered with
corded wire in spirals, white
and gray matte enamel in
spirals, high rectangular fiels
broken by carnelian.
Length 190, height 30, width
20 mm (one link).
Stamped: TF (linked) 935.
Marianne Geitel, Berlin.
Lit.: Die Dame, No. 8, 1929-
30, p. 55, picture in an
advertisement.

2.91 PENDANT late 20's
Silver, gilded, soldered with
corded wire lines and raised
spirals, rough graining, matte
enamel in black and green,
smoky quartz.
Height 45, width 35 mm.
Stamped: TF (linked) 935.
Württemberg State Museum,
Stuttgart, Inv. No. 1986-109.

2.92 PENDANT late 20's
Silver, gilded, corded wire for
stone setting and in parallel
lines, light blue matte enamel,
cut black glass, marcasite.
Height 70, width 35 mm.
Stamped: TF (linked) 935.
Marianne Geitel, Berlin.

2.93 PENDANT late 20's
Silver, gilded, soldered with
corded wire, beige and
orange-red matte enamel, cut
citrine quartz.
Height 70, width 27 mm.
Stamped: TF (linked) 935.
Marianne Geitel, Berlin.
Lit.: Ketterer Auction Cat. No
82, May 1984m p. 180, No.
831.

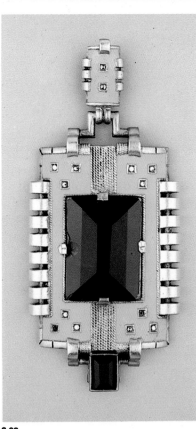

2.92

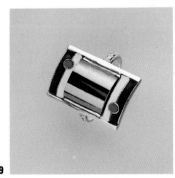

2.99

2.93

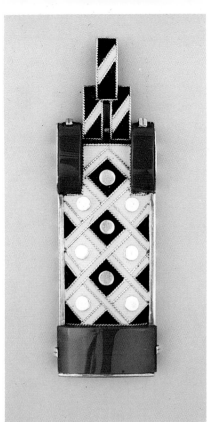

2.94

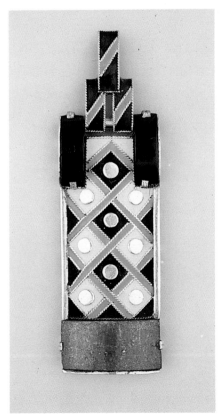

2.95

2.94 PENDANT ca. 1930
Silver, gilded, soldered with
corded wire, small flat metal
points, matte enamel in black,
pale yellow and lemon
yellow, three carnelians.
Height 75, width 22 mm.
Stamped: TF (linked) 935.
Marianne Geitel, Berlin.

2.95 PENDANT ca. 1930
Variation of Cat. No. 2.94.
Matte enamel in black, beige,
salmon, lapis lazuli, black
colored agate (?)
Height 75, width 22 mm.
Marianne Geitel, Berlin.

2.96 BROOCH ca. 1930
Silver, gilded, matte enamel
in beige and light blue, lapis
lazuli.
Width 60 mm.
Stamped: TF 935.
Astrid and Rainer Schill,
Heilbronn.

2.97 BROOCH ca. 1930
Designed by Gustav
Braendle, Jr.
Silver, soldered with corded
wire, matte enamel in black,
yellow, light and dark blue,
two corals, two hematite.
Height 25, width 50 mm.
Stamped: TF (linked) 935.
Marianne Geitel, Berlin.
2.97a Design original
drawing 5, No. 35, variations.

2.98 BROOCH 1930
Designed by Gustav
Braendle, Jr.
Variation of Cat. No. 2.97.
Matte enamel in black,
brown, beige, light blue,
pearls.
Marianne Geitel, Berlin.
2.98a Design, compare Cat.
No. 2.97a.

2.99 RING 1930
Designed by Gustav
Braendle, Jr.
Silver, matte enamel in black
and turquoise (stripes), red
(dots), hematite, the enamel
fields are surrounded by fine
corded wire, the ring bar is
decorated.
Height 20, width 13 mm (head
of ring).
Stamped: TF (linked) DEA
935.
Marianne Geitel, Berlin.
2.99a Design, Pattern Book II,
Model No. 5595.
Pencil, drawing ink, yellow
and blue pencils.
Dated "Jan. 15, 1930", drawn
full-size.
Original drawing 2, No. 10,
variations.

2.100

Matte Enamel Triangles

2.101

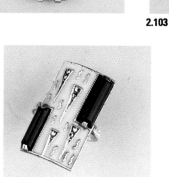

2.103

2.100 EARRINGS 1927
Silver, soldered with corded wire, red matte enamel, marcasite, onyx.
Height 35 (without attachment), 55 overall, width 20 mm.
Stamped: TF (linked) 935.
Beatrice Ost collection.

2.101 PENDANT 1927
Silver, gilded, soldered with corded wire, red matte enamel, marcasite, onyx.
Height 50, width 18 mm.
Stamped: TF (linked) 935.
Marianne Geitel, Berlin.
2.101a Design, Pattern Book I, Model No. 20520.
Pencil, black drawing ink.
Dated "May 5, 1927", drawn full-size.

2.102 RING 1928
Silver, soldered with corded wire, light green matte enamel, marcasite, onyx.
Height 25, width 15 mm (head of ring).
Unsigned.
Marianne Geitel, Berlin.
2.102a Design, Pattern Book II, Model No. 5419.
Pencil, drawing ink, red and blue pencils.
Dated November 1928, drawn full-size.

2.103 PENDANT ca. 1929
Silver, gilded, soldered with corded wire in parallel lines and as settings of stones and enamel, matte enamel in beige, brown and red (chevrons), three topaz.
Height 45, width 25 mm.
Stamped: TF (linked) 935.
Marianne Geitel, Berlin.

2.104 RING 1929
Silver, gilded, soldered with corded wire as settings of stones and enamel, matte enamel in brown, green, light blue and black (chevrons and rectangles), black glass stones.
Height 24, width 17 mm (head of ring).
Unsigned (bar was replaced).
Marianne Geitel, Berlin.
2.104a Design, Pattern Book II, Model No. 5491.
Pencil, drawing ink, red, yellow and blue pencils.
Dated "May 7, 1929", drawn full-size.
Pendant (Cat. No. 2.103 and ring (2.104 were part of a series, as shown by the decor and lateral edge formation.

2.105 BRACELET ca. 1929
Silver, soldered with corded wire around enamel, matte enamel in beige, black, red and light blue (diagonal wavy

2.102   **2.104**

2.106

2.105

lines, triangles), seven rectangular links, originally eight.
Length 180, link height 18, width 20 mm.
Stamped: TF (linked) 935.
Compare decor of Cat. No. 2.103.
Marianne Geitel, Berlin.

2.106 RING 1929
Silver, gilded, soldered with corded wire and grained triangles, yellow and black matte enamel, two lapis lazuli squares, red glass ball.
Height 18, width 22 mm (head of ring).
Stamped: TF (linked) DEA 935.
Marianne Geitel, Berlin.
2.106a Design, Pattern Book II, Model No. 5485.
Pencil, drawing ink, red, yellow and blue pencils (identical to actual piece).
Dated "April 25, 1929", drawn full-size.

2.107 PENDANT 1928-1929
Silver, gilded, soldered with corded wire, rough graining, gray and red matte enamel, three red glass stones, smoky quartz, marcasite.
Height 65, width 25 mm.
Stamped: TF (linked) 935.
Württemberg State Museum, Stuttgart, Inv. No. 1986-120.
Lit.: Die Dame, Vol. 56, 1929, No. 17, p. 39 (same decor).

2.107

2.110

Matte Enamel Oriental Style

2.108

2.109

2.108 BROOCH 1927
Silver, gilded, soldered with corded wire (flowers and waves), turquoise and brown matte enamel, smoky quartz, coral, coarse grain.
Height 25, width 38 mm.
Stamped: TF (linked) 935.
Antiquarius Gromotka/Dr. Westermeier, Munich.
2.108a Design, Pattern Book I, Model No. 20923.
Pencil, drawing ink. Dated "Sept. 24, 1927", drawn full-size.

2.109 BROOCH 1927
Silver, gilded, soldered with corded wires (flowers and waves), turquoise and brown matte enamel, smoky quartz, coral, coarse grain forming hexagonal outline of brooch.
Height 40, width 48 mm.
Stamped: TF (linked) 935.
See Pattern Book I, Model No. 20921, "Sept. 24, 1927."
German private collection.

2.110 PENDANT with chain 1927
Silver, gilded, soldered with corded wire (flowers and waves), red-brown and salmon matte enamel, light blue glass (triangles), turquoise, corded wire fringe.
Height 75, width 45 mm (pendant), length 360 mm (chain).
Stamped: STERLING GERMANY.
Private collection, Pforzheim.
2.110a Design, Pattern Book I, Model No. 20936.
Green and blue colored pencils.
Dated Sept, 1927, drawn full-size.

2.111 BRACELET 1927
Silver, gilded, soldered with corded wire (flowers and waves), black, blue and turquoise matte enamel, amazonite, marcasite, wire also in circles. The bracelet consists of five square and five rectangular links.
Length 180, width 24 mm.
Stamped: TF (linked) 935.
Galerie Urlass, Frankfurt.
2.111a Design, Pattern Book I, Model No. 20902.
Pencil, drawing ink, green and blue pencils.
Dated "Sept. 1927", drawn full-size (one link).

2.111

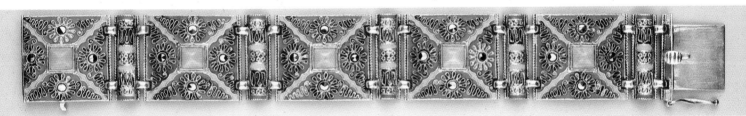

2.112

Matte Enamel Spiral Motifs

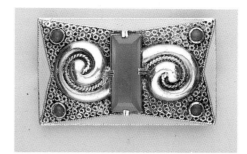

2.113

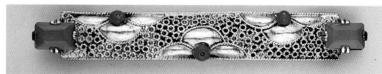

2.114

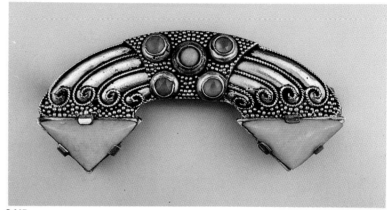

2.115

2.112 BROOCH 1926
Silver, gilded, turquoise
matrix, marcasite.
Height 33, width 33 mm.
Stamped: TF (linked) 935.
Antiquarius, Gromotka/Dr.
Westermeier, Munich.
2.112a Design, Pattern Book
I, Model No. 20230.
Drawing ink. Dated before
8/30/1926. Drawn full-size.

2.113 BROOCH ca. 1926
Silver, gilded, soldered with
corded wire in circles and as
settings for the stones, three-
dimensional spirals on both
sides of a blue glass stone,
four corals, turquoise matte
enamel in triangles along the
edges.
Height 25, width 40 mm.
Stamped: TF (linked) 935.
German private collection.

2.114 BROOCH 1926
Silver, gilded, soldered with
corded wire, partly in circles,
three corals, blue cut glass
rectangle, three half-flowers
as decor.
Height 13, length 70 mm.
Stamped: TF (linked) 935.
Marianne Geitel, Berlin.

2.114a Design, Pattern Book
I, Model No. 20266.
Pencil, black drawing ink.
Dated "9/22/26."
In the design, the rectangular
stones are replaced by round
ones but it is noted (also)
with outer cornered stones.
Both variations were
produced.

2.115 BROOCH 1927
Silver, gilded, amazonite,
chalcedony, soldered with
corded wire, grained.
Height 30, width 55 mm.
Stamped: TF (linked) 935 and
"Original Fahrner" seal.
Present from Gustav
Braendle, 1931.
City Museum in the Prediger,
Schwäbisch Gmünd, Inv. No.
1959/G 2406.
2.115a Design, Pattern Book
I, Model No. 20647.
Pencil, drawing ink. Dated
"Aug. 3, 1927." Drawn
full-size.

2.116

2.117

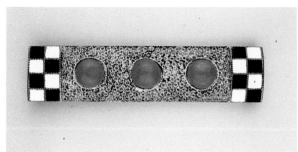

2.118

2.119

2.116 NECKLACE 1928
Silver, gilded, soldered with corded wire and coarse graining, black and white (circles) matte enamel, coral, lapis lazuli. It consists of four square and four raised rectangular links, connected by two rows of chain.
Length 365, links 27 x 27 or 25 x 15 mm.
Stamped: TF (linked) 935.
See same ring motif of Model No. 5373, dated "6/5/1928" (Pattern Book II).
Privately owned.

2.117 EARRINGS 1928
Silver, gilded, soldered with corded wire and graining, golden brown and turquoise matte enamel, two cut gold topaz, turquoise. The central part is shaped like a shield, and metal bars hang down from the bottom of it, forming a point.
Height 57, width 20 mm.
Stamped: TF (linked) 935.
Beatrice Ost collection.

2.118 BROOCH 1928
Silver, gilded, soldered with corded wire in circles and around squares, black and white matte enamel, three corals.
Height 12, length 55 mm.
Stamped: TF (linked) 935.
See Pattern Book II, Model No. 5395, June 1928.
Marianne Geitel, Berlin.
Lit.: Christie's Auction Catalog, Twentieth Century Decorative Arts, Geneva, Nov. 12, 1989; No. 189 is a pendant with the same checkerboard pattern.

2.119 PENDANT late 20's
Silver, gilded, soldered with corded wire in circles and around the enamel, dark and light blue matte enamel, blue glass stone.
Height 55, width 22 mm.
Stamped: TF (linked) 935.
Marianne Geitel, Berlin.
The same pendant in form, with black and blue matte enamel and smoky quartz, is in the Museum of Commercial Art, East Berlin, Inv. No. 1979, 177.

2.121

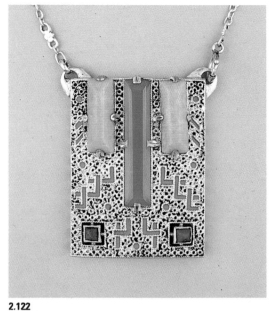

2.122

2.123

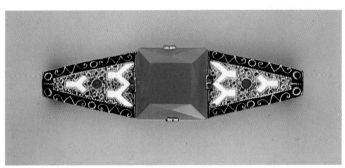

2.120

2.120 BROOCH late 20's
Silver, gilded, soldered with
corded wire in circles and
free lines, black matte
enamel edges, dots and Y-
shapes in white and red
matte enamel, a blue cut
glass stone in the center.
Height 16 (middle), width 60
mm.
Stamped: TF (linked) 935.
Marianne Geitel, Berlin.

2.121 PENDANT late 20's
Silver, gilded, soldered with
corded wire in circles, free
lines and around the enamel,
green, blue, salmon large cut
smoky quartz.
Height 50, width 25 mm.
Stamped: TF (linked) 935.
Marianne Geitel, Berlin.

2.122 PENDANT late 20's
Silver, gilded, soldered with
corded wire in circles and
around the enamel and
stones, two amazonite, lapis
lazuli, light blue glass stone,
blue matte enamel (chevrons
and dots).
Height 45, width 32 mm.
Stamped: TF (linked) 935.
Marianne Geitel, Berlin.

2.123 PENDANT late 20's
Silver, gilded, corded wire in circles and around the light green geometric enamel fields (dots, semicircles, rectangles, L-shapes), white gloss enamel, black glass squares.
Height 70, width 30.
Stamped: TF (linked).
Marianne Geitel, Berlin.

2.124 PENDANT with chain late 20's
Silver, soldered with corded wire and graining, red and black matte enamel, smoky quartz.
Height 50, width 28 mm below, 13 mm above.
Chain length 390 mm.
Stamped: TF (linked) 935 (pendant), 925 (chain).
Beatrice Ost collection.

2.125 PENDANT late 20's
Silver, gilded, soldered with corded wire, coarse graining, matte enamel in red and black (rectangles, triangles), lapis lazuli, coral and turquoise.
Height 58, width 27 mm.
Stamped: TF (linked) 935.
Marianne Geitel, Berlin.

2.124

2.125

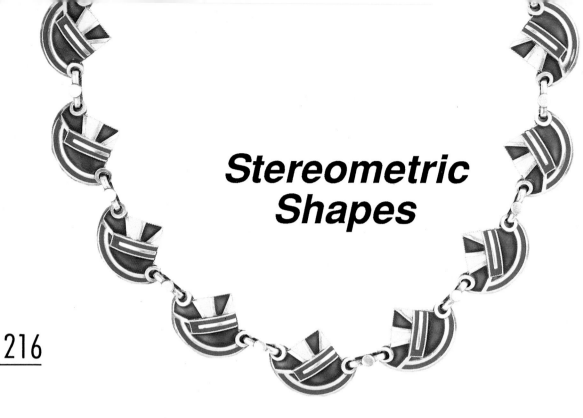

Stereometric Shapes

2.126 PENDANT late 20's
Silver, corded wire, black
matte enamel, two
rectangular carnelians,
raised metal bars.
Height 80, width 27 mm.
Stamped: TF (linked) 935.
Marianne Geitel, Berlin.

2.127 CHAIN ca. 1930
Silver, gilded, soldered with
corded wire, metal bars, red,
brown and beige matte
enamel, fourteen links in the
form of quarter-circles.
Length 400 mm.
Stamped: TF (linked) 935.
Marianne Geitel, Berlin.

2.126

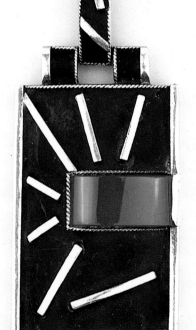

2.129

2.130

2.132

2.128

2.131

2.128 NECKLACE ca. 1930
Design attributed to Gustav
Braendle, Jr.
(Similar design, original
drawing 6, No. 50)
Silver, gilded, matte enamel
in black, red, ocher, light
blue, onyx.
Length 500 mm.
Stamped: TF (linked) 935.
Wiener Interieure, Vienna.
Lit.: Die Dame Vol. 56, 1929-
30, shown with the same
links, other decor
(advertisement).

2.129 BROOCH ca. 1930
Silver, gilded, matte enamel
in red, black, light blue,
brown, lapis lazuli.
Height 15, width 60 mm.
Stamped: TF 935.
Astrid and Rainer Schill,
Heilbronn.

2.130 BROOCH 1930
Designed by Gustav
Braendle, Jr.
Silver, lapis lazuli, red matte
enamel.
Height 15, width 65 mm.
Stamped: TF (linked) 935.
E. L. collection
2.130a Design, original
drawing 8, pencil sketch.

2.131 PENDANT with chain
ca. 1930
Silver, light blue and black
matte enamel, onyx.
Length 220 (chain), diameter
35 mm (pendant).
Stamped: TF (linked) 935.
Gabriela Arnold collection.

2.132 BROOCH 1930
Designed by Gustav
Braendle, Jr.
Silver, blue matte enamel,
onyx.
Height 15, width 50 mm.
Stamped: TF (linked) 935.
Beatrice Ost collection.

2.132a Design, original
drawing 2, No. 8.

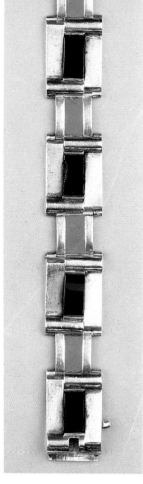

2.133

2.137

2.134

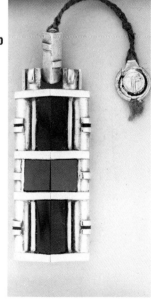

2.140

2.138

2.141

2.133 BRACELET ca. 1930
Silver, blue matte enamel,
onyx.
Length 200, height 15 mm.
Stamped: TF (linked) 935.
Private collection, Pforzheim.

2.134 PENDANT late 20's
With original silk cord.
Silver, black matte enamel,
turquoise enamel dots, two
round cut topaz.
Height 40, width 22 mm.
Stamped: ORIGINAL
FAHRNER (in octagon) 935.
Marianne Geitel, Berlin.

2.135 Pendant ca. 1930
Designed by Gustav
Braendle
With original silk cord.
Silver, black and red matte
enamel, three black glass
stones (colored agate?).
Slider attached to silk cord.
Height 60, width 20 mm.
Stamped: TF (linked)
STERLING GERMANY
Marianne Geitel, Berlin.
2.135a Design, original
drawing 11, variations.

2.136 BROOCH 1930
Designed by Gustav
Braendle, Jr.
Silver, beige, red and black
matte enamel, hematite as
raised ball, soldered with
corded wire, brooch formed
as triangle.
Lides 50 and 60 mm, ends 25
mm.
Stamped: TF (linked) 935.
See use of hematite ball on
Cat. No. 2.146.
Beatrice Ost collection.

2.136a Design, original
drawing 7 a & b, No. 59.

2.137 EARRINGS ca. 1930
Silver, coral, one clip
replaced.
Height 50, width 10 mm.
Stamped: TF (linked) 935.

Württemberg State Museum,
Stuttgart, Inv. No. 1986-119a,
b.
Lit.: Die Dame, Vol. 57, No. 5,
1930-31, p. 38.

2.135

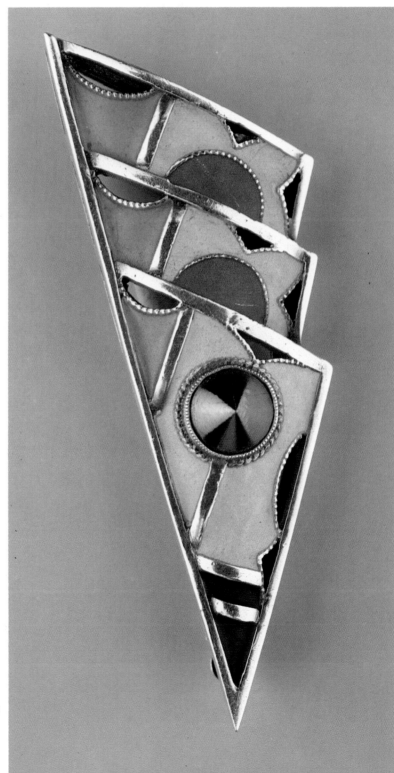

2.136

2.139 BRACELET ca. 1932
(not illustrated)
Silver, light blue matte
enamel, partly gilded.
Length 180, width 11 mm.
Stamped: TF 935.
Astrid and Rainer Schill,
Heilbronn.

2.140 PENDANT 1930
Designed by Gustav
Braendle, Jr.
Silver, smoky quartz.
Height 58, width 20 mm.
Stamped: TF (linked) 935,
with Fahrner seal.
Württemberg State Museum,
Stuttgart, Inv. No. 1986-116.
2.140a Design, original
drawing 11, variations.

2.141 PENDANT 1930-31
Silver, onyx, light blue matte
enamel.
Height 75, width 25 mm.
Stamped: ORIGINAL
FAHRNER 935.
Württemberg State Museum,
Stuttgart, Inv. No. 1986-117.
Lit.: Die Dame, Vol. 57, 1930-
31, advertisement, Model No.
23033, price RM 34.-

2.138 CHAIN 1931
Silver, oxidized, light brown
matte enamel, green glass
stone, three ornamental
hangings in front, the central
one in shield form, the others
square. The links of the
chain consist of flat rings and
oblong loops.
Length 420 mm.
Stamped: ORIGINAL
FAHRNER 935.
Württemberg State Museum,
Stuttgart, Inv. No. 1986-98.
2.138a Design, Pattern Book
IV, Model No. 1101.
Pencil, drawing ink. Dated
"Nov. 25, 1931."

2.143

2.144

2.142

2.148

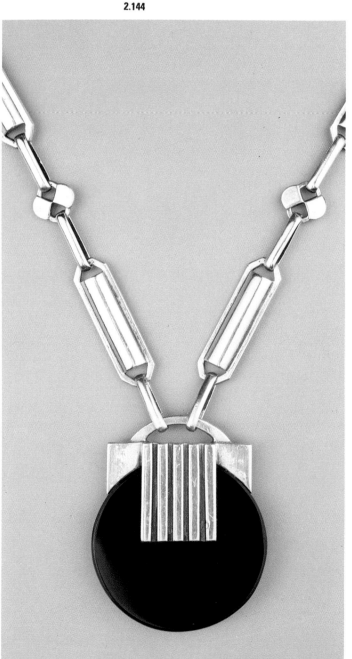

2.142 RING 1930
Silver, black matte enamel,
hematite.
Height 25, width 10 mm (head
of ring).
Stamped: TF (linked) 935.
Hans-Peter Callsen,
Bobb.2.142a: Design, Pattern
Book II, Model No. 5662.
Drawing ink, red pencil.
Dated "March 26, 1930."
Drawn full-size.

2.143 PENDANT ca. 1930
Silver, black matte enamel,
onyx.
Height 70 (52), width 20 mm.
Stamped: TF (linked) 935.
B. M. collection.
Lit.: Der Querschnitt, spring
1930, similar pendants in an
advertisement.

2.144 PENDANT ca. 1930
Silver, corded wire, black
matte enamel, hematite.
Height 60, width 18 mm.
Stamped: TF 935.
Astrid and Rainer Schill,
Heilbronn.

2.145 PENDANT ca. 1930
Silver, corded wire, black
matte enamel, hematite.
Height 64, width 20 mm.
Stamped: TF 935.
Astrid and Rainer Schill,
Heilbronn.

2.146 RING 1930
Designed by Gustav
Braendle, Jr.
Silver, black matte enamel,
hematite as raised ball.
Height 15, width 10 mm (head
of ring).
Stamped: TF (linked) 935.
Compare use of a hematite
ball on Cat. No. 2.136.
Flesser collection, Hof.
2.146a Design, original
drawing 7a + b, No. 57, with
similar cuff links.
Pattern Book II, Model No.
5649.
Pencil, drawing ink, red
pencil. Dated "March 12,
1930", drawn life-size.

2.150

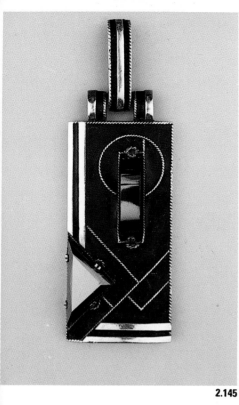

2.145   2.147

2.146

2.149

2.147 PENDANT 1930
Designed by Gustav
Braendle, Jr.
Silver, soldered with corded
wire, metal bars, black matte
enamel, matte rock crystal,
onyx.
Height 45, lower width 24
mm.
Stamped: TF (linked) 935.
B. M. collection.
2.147a Design, original
drawing 5, No. 41, variations.

2.148 PENDANT with chain
ca. 1930
Silver, onyx
Length 300 (chain), height 35
mm (pendant).
Unsigned.
Privately owned by a former
Braendle employee.

2.149 PENDANT with chain
ca. 1930
Silver, black enamel, onyx.
Height 40, width 20 mm
(pendant), length 180 mm
(chain).
Stamped: TF (linked) 935.
B. M. collection.

2.150 CHAIN ca. 1930
Silver, black matte enamel.
Length 380 (chain), height 35
mm (one ornament).
Stamped: TF (linked) 935.
Württemberg State Museum,
Stuttgart, Inv. No. 1986-95.

2.151 CHAIN 1932
Silver, onyx.
Length 420, height 15, width
10 mm (one ornament).
Stamped: DEA 935.
Württemberg State Museum,
Stuttgart, Inv. No. 1986-97.
2.151a Design (photocopy),
Pattern Book III, Model No.
279.
Dated February 1932.
Comment: "Chain 69 every
10 hrs. Strength 300 No., Ges.
250."
Lit.: Die Schaulade, Vol, 7,
1931, No. 2, p. 117.
Reference to DEA rings.

2.151

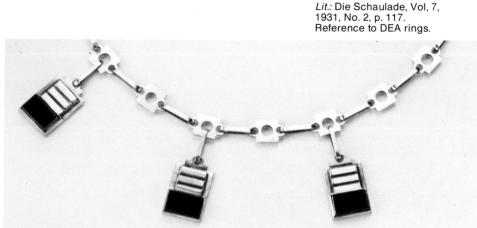

Men's Jewelry

2.152 CHATELAINE late 20's
Silver, gilded, corded wire,
coarse graining, red and gray
(semicircles) matte enamel,
black glass, hexagonal
ornament with black rep
band.
Length 125 (hexagon), height
35, width 30 mm.
Stamped: TF (linked) 935.
Marianne Geitel, Berlin.

2.153 CHATELAINE 1930
Designed by Gustav
Braendle, Jr.
Silver, black enamel,
hematite, black rep band.
Length 135, height 85, width
25 mm (ornament).
Stamp obliterated.
Hans-Peter Callsen, Bonn.
Lit.: Der Querschnitt, Vol. 10,
1930, No. 4, p. 263,
advertisement, showing this
piece in a case with a pair of
cuff links.
2.153a Design, original
drawing 7a + b, No. 54,
matching cuff links.

2.152

2.153

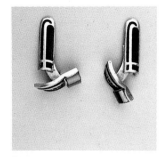

2.154

2.156

2.157

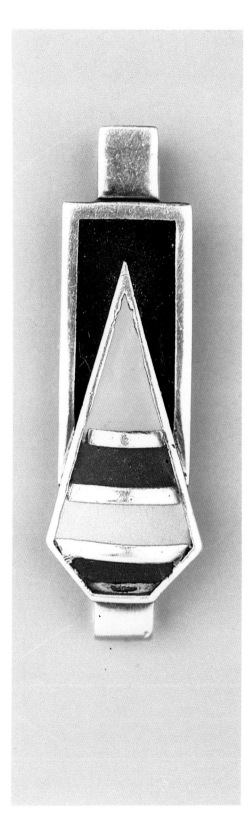

2.155

2.154 CUFF LINKS ca. 1930
Silver, black enamel,
hematite.
Height 12, width 8 mm.
Stamped: TF (linked) 935.
See Cat. No. 2.153.
Private collection, Pforzheim.

2.155 TIE CLIP 1930
Designed by Gustav
Braendle, Jr.
Silver, black, turquoise, red,
gray and brown matte
enamel.
Height 30, width 8 mm.
Stamped: TF (linked) 935,
Marianne Geitel, Berlin.
2.155a Design, original
drawing 4, No. 33.

2.156 MAN'S ONYX RING ca.
1936
Silver, onyx.
Height 20, width 12 mm (head
of ring).
Stamped: TF (linked) 935.
Private collection, Pforzheim.

2.157 MAN'S RING ca. 1936
Silver, lapis lazuli
Height 20, width 18 (head of
ring)
Stamped: TF (linked) 925
Private collection, Pforzheim

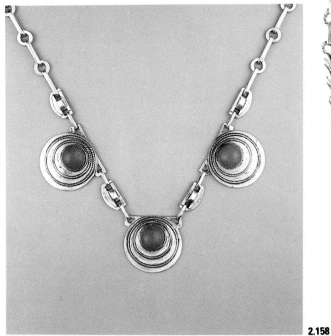

2.158

2.161

2.158 CHAIN ca. 1930
Silver, soldered with
corded wire, coral,
hematite, chain of metal
rings and oblong loops,
three round ornaments in
front.
Length 400, height 18 mm
(ornament).
Stamped: ORIGINAL
FAHRNER (in octagon)
935.
Privately owned.

2.159 PENDANT 1933
Silver, partly gilded, black
glass.
Height 50, diameter 30
mm.
Stamped: ORIGINAL
FAHRNER (in octagon)
935.
Marianne Geitel, Berlin.
2.159a Design, Pattern
Book IV, Model No. 1319.
Marking ink. Dated "Sept.
25, 1933." Drawn full-size.

2.160 BRACELET ca.
1933
Height 35, diameter 70 x
60 mm.
Stamped: FAHRNER 800.
Privately owned, Freiburg.

2.161 CHAIN ca. 1933
Silver, cut smoky quartz,
soldered with corded
wire.
Height 45 (center), length
240 mm (chain).
Stamped: ORIGINAL 935
FAHRNER.
Württemberg State
Museum, Stuttgart, Inv.
No. 1986-99.

2.162 RING 1932
Silver, chrysoprase.
Height 28, width 13 mm
(head of ring).
Stamped: FAHRNER 935.
Galerie Urlass, Frankfurt
on the Main.
Lit.: Die Dame, No. 1,
1932-33, p. 45, showing
three similar rings.

2.163 BROOCH 1933
Silver. Diameter 35 mm.
Stamped: ORIGINAL (in
octagon) 935 FAHRNER.
Marianne Geitel, Berlin.
2.163a Design
(photocopy), Pattern Book
IV, Model No. 1377.
Dated "Dec. 9, 1933."
Drawn full-size.

2.159

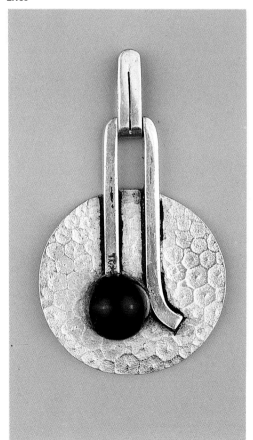

2.160

2.164 CHAIN ca. 1934
Silver, gilded, synthetic
amethyst.
Height 40, width 45 mm
(center), length 190 mm
(chain).
Stamped: ORIGINAL 935
FAHRNER.
Private collection,
Pforzheim.
Lit.: Picture in Die Dame
1934, p. 286.

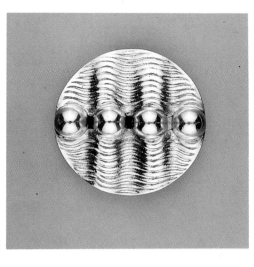

2.163

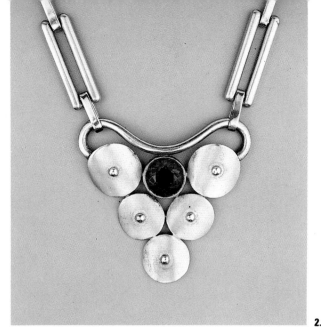

2.164

2.167

2.168

2.162

2.166

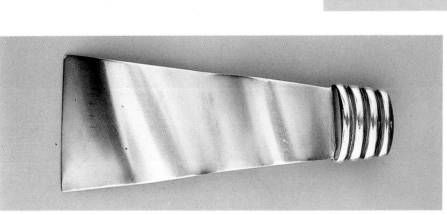

2.165

2.165 TIE CLIP 1934
Silver.
Height 68, width 13-28 mm.
Stamped: ORIGINAL
FAHRNER (in octagon), TF
(linked) 925.
Marianne Geitel, Berlin.
2.165a Design, Pattern Book
IV, Model No. 1573.
Drawing ink. Dated "Dec. 20,
1934." Drawn full-size.

2.166 PENDANT (cross) ca.
1935
Silver, cut topaz, marcasite.
Height 70, width 50 mm.
Stamped: TF (linked) 935.
Private collection, Pforzheim.
Lit.: Piece shown in a sales
brochure from the fifties,
Model No. 20970.

2.167 BROOCH 1936
Silver, amazonite (?)
Height 38, width 50 mm.
Stamped: TF (linked) 925.
Private collection, Pforzheim.
2.167a Design, Pattern Book
IV, Model No. 2065.
Drawing ink. Dated "July 4,
1936."
Drawn full-size.

2.168 BROOCH ca. 1936
Silver, hematite.
Height 30, width 50 mm.
Stamped: TF (linked) 925
ORIGINAL FAHRNER.
Private collection, Pforzheim.
2.168a Photo, Pattern Book
IV, Model No. 2624, no date.

2.170

Filigree Jewelry (Post-1932)

2.169 CHAIN ca. 1935
Silver, gilded, soldered with
corded wire (filigree), green
glass stones.
Length 430, height 15, width
30 mm (center).
Stamped: ORIGINAL
FAHRNER TF (linked) 925.
Private collection, Pforzheim.

2.170 CHAIN ca. 1935
Silver, gilded, soldered with
corded wire in spirals,
synthetic aquamarine.
Length 420 mm.'Stamped:
ORIGINAL FAHRNER TF
(Linked) 925.
Private collection, Pforzheim.

2.171 DRESS CLIP 1936
Silver, gilded, soldered with
corded wire spirals (filigree),
synthetic amethyst,
marcasite.
Height 48, width 20-40 mm.
Stamped: TF (linked) 935.
Private collection, Pforzheim.
2.171a Design, Pattern Book
IV, Model No. 1961.
Drawing ink. Dated "Jan. 2,
1936."

2.172 BROOCH ca. 1936
Silver, gilded, soldered with
corded wire spirals (filigree),
synthetic amethyst,
marcasite.
Height 50, width 60 mm.
Stamped: TF (linked) 935
FAHRNER.
Private collection, Pforzheim.
2.172a Design, Pattern Book
V, Model No. 2307.
Drawing ink. No date.

2.171

2.169

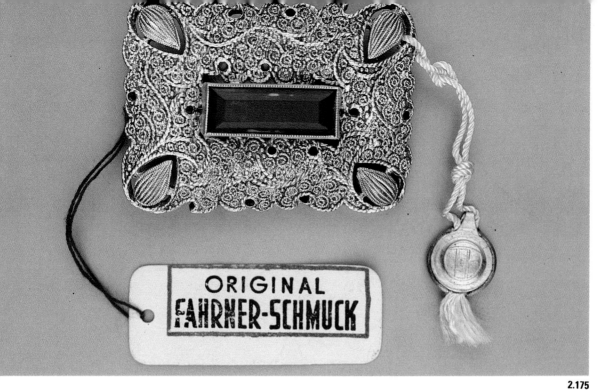

2.175

2.173 BRACELET ca. 1937
Silver, gilded, soldered with
corded wire spirals,
marcasite, three pearls.
Diameter 65 by 55, height 55
mm (center), height 18 mm
(ring).
Stamped: TF (linked)
STERLING GERMANY,
rounded label "ORIGINAL
FAHRNER", on back "Model
No. 3592/O E 118500."
Privately owned by Max
Hering.
2.173a Photo, Price Index I,
Model No. 3592, no date.

2.174 BROOCH ca. 1937
Silver, gilded, soldered with
corded wire spirals (filigree),
two pearls.
Height 57, width 40 mm.
Stamped: TF (linked) 935.
Private collection, Pforzheim.
Lit.: FAHRNER sales
brochure from the forties.

2.175 BROOCH ca. 1937
Silver, gilded, soldered with
corded wire spirals (filigree),
carnelian.
Height 28, width 35 mm.
Stamped: TF (linked) 935,
label "ORIGINAL FAHRNER-
SCHMUCK" and "TF" seal.
Private collection, Pforzheim.

2.173

2.174

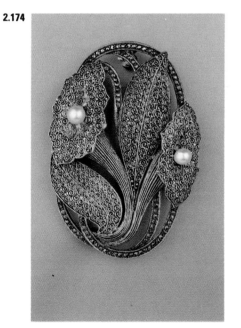

2.172

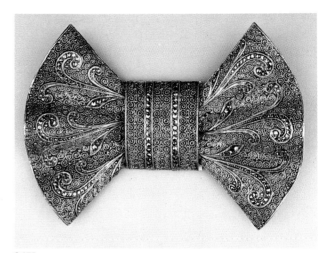

2.176

2.176 BROOCH "pussy-willow branch" ca. 1937
Silver, gilded, marcasite.
Height 20, width 90 mm.
Stamped: TF (linked) 935 FAHRNER.
Private collection, Pforzheim.
2.176a Design, Pattern Book V, Model No. 2329.
Drawing ink. No date. Earlier, circa 1905, pussy-willow brooches of silver with coral were made.

2.177 BROOCH ca. 1938
Designed by Gustav Braendle, Jr.
Silver, gilded (red and yellow gold), soldered with corded wire spirals (filigree), marcasite.
Height 50, width 70 mm.
Stamped: TF (linked) 935 FAHRNER.
Private collection, Pforzheim.
2.177a Photo, Price Index I, Model No. 2645, no date.
Lit.: FAHRNER sales brochure, forties, picture with caption: "Brooch 2645/2 v (= gilded; marcasite) M 40.50."

2.178 BROOCH "Bird"
Forties
Silver, gilded, soldered with corded wire spirals, coarse graining, light green glass stones, marcasite.
Height 40, width 70 mm.
Stamped: TF (linked) 925.
German private collection.

2.179 BROOCH "Snail"
Forties
Silver, gilded (red and yellow gold), soldered with corded wire spirals, marcasite.
Height 25, width 50 mm.
Stamped: TF (linked) 925 ORIGINAL FAHRNER.
Privately owned by Max Hering.

2.180 BRACELET Forties
Silver, gilded, soldered with corded wire, "millegriff" technique flowers, translucent turquoise, lilac and red enamel.
Length 180, height 25 mm.
Stamped: TF (linked) 925 ORIGINAL FAHRNER (in octagon), label with Model No. 4697 C.
Privately owned by Max Hering.
Lit.: FAHRNER sales brochure, forties, set of chain, brooch, bracelet, earrings, pendant.

2.177

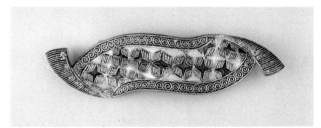

2.181

2.178

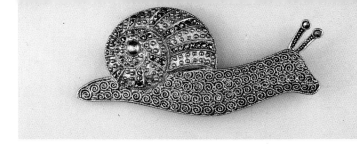

2.179

2.180

2.182

2.181 BROOCH Forties
Silver, gilded, soldered with
corded wire, "millegriff"
flowers, enamel in turquoise,
red and lilac.
Height 15, width 65 mm.
Stamped: TF (linked) 925
"ORIGINAL FAHRNER" (in
octagon), "TF" seal and label,
Model No. 2-4690.
Privately owned by Max
Hering.

2.182 CHAIN Forties-Fifties
Silver, gilded, "millegriff"
technique, marcasite.
Length 420 mm.
Stamped: TF (linked) 925
ORIGINAL FAHRNER (in
octagon), "TF" seal.
Privately owned by Max
Hering.

2.183 BROOCH
Forties-Fifties
Silver, gilded, "millegriff"
technique, marcasite.
Height 40, width 45 mm.
Stamped: TF (linked) 925
ORIGINAL-FAHRNER (n
octagon), "TF" seal and label,
Model No. 4934/0.
Privately owned by Max
Hering.
2.183a Photo (line drawing),
Price Index I, Model No.
04934, no date.

2.184 BROOCH Forties
Silver, gilded, partly
"millegriff" technique,
soldered with corded wire,
marcasite, translucent
enamel in various colors.
Height 45, width 40 mm.
Stamped: TF (linked) 925, E.
L. collection.
Lit.: FAHRNER sales
brochure, forties, piece
shown with Model No. 1.4647
v (= gilded).

2.184

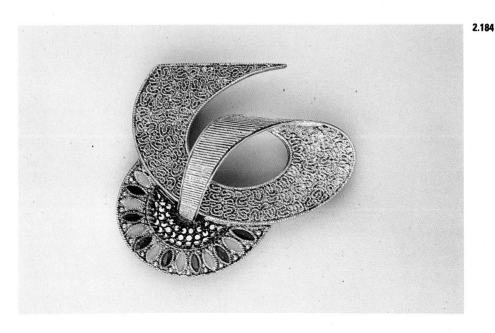

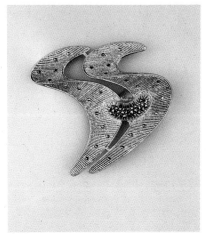

2.183

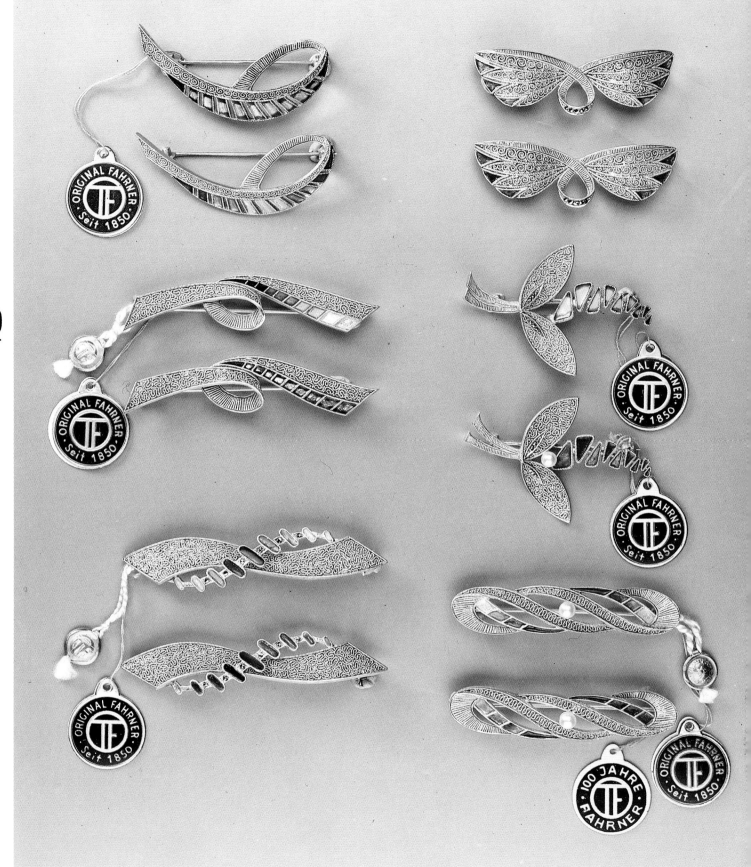

2.185 BROOCHES
Forties-Fifties
Half-moon, wavy stripe,
butterfly form, flowers.
Silver, gilded, partly
enameled.

Stamped: TF (linked) 925,
some with "TF" seal and
label.
Privately owned by Max
Hering.

The LastTwo Decades

2.188

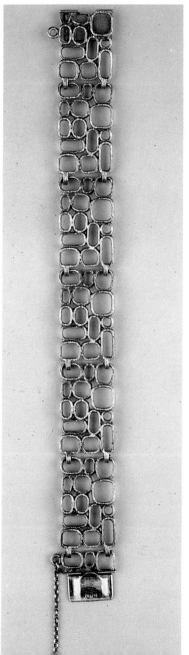

2.186

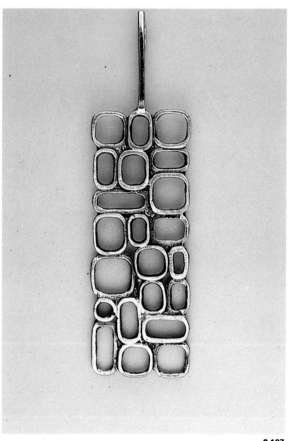

2.187

2.186 BRACELET Sixties
Silver, oxidized.
Length 200, height 18 mm.
Stamped: TF (linked) 925.
Privately owned by Max
Hering.

2.187 PENDANT Sixties
Silver, oxidized.
Height 70, width 20 mm.
Stamped: TF (linked) 925.
Privately owned by Max
Hering.

2.188 CHAIN Sixties
Silver, oxidized, rose quartz
balls.
Length 420, height 18, width
30 mm (one rectangle).
Stamped: TF (linked) 925,
label with Model No.
05654/3.
Privately owned by Max
Hering.
Lit.: See FAHRNER sales
brochure and price list of
1971.

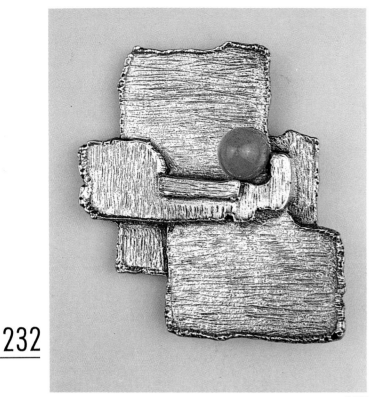
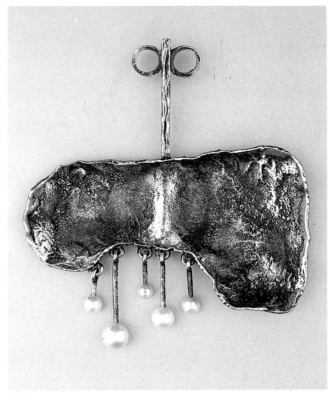

2.189   2.190

2.189 BROOCH
Sixties-Seventies
Silver, oxidized, green
colored agate.
Height 50, width 40 mm.
Stamped: TF (Linked) 925.
Privately owned by Max
Hering.

2.190 PENDANT
Sixties-Seventies
Silver, oxidized, pearls.
Height 70, width 65 mm.
Stamped: TF (linked) 925.
Privately owned by Max
Hering.

2.191 PENDANT with chain
Sixties-Seventies
Silver, oxidized.
Height 40, width 35-68 mm
(pendant), half-length 180mm
(chain).
Stamped: TF (linked) 925.
Privately owned by Max
Hering.

2.192 BROOCH 1971
Gold, rubies.
Height 22, width 45 mm.
Stamped: TF (linked) 585.
Privately owned by Max
Hering.

2.193 BROOCH 1971
Gold, pearls.
Height 30, width 40 mm.
Stamped: TF (linked) 585.
Privately owned by Max
Hering.
Lit.: FAHRNER 1971
Christmas brochure shows a
similar piece.

2.192

2.194

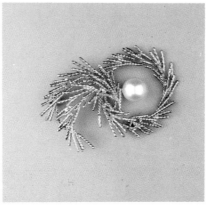

2.193

2.195

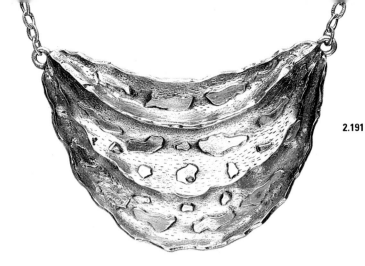

2.191

2.197

2.198

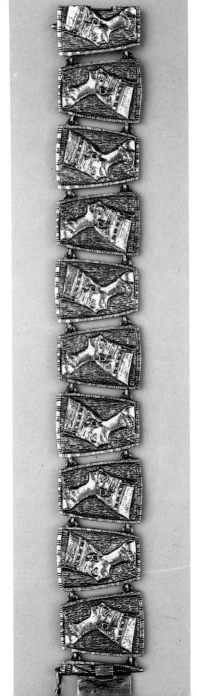

2.196

2.194 BROOCH "Spider"
Seventies
Gold, opal.
Diameter 40 mm.
Stamped" TF (linked) 585.
Privately owned by Max
Hering.

2.195 BROOCH Seventies
Gold, lapis lazuli, pearls.
Diameter 45 mm.
Stamped: TF (linked) 585.
Privately owned by Max
Hering.

2.196 BRACELET Seventies
Silver, oxidized.
Length 190 mm.
Stamped: TF (linked) 925.
From the "Antique Art"
series.
Model No. 10317, motiv:
Akhenaton's wife (Amenophis
IV).
Privately owned by Max
Hering.
Lit.: The "Antique Art" series
offered in 14- and 18-karat
gold in a 1972 sales
brochure.

2.197 PENDANT Seventies
Height 45, width 32 mm.
Stamped: TF (linked) 925.
From the "Antique Art"
series.
Model No. 10267, motif:
Tombstone of Upwatmose,
1400 B.C.
Reverse: Hieroglyphics.
Privately owned by Max
Hering.

2.198 PENDANT Seventies
Silver, oxidized.
Height 40, width 30 mm.
Stamped: TF (linked) 925.
From the "Antique Art"
series.
Model No. 10306, motif:
Etruscan, Turquinia, 470 B.C.
Privately owned by Max
Hering.

FASHION JEWELRY - or the Problem of Industrial Production of Luxury

Ingeborg Becker

Clothing and jewelry, at least in European fashions, play a symbiotic role. They depend on each other, a relationship that goes without saying in general terms but does not necessarily have to exist.

"There are peoples who wear practically no clothing but like to wear plenty of jewelry, and there are other peoples who are very heavily dressed for climatic reasons but have practically no jewelry. Still others wear little clothing and much jewelry, others much clothing and little jewelry."[1]

Along with such standardized ethnographic phenomena, the relationship between jewelry and clothing assumes another dimension in the context of changing fashions. It terms of a more and more strongly growing art industry in the late 19th Century, which involves the theme of jewelry and clothing production discussed here, it is no longer just "pure" jewelry that is passed on from generation to generation. To a growing degree, jewelry plays a role of meeting present needs. It is not the material value that necessarily decides the function of jewelry; rather the decorative aspect can dominate. Almost any material is acceptable in any combination. Porcelain, copper, brass, silver, gold, pearls, enamel, mosaic, as well as synthetic stones, marcasite jewelry, paste, paint. It is a development that set in more strongly after the end of World War I. Influenced by inflation and export bans, the conflict between traditional handmade jewelry and

an artistic industry intensified in Germany. The goldsmith also used growing amounts of silver, garnet, amber, onyx, chrysoprase, turquoise, stones and materials that had only gained entrance into the "high" art of jewelry since the days of Art Nouveau.

This is probably why a precise definition of "fashion jewelry" cannot be gained conclusively from contemporary statements.

Was it only the striking, large-scale, "ungenuine" jewelry that firms like Chanel and Schiaparelli designed in the twenties, or could the artists' designs of Art Nouveau claim this term for their own?

Was it rather the "cheap", inexpensively produced German jewelry of the thirties that allowed its wearers to follow every change in fashion, and of which it was said enthusiastically: "In contrast to the jewelry, made of precious metals and precious stones, that our mothers wore, our jewelry is not made for eternity. We change our jewelry with out clothes and with the styles." Such jewelry has been spared the obligation to be a "neutral creation", and "its forms have become more daring, more elegant and lively."[2]

Or was it jewelry that was integrated into clothing styles, such as the Parisian jewelers Cartier and Fouquet produced, particularly in the years from 1900 to 1930? The luxurious character of the epochs of Art Nouveau and Art Deco styles seem predestined to make for a close relationship among art, jewelry and fashion: Fouquet collaborated with the

236

1)
Rudolf Rücklin, Schmuck und Kleidung, in: DGZ No. 40, 1923, p. 275.

2)
Anni Bracht, Neue Schmuckmoden, in: Schaulade, Vol. 9 (1933), No. 8, p. 301.

fashion designer Patou, Cartier with Worth.

The high point was reached by the style-setting 1925 "Art Deco" Exhibition in Paris.[3] Cartier designed shoulder straps, "epaulettes" that ended in emerald pendants below the shoulder and formed an unbroken band over the whole neckline. There were also belts of rock crystal and diamonds with onyx tassels, "royal" jewelry that proclaimed Cartier's artistic credo of the unity of the decorative arts; Cartier's creations were always supposed to be presented in direct connection with the fashion in hats, hair styles, belts, fabrics and shoes.[4] Cartier was the only jeweler who, at the 1925 "L'Exposition Internationale des Arts Décoratifs et Industriels Modernes" in Paris, was not with the other jewelers and goldsmiths in the Grand Palace but in the "Pavilion of Elegance" with the rest of the fashion industry.

The question of "costume ornament or object of art?"[5] in this emphatic form concerns only the French clothing and jewelry styles at first, though since the

NUR ECHT MIT DIESER PLOMBE

beginning of the 20th Century they have set the standards for Europe and North America.

Fashion and Jewelry in Art Nouveau. Rarely has such intensive public consideration been given to fashion and jewelry as in the years between 1890 and 1910. The "Youth Style", a style that set out to be "modern" and also to penetrate all aspects of daily life, turned to questions of fashion with particular intensity in Germany. Discussion of up-to-date clothing was linked with outlooks on life almost from the start and also concerned questions of health and hygiene, women's emancipation and education.

Famous Art-Nouveau artists such as Peter Behrens, Henry van de Velde, Richard Riemerschmid, Bernhard Pankok and Alfred Mohrbutter designed clothing and in some cases also jewelry that was to correspond to a new ideal of beauty. In particular, Henry van de Velde also expressed himself on these questions

3)
Compare DGZ Vol. 28, No. 40, 1925, p. 380: "Suiting the jeweler's art to the prevailing fashion trends is clearly seen in all these costly, unusual pieces of jewelry that are displayed at "L'Exposition Internationale des Arts Décoratifs et Industriels Modernes." Jewelry is no longer seen as a treasure, a possession, although in our times of financial insecurity the possession of precious stones still seems to offer the greatest security, but rather as an enhancement and accompaniment for fashion."

4)
Compare Hans Nadelhoffer, Cartier, König der Juweliere — Juwelier der Könige, Herrsching 1984, p. 191.

5)
See Yvonne Delalandres, in Les Fouquets, Bijouteriers & Joailleriers á Paris 1860-1960, Musée des Arts Decoratifs 1983, pp. 34-39.

theoretically.[6] A "counter-style" that did not agree with the dictated fashion ideals of (French) Haute-Couture was demanded of all reformers. The first prerequisite for it was the wearing of a laced corset that bent the silhouette of the body into an S shape. The bust was pushed far forward, the abdomen and pelvis forced backward and the rump strongly stressed: "If one looks at a present-day stylish lady — by which I mean one who copies the bending of the body prescribed in Paris very conscientiously — then her upper and lower body do not seem to belong together. The bosom extends far out from the rest of the body, the lower body is forced to bend strangely backward, forming a terrible structure."[7] Wearing corsets was attacked from a medical standpoint as being unhealthy. The beauty of the unlaced feminine body was praised, and a natural way of life was advocated. When one argued from an artistic-esthetic standpoint, an undertone of patriotism was often heard. "Away with Paris" and its fashion dictates, it was said, suggesting a hint of German superiority in fashions too — an attitude that grew stronger in the last years before the outbreak of World War I.[8] But as early as 1902, van de Velde complained that the German woman was "bound to the will of a few big clothing firms — mainly in Paris" — playing a "ridiculous role" that made her a "slave" to the tyranny of season-oriented creations.[9] The clothing itself was also decried, as well as the malformation caused by the corset and the

surrender to every silly fashion fad. It was the overabundance of decoration that every reformer inveighed against. Lace, ribbons, straps, bands, embroidery, tassels, artificial flowers, buttons that had nothing to do with the cut of the dress, all strengthened the unnatural character of it. "And then all these things that are quite openly referred to as 'false'! False skirts, false seams, false sleeves, false collars, false pockets — I do not believe there is a single part of feminine clothing that does not live a double life!"[10]

Opposed to these foreign "trucs" were the organic beauty, the liveliness of the material, qualities that no "French cut"

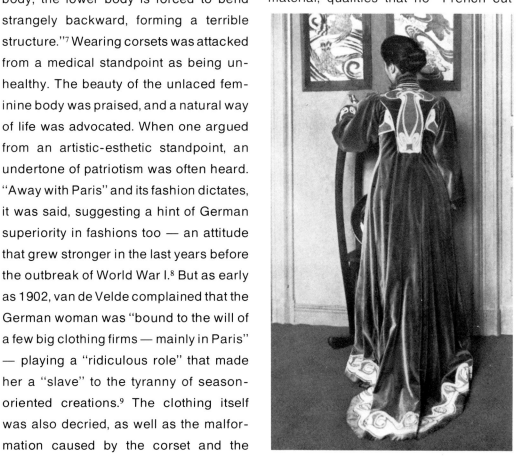

6)
Henry van de Velde, Die künstlerische Hebung der Frauentracht, Krefeld 1900.

7)
J. Mayer, Das neue Frauenkleid, in: Stuttgarter Mitteilungen über Kunst und Gewerbe, 1905-06, p. 101.

8)
Compare Sabine Sabor, Die Werkstatt der Emmi Schoch 1906-1916, Master's thesis, Heidelberg 1987, p. 53.

9)
Henry van de Velde, Das neue Kunst-Prinzip in der modernen Frauen-Kleidung, in: DKD, Vol, 10, 1902, p. 365.

10)
Henry van de Velde, Das neue Kunst-Prinzip, op. cit., p. 370.

had brought out for a long time. an de Velde designed numerous models that were shown along with other artists' designs at a very influential exhibition in Krefeld in the spring of 1900.[11] They were designs that were not created in a puritanical spirit of reform; quite the opposite, they were meant to be dedicated above all to the principles of beauty. Cut, workmanship and cloth had to change completely if the natural form of the body were to be retained. But even these clothes did not inspire unqualified admiration, even among partisans of the modern. Over and over, more naturalness was demanded, and even in the Krefeld show one sees only a "reformation of accessories and nothing more, otherwise just the same old pedestrian forms that could just as well have been born in the imagination of a tailor in Paris."[12] It was also said that "we might well keep in mind the fact that a beautiful woman is most beautiful undressed . . . and choose our clothing so that it does not conceal our bodies and distort their real lines." The creations of van de Velde and Mohrbutter were criticized from precisely this point of view.[13]

In all the various conceptions of "modern women's clothing", which was often referred to deliberately by the term "Tracht" (peasant costume), the "artist dress" or "individual dress" stressed the construction of it, the push for "the essence of the matter. This essence of the matter is seen properly in the structure, the nature of the cloth and the individual

suitability to the wearer."[14] Seams and cut are stressed, and thus the ornament takes on a special significance here too.

Just as fashion provided food for thought, attention was also drawn to jewelry. The striving for modernity in clothing and jewelry must be seen first of all in the light of the still-present Founding Years (post-1871) with their confusion of tastes, their opulence and love for falseness. Jewelry was meant "to show off" then, to demonstrate the wealth and social position of the wearer. In this area too, emphatic articles advocated a new style, a new striving for simplicity and artistic design. "One dared to strive for an intimate effect that revealed itself only to the eye trained not to rely on the number of carats" — here too we see the move from "illusion to reality."[15]

Haute Couture Ready-to-Wear Clothing - or Opposites Attract. The artistic "individual dress" was worn by few women of a certain level of society. "Hidden in intimate circles, where the success of the commercial-art movement is to be sought to this day,"[16] such an individual style did not represent a general consensus. An important factor, since one must proceed from a standpoint of absolute obligation, of public fashion laws. The fashion around 1900, Haute Couture or "Eigenkleid", essentially met the expectations of a financial and cultural upper stratum, but ignored the needs of most women. The role of the woman in the rapidly developing industrial

11)
The exhibition opened at the Krefeld City Hall on April 4, 1900 and closed on April 13. Forty objects were shown, including 24 toilettes and 16 design drawings by van de Velde and Alfred Mohrbutter, see van de Velde, as above, p. 370.

12)
Margarete Bruns, Der Stil in der modernen Kleidung, in: DKD, Vol. VIII, 1901, p. 476.

13)
"Henry van de Velde broadens the shoulders of an already powerfully developed woman with big flaps and pads. Instead of allowing us to observe her probably nicely developed bosom, though, he presses it down by a very deep-seated square yoke that ignores her figure, so much so that one can barely tell that she has a bosom. Alfred Mohrbutter goes even farther, going so far as to present a long-known tailor's version of a waistline . . . as an artistic design . . .", as above.

14)
Anna Muthesius, Die Ausstellung künstlerischer Frauen-Kleider im Warenhaus Wertheim-Berlin, in: DKD, Vol. XIV, 1904, p. 443.

15)
Hans Schliepmann, Moderner Schmuck, in: DKD, Vol. V, 1899-1900, p. 61.. "When the lovely little brooches by Chéret, Vernier, van de Staeten, etc., first appeared in Berlin about two years ago, scarcely more than a button with a somewhat lively outline and an unbelievably delicate relief design on a slightly sunken surface", the high prices charged for them inspired ridicule and annoyance. Only slowly did one come to understand the "actual value of the piece of jewelry, its independent artistic charm and the individual note that it is capable of providing."

16)
Anna Muthesius, op. cit., p. 441.

process was not taken into consideration. What with the validity of fashion dictates, the ideas of the great fashion houses thus had to be translated into mass-production. Berlin-Hausvogteiplatz became the fashion center of Germany, where fashion came "from the rack" and the models of Paris Haute Couture were adapted and put into production as reasonably priced mass-produced clothing.[17] These circumstanced have been bemoaned over and over. All the requirements of an individual style seemed to be missing: Soft, flowing fabrics in "unusual colors" could not be had in the shops, the modern velvet and silk fabrics had to be imported from England, lace and small items from Paris. The inevitable high price stood in the way of a wide distribution of modern, individual clothing. Anna Muthesius ended her appeal militantly: If one could, first of all, buy good yarn and fabrics at reasonable prices in any shop as German products, then not only the grand wardrobes of rich women, but even the dress made in a back room of the house by a little seamstress would be done a great service."[18]

It was just this individualization of style that was to be thwarted by the binding dictates of fashion. For from a sociological standpoint, styles took on a particular function around 1900 in view of the role of the woman in society. Her separation from the everyday (masculine) world of work and its representative function, which indicated the social status of the man, was to be made obvious. The luxurious nature of fashions thus gave evidence of "demonstrative extravagance", which went hand-in-hand with "demonstrative indolence" — factors that gave evidence of financial strength, power and success, and that could not normally be displayed by the woman herself.[19]

The situation in jewelry production looked similar. In the luxury class, diamonds, gold, pearls, rubies, sapphires and emeralds were mainly used. Jewelry in this category was reserved from the beginning only for a financially strong upper class. This was definitely jewelry that did not necessarily represent artistic criteria.[20] Modern exclusive jewelry was created in exemplary form by Lalique in Paris and, with another goal and another public in mind, by the artists of the Wiener Werkstätte. This jewelry also depended on individual production and was consequently expensive. There was also the jewelry production that, in Germany, was centered in Pforzheim. Just as mass-production of clothing adapted and cheapened high fashion for manufacturing, the industrial production of jewelry at first merely adopted the external appearance of expensive jewelry. If the expensive jewelry could not always stand out in terms of artistic sensitivity, this was even less true in the case of inexpensive goods. The costliness of precious materials and the glow of diamonds were no longer present to create the effect. Imitation, surrogate, the key words, the magic words of Historicism, had long played a role in

17)
Compare Brigitte Stamm, Berliner Chic, in: Berlin um 1900, Exhibition Catalog, Academy of the Arts, Berlin 1984, pp. 105 ff.

18)
Anna Muthesius, op. cit., p. 443.

19)
Compare Brigitte Stamm, Auf dem Weg zum Reformkleid, in: Kunst und Alltag um 1900. Yearbook 3 of the Werkbund Archives, Lahn-Giessen 1978, p. 143.

20)
Rudolf Rücklin, Pforzheimer Schmuck modernen Stils, in: DKD, Vol. IV, 1899, p. 467.

jewelry mass-production. And the repertoire of forms in Art Nouveau was particularly suited to being made by machine, and for these reasons it was not surprising that around 1900 a crisis in German jewelry production can be sensed. The mass-production of "scarcely pleasant naturalistic and fleetingly 'stylized' products" was being decried in that sector, and it was vital that the mass-industry rise above the exploitation of the so-called "Youth Style" tendency, also known as "Secession."[21] But there were exceptions. In Pforzheim it was the firm of Theodor Fahrner that stepped forward with modern jewelry that was being produced in quality.

Fahrner understood the nature of the machine and the possibilities of machine production, and could come to terms with the artistic goals of Art Nouveau.

At the 1900 World's Fair in Paris, the firm of Theodor Fahrner first stepped forth in grand style. The newness of his work was noticed at once. He owed his success primarily to his employment of recognized artists who, to be sure, were close to the applied arts but not necessarily willing to subordinate themselves only to the realm of jewelry, for example, Max Joseph Gradl and Patriz Huber. In addition, Fahrner himself had sufficient artistic sensitivity to know exactly which forms and materials were suitable for industrial production. His jewelry stood out for its simple forms and simple materials.[22] In 1904 Fahrner had appeared again, at the World's Fair in St. Louis, this time with works by Georg

Kleemann, Fritz Wolber, Julius Müller-Salem and Franz Boeres. A "corporative representation by the Pforzheim art-industrialists" was ruled out by customs laws, and only those artists who worked as teachers at the Pforzheim Kunstgewerbe School had joined together to document in exemplary form, with a few pieces, the achievements of jewelry production. For they wanted to counteract Pforzheim's bad reputation "as a place where cheap and poor-quality mass goods were produced."[23]

Three years before that, Fahrner had been able, by participating in the exhibition of the Darmstadt Artists' Colony at the Mathildenhöhe, to share in the fame of the new "Secessionist" art with designs by Patriz Huber, Paul Bürck and Ludwig Habich.

This collaboration with representatives of the avant-garde in commercial art was cleverly integrated into the firm's advertising by Fahrner.[24] The TF trade mark plus the equating of "Fahrner Jewelry" with "genuine artistic jewelry" "to designs by leading artists" lifted production to the level that jewelry made by jewelers once had all to itself. The modern artist jewelry was made chiefly of silver, a fact that appears interesting in esthetic-artistic, customer-sociological and economic terms alike.

The artistic designs of Gradl and Habich were generally made three-dimensionally. Designs by Huber, Boeres and Kleemann stressed geometrical lines. Elements of

21)
Moderner Deutscher Schmuck, in: DKD, Vol. VI, 1900, p. 518; see also Ulrike von Hase-Schmundt, Massenproduction als Stil, Zur Entwicklung des Gablonzer Schmucks im 19. Jahrhundert und um 1900, in: Weltkunst 1986, Vol. 56, No. 23, pp. 3776-3781.

22)
"A profitable concentration on simple problems is shown, whose solution . . . has proved to succeed in outstandingly beauty, thoroughly tastefully, in individual objects. Here too, Fahrner shows esthetic sensitivity in choosing the right material for the artistic design without prejudice, and when precious metal is not appropriate in terms of style, he turns to steel . . ." see Moderner Deutscher Schmuck auf der Weltausstellung, in DKD, Vol. VI, 1900, p. 524.

23)
Rudolf Rücklin, Pforzheimer Feinmetallarbeiten auf der Weltausstellung St. Louis, in: DKD, Vol. XIV, 1904, p. 502.

24)
Rudolf Rücklin, Das Werk Theodor Fahrners, in: DGZ, No. 39-40, 1919, p. 268: "He does not avoid making business advertisements, but here too, as in everything, he is noble and restrained. He introduced the term "Fahrner-Schmuck." That was enough of an advertisement."

Celtic-Germanic culture were often adapted for this jewelry, most of which could be conceived only in silver. The colorful quality of the preferred stones, such as lapis lazuli, turquoise and onyx, was particularly effective on silver. In addition, this jewelry with a "Germanic" flavor represented in an understated but direct way the "away from Paris" slogan of German fashion and implied the esthetic and moral superiority of its wearer. On the other hand, silver is naturally much less expensive in material value than gold. The many pieces of jewelry made of gilded silver also point in this direction. Such a material was very suitable for mass production that had to be done as economically as possible. For the retailers and customers had to calculate too. It was known from the start which customers were involved: The buyers of this modern silver jewelry were the educated civil servant and the bourgeois who liked art,[25] who strove deliberately to distance himself from the general "masses" just as did those who wore gold and jewels. By making a display of riches and obvious money to spare, the wearer of modern artist jewelry could show herself to be cultivated, tasteful and esthetically sensitive.[26]

Fahrner Jewelry contributed to the "democratization of luxury" that became the characteristic of German jewelry after 1900. These early Fahrner products were mainly clothing jewelry, belt buckles, brooches, cuff links, hatpins. Yet one can

25)
Rudolf Rücklin, 25 Jahre deutscher Schmuckkunst, in: DGZ No. 9, 1923, p. 71, and Pforzheimer Feinmetallarbeiten, in: DKD, Vol. XIV, 1904, p. 500: "But it is also the sales conditions that have an important effect here. That public that comes into the picture chiefly for the sale of fine gold jewelry is only involved in exceptional cases with modern ornamentation, modern creations."

26)
Re the problems of "distancing", see the amusing study by Roland Girtler, Die Feinen Leute. Von der vornehmen Art, durchs Leben zu gehen, Frankfurt-New York 1989.

27)
See Wolfgang Georg Fischer, Gustav Klimt und Emilie Flöge. Genie und Talent, Freudnschaft und Besessenheit, Vienna 1988, pp. 65 ff, and Hermes Villa Exhibition Catalog, Vienna 1988, Emilie Flöge und Gustav Klimt, double portrait in ideal landscape, pp. 26 ff.

scarcely find a contemporary fashion photograph in which these items are worn. They simply do not have that accentuative effect that is inherent to the Wiener Werkstätte jewelry. The symbiotic effect of avant-garde fashions and the same kind of jewelry is shown clearly in a photo documentation owned by Gustav Klimt's life companion Emilie Flöge.[27] She owned one of Vienna's first fashion salons. Her merchandise was exclusive and expensive, though it had only vague tendencies toward the new fashion trends. Privately, though, she wore a series of reform dresses that were inspired by the artistic impetus of the Wiener Werkstätte. The photos that Klimt and others took of her in these dresses almost always show her wearing jewelry designed by Josef Hoffmann, Kolo Moser, Otto Prutscher or the anonymous artists of the Vienna Workshops. In the artistic pictures that the renowned photographer D'Ora (Dora Kallmus) took of her, she also wore —

with more conventional fashions — the well known dog-collar, square brooches or fine-link chains of the Wiener Werkstätte.[28] Emilie Flöge was regarded as a muse who interpreted the art of the Klimt circle. In that way, and through her own creative activity, she had an exalted position. She is a fine example of what Anna Multhesius said of the role of the new women's clothing, especially that it existed only in small circles (see #16). Her closeness to Klimt and her acquaintance with the most important woman photographer of the time provided the necessary publicity for her.

The wearers of Lalique jewelry appear to be just as exclusive: "Of course one sees Lalique's jewelry neither on the street nor in the theater nor at grand soirées. But this only proves that the master's customers understand his intentions clearly. For Lalique does not want to create parade jewelry that shows off its wearer's wealth, ...rather he creates...intimate jewelry that is meant to be worn in small circles and, above all, to please its wearer herself..."[29] Fahrner's jewelry too can be found only rarely in fashion photos. It seems as if the modern artist jewelry, whatever its origin, has too private a life style to be seen in typical fashion photos.

A small special borderline realm in which the Fahrner firm also made an appearance in the fashion and jewelry sector may also be mentioned. In "Die Goldschmiedekunst" in 1912 (below) "new practical ladies' purses" were shown, woven of "precious metals" and featuring a special patent. By a special process, the metal weave is always held tense, thus allowing a division into inside compartments. There is also a "modern", rigid curved bow that replaces the old carrying chain of this type, former just called a "bag." The form can go with the prevailing fashions —whether it is a simple rectangle or a polygon with metal chain and ornaments on the edge: "The new ladies' purses are only of the finest type, like all products that the well-known firm of Theodor Fahrner has put on the market in gold and silver."[30]

Fahrner is an ideal example of the type of "art industrialist" of the turn of the century.[31] It was a concept that was used as a harmonizing factor to conciliate the opposing poles of art and industry, a basic problem that was not very easy to solve in the Machine Age. Rudolf Rücklin, a teacher at the Goldsmithing School with a deep knowledge of the Pforzheim jewelry industry, described Fahrner as a man with the soul of an artist, who strove more and more to realize the "ideal of an artistic workshop industry." Fahrner always wanted, as Rücklin says, to scale down, but collaborated with a wholesaler and later sold di-

28)
See also the list of their legacy of jewelry and related articles listed in the publications cited above.

29)
KuKH, Vol. III, 1900, pp. 494 ff.

30)
Die Goldschmiedekunst, 1912, No. 9, p. 127 (with three pictures).

31)
Rudolf Rücklin, Das Werk Theodor Fahrners, in: DGZ 1919, No. 39-40, pp. 268 ff.

rectly to the retailer. The field of tension between the artistic design and mass production resulted for Fahrner's production in an ambivalence that seemed unavoidable.

For it was said categorically in 1908: "In reality, the industry can never produce art. Art industry is non-existent . . . The artistic problem of industry can only be solved if industry is determined to serve not a falsified art but good taste . . . The artist associates with industry not to produce art, but to spread the culture of good taste. Let it be said again that art has nothing to do with industry."[32]

Fahrner's artist jewelry was an attempt to put new artistic ideas into series production. The reformer-like basic idea of Art Nouveau, that an esthetic education can also include a moral category for the

32)
Josef August Lux, Das neue Kunstgewerbe in Deutschland, in it, Industrie und Kunst, pp. 241 ff.

average person, was to be realized through his series production of jewelry in an indirect way and in an admirable manner.

Jazz Age and False Glitter - Fashions and Jewelry of the Twenties. The first few post-war years resulted in a completely new feeling for life. Nothing was as it had been before, and the fashions showed the dramatic, earth-shaking changes in the times.

The position of the woman had changed. On account of many women having worked during the war years, better education being available, and sports activities, a new feminine ideal with a new style crystallized. At first, of course, it had to give way to the shortage of materials caused by the war. Simple, unpretentious cuts that spared material were proclaimed, the skirt ended about at calf-length. As opposed to the extravagance of fabric, appliques, attachments and lace of the fashions that were worn just ten years before, a definite "severity of line" appeared. But an essential component of the styles of the following years was its "fast living", its proverbial changeability. The general dynamics that characterized the new decade in general could also be seen in this sector, and the spectrum was expanded. Now clothing was needed for sports such as golf, tennis, riding, skiing, bicycling and motoring, for flying, for elegant ocean-liner travel, railroad trips, tea-dances, cocktails, soirées, but also for

the office and everyday business. The mobility, the urge to move ahead that became the "catchword of the century",[33] demanded that clothing should know no enclosing, limiting bounds. Fashion also became an exciting situation that could affect a receptive public through numerous newspapers and magazines. The jewelry industry sensible reacted to this generally increased interest in what was fashionable. In the winter of 1921-22 the Pforzheim Kunstgewerbe School — with the collaboration of Vera Joho-Fahrner, was already offering courses in jewelry designing that were directly related to the clothing fashions of the times (left, also Cat. No. 1.68).

The fluctuation of styles in jewelry and clothing caused the opposition between artistic handicraft and industry to become visible in particular virulence: "But today, in this feverish business life in which jewelry is no longer made with love and pride by a few careful artisans, in which styles change four times a year, become completely different, today is no time for individual jewelry styles to arise, live and die out. Everything rushes, everything is in motion, people have neither time nor patience to go on wearing the tried and true styles of twenty to thirty years ago simply because they know their value."[34]

Not only in all-out fashion periodicals or inserts were the styles of the season open to debate. The trade papers of the jewelry industry, such as the "Deutsche Goldschmiedezeitung" or "Die Goldschmiedekunst", also discussed fashion problems regularly. The length of skirts. the form of necklines, the position of the waistline, the nature of the sleeves, the composition of the hat, the colors of the season, all this was important and had its effect on jewelry design. Historic, inherited jewelry was regarded as antiquated and worthy of being "preserved religiously among other old valuables and trinkets in showcases as monuments to earlier culture."[35] Above

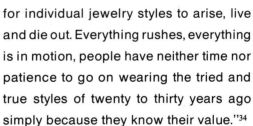

33)
Sabine Runde, Welt ohne Alltag. Modegrafik der 20er Jahre von Anni Ofterdinger, Exhibition Catalog, Museum of Arts and Crafts, Frankfurt on the Main, p. 109.

34)
Vera Joho-Fahrner, Mode und Schmuck, in: Blätter des Kunstgewerbevereins Pforzheim, New Series, Vol. 23, 1921-22, No. 1, page 1.

35)
In: Die Goldschmiedekunst, 1926, No. 20, p. 407.

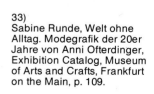

all else, the dictates of fashion also required certain forms of jewelry, the deep back neckline of a dress required stylish jewelry that was hitherto unknown. The popular sleeveless dresses also called for striking bracelets. A decorative headband looked particularly good in bobbed hair, and long earrings took on the job of linking the face to the desirable stretched silhouette of the body.

The jewelry industry, though, found itself in an extremely precarious position during the war and in the postwar era. Various restrictions were placed on the use of precious metals. Then too, the use of Imperial coins was allowed only as of 1919. It was a law that lifted a necessary wartime regulation which made the melting down of silver coins for reworking by jewelers and goldsmiths a punishable offense.[36] During the war a luxury tax had also been introduced, amounting to 20% of any sales price over twenty Marks and covering gold and silver articles, watches, precious and semi-precious stones and pearls. In 1917 all German branches of the precious-metal business petitioned against this and suggested a 1% sales tax instead.

There was also a rise in silver prices in 1919. This was caused by the decrease in silver production in the major producing countries such as the USA, Mexico and Canada and the simultaneous increase in demand in such countries as British India and China. Germany's rate of exchange was weak outside the country, and was

prey to constant fluctuations. The prospects of the silver market for the industries that used it were "heartily bad", assuming that the economic situation would not improve in the foreseeable future. German silver prices were not equal to those on the world market, and the enormous increase made any exact calculation impossible. It was necessary to deal with the shortage caused by lack of raw materials and higher prices while simultaneously staying afloat on the world market. The primary requirement for the survival of the German jewelry industry was thus, first of all, that the connection with the international standard had to be established again after the war. For as early as February of 1918 it was said that high-quality work would be the only means of economic consolidation and progress. It was admitted realistically that Germany would be dependent on the outside world, "whose attitude after peace had been made will not be friendly," for importing raw materials, and that therefore only respect for German achievement would guarantee success. The derogatory term of "camelote allemande", German trash, that the French competitors had come up with, was not to be denied. "We cannot wait until the war is over, but must show the rest of the world now what German quality work can achieve. Of course our sources of help are closed, our capability is limited. But the artistic perfection of our products is not limited by the war."[37]

The reports on fashion and jewelry that

36)
The regulation of May 10, 1917 decreed that anyone who melted or otherwise adapted coin of the realm without special permission from the Chancellor "for the purpose of commercial revaluation" was to be punished with imprisonment for up to one year and/or a fine of up to 50,000 Marks. Any articles thus made were to be confiscated. In: DGZ, 1919, No. 51-52, p. 351.

were published in many periodicals said nothing of these limitations, fears and hopes. Here an unreal world was portrayed that related to only a small percentage of the buying public. It was the setting of an artificial play that had more relevance to the illusionary world of the cinema, the stage and drama than to reality. And it was generally accepted at that.[38] The social climb from shopgirl to movie star, with Greta Garbo as a shining example, became the dream that was supposed to become reality. The novel "Das kunstseidende Mädchen" by Irmgard Keun (1932) illustrates in exemplary fashion the strivings of an untalented little actress "to become a star" and her pre-programmed failure in the face of society's brutal reality.

The movie star could, on the basis of certain factors, be regarded as the modern ideal of feminine self-perception. Her social prestige was no longer dependent on a prosperous husband, but was based on her own income and ability. At the same time, this profession was not linked with monotonous or "unfeminine" work, but corresponded to the traditional role with its emphasis on beauty and fine appearance. A visible sign of this social rise (status) included extravagant clothing, expensive cars, houses, all of which could be afforded thanks to the salaries that were — from the normal consumer's point of view — astronomically high. The often-hysterical reception of the film star at public appearances also showed to some extent that the "goddess" was seen as the personification of these longings and wishes.

In such a world of glamour and glitter it was only natural that fashion and jewelry should go hand in hand internationally. Paris was still setting the tone as before, and the American influence was also growing in importance, reaching out to all of Europe from the many "Americans in Paris." The young American women represented a new type of woman, sporting, natural, quite at home with their freedom of movement. Coco Chanel varied the jumper introduced from America with simple jerseys and laid the groundwork for a general ready-to-wear style, an area that none of the leading fashion houses could ignore.

The fashion creations of the twenties grew out of this tension between demonstrative exclusivity and suitability to mass taste. The artistically dominant jewelry of the time was likewise internationally oriented. It was dominated by geometric patterns, strongly contrasting colored surfaces and the glitter of sparkling stones, of whatever kind. Exotic influences, especially from China and Egypt, aroused the general imagination.[39] There are two realms of culture whose art shows strongly decorative elements while at the same time having a hermetic character. The fascination with such art is shown in the choice of materials for jewelry. Lacquer, ivory, coral, shell cameos, jade, turquoise, onyx, ebony were preferred. Sharp con-

37)
In: Das Schaufenster des deutschen Geschmacks, in: DGZ, No. 9-10, Feb. 23, 1918, pp. 41 ff.

38)
See also B. Mundt, Metropolen machen Mode, 3rd revised edition, Berlin 1989, introduction, p. 10.

39)
Tutankhamun's tomb was discovered in 1922.

trasts such as red and black —originally achieved by combining coral and lacquer — or black and white (rock crystal), green and black (jade), as well as turquoise and gold, were popular combinations that are found in Cartier of Fouquet jewelry just as in "Fahrner Jewelry" or anonymous jewelry designs of the twenties that already used artificial materials.[40] The dynamics of the "new world" produced stereometric forms that were composed tectonically, and forms emerged that were reminiscent of the Chrysler Building or similar Art-Deco architecture (see Cat. No. 2.135). The ideal range extended from the skyscrapers of New York to the steppes of Asia and the tombs of Egypt — a cosmorama of space and time that came out in colorful and glittering jewelry.

Fashion too knew the strong contrast of colored surfaces, the geometric pattern, the cascading fall of fabrics and the asymmetrical cut. The Oriental influence on fashions was already mentioned in the influential journals in 1920, an inspiration that lasted through the whole decade, strengthened by films and shows.

Much as fashion and jewelry corresponded in Art Nouveau, the two genres also interpreted the artistic tendencies of the time in Art Deco. In Art Nouveau it was the ornamental lines of the cloth that were translated into three-dimensional metal;

in Art Deco it was the strict "cubistic" transposition of decor into the three tangible dimensions of the piece of jewelry.

There are always objects that, seen for themselves, have an autonomous effect as small objects of art per se — without needing to have a direct relationship to the clothing or the wearer. This is not negated by the fact that the background surely can be seen very concretely, for "necklines, sleevelessness, and hair styles that leave the ears free all require jewelry, and plenty of it. One wears "jewelry ensembles" of chains, earrings and many bracelets that match each other as well as the color of one's clothing. Strong-colored semi-precious stones (onyx, lapis lazuli, malachite), coral and jade are popular, they are worked in large rings, diamonds, short pyramids, cabochons and square frames and trimmed with pearl fringes and loops. Ropes of pearls hang together, the third one down to the waistline and even lengthened by a big rectangular unset aquamarine, emerald or sapphire.

All this does not need to be genuine: paste, colored glass, rhinestones and tiny crystals (marcasite) are easier to come by and almost as effective."[41] In addition, the taste of the times for glamour is integrated directly with fashion. Dancing and socializing clothes are preferentially given colored glass and steel pearls, metal plates, paillettes, gold and silver embroidery, rhinestones, cultured pearls or jet as sparkling decoration.

40)
Compare B. Mundt,
Metropole machen Mode,
color plate, p. 136, Galalith
Jewelry.

41)
B. Mundt, op. cit., p. 69.

The German Jewelry of the German Woman.

The change in stylistic tendencies that was to determine the appearance of women throughout the decade had already made itself known by 1930. "Die Goldschmiedekunst", which always took up fashion questions intensely, acknowledged: "Slowly but surely, fashion has developed a new type of the boyish woman. Step by step, scarcely recognizable as a movement, this significant change proceeded.

The effect is ". . . perfection in the evenness of everything that is feminine." The garconne look was thus passé. Inside and out, genuine femininity was treasured, all exaggerations were done away with and a new, "proper" relationship to clothing and fashion was found.

The fashion ideal first put emphasis on a moderated, natural and elegant line. The feminine figure was intentionally accentuated, and for "those less well-proportioned", the corset was once again a threat.[42]

Special emphasis was given to the hat at the beginning of the decade, a fact that the jewelry industry recognized with annoyance and ascribed merely to a good advertising campaign by the hat manufacturers. Again and again the necessity to cooperate with fashion and advertising was stressed — a connection that "Fahrner Jewelry" made good use of in its advertising from the start. The fashionable jewelry of the time also achieved a withdrawal from everything expressive, colorful and eccentric: gold jewelry and gilded silver jewelry in all shades were dominant.

It is noteworthy that this jewelry achieved its effect mainly from its relationship to clothing. The autonomous character of Art Nouveau and Art Deco jewelry is no longer found in the jewelry of the thirties. The close relationship to clothing also became clear in that shapes came into being that looked like cloth translated into metal: bows as brooches (Cat. No. 2.177), bracelets that took the place of cuff links, patterned metal bandeaus, pearl or gold collars, an accessory that head been created by Coco Chanel in 1925. Along with these more conventional but not undecorative forms there came, in ever-increasing quantities, forms that were natural. Inexpensive motifs like flowers, leaves, sheaves, starfish were used as decorative elements and gave their wearers a modest glitter.

After 1933 Germany left the international fashion scene and subscribed to its own national style. Then came the "Arianizing" of the clothing, fashion and tailor shops, most of which were Jewish.

Berlin had ceased to be an international clothing center.

Fashion itself, that gave visible evidence of the social role of the woman, underwent — as did all other areas of daily life — a strict indoctrination of National Socialistic propaganda. The required return to home and hearth in the role of housewife and mother made an end to all extravagance.[43]

42)
In: Die Goldschmiedekunst, 1930, p. 401.

43)
Compare Christianne Weber, Schmuck der 20er und 30er Jahre in Deutschland. Stuttgart 1990.

The ideology involved gave the discussion of fashion and jewelry a direction that once again involved an outlook on life. The aversion to French fashion dictates, now a part of history, was renewed vehemently with unmitigated harshness, in language that scarcely differed from that of the pre-war "reformers." At the focal point of this discussion was the question of a moral and ethical position on fashion, rather than an esthetic one. It was of being flighty because its seasonal changes lacked any seriousness. Maria van de Velde had already written in 1901 that in modern times the "fate of the dress had fallen into the professional and dangerous hands of the tailors and milliners", and went on to say: "The viewpoints of business thought up new changes of fashion for every season and forced their laws on women and men. Gradually they lost any consideration for art and for the morality of beauty. For fashion is the thoroughly lost one who is to blame for all the ugliness that the decade has accumulated. All of her creations bear the unmistakable signs of whim and chance . . . With the morals of our times and the condition of our art, it could scarcely be otherwise." Thus the ethical character of clothing reform was thrust clearly into the middle of all imaginable considerations.[44]

What is implied is the economic aspect of seasonal changes in the changeable nature of fashion, a condition that, under the pretext of social assistance, gave reason to preserve resentment. For the economic demands of the market and the financial dependence of the worker were transferred into a purely moral dimension. Consider a statement from 1914 that, in polemic manner, described the nature of fashion: "Fashion is the last triumph of flightiness, the deepest and most generous source of surrogate economy . . . The favorite element of fashion is change. But its result is seasonal work, with its great economic harm to the seasonal workers."[45] As an alternative there is only the turn back to "quality work." In the "social reorganization of all conditions", as it was called in 1934,[46] the backward-looking ideology of National Socialism looked forward to the "turning away from the sham approach to household goods, clothing, jewelry" and a turn to genuine, dedicated workshop work was promoted. Material feeling, viewed now as a "tender sprout", could develop when, as it was said, the German woman turns away from stylish trash and false jewels in the department store (which at that time was often Jewish-owned).

Although the veiled (anti-Semitic) criticism of capitalism and the equation of "quality" with "German" appeared as tangible formulas, nothing changed the basic requirement that high-quality artistic work is justified. It still seemed valid that only work of high artistic value — to a certain extent — could help an industry that, like the manufacturing of jewelry, was fighting hard to survive. The tension

44)
In: Wiener Rundschau, Vol. V, No. 10, May 1901, p. 204.

45)
It is further said: "If the development of fashions were merely a case of satisfying extravagant tendencies in a small upper level of the population, one would not need to pay any great attention to it. But it is a cult of the external that has become its own justification and gone to extremes, drawing all levels of the population under its spell and, in addition to the mental anguish of those tyrannized by it, consumes a huge amount of productive human working energy." in: Kunstgewerbeblatt Vol. 25, 1914, p. 28.

46)
H. Rothenbüchler, Qualitätsschmuck, in: Die Schaulade, Vol. 9, 1933, p. 300.

between production quantities that were calculated according to cost-efficient, market-oriented and profit-maximizing principles, and studio work, that was naturally based on other laws, can be traced as a constant factor through decades of discussion. Thus in the thirties, progressive designers like Wilhelm Wagenfeld and Wolfgang Tümpel were regarded as very exemplary in their jewelry designs,[47] and seemed to contradict the narrow-mindedness of general artistic taste. The mixture of economic and moral categories, of course, confused the situation, a condition that may distract one from the mongrel status of fashion and jewelry production. Both possess a high degree of artistic handiwork, but it must be devoted to meeting the demands of the market, and yet it reacts seismographically to political situations. It is obvious that this ever-present tension between artistic handicraft and artistic industry continued to exist — a dualism that could always be harmonized only with difficulty. In the article "Die Grenzen zwischen Kunst-handwerk und Kunstindustrie"[48], Rudolf Rücklin, the great admirer of Theodor Fahrner's achievements, took up this theme once again. Still obligated to the tradition of the Kunstverein and Kunst-gewerbe movement in the late 19th Century, Rücklin tried to avoid those mystifying components of this emotion-packed subject. The manufacturing of jewelry always included a high degree of mass-produced reproduction resulting

from the use of mechanical processes; that was part of its character.

The replacement of high-priced natural materials by cheap synthetic products for decorative effect is also, according to Rücklin, as old as jewelrymaking itself. The work involved in production and the influence of trade are also important factors. For "the artistic handiwork has always led, necessarily and naturally, to the activity of the art industry, in and of itself."[49] The art industry always discovers the "need of the people, which has only an instinctive rather than a conscious and trained relationship to are."[50] The buying public for this category is moved less by artistic intentions than by considerations of fashion. According to Rücklin, "fashion" means a degradation, a sinking of artistic trends into the awareness of the masses. According to this, artistic handiwork and artistic industry are expressions of the cultural makeup of a people, fashion taste, artistic taste and artistic needs are elements of the people's soul that follow their own laws and should not be regi-mented. Behind them there hides the demand for the exemplary quality of good artistic handicraft designs that can be adapted to a broad basis. Not by chance does Rücklin choose, as the first il-lustration to his lecture, a picture of silver filigree jewelry from the firm of Gustav Braendle, Theodor Fahrner's Successor. Rücklin's concept of a "people's soul" was surely influenced by the cultural ideals of the 19th Century. In such a

47)
ibid.

48)
In: DGZ 1934, No. 45, pp. 464-467.

49)
Op. cit., pp. 464-465.

50)
ibid.

and morning and afternoon fashions ranged from sporting to timelessly elegant. Coral and turquoise, lapis lazuli, enamel, crystals, marcasite and garnet were used in jewelry, and naturally so was amber, "German gold." Of course gold jewelry was the absolute favorite, its special feature being its timelessness, which never became unmodern in an overall sense; it seemed to be ideal for the moderate fashions of the thirties, for it proved to be suitable as jewelry for every time of the day and every occasion and thus was really useful.

context, the linking work "Volk-" means the same thing as "popular" or "universal."[51] In extreme and emotional form, as a unity of all Germans, the propaganda of the National Socialists took up this concept. Even in their observations on jewelry, the folk aspect is not missing. Thus the German people as a unit are exhorted again and again, and German decorative stones are conjured up out of German Mother Earth, so that the German woman can wear them with pride and joy.[52]

Such curiosities seemed interesting only because they seemed to anticipate the avalanche of special regulations concerning precious metals and stones, and because they set up a fictional position opposed to the realities of the jewelry and fashions of the times. For although Germany had left the international fashion scene on account of its political development, German fashions did not look essentially different from those of Paris, London, New York or Nice.[53] Until well into the thirties, correspondents reported on the fashion trends in those places. Something exotic — within reason — still appeared to be wanted for evening wear,

But even these small, unpretentious pieces of gold jewelry were adapted to fit into the awareness of the political mission of the times. The qualities attributed to gold were now attributed to the German character and German handiwork: honesty and sincerity were associated with it, genuine ability documented and the permanence of the German people's cultural values brought to the fore. Once again the differences between the national characters of France and Germany were cited; it was said: "We cannot ask that our style should become the whole world's style, and we do not want to throw out golden lures and silken snares of our style to gain that, as France does. But we do want to show the world, especially in art and commercial art, what German ability and German will are able to accomplish in

51)
Compare the concepts that resulted in 19th-Century terms such as folk school, folk library, folk song, folk books.

52)
Deutsche Schmucksteine, in: DGZ No. 8, 1934, p. 341; an article signed only with "S" and closing with the following anthem in verse: German stone from German soil,/ Nobly formed by artist's hand,/ He who recognizes your value/ Loves the German Fatherland./ Mighty powers that created/ simple German precious stones/ Radiate from you and cry out:/ My wearers shall be German too."

53)
See Mode, Modeschmuck und Schmuckstil, in: DGZ, No. 49, 1936, p. 501: "Fashion is international today in that the cut or the type of the dress is much the same . . . a German woman would not attract attention by looking strange either in Paris, London or Vienna."

stubborn striving and patient endurance."[54]

Prophetic words that were to be fulfilled, though in other areas than this.

The Graphic Appearance of Fahrner Jewelry in Advertising. Theodor Fahrner was one of the first entrepreneurs who called the buyer's attention to his mass-produced jewelry in advertisements. The first inexpensive advertisements appeared in 1901. In the advertising circulars included with "Deutsche Kunst und Dekoration" as of 1906, Fahrner used graphic "essentials" that remained the same over the years.

The "TF" linked in a circle was also used on the seal that was hung on every piece of original Fahrner Jewelry.

This advertising made use of the Eckmann script, a form characteristic of Art Nouveau and made to look like the brush writing of East Asian calligraphy.

The message of the advertisement already proclaimed Fahrner's credo: This jewelry, though machine-made, was created from the "designs of leading artists", and buying Fahrner Jewelry implied, in a kind of circular reasoning,

that one was buying "genuinely artistic" jewelry. Not only did the stamp of purity thus become important, but the TF monogram was even more so. Only in this way — so it seems — could it be seen that it possessed an inherent quality. Fahrner's advertising of his jewelry with his signet and name followed the trend of the times in creating brand-name articles. Products still well-known today, such as Persil, Odol, Sarotti and Sanella, gained their characteristic brand-name image around the turn of the century. The basis of "modern" advertising strategy was the idea that the buyer was not necessarily being offered a specific article, but rather, with the help of advertising, the public was being induced to create a demand. For the first time, the solid line from manufacturer to consumer via middlemen such as wholesalers, agents and retailers was broken as the manufacturer turned directly to the consumer.

It was not just the product itself that was important; the desire to buy it had to be mobilized. Aspects of psychology, especially mass psychology, suddenly played a role in gaining attention and thus business success.[55]

As of 1890 the art of the placard advanced quickly, helped by improving graphic techniques and artistic interest in this medium. Advertising with placards and graphically effective designs, at first the only means of advertising, soon attracted the attention of sociologists, art historians and marketing specialists. This

54)
Ludwig Segmiller, Goldschmuck, in: DGZ No. 3, 1936, p. 25.

55)
Victor Mataja, Reklame und Publikum, in: Die Reklame, Mitteilungen des Vereins deutscher Reklamefachleute, No. 26, 1912, p. 7.

resulted in early theories of mass communication and publicity. It was soon recognized that the signet, the trade mark, took on a special significance. It fulfilled the important task of differentiating one firm's goods from those of another, namely the competition. "The livelier, more striking and meaningful such a signet is, the more harmoniously this little form is made into a work of art, the more impact this identifying mark has in advertising."[56]

Of course the goods and the offer had to agree over time; only then was success guaranteed. The trade mark thus required quality in and of itself.

The simple but tasteful words of the early advertising gave way at the beginning of the twenties, the beginning of the Braendle era, to striking large-format advertisements for Fahrner Jewelry.[57] The firm, which at this point could already look back on tradition, honors and awards, used graphic art to advertise the highest quality for itself and its products. With a commanding attitude like that of a Baroque heraldic emblem, the observer-buyer was vividly shown the high rank of Fahrner Jewelry: At the midpoint of an oval, ornamented shield — under a realistic, precisely delineated crown — there appeared the TF trade mark. The term "Fahrner Schmuck" was present in conventional, lively cursive script, with stylized crossed laurel branches below it. Linked, script and laurel motif appeared on an octagonal dark background, its points bearing the names of cities that were the

sites of important competitions for art and industry: Paris (1900 World's Fair), Darmstadt (1901), Karlsruhe (1904 Jubilee Exhibition), St. Louis (1904 World's Fair), Dresden (1906 Kunstgewerbe Exhibition), Brussels (1910 World's Fair). Though this design is unique as compared to the firm's later avant-garde advertising, it makes certain aspects clear: Even in times of decline and "lack of monarchy", such as existed in Germany after 1918, there were obviously "lasting values." The primacy of art, which was stressed by Fahrner Jewelry again and again, obviously could no longer be used effectively in politically uncertain times.

Modern principles of design and targeting of a particular level of consumers played a role in the advertising of the twenties.

These Fahrner advertisements often utilized the artistic method of montage, the combination of photos and graphic elements, as dominating characteristics of advertisements in the magazines "Die Dame" and "Der Querschnitt."

In the large-format advertisements in "Die Dame", graphics made motifs and themes visible that were also spoken of in the wording: The lady was shown at the golf course, in the theater box, at the party — naturally, always with Fahrner Jewelry. The graphic drawing that contained the narrative, generic element was equated with the documentary level. The jewelry appeared as a documentary representation, often with the added note,

56)
Paul Ruben, Das Signet und die Reklame, in: Die Reklame, ihre Kunst und Wissenschaft, hrsg. von P. Ruben, Berlin 1913, Bd. 1, P. 153

57)
in: DGZ, Jg. 1921, Nr. 5, P. 66

"approximately 3/4 actual size."

The most precise information about the product was thus linked with suggestions that were meant to communicate such hard-to-define concepts as elegance, status, individuality and exclusivity. The vitalization of these two levels, the suggestive and the informative, was accomplished with the help of montage. Almost in the manner of a "cubistic" technique, the photo was related to the drawing, linked by the words "Fahrner-Schmuck." Now it appeared as a three-dimensional line of letters, often enhanced with dramatic lights and shadows. In a "tangible" way, the point of it was to be made clear. The little monogram had also developed into the seal that was related to every piece of "Original Fahrner Jewelry." The advertisements in "Der Querschnitt" used the photo more powerfully as the transmitter of the advertising. These advertisements, one column wide, often combined photographs of particular pieces of jewelry with relatively extensive texts. The main point of this advertising was supposed to be the information, since the readers of "Der Querschnitt" were supposed to be more intellectual than those of "Die Dame." Mixtures of graphics and photos appear here too. Again and again, fashion information was used as advertising, which was also seen in "Die Dame", and the fashions of various times of the day were shown: "The style of sport clothes", "for the afternoon", "the lady's evening gown", always combined with

jewelry. These advertisements were designed so that the jewelry in question was portrayed in a detailed photo showing its function on the neck or ear, combined with a sort of negative of a feminine face. Simple but elegant line drawings were also used, again combined with a photo.

Since "Der Querschnitt" reached a more masculine public, the theme of jewelry as a gift appeared here too, with the slogan of the advertisement cleverly included in the following text, simultaneously conjuring up associations with jewelry, especially Fahrner Jewelry. Thus lines like "respectable and genuine" or "the value of a gift" were stressed typographically, along with the name "Fahrner-Schmuck." In between, in smaller type, was the text in between, in smaller type, was the text in which the buyer was assured that such a gift would mark him as a person with tact and taste, and that with the firm's large and modern assortment of jewelry, the choice would be easy. Naturally the silhouette drawing behind the photographed jewelry was that

of a couple: the purchaser and recipient of the jewelry were portrayed here.

The pure photo advertisement, the portrait of the buyer-wearer with her jewelry, as used relatively seldom and did not attain the same suggestive effect. The effect on the female purchaser is more penetrating in the abstract, stylized portrayal. The possibilities of identification are greater. Here, of course, only a certain type is portrayed, the embodiment of fashion, whereas a photograph seems too cut and dried. In addition, the combined advertisement show the meaningful touch of a commercial artist, while the photograph bespeaks a less artistic level. The possibilities of identification are limited, even when exemplary character is represented. The most meaningful, though at the same time not very convincing, example appeared in "Die Dame" (1930-31) with the original photo" Frau von Stetten wears Fahrner Jewelry." Next to it there appeared, as if in a sales brochure, various pieces of jewelry with their prices. The feeling of exclusivity and taste that the photo of the noble wearer of Fahrner Jewelry was meant to suggest was made ridiculous through the listing of prices. Advertising with portrait photos, though in impersonal form, appeared in later years too, though rarely.

In Fahrner Advertisements the Following Complexes Crystallize:

Information about fashion and jewelry. This includes advertisements that combine an extensive text, a documentary photo of jewelry and the graphic image of a woman. Specific forms of jewelry can be promoted. There is an advertisement for "beautiful necklaces" (1930-31) saying that "fashion requires neck jewelry" and "primitive jewelry is passé." One could also request of the Fahrner firm a jewelry fashion booklet showing the new directions in fashion with the appropriate jewelry (in, among others, "Der Querschnitt" 1931-32).

Identification: This concerns what one still tries to buy today with a certain brand-

Woman from Stetten wearing Fahrner jewelry.

name image: above and beyond the actual object, the buyer and wearer of such jewelry take on a social status and background that corresponds to their concepts and desires. This includes the level of society and the elegant world, as shown by the little impressions of the golf course, theater box and party. To a great degree, the stylized drawing focuses on the woman as recipient. Thus she becomes — in a particularly clever advertisement in "Die Dame" in 1929-30 — the elegant lady who is seen from the back before a jeweler's display, in which the play of various levels is introduced in a particularly refined way. Her reflection appears to her as a placard advertising Fahrner Jewelry within the display — now seen from the front. The slogan: "Why wonder? Fahrner Jewelry, the most desirable Christmas gift", is dictated to her by a shopping list, and alluringly near, almost tangible, lifted out of the picture, are the real pieces of jewelry.

Photos of women used for advertising were also utilized in more old-fashioned ways. The principles of modern fashion and jewelry photography had not yet been applied. The advertisements appear, at least from a present-day point of view, as not so effective or interesting.

The Image of the Lasting Value of Fahrner Jewelry: In early Fahrner advertising the emphasis was on "artist jewelry." According to the "cultivated bourgeois" trend of the 19th Century, which made science and art of primary importance, such jewelry implied value and excellence — irrespective of the material. In addition, according to classic principles of advertising, "advertising and offering" were one and the same. Fahrner really could gain the services of leading artists of the new style for his production.

Even before 1910, though, the artist's name no longer mattered, and thus the advertisements slowly changed their concept. This downplaying was accomplished by using the term "artists' designs" of "to the designs of leading artists." The reference to the awards that Fahrner Jewelry had won at all the significant exhibitions of the century (see pp. 30-31) offer, in addition to the information, an impression of absolute values that such jewelry could claim for its own.

The advertising that appeared at the end of the twenties implied the taste, individuality and elegance of the wearer of Fahrner Jewelry: "Fahrner Jewelry singles out the elegant woman. She is admired by those around her because of her individual taste." (Die Dame, 1930-31) Fahrner Jewelry became the "genuine, the Original Fahrner Jewelry, what with its trade mark, its seal. The very authenticity was stressed again and again in advertisements as a quality that made jewelry truly valuable. A "Querschnitt" advertisement in 1930, for example, said: "The genuine stones and genuine metals used" afforded buyers of Fahrner Jewelry a "higher inherent value" than the actual purchase price. And the question of "why

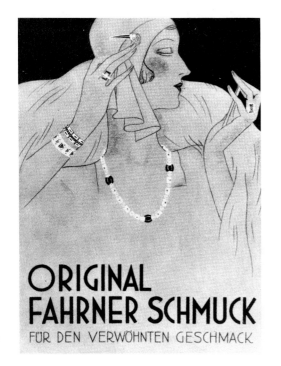

ORIGINAL
FAHRNER SCHMUCK
FÜR DEN VERWÖHNTEN GESCHMACK

Fahrner Jewelry?'' could also be answered simply: "The variety of designs, expert work based on decades of experience. Every piece produced in limited numbers, prices kept low, assortments of masterfully designed jewelry in original versions." It was summed up as follows: "A requirement of our time is fulfilled. A special class at moderate prices." (Der Querschnitt, 1932).

Following the general tendency of the late thirties, a photo advertisement stressed the obligation of Fahrner Jewelry "to offer more than quickly outmoded fashion decoration. Made of genuine silver, the noble material of the German goldsmith's art, along with gold and genuine or synthetic stones."

The incompatibility of art and machine work cannot be escaped by the partially machine-made Fahrner Jewelry by words alone. For the wording of the advertisement almost always tried to deal with the great question, "Gretchen's question" of the 19th and early 20th centuries. "That it was particularly the machine that, through commerce, killed the sense of excellent workmanship, is a known fact. But one must beware of seeing machine work as a necessary evil by taking that which British social-commercial artists have done as a condemnation of the machine itself. . . .

58)
Quoted from Julius Posener, Anfänge des Funktionalismus. Von Arts und Crafts zum Deutschen Werkbund, Berlin, 1964, pp. 166 ff.

Obviously the machine is not there the produce art. This is a privilege of the human hand." Thus spoke Muthesius in 1903.[58]

The fact of industrial necessity thus was not in the "bedevilment" of the machine but rather the sensitive use of functional forms. If the early Fahrner Jewelry could still come from artists' designs and be transmitted into machine-made linear, geometric ornamentation, then the advertising of later years, especially, of course, in the thirties, imagines an aura of authenticity, excellence, luxury as moderate prices — an impossibility in and of itself.

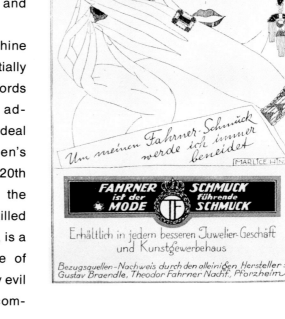

Um meinen Fahrner-Schmuck werde ich immer beneidet

MARLICE HINZ

FAHRNER SCHMUCK
ist der führende
MODE SCHMUCK

Erhältlich in jedem besseren Juwelier-Geschäft und Kunstgewerbehaus

Bezugsquellen-Nachweis durch den alleinigen Hersteller: Gustav Braendle, Theodor Fahrner Nachf., Pforzheim

The Fahrner advertisement relates to traditions that do not amount to the actual, true "artistic heritage", namely the handiwork of the talented gold- and silversmith. It had taken on the task of portraying the noble niveau of this jewelry, through prices that were moderate though still not easy for broad levels of the population to pay. For in these economically difficult times of the twenties and thirties, with three million people out of work, it was naturally not easy to make costly jewelry of this type available to the woman, or the man.

With a clever combination of fashion and jewelry to be regarded as a single entity, Fahrner advertising succeeded in making its offerings appear to be part of the "dictates of fashion": the elegant and well-dressed woman wore Fahrner Jewelry. Thus she wore "genuine" jewelry, namely the genuine "Original Fahrner Jewelry."

Die Schönheit der Kleidung wird durch die aparte Wirkung des *Fahrner Schmuckes* in außerordentlichem Maße gehoben. Keine Dame von Geschmack wird in Zukunft darauf verzichten wollen

Sample card (photo) 1929-30.

Appendix

The Use of the "TF" Trade Mark (1901-1979)

Dieter Zühlsdorff

a. Stampings   Artist Monograms: see pp. 68 ff.

1. Cat. No. 1.74 (1901)

2. Cat. No. 1.37 (ca. 1903)

3. Cat. No. 1.129 (1908-1910)

4. Cat. No. 1.154 (1914)

5. Page 150 (post-1914)

6. Cat. No. 1.147 (Post-1910)

7. Cat. No. 1.162 (Post 1910; "EX" probably   Export)

8. Cat. No. 1.109c (twenties)

9. Cat. No. 2.27 (1926)

10. Cat. No. 2.67 (1927)

11. Cat. No. 2.134 (late twenties)

12. Cat. No. 2.151 (1932)

b. "TF" trade mark registrations and "TF" trade marks in print.

THEODOR FAHRNER
PFORZHEIM
Gold- und Silberschmuck
nach Künstler-Entwürfen
Fabrik gegründet 1855

Schutz-　Marke

Man verlange nach meiner Schutzmarke
bei ersten Juwelieren u. Kunsthandlungen.
An Private wird nicht verkauft.

1. Trade mark registered at the Imperial Patent Office in Berlin, July 22, 1901. Entered on August 25, 1902 as No. 55308 (F. 3819/17). Published in WZB, Vol. IX, 1902, p. 767.

2. Advertisement in: Joseph M. Olbrich, Die Ausstellung der Künstlerkolonie 1901, Darmstadt Mathildenhöhe, p. 136 (advertisers' appendix).

3. Entry in the Adress- und Handbuch für das deutsche Goldschmiedegewerbe, Leipzig 1903, pp. 7 and 256 (illustration).

FAHRNER SCHMUCK
NACH ENTWÜRFEN ERSTER KÜNSTLER

WOLLEN SIE GEWÄHR FÜR ECHT KÜNSTLERI:
SCHEN SCHMUCK SO ACHTEN SIE BEIM KAUF
DARAUF, DASS ER MIT (TF) GESTEMPELT IST.

4. Advertisement in: Advertising circular in DKD, 1906, No. 2.

MAN BEACHTE DIE
SCHVTZMARKE :

5. Advertisement in: Kochs Monographien IX, Schmuck- und Edelmetallarbeiten, Darmstadt 1906, p. 108 (excerpt).

FAHRNER SCHMUCK

6. Trade mark registered at the Imperial Patent Office in Berlin on May 19, 1910. Entered on August 1, 1910 as No. 132886 (F. 9731/17). Published in WZB, Vol. XVII, 1910, pp. 1614 ff.

THEODOR FAHRNER
◎◎ PFORZHEIM ◎◎
GOLD- UND SILBERWAAREN-
FABRIK · GEGRÜNDET 1855 ∾

7. Theodor Fahrner's letterhead, handwritten letter by Theodor Fahrner (attestation for Friedrich Katz), dated July 4, 1913.

Fahrner-Schmuck
D.W.B.
Theodor Fahrner · Kunstwerkstätten

Postscheckkonto 1374
Fernsprecher Nr. 76

Preisgekrönt: Darmstadt / Paris
St. Louis / Dresden / Karlsruhe
Brüssel / Malmö
Gegründet 1856

Pforzheim

Fabrik-  Marke

8. Theodor Fahrner Letterhead, dated December 31, 1919.

9. Advertisement in: DGZ, 1920, No. 12, p. 52.

Note: No piece of jewelry signed with this mark has been found.

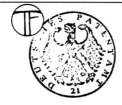

264

10. German Patent Office, patent roll (Warenzeichenregister), Berlin, registered on July 15, 1921, No. 273516, entered on October 14, 1921 (document number B 41165): Gustav Braendle, Theodor Fahrner Nachf., Pforzheim. Protection extended through July 15, 1971.

11. Advertisement in: DGZ 1922, No. 3, p. 48.

GUSTAV BRAENDLE, THEODOR FAHRNER NACHF., PFORZHEIM
FABRIK FEINER GOLD- UND SILBER-WAREN
DEUTSCH / EXPORT

Fabrik- TF Marke

12. Gustav Braendle, Theodor Fahrner Nachf. Letterhead, dated May 1, 1925.

FAHRNER SCHMUCK ist der MODE führende SCHMUCK

Erhältlich in jedem besseren Juwelier-Geschäft und Kunstgewerbehaus

13. Advertisement in: Die Dame, Vol. 54, No. 20, 1927, p. 43.

FAHRNER-SCHMUCK
MIT DER PLOMBE

14. Advertisement in: Der Querschnitt, Vol. X, No. 8, 1930, p. 543.

15. Brochure "J 62" (probably 1962).

FAHRNERSCHMUCK-FABRIK
Factory of Fahrner Jewelry

GUSTAV BRAENDLE · THEODOR FAHRNER NACHFOLGER · PFORZHEIM

16. "Fahrner Jewelry Factory" Letterhead, dated May 25, 1972.

c. "TF" seals and "TF" labels

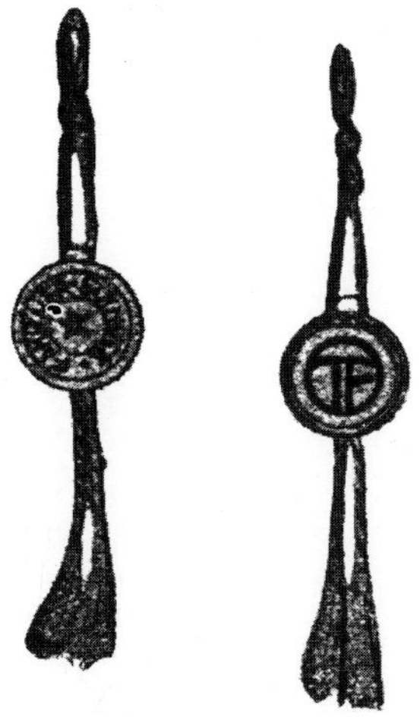

1. "TF" seals as trade marks registered at the German Patent Office in Berlin on September 19, 1928, entered in February 14, 1929, published in WZB Vol. XXXVI, No. 5, 1929, p. 495 (see Cat. No. 2.146).

2. DEA seal as trade mark, registered at the German Patent Office in Berlin on January 27, 1932, entered on November 1, 1932 as No. 449837 (B 67260), published in WZB, Vol. XXXIX, No. 22, 1932, p. 1625.

3. Etikette "ORIGINAL FAHRNER-SCHMUCK". Roter Aufdruck auf Papier-Etikette. An Schmuckstücken aus dem Nachlaß Gustav Braendle. Vermutlich 30er-/40er Jahre.

4. Labels "TF ORIGINAL FAHRNER since 1850", reverse: "100 Years of FAHRNER", silver label for silver jewelry, gold label for gilded silver jewelry, used since early fifties.

5. Labels "ANTIKE KUNST", paper labels with "TF" and notation of gold content; reverse: Model number plus exact description of motif shown on the piece of jewelry.

d. *Advertising Slogans*

„Fahrnerschmuck"

1. "Fahrnerschmuck", registered as a trade mark at the German Patent Office in Berlin on July 15, 1921, entered on October 28, 1921 as No. 274300, Group 17 (B. 41164), published in WZB, Vol. XXVII, No. 11, 1921, p. 3157.

Fahrnerschmuck mit der Plombe

2. "Fahrnerschmuck with the seal", registered as a trade mark at the German Patent Office in Berlin on December 10, 1930, entered on March 10, 1931 as No. 430298, Group 17 (B 65252), published in WZB, Vol. XXXVIII, No. 7, 1931, p. 611.

266

Original-Fahrner-Schmuck

3. "Original-Fahrner-Schmuck", registered as a trade mark at the German Patent Office in Berlin on December 10, 1930, entered on February 13, 1931 as No. 429197, Group 17 (B 65208), published in WZB, Vol. XXXVIII, No. 5, 1931, p. 414.

DEA-SCHMUCK

4. "DEA-SCHMUCK". Registered in Der Querschnitt, 1932, H.3 (March 1932), o.S.

5. "Fahrner Schmuck entzückt beglückt", registered as a trade mark at the German Patent Office in Berlin on March 30, 1935, entered on May 31, 1935 as No. 476215, Group 17 (B 72409), published in WZB, Vol. XXXXII, No. 12, 1935, p. 795. Next page: Advertisement with this slogan in: DGZ 1935, No. 35, p. 5.

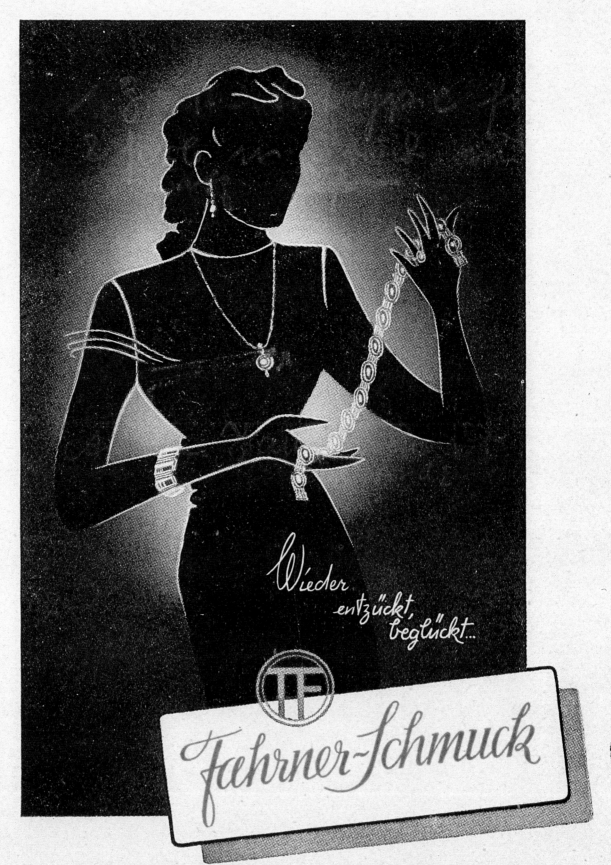

Wieder entzückt, beglückt...

Fahrner-Schmuck

ALLEINIGER HERSTELLER GUSTAV BRAENDLE THEODOR FAHRNER NACHFOLGER

Fahrner Family Tree (four generations)

1. Generation

1 *Gustav Adolf Faber*
Kreisgerichtsrat
✳ 18.11.1829 Stuttgart -
† 13.5.1871 Stuttgart,
Heirat mit

2 *Amélie Gschwindt*
✳ 4.6.1844 Pforzheim -
† 2.1.1902 Pforzheim

2. Generation

1 *Albert Faber*
✳ 1867 - † 1951

2 *Martha Faber*
✳ 12.5.1869
Stuttgart -
† 20.12.1940
Zürich,
Heirat am
12.7.1890
mit

3 *Theodor Fahrner*
✳ 4.8.1859 Pforzheim -
† 22.7.1919 Pforzheim

3. Generation

1 *Bert (Albert) Joho*
✳ 23.2.1877 Bruchsal -
† 6.10.1963 Zürich
Heirat am
20.7.1916 mit

2 *Vera Fahrner*
✳ 23.1.1895 Pforzheim -
† 19.9.1987 Mexiko

3 *Yella Fahrner*
✳ 12.10.1897
Pforzheim -
† 8.1.1977
Heirat am 2.7.1921
mit

4 *Dr. Hans Curjel*
✳ 1.5.1896 Karlsruhe -
† 3.1.1974 Zürich

4. Generation

1 *Virginia Joho*
✳ 20.3.1927 Karlruhe -

2 *Luzia Curjel*
✳ 5.2.1926 -

3 *Caspar Robert Curjel*
✳ 21.11.1931 -

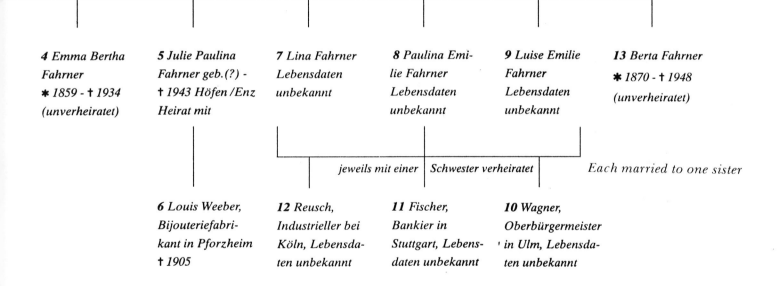

3 Theodor Fahrner sen.
✴ 2.4.1823 -
† 11.7.1883 Pforzheim
Heirat mit

4 Pauline Schweikert
✴ 8.5.1828 -
† 27.9.1886

4 Emma Bertha Fahrner
✴ 1859 - † 1934
(unverheiratet)

5 Julie Paulina Fahrner geb.(?) -
† 1943 Höfen/Enz
Heirat mit

7 Lina Fahrner
Lebensdaten unbekannt

8 Paulina Emilie Fahrner
Lebensdaten unbekannt

9 Luise Emilie Fahrner
Lebensdaten unbekannt

13 Berta Fahrner
✴ 1870 - † 1948
(unverheiratet)

jeweils mit einer | Schwester verheiratet   *Each married to one sister*

6 Louis Weeber,
Bijouteriefabrikant in Pforzheim
† 1905

12 Reusch,
Industrieller bei Köln, Lebensdaten unbekannt

11 Fischer,
Bankier in Stuttgart, Lebensdaten unbekannt

10 Wagner,
Oberbürgermeister in Ulm, Lebensdaten unbekannt

The grave of Theodor Fahrner, Sr. and his wife Pauline, as well as their daughters Emma and Berta, is found in the main cemetery in Pforzheim. The grave of Theodor Fahrner, Jr. was also in this cemetery but was moved some years ago.

Martha Faber (ca. 1883), later the wife of Theodor Fahrner, Jr.

the Joho Family

Vera and Yella Fahrner, Christmas 1899

Gustav Braendle, Sr., circa 1929

Martha Fahrner (1940).

Hans Braendle, circa 1929.

Gustav Braendle, Jr., circa 1929

Herbert Braendle, circa 1960.

Documents

Ulrike von Hase-Schmundt

1)
V. Becker, Murrle, Bennett & Co. — are they the German links with Liberty Jewellery? in: Art Collector 11, 1980, pp. 72 ff (with illustration), similarly in: Antique & 20th Century Jewellery, London 1980, pp. 255 ff.; John Culme, The directory of gold- and silversmiths, jewelers and allied traders 1838-1914 (from the London Assay Office registers), 2 vol., Woodbridge 1987.

2)
Died April 4, 1950; son of the tin founder Jakob Mürrle.

3)
Born ca. 1842, died Nov. 17, 1920. Since 1877 Wilhelm Fühner directed the treasury of the Kunstgewerbeverein. Data in Pforzheim City Archives, Address Book and: Fünfzig Jahre im Dienst der Pforzheimer Kunstindustrie 1877-1927, Pforzheim 1927.

4)
My viewpoint expressed in the first edition of "Schmuck in Deutschland und Österreich" that it was a case of partial manufacturing proved to be incorrect. Immanuel Saake, ca. 1864-May 12, 1927, son of Georg Christian Saake, 1819-1879, brother of Karl Julius and Paul Saake, who owned the "Saake Brothers" tool factory. Addressbuch 1900: "Immanuel Saake, representative of Murrle, Bennett & Co., London, jewelry buyer, Bahnhofstrasse 11:. Addressbuch 1914: "Immanuel Saake, Commission and Export, representative of Murrle, Bennett & Co, London, Artistic Novelties Ltd., London, The L. F. Brenner & Co, jewelry buyer, Bahnhofstrasse 11." In 1905 "Mrs. M. Saake" was listed as a part-owner of the firm of Murrle, B. & Co. After 1919 the business was rebuilt. In the Pforzheimer Kurier 196, August 22, 1953, a precious stone business was cited in addition to the export business.

5)
Adressbuch 1895 and R. Rücklin, in: DGZ XXII, 1919, p. 268.

6)
There he met Archibald Knox, who presumably had also made designs for his firm, and who worked in "Alien's Detention."

Murrle, Bennett & Co, London. *Closely related to the history of Theodor Fahrner is that of the British firm of jewelry and silver goods importers, Murrle, Bennett & Co. A brief look at it shall be offered here, for on the one hand it was an important business partner to Theodor Fahrner, and on the other a carrier of the concept of the "artist-manufacturer" to Britain in an interesting way. The British authors Vivienne Becker and, in particular, John Culme, a chronicler of incredible precision, have studied the history of this London firm, which had been mentioned only fleetingly in the literature previously.[1] John Culme lists the following titles of the firm up to 1916:*

Siegele & Bennett: 1884-ca. 1894

Siegele, Bennett & Co.: ca. 1894-1896

Murrle, Bennett & Co.: 1896-1905

Murrle, Bennett & Co. Ltd.: 1905-1916

White, Redgrove & Whyte (Murrle, Bennett's successors) 1916-17

White & Redgrove Ltd.: 1917 to the present

Subsidiaries: Artistic Rolled Gold Co

Murrle, Bennett Export Ltd.: 1916

The relationship of the firm of Murrle, Bennett & Co. to Pforzheim is a close one. Except for the British family of John Baker Bennett and Elizabeth Bennett, partners until 1907, the proprietors were born in Pforzheim; as V. Becker writes, Siegele and Mürrle were cousins, and both were friends of Theodor Fahrner.

The merchant Ernst Mürrle, born on September 1, 1861, went outside the country on business quite early.[2] In 1896, when Siegele withdrew, he became a partner in the firm, which was then called "Murrle, Bennett & Co." Up to 80% of the wares in the stately three-story shop at 13, Charterhouse Street in London were ordered from Pforzheim from then on, especially from the firms of Wilhelm Fühner[3] and Theodor Fahrner. The firm also exported to France and had representatives in Edinburgh and South Africa. Up to six times a year Mürrle traveled to Pforzheim to examine the new assortments and export the finished products via the firm's sales agency of Immanuel Saake, Bahnhofstrasse 11.[4] Immanuel Saake was the buyer and part owner of the firm of Murrle, Bennett & Co., he directed the export business even before Mürrle's entry in 1895. He may also have been the wholesaler through whom Fahrner originally sold before selling directly to his retailers.[5]

A subsidiary firm of Murrle, Bennett & Co. was the "Artistic Rolled Gold Co.", in 1909 "Artistic Novelties Ltd.", with Ernst Mürrle as its chairman, Immanuel Saake as director and Carl Hirth as business manager. This subsidiary firm imported gold-plated jewelry almost exclusively from Germany.

The outbreak of World War I meant the end of the firm of Murrle, Bennett & Co. under German leadership. Ernst Murrle was interned on the Isle of Man and released in an exchange with Germany in 1916.[6] In the same year, the shop and stock passed into the hands of the British colleagues. The firm was now called "White, Redgrove & Whyte." Mürrle and Saake had to take large losses, but both built up new export and wholesale firms after the war.[7] This

JEWELS BY MODERN ARTISTS

PENDANT in 15 carat Gold,
with Turquoise Matrix and
Pearl Drop

BROOCH, conventionalized
flower design with Lapis

BROOCH, hand chased,
with Opal Matrix centre

BROOCH, in 15 carat Gold
with Opal Matrix centre
and Blister Pearl Drop

BROOCH, hand chased,
of Celtic character

BROOCH, hand chased,
of Celtic character

These Designs are
the Property of and
are made up by
MURRLE,
BENNETT
& Co.
13 CHARTERHOUSE ST.,
LONDON. E.C.
WHOLESALE AND
SHIPPING ONLY.

BRACELET, flexible, with four
Matrix Turquoises and
Matrix Turquoise Snap,
mounted in 15 carat Gold

Obtainable only through high-class Jewellers.

*provides a brief outline of the firm's history,
which is very typical of the fates of worldwide
export connections of Pforzheim manufacturers.[8] Important to our observation of the
two firms' cooperation: A large portion of the
jewelry bought by Murrle was manufactured by
Theodor Fahrner and bears the characteristic
trade marks of Theodor Fahrner and Murrle,
Bennett 7 Co. (below). At the beginning of the
century, artists' monograms often appear as a
third mark; they have been found on pieces by
M. J. Gradl and Patriz Huber. In certain
designs, both came very close to British jewelry
designs. Possibly they were assigned to design
specifically for the British market. It is striking*

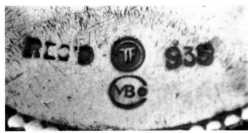

*that, for example, one of Gradl's most inter-
esting pieces (Cat. No. 1.29) was not mentioned
in the German publications of the time,
although Gradl's work was otherwise depicted
in great numbers. A jewelry advertisement of
the firm of Murrle, Bennett & Co. in "The
Studio" in 1900 shows that quantities of
second-rate goods were also offered for sale.[9] To
what extent they also bore the "M B & Co" trade
mark is not known. In this respect, Mürrle's
involvement with Theodor Fahrner's artist
jewelry appears to be more important, whether
it was sold with the artist's monogram or not.
The application of both trade marks in itself
documents the desire for connections with the*

*British arts-and-crafts movement, which —
excellently represented in all areas of artistic
handiwork by the firm of Liberty — promoted
the preparation of artistic designs, suitable for
the material, for industrial series production.
Surely the success of Fahrner Jewelry in Britain
was not just the result of good business between
longtime friends, but was based on the fact that
the British buying public saw their wish for
high-quality, moderately-priced Jewelry fulfilled in the artistic jewelry of the Pforzheim
firms, above all that of Theodor Fahrner.*

*Up to now it has been difficult to recognize a
system in the stampings — superficially seen,
deliberately varying — on the merchandise. Are*

7)
The jewelry wholesalers Murrle,
Bennett & Co. in Pforzheim,
Luisenstrasse 35, was dissolved in
1926. Ernst Mürrle remained the
proprietor of the firm. DGZ
XXIX, 1926, p. 11.

8)
Here we cannot go into the
interesting relations of Murrle,
Bennett & Co. with the firm of
Liberty. V. Becker believes, and
has proved in individual cases,
that Murrle also supplied the
Liberty firm and did not copy its
designs. See Note 1 for sources.

9)
Modern Designs in Jewellery and
fans, Special Winter number of
"The Studio", 1901-02. The
advertisement is not included in
the 1973 reprint. Another
advertisement is shown in Adrian
Tilbrook, The Designs of
Archibald Knox for Liberty & Co.,
London 1976, p. 184 (picture
above).

trade marks of other German firms also found, or was it only Theodor Fahrner who prevailed? Were all of Max J. Gradl's pieces marked with his "MiG" monogram? Many questions remain open.

The Patent Rights

a) Patent Law of 1877

Until 1871, varying possible means of acquiring regulated commercial protection prevailed in the various German states. Prussia's "Technical Deputation" in particular, an organization of experts, set the most stringent rules, so that the right to a patent was sometimes not applied for. In 1863 the "VDI" (Verein Deutscher Ingenieure) therefore presented a petition that complained of the hostility of entrepreneurs that led to the all-too-frequent rejection of registered patents. Under the pressure of this and similar protests, the creation of a patent law for the entire German Empire took place in 1875, resulting in the proclamation on May 25, 1877 of an Imperial law that went into power on July 1, 1977. According to this law, an object to be patented was subjected to an examination and was published in the form of technical drawings in the patent rolls of the Imperial Patent Office in Berlin. The patent existed as long as a yearly fee was paid, in the first year 30, in the second year 20 Marks. The patent number could be placed on the patented object, but this was not required.

b) The "Registered Patent" DRPa

In an article in the "Journal der Gold-schmiedekunst" in 1905 it was noted that the patent law included no provision for how it could be indicated on the object. Out of this indefinite situation there arose the improper use in the jewelry industry of marking an object for which a patent had been applied but not yet received with the letters "D.R.Pa." (English: PATT.APPLied). At first it was shown on the part of the manufacturer that the piece had been registered for patenting, though at times this could mean only a registration for sample protection. Then the "a" was capitalized to read "D.R.P.A.", which could easily be identified as an abbreviation for "Deutsches Reichs-Patent-Amt", To avoid misunderstandings of this kind, this practice was banned by the State Courts in Aachen and Berlin I, in 1898 and 1900, as "unconditionally dangerous and deceptive", although the defendants cited that it was a general custom. The abbreviation "D.R.Pa." was also banned, but that of "D.R.P. angemeldet" was allowed.

In the same article it is also mentioned that many pieces marked with "D.R.P.", "Patent" or "patentiert" were actually only protected as samples. The expression "officially protected" also had to be treated with caution. Generally this referred only to a trade name or trade mark, for example, that of a placard, that made it seem as if the product advertised on it was itself protected. A designation such as "Name protected", "Trade Mark Protection number..." or "W.Z.Protection No...." was clearer.[1]

c) Business Model Protection (D.R.G.M.) 1891

On October 1, 1891 the patent law was expanded with a law to protect business models, small

Waarenzeichenblatt

Das Blatt erscheint monatlich zum Preise von 20 Mark für den Jahrgang. Anfragen und Bestellungen sind zu richten an die Verlags-Buchhandlung.

Das vom Kaiserlichen Patentamt herausgegebene Blatt für Patent-, Muster- und Zeichenwesen wird dem Waarenzeichenblatt kostenfrei beigegeben.

Herausgegeben vom Kaiserlichen Patentamt.

II. Jahrg.   Januar 1895.   Heft 1.

technical developments that, unlike patents, did not need to be examined again. "Models of working apparatus or utensils or parts of the same are protected as business models according to this law as long as they are supposed to serve their purpose in work or use through a new formation, arrangement or design protected as business models according to the stipulations of this law.[2] Like the patent, the business model was registered with the Imperial Off. and put in the appropriate section of the "Patentblatt." In addition, an object could have dual protection as both a patent and a model. The protection period covered three years, with a few of 15 Marks. An extension for three years could be obtained for a fee of 60 Marks.[3]

d) Trade Name and Trade Mark Protection 1874 and 1894

Even before the newly formulated and unified patent law of 1877, on November 30, 1874, a trade-mark protection law was proclaimed, and was expended on May 12, 1894. According to the 1874 law, the name to be protected was included in the commercial register of the city in which a firm's main office was located. The protection period was ten years. The registration was rejected if "the mark consisted exclusively of numbers, letters or words."[4] The new 1894 law on trade marks concerned the registration of a name in words, as long as it said nothing of the means of manufacture. It governed the role of the Patent Office concerning symbols.

Despite specific laws, it was seen that there was confusion in some firms. To help avoid offenses, both the "Journal der Goldschmiedekunst" and the "Deutsche Goldschmiedezeitung" discussed this problem frequently in their "Patent News" or "Patents Etc." columns.

1)
Patent Bureau O. Krueger & Co., Dresden, D.R.P.A., in: JGK 26, 1905, pp. 138 ff.

2)
Reichsgesetzblatt 1891.

3)
From 1891 to 1907, more than 30,000 such models were registered. Most of them were household articles. Lit.: Paul Hennig, Geschmacksmuster und Gebrauchsmuster, in: GK 43, 1910, pp. 404 ff. (The models themselves, up through No. 1,000,000, were lost in World War II and exist today only as descriptions in the "Patentblatt.")

4)
Lit.: Nachweisung der im Deutschen Reich gesetzlich geschützten Waarenzeichen, published by Robert Fickert for the Imperial Department of the Interior, 1875 ff, Berlin. (Jewelry is in Group V: Metal Utilization). Waarenzeichenblatt, published by the Imperial Patent Office, No. 1, 1894 (Jewelry is under Section 17: Gold and silver goods).

Abbreviations

Abb.	Abbildung		KGV.	Kunstgewerbeverein
Auk.-Kat.	Auktionskatalog		L.	Länge
Ausf./ ausgef.	Ausführung/ ausgeführt		lt.	laut
Ausst.	Ausstellung		m.	mit
B.	Breite		Nachf.	Nachfolger
Bd./Bde.	Band/Bände		Nr.	Nummer
Bez./bez.	Bezeichnung/bezeichnet		o.	ohne
BMV-Nr.	Beschlagmarken-Verzeichnis-Nr.		o.A.	ohne Autor
Br.	Breite		o.B.	obere Breite
bzw.	beziehungsweise		o.g.	oben genannte
cm	Zentimeter		o.J.	ohne Jahr
d.Ä.	der Ältere		o.S.	ohne Seitenangabe
Darst.	Darstellung		Pfh.	Pforzheim
dergl.	dergleichen		Prof.	Professor
d.J.	der Jüngere		Rs.	Rückseite
Dm.	Durchmesser		s.	siehe
Dt.	Deutsche/er		S.	Seite
erw.	erwähnt		s.a.	siehe auch
Fa.	Firma		Sa.	Sachsen
F.N.	Fahrner - Nachlaß		sen.	Senior
franz.	französisch		Slg.	Sammlung
F.St.	Fahrner - Stiftung		^T.	Tafel
geb.	geboren		TH	Technische Hochschule
gest.	gestempelt		u.a.	und andere
g.H.	gesamte Höhe		u.a.O.	und an anderen Orten
gr.Br.	größte Breite		u.B.	untere Breite
H	Höhe		v.	von
H.	Heft		versch.	verschiedene
h.L.	halbe Länge		vgl.	vergleiche
Hl.	Heiliger		v.l.n.r.	von links nach rechts
Hrsg./hrsg.	Herausgeber/herausgegeben		Vorber.	Vorbereitung
Inv.	Inventar		Vs.	Vorderseite
Jg.	Jahrgang		w.Lit.	weitere Literatur
jun.	Junior		Württ.	Württembergische/er
Kat.	Katalog		Wwe.	Witwe
Kgl.	Königliche/er		zit.n.	zitiert nach
KGS.	Kunstgewerbeschule		zugeschr.	zugeschrieben

Bibliography

Abbreviations for Literature

Berichte *Royal State Commercial Museum, Stuttgart, Reports per year, as of 1906.*

DGZ *Deutsche Goldschmiedezeitung, Leipzig, as of 1898.*

DK *Dekorative Kunst, Illustrierte Zeitung für angewandte Kunst, Munich, as of 1897-98.*

DKD *Deutsche Kunst und Dekoration, Darmstadt, as of 1897.*

GK *Die Goldschmiedekunst, Leipzig, as of 1910.*

JG *Journal der Goldschmiedekunst (Amtliches Organ des Verbandes und der meisten Innungen und Vereinigungen), Leipzig, as of 1881 (became "Die Goldschmiedekunst" in 1910).*

Inv. KGS *Inventar der Kunstgewerbeschule Pforzheim, 1880 to 12.3.1922.*

KGB NF *Kunstgewerbeblatt, Monatsschrift für Geschichte und Literatur der Kleinkunst. Organ für die Bestrebungen der Kunstgewerbe-Vereine, Leipzig, as of 1885, Neue Folge as of 1890.*

KGB Pfh. *Kunstgewerbeblatt für das Gold- Silber- und Feinmetallgewerbe, Fachzeitschrift des KGV Pforzheim, Gewerbemuseum zu Schwäbisch Gmünd, des Kunstvereins zu Hanau, der freien Vereinigung des Gold- und Silberwarengewerbes zu Berlin, Berlin, as of 1894.*

KuH *Kunst und Handwerk, Zeitschrift des Vereins zur Ausbildung der Gewerke in München, Munich, as of 1851.*

KuKH Kunst und Kunsthandwerk, Vienna 1898.

Das Kunstgewerbe in Elsass-Lothringen, *Strassburg, as of 1900.*

Mitt. Württ. Mitteilungen des Vereins für decorative Kunst und Kunstgewerbe, Stuttgart, as of 1900.

The Studio The Studio, London, as of 1893.
V & K Velhagen & Klasings Monatshefte, Bielefeld-Leipzig, as of 1888.

Bibliography used for Theodor Fahrner (to 1919)

1 a) Original Sources
Family tree of the ancestors and descendants of Martha Fahrner, née Faber, Pforzheim (privately owned).
Chronicle of the Braendle family, Pforzheim, privately owned.
Adressbücher (directories) of the City of Pforzheim, 1859-1933.
Adress- und Handbuch für das deutsche Goldschmiedegewerbe, Leipzig 1903.
Membership list of the Deutsche Werkbund, May 1, 1914.
Information in the Pforzheim City Archives.
Iventare of the Grossherzoglichen Kunstgewerbeschule Pforzheim (now Institute of Artistic Design): Inventory of Metal Models II and 2, 1880 to Dec. 3, 1922.

1 b) Journal articles, illustrations and notes not cited or briefly cited in Catalog Part I, the artists' biographies or notes (in chronological order):
Rudolf Rücklin, Der Künstlerfabrikant, in: DGZ III, 1900, pp. 188-190, 199-200 and DGZ IV, 1901, p. 8.

Von der Pariser Weltausstellung, in: DGZ III, 1900, p. 191, picture on p. 5.
KGB Pfh., 7, 1900, pp. 66 ff, Plate 1.
Ostwald, Moderne deutsche Goldschmiedekunst, in: Westermanns Monatshefte 45, 1901, pp. 797 ff.
Rudolf Rücklin, Die Resultate der Ausstellung der Darmstädter Künstlerkolonie, in: KGB Pfh. 8, 1901, no page number.
KGB Pfh. 9, 1902, picture on p. 8.
Rudolf Rücklin, Pforzheimer Fein- und Metallarbeiten a.d. Weltausstellung St. Louis, in: DKD XIV, 1904, pp. 503 ff, with picture.
Zeitschrift des Mitteldeutschen Kunstgewerbevereins zu Frankfurt am Main, 1904-05, pp. 159 ff.
Hanns von Zobeltitz, Die Pforzheimer Schmuckindustrie, in: Velhagen & Klasings Monatshefte XIX, 1904-05, Vol. 1, pp. 549 ff (with picture).
Rudolf Rücklin, Berichterstattung der von dem Kunstgewerbe-Verein Pforzheim nach der Weltausstellung in St. Louis entsandten Herren, in: KGB Pfh. 12, 1905, pp. 1 ff.
Personal- und Geschäftsnachrichten, in: JGK 26, 1905, p. 161.
Das 50jährige Geschäftsjubiläum, in: Pforzheimer Generalanzeiger, 99, 4.28.1905.
Rudolf Rücklin, Die Moderne Schmuckkunst im Lichte der Weltausstellung in St. Louis, in: KGB NF 1905, pp. 146 ff, with picture.
Rudolf Rücklin, Unsere Bilder, in: DGZ IX, 1906, p. 149, pictures on pp. 145, 152.
Verzeichnis der auf der 3. Deutschen

Kunstgewerbe-Ausstellung Dresden 1906 mit Preisen ausgezeichneten Aussteller . . . in: JGK 27, 1906, p. 264.

Die dritte deutsche Kunstgewerbeausstellung, Dresden 1906, in: KGB NF 1906, pp. 210 ff.

Rudolf Rücklin, Pforzheim auf der Jubiläumsausstellung für Kunst und Kunstgewerbe in Karlsruhe 1906, in: KGB Pfh. 13, 1906, pp. 24 ff and 147, picture on p. 21.

Rudolf Rücklin, Moderner Silberschmuck von Theodor Fahrner in Pforzheim, in: DGZ XII, 1909, pp. 37 ff, pictures on pp. 311, 313, 315.

Rudolf Rücklin, Die Metallkunstausstellung im Kgl. Landesgewerbemuseum Stuttgart, in: DGZ XII, 1909, pp. 347 ff.

Fritz Hellwag, Die Pforzheimer Schmuck-Industrie, in: KGB NF 1909, pp. 81 ff, pictures on pp. 82 ff.

KGB Pfh. 16, 1909, pp. 5 and 32.

JGK 30, 1909, pictures on pp. 160 ff.

Kgl. Landesgewerbemuseum Stuttgart, Berichte über das Jahr 1909, pp. 15 and 59, Berichte über das Jahr 1910, p. 40.

DK XXII, 1909-1910, picture on p. 583.

DGZ XIII, 1910, Pictures on pp. 169, 170.

Fahrner-Schmuck, in: GK 31, 1910, p. 37, pictures on pp. 36, 39.

L. Segmiller, Pforzheim in Brüssel 1910, in: GK 31, 1910, pp. 251 ff.

L. Segmiller, Die Ausstellung neuzeitlicher Erzeugnisse der Pforzheimer Edelmetallindustrie 1911, in: KGB Pfh. 18, 1911, pp. 2 ff.

DGZ XIV, 1911, picture on p. 359 (Arbeiten der Werkstätten für Metallbearbeitung Prof. A. Schmid),

GK 32, 1911, picture on p. 243.

Rudolf Rücklin, Die Pforzheimer Schmuckindustrie, Stuttgart 1911, p. 35.

Fahrner-Schmuck, in: GK 34, 1913, p. 403, pictures on pp. 394, 395.

Rudolf Rücklin, Pforzheim auf der Werkbundausstellung in Köln, 1914, in: DGZ XVII, 1914, picture on p. 83; Zu unseren Abbildungen, p. 126, pictures on pp. 49-51.

L. Segmiller, Die Pforzheimer Gold- und Silberwarenindustrie auf der Werkbundausstellung in Köln 1914, in" KGB NF XXVI, pp. 161 ff, picture on p. 175.

Zu unseren Abbildungen, in: DGZ XVIII, 1915, pp. 66 ff, pictures on pp. 18, 19 and 83.

Zu unseren Abbildungen, in: DGZ XX, 1917, pp. 180 ff, pictures on pp. 46, 47.

L. Segmiller, Pforzheimer Kunstleben im Kriege, in: DGZ XXI, 1918, pp. 75 ff.

Zu unseren Abbildungen, in: DGZ XXI, 1918, pp. 136 ff, pictures on pp. 30, 31.

Theodor Heuss, Werkbund-Ausstellung in Kopenhagen, in: DKD XLIII, 1918-1919, pp. 253 ff, picture on p. 263.

DGZ XXII, 1919, p. 215 (announcement of death with brief biography).

Rudolf Rücklin, Das Werk Theodor Fahrners, in: DGZ XXII, 1919, pp. 268 ff.

Freie Presse, Pforzheim, 7/24/1919 (announcement of death).

GK 40, 1919, p. 226 (announcement of death with brief biography).

Handelsregisterliche Eintragungen, in: DGZ XXIII, 1920, p. 66.

Rudolf Rücklin, *25 Jahre deutscher Schmuckkunstm in: DGZ XXVI, 1923, pp. 69 ff.*

Kunstgewerbemuseum der Stadt Köln, *Schmuck II, Cologne 1985, p. 265 (biography).*

1 c) Catalogs for Exhibitions at which Theodor Fahrner was represented.

Paris World's Fair 1900, *Amtlicher Katalog der Ausstellung des Deutschen Reiches, Berlin (1900), Klasse 94 Sammelausstellung der Pforzheimer Bijouterie-Industrie, Th. Fahrner is Exhibitor No. 4402.*

Joseph Maria Olbrich, *Die Ausstellung der Künstlerkolonie Darmstadt 1901, Hauptkatalog, pp. 40, 42, 44, 47, 103, 108, 132 (advertisement), cited as: Kat. Olbrich 1901.*

Offizieller illustrierter Katalog *der Jubiläums Kunstausstellung, Karlsruhe 1902, p. 58.*

World's Fair in St. Louis 1904, *Amtlicher Katalog, Berlin 1904, Group 31, No. 2309, p. 450; Group 37, No. 2448, p. 456.*

1. Ausstellung der Münchener Vereinigung *für angewandte Kunst, Munich 1905, p. 35, No. 44-46.*

Das deutsche Kunstgewerbe 1906, *Dresden 1906, pp. 247, 252, 291.*

Weltausstellung Brüssel 1910. *Deutsches Reich. Amtlicher Katalog, Berlin 1910. Class 94 "Gold- und Silberschmiede-arbeiten", Th. Fahrner, Exhibitor No. 3499. Class 95, "Juwelierarbeiten und Schmucksachen", Th. Fahrner, Exhibitor No. 3450: "Theodor Fahrner Kunst-gewerbliches Atelier, Pforzheim", p. 41, Room 15: "non-precious metals."*

Deutschland in Brüssel. *Die deutsche Abteilung der Weltausstellung, Köln 1910, (p. 23, list of honors, in appendix).*

Werkbundausstellung Köln 1914, *pp. 122-123.*

Amtlicher Katalog *für die Deutsche Abteilung der Baltischen Ausstellung, Malmö 1914, Berlin 1914.*

2) General literature and reference works mentioning Theodor Fahrner.

Becker, Vivienne, *Antique and 20th Century Jewellery, London 1980, quoted from 2nd edition, 1987, pp. 258 ff, il-lustrated.*

Becker, Vivienne, *Murrle Bennett, are they the German link with Liberty Jewellery? in: antique collector 11, 1980, pp. 72 ff, illustrated.*

Becker, Vivienne, *Art Nouveau Jewellery Made in Germany?, in: antique collector 9, 1982, pp. 65 ff, illustrated.*

Becker, Vivienne, *Art Nouveau Jewellery, London 1985, pp. 111.130, 136, 160, 218, 234, with numerous illustrations.*

Black, Anderson, *Die Geschichte des Schmucks, Munich 1976.*

Canz, Sigrid, *Symbolistische Bild-vorstellungen im Juwelierschmuck um 1900, dissertation, Munich 1974, Kochel 1976.*

Culme, John, *The directory of gold and silversmiths, Jewellers and allied traders, 1838-1914, Woodbridge 1987 (2 vol.).*

Falk, Fritz, *Schmuckkunst um 1900, in:*

Goldschmiedezeitung 1969, pp. 640 ff.

Falk, Fritz, *Europäischer Schmuck, Königsbach-Stein 1985, pictures no. 178-187, 192, 194.*

Gailing, Monika, *Ein Art-Nouveau-Schmuckstück von René Lalique im Pforzheimer Schmuckmuseum, master's thesis, Tübingen 1982.*

Gerstner, Paul, *Die Entwicklung der Pforzheimer Bijouterie-Industrie von 1767-1907, in: KGB Pfh. 14, 1907, pp. 11 ff, and Tübingen 1908.*

Haberlandt, Michael, *Völkerschmuck, Vienna 1906.*

Handbuch *des Kunstmarktes, Berlin 1926.*

von Hase, Ulrike, *Schmuck in Deutschland und Osterreich 1894-1914, Munich 1977, re Th. Fahrner pp. 86, 90, 93, 95, 97, 99, 105, 107ff, 112ff, 120ff, 124, Cat. No. under Th. Fahrner: Benirschke, von Berlepsch, Boeres, Bürck, Gradl, Habich, Huber, Kleemann, Kleinhempel, Kunstgewerbeschule Pforzheim, Matz, Morawe, Müller-Salem, Wolber.*

Holme, Charles, *Modern Design in Jewellery and Fans, London, Paris, New York 1902 (The Studio, Special Number 1901-02).*

Hoffmann, Julius, *Der moderne Stil, Stuttgart 1905.*

Joppien, Rüdiger, *Deutsche Goldschmiedekunst bis 1914, in: Der westdeutsche Impuls 1900-1914. Die deutsche Werkbund-Ausstellung 1914. Kat. Ausst. Köln 1984, picture on p. 253.*

Koch, Alexander, *Die Ausstellung der Darmstädter Künstlerkolonie, Darmstadt 1901, Reprint Stuttgart 1989.*

Koch, Alexander, *Schmuck und Edel-metall-Arbeiten, Darmstadt 1906, Reprint Hannover 1985, richly illustrated.*

Maschke, *Die Pforzheimer Schmuck- und Uhrenindustrie, Pforzheim 1967.*

Meier, Graefe Julius, *1900 Die Welt-ausstellung in Paris, Paris and Leipzig 1900, pp. 111 ff.*

Niggl, Reto, *Theodor Fahrner: Schmuck mit Geschmack, in: Antiquitäten-Zeitung 11, 1978, pp. 10 ff, illustrated.*

Niggl, Reto, *Maschinenschmuck in Auktionen — Theodor Fahrner, in: Antiquitäten-Zeitung 24, 1988, pp. 736, 750, illustrated.*

Niggl, Reto, *Kastanie und Flugkörper, in: Antiquitäten-Zeitung 3, 1989, pp. 82 ff, illustrated.*

Pieper, Wolfgang, *Geschichte der Pforzheimer Schmuckindustrie, Gernsbach 1989.*

Pforzheim *— Stadt und Landkreis, Stuttgart 1953, pp. 36 ff.*

Pforzheim: *Denkschrift über die Grossherzogliche Kunstgewerbeschule zu Pforzheim, Pforzheim 1911, in: DGZ XIV 1911, pp. 341 ff.*

Pforzheim: *Einhundertfünfundzwanzig Jahre Gewerbeschule 1833-1958, Pforzheim 1958.*

Pforzheim: *75 Jahre Goldschmiedeschule Pforzheim, Pforzheim 1980.*

Rücklin, Rudolf, *Das Schmuckbuch I, Leipzig 1901 (2 vol.), Reprint Hannover 1988, p. 249.*

Rücklin, Rudolf, *Die Pforzheimer Schmuckindustrie, Stuttgart 1911, picture on p. 35.*

Rücklin, Rudolf, *Städtisches Schmuck-*

museum Pforzheim, Führer durch die Historische Abteilung, no year (1930-1940?), no page.

Stöckig & Co., Kat. des Versandhauses Stöckig & Co., Dresden, ca. 1911, Modern Jewelry section.

Tauch, Peter, Die wirtschaftliche Entwicklung der Pforzheimer Bijouterie-industrie im 19. Jahrhundert und ihre wesentlichen Bestimmungsfaktoren, dissertation, Tübingen 1982.

Ulmer, Renate, Patriz Huber, master's thesis, Heidelberg 1982.

Zier, Hans Georg, Geschichte der Stadt Pforzheim, Stuttgart 1982, p. 249.

3) Museum, Exhibition and Auction Catalogs

Jablonecká secése, Kat. Ausst. Gablonz Neisse, 1972.

Ein Dokument Deutscher Kunst 1901-1976, Kat. Ausst. Darmstadt 1976, 5 vol.

Jugendstil, Kat. Ausst. Brussels 1977.

Silber des Jugendstils, Kat. Ausst. Munich 1979.

Falk, Fritz, Von der Antike bis zur Gegenwart, 2nd ed., Pforzheim 1981.

Chadour, Anna Beatriz and **Joppien, Rüdiger,** Schmuck I und II, Kunstgewerbemuseum der Stadt Köln, cologne 1985.

Franzke, Irmela, Jugendstil, Bestandskatalog des Badischen Landesmuseums Karlsruhe, Karlsruhe 1987, 2nd ed.

Schmuckkunst im Jugendstil, Kat. Ausst. von Ingeborg Becker, Berlin 1988.

Umelecká, Kolonie Darmstadt 1899-1914, Kat. Ausst. Prague 1989.

The Art of Cartier, Paris 1989, text by Thérèse Burollet and Gilles Chazal.

Fahrner-Schmuck, Auktions-Katalog 153, Wolfgang Ketterer, Munich 1990.

Literature on Gustav Braendle, Theodor Fahrner's Successor (1919-1979)

1) Original Sources

Chronicle of the Braendle family, Pforzheim, privately owned.

Fahrner Sales Literature, no dates.

Pattern Books, see pp. 164 ff.

2) Literature not cited or briefly cited in the text and catalog.

Becker, Vivienne, Antique and 20th Century Jewellery, London 1980, pp. 256-261.

Bott, Gerhard, Ullstein Juwelenbuch, Abendländischer Schmuck von der Antike bis zur Gegenwart, Frankfurt-Berlin-Vienna 1972, p. 216.

Bruckmanns Handbuch des Schmucks, Munich 1977.

Chadour, Anna Beatriz and Rüdiger Joppien, Schmuck I und II, Kunstgewerbemuseum der Stadt Köln, Cologne 1985, Vol. I, No. 25, 235, 275, 276, 278, Vol. II, pp. 265, 266.

Gabardi, Melissa, Les Bijoux de l'Art Dèco aux années 1940, Paris 1986, p. 189.

Gabardi, Melissa, Art Deco Jewellery 1920-1949, London 1989, p. 180.

Illustriertes Jahrbuch und Führer durch die deutsche Schmuckwaren-Industrie, Pforzheim 1922.

Kunst und kunsthandwerk am Oberrhein 1925, Vol. I (Jahrbuch des Badischen Kunstgewerbevereins und des Kunstgewerbevereins Pforzheim), p. 93.

Taschen-Addressbuch für die Bijouterie Branche, Pforzheim 1921-22, p. 14.

Raulet, Sylvie, Schmuck Art Dèco, Munich 1987.

Reichshandbuch der Deutschen Gesellschaft, Das Handbuch der Persönlichkeiten in Wort und Bild, 1 vol., published by the Deutsche Wirtschaftsverlag, Berlin 1930, p. 195.

3) Auction Catalogs

Christie's, Twentieth Century Decorative Arts, Geneva, 11/12/1989, p. 219.

Auktionskataloge Ketterer, Munich, 1977ff.

Auktionskataloge Dr. Fritz Nagel, Stuttgart, 325. Auktion, 1988, pp. 194-199, 328. 1989 Auction, p. 219.

4) Journals named in the text but only cited briefly.

Antiquitäten-Zeitung, Munich: No. 11, 1978, pp. 10-11, No. 20, 1978, pp. 18-19, No. 21, 1982, p. 525, No. 16, 1984, pp. XXVI-XXVII, No. 24, 1988, pp. 736, 737, 750.

Deutsche Goldschmiedezeitung, Leipzig, 1898ff, cited 1919ff.

Deutsche Kunst und Dekoration, Darmstadt, 1897ff, cited 1919ff.

Die Dame, Illustrierte Frauenzeitung, Ausgabe der Modewelt mit Unterhaltungsblatt, Berlin, 1872ff, cited 1931ff.

Die Schaulade, Bamberg, cited 1931ff.

Gold und Silber, Vol. 3, No. 10, 1950, p. 25.

Photo Credits:

We thank the museums and private collectors named in the photo captions and catalog numbers for their friendly provision of photographic material, as well as the following photographers, archives and publishers (the citations are page numbers).

Peter Frankenstein, Marbach, all jewelry photographs.

Baden State Museum, Karlsruhe: 101 (below).
British Museum, London: (XLV III C II): 59.
Institute for Design, Pforzheim, 189 (left)
Mrs. Gabel, 161
Gulbenkian Foundation, Lisbon, 48
Max Hering, Pforzheim, 162, 166-169
Huwald Collection: 270-271.
Library of Art, Berlin (Kasten 5950v/161): 51.
Austrian State Museum, Linz: 57.
Austrian Museum of Applied Art, Vienna: 58 (#48), 189 (right).
Private collection, Pforzheim: 160, 178, 180 (above), 181, 185, 260, 267.
Private collection (F.N.): 17, 20-21, 25 (#6-7), 40, 41, 42-43, 66, 77, 159, 171, 184, 235, 237, 244, 256, 268-269.
Hans Schöner Verlag, Königsbach-Stein: 34 (#16), 80, 92 (above), 93 (above), 97 (above), 127 (above), 132, 133 (both below), 140 (lower right). Mr. Scho³ner kindly supplied duplicates from the book: F. Falk, Europäischer Schmuck, Königsbach-Stein 1985.
Ullstein-Bilderdienst, Berlin: 172, 175, 179, 198 (upper right), 258.
Wiener Interieur, Vienna: 157.
Württemberg State Museum, Stuttgart: 155, 210 (lower right), 218 (all b/w), 220 (#2.150), 221 (#2.151), 224 (upper right).

Index